Library of
Davidson College

Against Fascism and War
Ruptures and continuities in British Communist politics, 1935–41

KEVIN MORGAN

Manchester University Press
Manchester and New York

Distributed exclusively in the USA and Canada by St. Martin's Press

Copyright © Kevin Morgan 1989

Published by Manchester University Press
Oxford Road, Manchester M13 9PL, UK
and Room 400, 175 Fifth Avenue,
New York, NY 10010, USA

*Distributed exclusively in the USA and Canada
by* St. Martin's Press, Inc.,
175 Fifth Avenue, New York, NY 10010, USA

British Library cataloging in publication data
Morgan, Kevin
  Against Fascism and War: ruptures and continuities in
  British Communist politics, 1935–1941.
  1. World War 2. Attitudes of Communist Party of Great
  Britain
  I. Title
  940.53

Library of Congress cataloguing in publication data
Morgan, Kevin, 1961–
   Against fascism and war: ruptures and continuities in British
  Communist politics, 1935–41/Kevin Morgan.
     p.   cm.
   ISBN 0–7190–3078–1
   1. Communist Party of Great Britain—History—20th century.
2. Great Britain—Politics and government—1936–1945.   I. Title.
JN1129.C62M67   1989
324.241'0975'09043—dc20   89-36488

ISBN 0 7190 3078 1 *hardback*

*Photoset in Linotron Times
by* Northern Phototypesetting Co, Bolton
*Printed in Great Britain
by* Billings & Son Ltd, Worcester

Contents

Preface and acknowledgements   v

Abbreviations   vii

Introduction   1

1   Capitalism's last resort: British Communists and the threat of Fascism, 1934–38   19

2   The Communist Party and the Popular Front, 1935–38   33

3   Britain: the centre of gravity, 1935–38   56

4   The last year of 'peace', 1938–39   69

5   For or against? The Communist Party and the outbreak of war   85

6   From the Soviet–German peace offer to the Blitzkrieg: the CPGB, 1939–40   105
    6.1   Revolutionary defeatism   106
    6.2   The British precedent   110
    6.3   Why this war?   112
    6.4   The rich man's luxury   122
    6.5   Engineers in the front line   128
    6.6   War! and the Welsh miner: Hornerism resurgent   134
    6.7   Imperialist war, anti-Soviet war   146
    6.8   May Day 1940   148
    6.9   Electoral contests   153

7   From the fall of France to the invasion of the Soviet Union: the CPGB, 1940–41, and some general themes from the 'imperialist war' period   171
    7.1   The 'Party line' turns a circle   171
    7.2   A summer of discontent   174
    7.3   One step back?   180

	7.4	A war for empire	185
	7.5	The 'new order' in Britain	189
	7.6	Labour movement or Labour Front?	196
	7.7	The People's Convention	201
	7.8	People's Peace, People's War	213
	7.9	A People's Government	218
	7.10	Communists and the war effort, 1940–41	225
	7.11	The Communist Party and the establishment	236
	7.12	Postscript: towards 22 June 1941	242
8		**Ruptures and continuities: two case studies**	**254**
	8.1	The rise and fall of the Left Book Club	254
	8.2	Mass struggles in Birmingham, 1939–41	277

Postscript and conclusion — 303

Appendix: Communist Party membership, 1939–41 — 311

Select bibliography — 319

Index — 323

Preface and acknowledgements

The study which follows is a revised version of my 1987 Manchester University doctoral thesis of the same title, structured in much the same way even if somewhat reduced in length and somewhat less exhaustive in its detail. My thanks should therefore go first of all to my thesis supervisor, David Howell, for his open-minded encouragement and guidance ever since the project's inception and to Lewis Minkin and James Hinton for the warm but critical reception they gave the thesis as its examiners.

I should like also to express my great debt of gratitude to all the Communists, ex-Communists and other Socialists interviewed during the course of this study, whose names are given at the back of this book. My debt to their helpfulness and hospitality, occasionally in very difficult circumstances, is all the greater in that none of those concerned would endorse everything written here and some would probably endorse very little of it. Of those interviewed I owe special thanks to Betty Reid, Malcolm MacEwen and the late Ted Bramley, all of whom read and commented upon parts of the original thesis, to Arthur Exell, who provided me with detailed references and information for the CP in Oxford, and to Eddie Frow, from whose encouragement and conversation over a number of years I derived so much benefit. Without the advantage of the splendid Working Class Movement Library built up by Eddie and Ruth Frow in Manchester, this book would have been very much the poorer.

Thanks are due also to the many other people who have helped me in various ways over the past few years, including members of my family, June Henderson, John Moorcroft, Mark Pinney and, especially, Julie Johnson.

The reader will notice how greatly chapters 6 and 7 benefit from the use of the files amassed by Mass-Observation and I would like to acknowledge the permission of the Tom Harrisson Mass-Observation Archive to reproduce this material.

I ought finally to clarify the criteria by which I have defined somebody as a Communist in this book. The need arises because, as is well known, it was commonplace during this period for individuals owing allegiance to the Communist Party to forbear from proclaiming this allegiance. In some cases this was in the belief that such individuals would enjoy a wider influence, or at least arouse fewer suspicions, than if they were publicly identified as Party members. A good example was the intellectual John Strachey, who, as Dutt wrote in 1935, had by that time 'either joined the Party or is at any rate regarding himself as under the same responsibility as a party member' (Dutt to Varga, 12.3.35, in the Dutt papers). In fact the latter was the case. Other Communists went 'undercover' in order to participate and gain influence in organisations such as the Labour Party and many trades councils from which they were formally excluded. In other cases individuals publicly identified with the Party had simply not got round to getting their Party card; thus the *Daily Worker*'s cartoonist 'Gabriel' (James Friell) did not join the Party until eighteen months after joining the *Worker*, while Malcolm MacEwen stood as Communist candidate in a Parliamentary by-election in 1941 without having yet joined the Party. In this book I have throughout referred to all such individuals as Communists, without inverted commas or a small 'C'. Thus the designation of somebody as a Communist should not be taken to mean that he or she necessarily held a Party card but that, *in the author's judgement*, he regarded himself as 'under the same responsibility as a party member'. I trust that I have not adopted this usage so indiscriminately as to brand mere 'fellow-travellers'. Certainly, I have used it only where, as for instance in the cases of Strachey and Pritt, the evidence, even if sometimes circumstantial, seemed to me overwhelming.

For this judgement, as for the interpretation presented in this book and for any errors of fact or omission, I am alone responsible.

K. M.
March 1989

Abbreviations

AEU	Amalgamated Engineering Union
AIA	Artists International Association
ASSNC	Aircraft Shop Stewards' National Council
BLP	(Birmingham) Borough Labour Party
BMTA	Birmingham Municipal Tenants' Association
BSP	British Socialist Party
BUF	British Union of Fascists
CC	(Communist Party) Central Committee
(EC) CI	(Executive Committee of the) Communist International
CP (GB)	Communist Party (of Great Britain)
CPSU	Communist Party of the Soviet Union
CWC	Clyde Workers' Committee
DC	(Communist Party) District Committee
Disc.	*Discussion*
DLP	Divisional Labour Party
DNP	D.N. Pritt papers
DW	*Daily Worker*
EATSSNC	Engineering and Allied Trades Shop Stewards' National Council
IBA	International Brigade Association
ILP	Independent Labour Party
JEC	(Birmingham Labour) Joint Emergency Committee
KPD	German Communist Party
LBC	Left Book Club
L(B)N	*Left (Book) News*
LLY	Labour League of Youth
LM	*Labour Monthly*
LNU	League of Nations Union
MFGB	Miners' Federation of Great Britain
MML	Marx Memorial Library
M-O	Tom Harrisson Mass-Observation Archive
MOI	Ministry of Information
NCL	National Council of Labour
NEC	(Labour Party) National Executive Committee

'Notes'	Palme Dutt's 'Notes of the Month' in the *Labour Monthly*
NP	*New Propellor*
NUS	National Union of Students
NUWM	National Unemployed Workers' Movement
PB	(Communist Party) Political Bureau
PC	People's Convention
PCF	French Communist Party
PCI	Italian Communist Party
PO	*Party Organiser*
PRO	Public Record Office
RIO	(Ministry of Information) Regional Information Officer
RPD	R. Palme Dutt papers
SDF	Social Democratic Federation
SWCA	South Wales Coalfield Archive
SWMF (EC)	South Wales Miners' Federation (Executive Council)
TC	*Town Crier*
TGWU	Transport and General Workers' Union
VG	Victor Gollancz papers
WCML	Working Class Movement Library
WNV	*World News and Views*
YCL	Young Communist League

Introduction

Over the past couple of decades there has emerged a substantial and heterogeneous corpus of writings on the British Communist Party during the period of the Comintern. Sadly, although the early history and pre-history of British Communism have given rise to a lively, informed and wide-ranging debate, much less of real value has been written on the CP during its 'Stalinist' period from the mid- to late 1920s onwards. By assessing the achievements and shortcomings of some of the most representative writings on Communism in Britain, it is intended in these preliminary comments to indicate the assumptions and methodology which have shaped the present study. The gravest of the faults which mar these writings are rooted in a distorting political prejudice and, in the cases of those writing within the Leninist tradition, questionable postulates as to the character of the revolutionary party and the nature of revolutionary change. It is worth beginning these opening comments by tracing these postulates back to their Leninist origins, for they were also fundamental to the ideology of the Communist Party during the period covered by this study. On this basis, I shall proceed to a brief discussion of the main approaches taken to Communist Party history, and thus to an explanation of the particular approach attempted in the chapters which follow.

The formation of the Comintern in 1919, and of its British section in 1920, was a recognition of and disengagement from the historical crisis of European Social Democracy revealed by the First World War. This crisis brought to a head a longstanding problem for Marxists: the relationship between 'determinism' and 'voluntarism'. The leading parties of the Second International had espoused a rigidly deterministic form of Marxism, most notably manifested in the SPD's Erfurt Programme of 1891, which proclaimed the inevitability of the supersession of mature capitalism by Socialism. The ideological custodians of German Social Democracy sanctimoniously rebuffed 'revisionist' attempts to tamper with this programme, but its revolutionary prognostications remained remote from the SPD's minimum, day-to-day programme, which presupposed the continued existence of capitalism for the foreseeable future. This disjunction was demonstrated conclusively on the outbreak of imperialist war in 1914. Despite having affirmed and confirmed its opposition to such a war at successive international congresses, the SPD offered its services to the Kaiser, just as its comrades abroad offered their services to the Kaiser's enemies. As empires clashed and empires tumbled, the main body of Social Democracy continued, as Rosa Luxemburg had warned it should not, to 'fold its arms and wait with fatalistic resignation for the arrival of a "revolutionary situation", for a spontaneous mass action of the people to fall from the clouds'.[1] But at times of social and political upheaval no mass political organisation can simply procrastinate. It was the recognition that the arms of Social Democracy were not so much folded as propping up the tottering structure of capitalism that led to the formation of a new International which would pull away the props and bring the whole edifice crashing down.

Internationally, August 1914 was the moment of disillusionment for Lenin, but within Russia he had long since declared war on 'economism' and it was this controversy that prompted his exposition of the role of the revolutionary party in *What Is To Be Done?* (1902). In this seminal pamphlet Lenin ridiculed the economists for their 'slavish cringing before spontaneity', meaning their abjuration of the responsibility to give political leadership and their veneration for the immediate economic struggles of the working class. These struggles, insisted Lenin, echoing Kautsky, could of themselves give birth only to 'trade-union consciousness'. 'Class political consciousness' would have to be imparted to the workers 'from without', for the doctrines of Socialism 'grew out of the philosophic, historical and economic theories elaborated by educated representatives of the propertied classes, by intellectuals'. Just as Socialist consciousness arose in the realm of ideas, rather than from the workers' experiences of struggle against capital, so would the party which was to embody that consciousness exist independently of that struggle, of its spontaneous ebb and flow. To put matters crudely, in terms of the difficult relationship between 'subjective' and 'objective' factors in history, 'between consciousness and spontaneity', Lenin regarded the Social Democratic Party as the subjective factor, the agent of historical change, the 'conscious element'. The workers themselves were very much 'objective' factors, incapable of developing their own ideologies or formulating their own political interests. The dichotomy between Social Democrat as agent and worker as object was vividly expressed:

> Marxism . . . gives a gigantic impetus to the initiative and energy of the Social-Democrat, opens up for him the widest perspectives and (if one may so express it)

places at his disposal the mighty force of millions and millions of workers 'spontaneously' rising for the struggle!

The Leninist party was almost an embodiment of historical will, the element of voluntarism required for revolutionary change. 'Give us an organisation of revolutionaries, and we shall overturn Russia!' said Lenin,[2] and his words acquired their unique resonance as he proceeded to do exactly that, in what Gramsci, representing those eager to break through the sterile determinism of the Second International, described as the 'Revolution against *Capital*'.[3] For the revolutionary looking across war-ravaged Europe in 1918 or 1920, it must have been easy to conclude that the factor which distinguished backward Russia from the 'objectively' more promising battlegrounds in the West was the existence of a resolute Bolshevik Party, a tried revolutionary leadership ready to unfold its arms and seize power the moment it fell within reach. Thus could the Communist Party appear as the means by which the worker was 'transformed from *executor* to *initiator*, from *mass* to *leader* and *guide*, from brawn to brain and purpose'.[4] The revolutionary international tended to be seen by its founders as the conscious, directing force of history rather than its product. If the history of the Comintern demonstrates anything, it is the fallacy of this conception; but this conception is implicit in the monodimensional view of Communist politics presented in many Marxist writings on the British Communist Party.

This brings me to the second thread of my argument. If the duty of the revolutionary vanguard was consciously and scientifically to exploit all favourable objective circumstances in the interests of Socialism, it was further held that, in the period opened up by the First World War, all the objective circumstances were conducive to revolutionary change. The fate of the revolution depended on the subjective factor, the question of leadership, alone. These assumptions were grounded in Lenin's analysis of imperialism, 'the highest stage of capitalism' and therefore, because it could develop no further, 'parasitic or decaying capitalism'. 'Imperialism', Lenin asserted in 1920, 'is the eve of proletarian social revolution. This has been confirmed since 1917 on a world-wide scale.'[5] Objectively, capitalism had reached breaking point; it was now 'anti-historical'.[6] The character of the epoch was expressed in its wars and revolutions, and the paramount need was to fill the vacuum left by the degeneration of Social Democracy. Thus the founding of the Comintern, which was heralded with much optimism of the will as the harbinger of 'the epoch of proletarian communist revolution'.[7] As a British participant in the Comintern's Second Congress recalled, 'we were playing leap-frog with history and did not know it'.[8] Nevertheless, despite the unwillingness of history to join in with this game of leapfrog, the

Comintern did not formally revise its estimation of the trajectory of history for more than two decades; and when it did so, it decided to revise also its own organisation and programme – out of existence. The Comintern, and not capitalism, had become anti-historical.

It should be noted in passing that these beliefs remained axiomatic for the British Communist Party, through all its tactical shifts, up to 1941. The Party's vaunted indispensability lay in its understanding:

> that the epoch which had opened with the war of 1914 was a revolutionary epoch; that imperialism could offer nothing but chronic decay, deepening crises, wars and catastrophe for mankind; that the task before the working class was the task of destroying capitalism and establishing their own revolutionary dictatorship in order to build socialism with the minimum of delay and suffering; and that every phase and aspect of the working class struggle and every section of the working class army needed to be subordinated to this supreme aim.[9]

Even the advance of Fascism, which prompted such a dramatic reappraisal of the Party's immediate tasks, signified 'the weakening of the basis and stability of capitalist-class power in its last stages. . . . The blows of the counter-revolution help to forge the army of the future victorious revolution.'[10] The condition for victory was to provide this army with its General Staff,[11] a revolutionary party based on 'the impregnable rock of the theory of Marxism–Leninism . . . [and] completely united in the outlook of its membership on the basis of this theory'. Without the leadership of such a party, the workers were doomed to defeat, to the horrors of Fascism and war; with it, their final victory was certain.[12] The historical crisis of mankind was reduced to the problem of revolutionary leadership.

This was also the conclusion, albeit with a very different emphasis, of Lenin's only peer as a revolutionary leader, whose ideas have exercised a hypnotic influence on a number of historians of British Communism. Throughout the 1930s, Trotsky remained convinced that the 'objective prerequisites for the proletarian revolution have not only "ripened"; they have begun to get somewhat rotten'. By 'objective prerequisites', Trotsky referred not only to the economic 'substructure' but to the 'subjective' attitudes of the 'multimillioned masses' who 'again and again enter the road of revolution. But each time', Trotsky went on, 'they are blocked by their own conservative bureaucratic machines'. The world stood on the brink of revolution and the approaching war brought with it the promise of the overthrow of capitalism. But the mass organisations of the working class, most deleteriously the Stalinist Communist Parties, far from taking the struggle forward, actually stood for the maintenance of bourgeois order. Just as in 1914, the problem was wholly one of leadership. The solution offered was consequently the same, even if – the first time as tragedy, the second time as farce – not quite the same. In 1938 Trotsky unveiled his new programme for revolution, *The Death Agony of Capitalism and the Tasks of the Fourth International*, in the anticipation that within a decade the new international would gain the allegiance of millions.[13]

Towards the end of his life, Trotsky was prone to occasional misgivings that his grand historical scheme might peter out as a utopia.[14] However, his brutal murder in 1940 meant that he was never to revise his fundamental political conceptions, and the movements which have since borne his name have never felt it necessary to do so. Their attempts to grapple with the history of the Comintern have therefore, as we shall see, been a parody of Marxist historical analysis.

The best Marxist historical writing is based on a comprehension of the relationship, dialectical if you like, between 'determinism' and 'voluntarism'. In broad terms the field of political struggle may be determined by the development of the forces of production and economic relationships, but that struggle is the conscious activity of human agents capable of challenging, and thereby changing, the logic of determinism. History is not a laboratory, and scientific Socialists, if such exist, do not stand above the raw material of the class struggle adding the combustible element which will bring the historical process to the desired conclusion. Only 'the philistine thinks that it is the revolutionaries who make a revolution and who can call it off at any point as they wish'.[15] History is rather the outcome of the struggle between rival classes challenging the logic of determinism in diverse ways. For whatever is determined does not need to be struggled for; and yet the struggle itself is, in broad outline, determined by the objective clash of interests. This paradox lies at the heart of the Marxist view of history. Men make history, but not as they please.

But the best Marxist historical writing has rarely resulted from the study of the Communist movement. Based on the conceptions we have already described, Trotskyist writings on British Communism do not trace the relationship between 'objective' and 'subjective' factors, but tend rather to assume a rigid dichotomy between them. On the one hand, the objective relations of class forces – in which are subsumed the 'subjective' attitudes of the multi-millions – are taken for granted. The epoch was one of capitalist stagnation and immanent proletarian revolution, requiring only the correct revolutionary leadership. An intelligent appreciation of the changing political environment – the objective framework – in which the CP operated is thus ruled out. Moreover, the Party itself is treated as something quite apart from this framework, as an organisation of professional revolutionaries to be judged by the correctness of its line. In reality, of course, the CP was an organisation of men working in munitions factories and women working in cotton mills, of the sons of Oxford dons and of South Wales miners, of soldiers and air-raid victims, of Jews and Catholics, of co-operators and trade unionists;[16] and it cannot be understood apart from this. The Party was not a General Staff, consulting its maps and deploying its troops. It was the political expression of the struggles and aspirations of thousands of ordinary, and yet at the same time exceptional, British people – ordinary in their experiences of the iniquities of capitalism and exceptional in their wholehearted refusal to accept their inevitability. However, our Trotskyist historians give us little idea of the motivations of those who joined the Party, of the nature and complexity of their allegiances or of the practical and political pressures to which they were subjected. All we get is a critique of the Party line, and usually a very poor one.

Even the ablest of these historians, Michael Woodhouse, cannot cope with the history of the Communist Party satisfactorily.[17] Woodhouse sets out to show why the CP was unable to develop the supposedly revolutionary potential of the General Strike and 'at least win from this struggle the basis for its emergence as a mass revolutionary Party'. His explanation, very crudely, is that the CP adopted the wrong line, and did so because the Comintern had fallen under the influence of Stalin: the CP's 'non-revolutionary interpretation of the British situation . . . flowed directly from the policy of Socialism in One Country . . .' The poverty of this analysis is all the more remarkable in that it follows a lengthy introduction in which Woodhouse dissects with precision and great insight the political and industrial tendencies which merged into the CP in 1920. 'The powerful impulses towards spontaneity and the various syndicalist forms of action', he concluded, 'were deeply ingrained in the traditions of important sections of the working class'; and 'it was to be one of the most fundamental tasks of the party in the early 1920s to fight this tendency'. but how was this to be achieved when 'the CPGB was as much a reflection of these tendencies as it was a conscious participant in them'?[30] The answer could only be a *deus ex machina*; with its wealth of revolutionary experience and above all revolutionary theory the Comintern was to uproot British Communists from their deeply ingrained traditions and transform them from brawn to brain. And indeed at first, while Stalin remained in the wings, the *deus ex machina* did the trick; by 1925, thanks largely to the guidance and assistance of the Comintern, the Party had been able 'to proceed towards the establishment of conditions for effective mass Communist work'. Thus can Woodhouse ascribe much decisive significance to the policy of Socialism in One Country and the 'Stalinisation' of the Comintern. Woodhouse's sophisticated treatment of the pre-Communist left gives way to a basically monocausal explanation of Communist politics which fails to probe the Party's relationship to wider social and political forces. This oversight is no reflection on Woodhouse's abilities as a historian, but rather on the distinctive conception of the role of the Comintern already described.[18]

The treatment of the Party as the disembodied incarnation of a political 'line' and the realisation that this line was formulated in Moscow led inevitably to the conclusion that the paramount question posed by a study of the CP – of any CP – was to ascertain how the Soviet leadership arrived at a particular policy. The most ludicrous manifestation of this approach is Black's lengthy diatribe against *Stalinism in Britain*,[19] but this volume merely reduces to an absurdity the preconceptions of other Trotskyist historians like Dewar and Pearce. Dewar, for example, is concerned wholly with 'the party's political reaction to events and the extent to which this expressed or failed to express revolutionary socialist principles; that is, the broad course taken by the party "line" '.[20] In charting this course, Dewar deems it sufficient to assemble a series of quotations from the Party press interspersed with lengthy disquisitions on the internal and external policy of the Soviet Union, and Pearce's methods are much the same.[21] These writers do not even succeed in their limited task. Dewar, for instance, exhausts the complexities of the Communist analysis of international affairs in the late 1930s by citing a communiqué issued at the close of Eden's visit to Moscow in 1935.[22] His discussion of the Popular Front fails even to mention the CP's contribution to industrial struggles during that period, while Pearce deliberately misleads the reader into thinking that the CP at that time opposed strikes 'as inimical to the true interests of the working class'.[23] Bornstein and Richardson, with similar intent, devote eleven lines to the CP's industrial activities between 1935 and 1941 and thirty-six pages to its opposition to strikes in the latter part of the war.[24] Despite their polemical vigour, these last works, which include the most detailed accounts of Communist politics in the 1930s and the 1940s, can hardly be considered as serious contributions to the history of the Party.

In their failure to locate the CP in the wider social and political context of which it formed a part and at the same time aspired to transform, the works mentioned so far differ little from more conventional histories of the Party. The best of these, Macfarlane's study of the Party's early years, is at least distinguished by its scholarship, its thoroughness and its author's worthy attempt to convey a sympathetic, but critical, understanding of Communist politics.[25] This is more than can be said for Henry Pelling, the author of the only academic study of the Party's long-term development. Pelling's work, a late product of the Cold War informed by a fervent dislike and suspicion of Communism, is basically a tendentious explanation of 'how it came to pass, that a band of British citizens could sacrifice themselves so completely over a period of almost forty years to the service of a dictatorship in another country'.[26] But, as is also the case with the Trotskyist histories of the Party, one puts Pelling's book down with no clearer idea as to how exactly this did come to pass. His work, to cite the words a historian of the American CP has used of Pelling's American contemporaries, 'makes it hard to understand why anyone with intelligence and integrity would have remained in such a movement for more than the few days or weeks required to discover its gross inadequacies'.[27] Pelling's analysis is always superficial and numerous errors of historical interpretation arise from his inability to conceive of the Party as a genuine product of and challenge to the conditions of life in capitalist Britain. One of the book's greatest failings, which it shares with most of the other works mentioned here, was clearly identified by the Communist theoretician, R. Palme Dutt:

> It is as if a cinematograph film were to be made of a wrestling match, and then all the representation of one opponent blocked out from the film, so that by this means all the violent exertions, writhings and contortions of the single figure in a vacuum could be presented as something highly absurd and purposeless.[28]

This is an intelligent point graphically put. The problem is Dutt's implication that the CP's 'writhings and contortions' can be explained simply by its ceaseless struggle against capitalism. Perhaps he forgets the time when his Bolshevik wrestler warmly embraced his opponent. Or the time when he had an ally in the ring and kicked him in the groin. This brings us to a third school of Communist Party history.

It is one of life's ironies that an organisation which has produced so many brilliant historians has, until very recently, had the greatest difficulty in coming to terms with its own history. Sadly typical are the first two volumes of the CP's official history which, whatever their merits, are characterised chiefly by their author's determined and sometimes devious refusal to address unflinchingly the most fundamental questions concerning Communist politics in the 1920s.[29] By the time a third volume came to be added to the series some two decades later, however, the CP had undergone a series of changes conducive to a more frank and critical assessment of its own past. One result was that the author of this volume, Noreen Branson, felt far fewer inhibitions than Klugmann about discussing the more contentious issues in the Party's history: the genesis of 'Class Against Class', for example, or the Moscow Show Trials.[30]

The problem with Branson's book, some two-thirds of which is devoted to the period covered by the present study, is not so much that she fails to address the 'difficult' questions in the Party's history as that she regards the 'less difficult' questions as quite unproblematical. The ambiguities of the Party's stance on international affairs in the late 1930s, to give one example, are lost; the Party is presented simply as the most forthright and most consistent opponent of appeasement. Similarly, Branson writes as if the CP in the 1930s identified the threat of Fascism solely with the continental dictators and with their British imitator; its characterisation of Fascism as an inevitable stage in the development of monopoly capitalism, in Britain as elsewhere unless forestalled by popular action, is more or less ignored. Like so many historians, Branson seems to view the 1930s from the standpoint of 'what happened next', of the wartime alliance of the 'democratic' powers against Fascism and of post-war Communist politics; and this teleological approach tends to overlook whatever – and there was much – did not lead in this direction. Moreover, there are serious omissions of 'uncomfortable' facts, though these are less glaring than Klugmann's.[31] Branson's main and considerable virtue is that she uses her wider knowledge of the period to great effect in sketching the CP's relations with the state and with the Labour and democratic movement; and she gives a vivid account of the CP's multi-faceted campaigning on the political issues of the day. But it would be unwise to leave the history of the Communist Party entirely in its own hands just yet.

On this interpretation, the study of Communist Party history, particularly of its 'Stalinist' period, has produced a number of flawed works and far fewer of real value. In 1939, a *Daily Worker* reviewer complained of one novelist that his Communist characters came over as 'little more than political mouthpieces – not personalities so much as speeches. Yet Communists are really quite human; some of them are even bus conductors and unemployed men.'[32] The same criticism could be made of many of the works discussed here; so often the Party is treated as little more than the political mouthpiece of the Soviet Government. This is not to suggest that these studies should necessarily be enlivened by a bit of human interest, but that to consider the enunciation of the Party line by its leaders is inadequate without also considering its application by 'really quite human' Communists in social and political contexts which were not laid down by Moscow and did not conform neatly to dogmatic preconceptions as to the general crisis of capitalism. And in fact, the most enlightening works on British Communism have been studies, not of the Party 'line', but of specific areas of Communist politics or particular industries and communities in which its members were firmly embedded.

The earliest of these was Martin's study of the Minority Movement. Martin regards the movement as 'an uneasy alliance between the Communist International and the extreme left wing of the British trade union movement' and his scholarly treatise is full of insights into 'the ambiguities, the tensions, the conflicts of loyalty and aspiration which stemmed from this fundamental dualism'.[33] More recently there have appeared a number of fine studies which throw light on the activities of Communists as working-class autodidacts and educationalists;[34] as the defiant vanguard of communities ravaged by capitalism;[35] and as South Walian miners, mobilising resistance to reaction at home and abroad.[36] Especially helpful in the preparation of this book were Croucher's absorbing account of *Engineers at War*[37] and Stuart Broomfield's fine doctoral thesis on the South Wales coalfield during the Second World War.[38] These are not histories of the Communist Party and should not be treated as such, but to a greater or lesser extent they all give some indication as to why people joined the Party, their activities and their beliefs as Party members, the conditions they aspired to change and the methods and organisations through which they hoped to change them. Above all, we catch a glimpse of the Party not just as a set of phrases and fancies, but as a real organism with real interests located in a real society.[39] The aim of this book is to incorporate this sort of perspective into a study focusing on the Party itself, as Hinton has done so well in his *History Workshop* article on Coventry Communism,[40] but has yet to be achieved in a full-length work adopting a national perspective. The objective is not simply a history 'from above', nor one 'from below', but a synthesis of the two, even if this objective is more easily formulated than attained.

The core of this book is provided by a discussion of the Party 'line' in the narrow sense and of its relationship to the fundamental and strategic objectives of the Communist Party. The unavailability of internal Party records obviously poses problems in this respect, but these are not insuperable given the wealth of printed sources. The *Daily Worker* especially provides an invaluable fund of information. 'In a communist paper', Palme Dutt reminded its editor just after it first appeared in 1930, 'every single column, item, headline and line has got to express the paper, express the party';[41] and the *Worker* provides the historian with the CP's immediate reaction to every major development in national and international politics until its suppression in January 1941.

The writings and papers of R. Palme Dutt, the CP's *eminence rouge*, provide the other major source for official Communist policy and its theoretical foundations. Dutt was the most important figure in the Party and his name crops up more than any other in this book, and so it is perhaps worth providing some biographical information on this elusive character. In 1949, Dutt himself described his family background:

My mother's family migrated from Holland to Sweden in the seventeenth century; my grandfather was a judge, one uncle a banker, another the founder of an insurance company and a Liberal Cabinet Minister, and a cousin, I regret to say, Ivan Kreuger, whom I chiefly remember for the lavish treats he gave us as children before he entered on his wilder speculations and collapse. My father left India in 1875 at the age of 18 years, with a Gilchrist Travelling Scholarship, of which there was then only one to be competed for from among the 300 millions of India, and never saw India again, living and practising as a doctor in the railwaymen's quarter of Cambridge.

It was into this background that Dutt was born in 1896. From an early age he was acutely aware of the contrast between the 'prejudice in the upper class sections of the town against the coloured doctor' and the 'deep affection in which he was held by the workers' and recalled that 'these early impressions of questions of class and of colour deeply affected our early childhood conceptions of life'. These impressions were reinforced by the quality of Dutt's home life, where 'mixed national traditions' were reflected in 'a strong current of hostility to the British Empire and to ruling class institutions in Britain. Many Indian nationalists passed through our home and stayed with us.' However, it was not until 1914 that Dutt, having 'read independently very widely since the age of six', began a serious study of Marxism and joined the ILP. His formative political experiences were thus those of opposition to the First World War; in 1916 he was jailed for resisting military orders and in 1917 he was expelled from Oxford University for disseminating anti-war propaganda. As a full-time worker for the Labour Research Department and a member of the National Guilds League, Dutt joined the CP on its formation in 1920.[42] His rapid ascendancy in the Party was only partly interrupted by his prolonged exile on grounds of ill-health as from 1924. Although he relinquished editorship of the *Workers' Weekly*, he continued to exert tight editorial control over the theoretical journal he had founded in 1921, the *Labour Monthly*. Moreover, Dutt's 'Notes of the Month' for this journal, usually lucid, always logical, and occasionally exhibiting 'all the lucid logic of insanity',[43] provided Communists with the most authoritative exposition of the Party line at any given moment; as one Communist recalled, 'people used to swear by them'.[44] Dutt was also the dominant figure on the Party's Central Committee and Political Bureau. Even during his lengthy sojourn abroad Dutt could claim that 'the majority of the leading party documents during this period [the previous six months] have been directly drafted by me';[45] and as from 1935 his supervision of the Party's affairs was to be made still more effective by his presence in King Street. Dutt was never one of the CP's more charismatic leaders – a Manchester Communist recalled that 'he was bloody awful; he'd have made as much impact if you'd stuck him in a back room of the Free Trade Hall and let him talk to himself'[46] – but his intellectual dominance within the Party and his authority in the back rooms of Communist politics were unchallengeable. Not surprisingly, Dutt's papers in the British Library have proved, despite their having been rigorously sorted by Dutt before binding, a major primary source for this study. John Saville has recently commented that 'there can be no major assessment of communist history without a large-scale exegesis of Dutt's writings and of his political position over forty years',[47] and this book is, in part, a contribution to that task.

But if Dutt's presence inevitably looms large in this study, an endeavour will also be made to give some idea of the 'Party line' in the broader sense suggested by a Communist journal in 1937:

> The Party line is made up of the voices in the coal mines, the dockyards, in the Trade Union Branches, and Co-op. Guilds; of the arguments which take place at the factory benches and at the street corners, in the pubs, by the firesides . . . How else, conceivably, could the Party line have any bearing on conditions and situations as we know them, in their ever-changing complexity?[48]

It is especially important that a study of the CP during the Popular Front period should take cognisance of this dimension of Communist politics. In the mid-1930s the Party effectively abandoned any attempt to sustain a distinctively Communist oppositional culture, resistant to contamination by bourgeois or social-democratic influences.[49] On the contrary, the essence of the new strategy was that Communists should work in a non-sectarian way in broad organisations which stood for far less than Communism. In doing so, Communists acquired new responsibilities and priorities, not as Party members but as, say, trade unionists or tenants; but at the same time they were to remain first and foremost *Communists*, members of a disciplined revolutionary vanguard who regarded all such movements as 'merely different aspects of one single and indivisible struggle of the working class for power'.[50] The 'new model party', wrote John Strachey, had at the same time to set itself apart from and immerse itself in the mainstream of political culture:

> it is necessary to cut oneself off from a thousand ties and influences which prevent anyone brought up in the British and American environment from becoming a scientific Socialist. And yet at the same time it is almost useless to become a scientific Socialist if in the process one cuts oneself off from full, effective participation in contemporary life in general and the life of the Labour movement in particular.[51]

In practice, as Strachey acknowledged, Communists could only hope to approximate to this ideal. By their effective participation in contemporary life Communists came to develop or reinforce countervailing loyalties and a sense of what was politically feasible which did not always conform to King Street's unpredictable conception of the 'single and indivisible struggle of the working class for power'; and, occasionally, effective participation in the broader movement and the Party line seemed quite incompatible. The Party leadership was well aware of, and perturbed by, the 'tendency on the part of some comrades in these organisations to separate themselves from the Party', to 'get immersed in practical affairs and neglect to relate the practical fight to the aims of the Party'.[52] Many active Communists would drop out of organised Communist activity altogether, not out of apathy but because *their* Party work was in the union, or some other organisation. 'It appears to me', complained one Communist, 'that the Party is of secondary importance to this type of member.'[53] Thus there existed the potential for some discrepancy between the official Party line, set out in sacred texts by Party leaders, and the line actually followed by Party members. That is one reason why it is so inadequate to write a history of the CP based solely on its official and quasi-official statements of policy, with the sometimes implicit and sometimes explicit assumption that its membership consisted of docile, or steel-hardened, cadres subordinating all other interests to the current Party line. To write Communist history is, in part, to trace the relationship, not always a harmonious one, between the Party's official pronouncements and the activities of its members. The decisive influence on the former was the stated policy of the Comintern, whose decisions were binding on the British Party, even though it enjoyed a substantial degree of autonomy in running its day-to-day affairs by the late 1930s. Party activists, on the other hand, were subject to a variety of influences, their own political inclinations included, and this book will try to give due weight to these.

The first four chapters of the book, which draw heavily on Dutt's writings, provide the reader with an outline and appraisal of the nature of Communist politics in the late 1930s, bringing out especially some of those themes which have been neglected in conventional studies of the period.[54] On this basis I proceed to a more detailed examination of Communist politics during the period of almost two years in which it opposed what it described as the 'imperialist war'. There are a number of reasons why a study of this period is particularly desirable:

1 The CP's policies and activities at this time are subject to widespread misconceptions. The main detailed analysis of the Party's opposition to the war is that published by Victor Gollancz at the time in which he and a number of other left wingers argued that the CP had adopted a Leninist policy of revolutionary defeatism.[5] This work has frequently been cited,

and its allegations repeated, by later historians; but a juxtaposition of Leninist theory and Communist practice will reveal that its main thesis is untenable.

2 In following the Comintern's instructions to oppose the war, the CP seemed to have adopted a policy quite opposed to that it had followed before the war. It was because of its various changes of line on the war that the CP came apparently to be known as the Picture Palace Party – 'because it has a brand new programme each week'.[56] In fact, an examination of the Party's literature and activities across this change of line enables us to pick out the enduring features of its programme and strategy, those which did not alter with every twist in Soviet foreign policy. In the field of immediate struggles especially, the continuities in Communist politics will be more apparent than the ruptures, as the sections on the CP's industrial politics and on mass struggles in Birmingham before and during the war will indicate.

3 Since the Comintern's instructions on the war did not fully accord with the political perspectives and long-term aims of British Communists, the period gives us an opportunity to examine how far 'Bolshevik discipline' worked in practice, and how far Communists tended to evade the implications of the new line, even when they did not actually resist it.

4 The period of the Nazi–Soviet Pact is a crucial one in the history of the Comintern, and yet only in Britain of all the belligerent countries was Communist policy expressed continuously and (for the most part) legally. As Borkenau has commented, 'it was in London that the communist policy was throughout most clearly formulated with the least disturbance by local and passing incidents'.[57] Thus the historian of the British Party is in a favourable position to establish how far, in the words of Fernando Claudin, the Comintern did indeed brandish once more the spectre of revolution, particularly in the metropolitan centres of the British and French Empires.[58]

5 During the 1930s there had been a constant tension between the CP's characterisation of the epoch as one of the revolutionary transition to Socialism and the more limited, defensive objectives it set itself. With the decision to oppose the war, this discrepancy became more marked, as Party leaders injected a note of revolutionary optimism into their speeches and writings, describing the war as the last throes of a doomed social order. In reality, whether one looked for divisions within the ruling class, the radicalisation of the masses, disenchantment with Social Democracy, mass strikes, mutinous troops, civil unrest or the growth of the revolutionary party, there were few indications that Britain was heading towards revolution; the only threat to the established order came from

without. This situation of extreme divergence between reality and Communist dogma enables us to assess how far the CP's activities were based on its own flights of rhetoric and how far on a more perceptive, more pragmatic appraisal of what was politically possible. We shall discover, as a French Communist historian has discovered of his party, that the CP's calls for 'action' were mostly 'incantatory' and that its 'verbal vigour contrasted sharply with the modesty of the concrete forms of struggle proposed'.[59]

The picture which emerges is a confused one, of a revolutionary party acclimatising itself to a situation offering few opportunities for revolutionary activity without abandoning its fundamental conceptions and expectations. This contradiction would be resolved, if only partially, in the period after June 1941 when the CP came not only to support the war but to revise many of the assumptions which had formed the theoretical basis of Communist politics for two decades. This period will be considered very briefly in the conclusion.

Some years ago Perry Anderson posited three basic requirements for 'an adequate historical reconstruction' of a Communist Party. The first was an accurate account of its 'membership, organisation, leadership, tendencies and policies'; the second, an assessment of its position in and relationship to the 'national balance of forces'; and the third, a description of its relations with the Comintern.[60] The encyclopaedic work which would meet these requirements will, perhaps, never be written, if only because the historian prepared to fulfil all these conditions is unlikely to be given access to the archive sources necessary to carry out fully the first and especially the third of these tasks. But if any such history is ever to be written of the British Party, it can only be a work of synthesis drawing on a great deal of painstaking collective research. It is as a contribution to that task, focusing on a particularly crucial period in the Party's history, that this book is intended.

Notes

1 Cited by P. Frolich, *Rosa Luxemburg* (1940), 162.
2 Lenin, *What Is To Be Done? Burning Questions of Our Movement* (1976 edn), 36–41, 47–9, 60, 99, 118, 157.
3 Article written 24.12.17 in A. Gramsci, *Selections from Political Writings 1910–1920* (1977), 34–7.
4 Gramsci, 'The Communist Party' (4.9.20), *ibid.*, 393.
5 Lenin, *Imperialism, the Highest Stage of Capitalism* (written 1916; 1944 edn), 109, 10. For an excellent discussion of Lenin's view of 'moribund capitalism', see F. Claudin, *The Communist Movement: from Comintern to Cominform* (1975), 56–62.
6 Gramsci's expression, 'The instruments of labour' (14.2.20), *op. cit.*, 166.

7 Manifesto of CI Foundation Congress, cited J. T. Murphy, *Preparing For Power* (1972 edn), 197. For a selection of Lenin's optimistic predictions at this time, see L. Kolakowski, *Main Currents of Marxism: 2. The Golden Age* (1981 edn), 476.
8 J. T. Murphy, *New Horizons* (1941), 135.
9 'Notes', Aug. 1940, 422–3. For a concise statement of the CP's fundamental beliefs, see R. P. Dutt, *The Political and Social Doctrine of Communism* (written 1938; 1942 edn).
10 *Ibid.*, 26–7.
11 Stalin's phrase, cited in *For Soviet Britain. The Programme of the Communist Party adopted at the XIII Congress* (CPGB, 1935), 47.
12 CPGB PB statement on the 'Twentieth anniversary of the Communist Party of Great Britain', *LM*, July 1940, 410–11.
13 Trotsky, *The Death Agony of Capitalism and the Tasks of the Fourth International* (written 1938; 1978 edn); I. Deutscher, *The Prophet Outcast. Trotsky: 1929–1940* (1970 edn), 476.
14 *Loc. cit.*
15 Trotsky (1916), cited Deutscher, *The Prophet Armed. Trotsky: 1879–1921* (1970 edn), 245.
16 To refer only to some of those interviewed for this study.
17 'Marxism and Stalinism in Britain, 1920–1926' in Woodhouse and Pearce, *Essays on the History of Communism in Britain* (1975).
18 *Ibid.*, 3–4, 41–3, 60–1, 65–9, 91 and *passim*.
19 R. Black, *Stalinism in Britain: a Trotskyist Analysis* (1970).
20 H. Dewar, *Communist Politics in Britain: the CPGB from its Origins to the Second World War* (1976), 9.
21 See his essays in Woodhouse and Pearce, *op. cit.*
22 *Op. cit.*, 129.
23 'From "Social-Fascism" to "People's Front" ' in Woodhouse and Pearce, *op. cit.*, 205.
24 S. Bornstein and A. Richardson, *Two Steps Back. Communists and the Wider Labour Movement, 1935–1945* (n.d.).
25 L. J. Macfarlane, *The British Communist Party: its Origin and Development until 1929* (1966).
26 H. Pelling, *The British Communist Party. A Historical Profile* (1975 edn), 191.
27 M. Isserman, *Which Side Were You On? The American Communist Party During the Second World War* (1982), viii–ix. The author's preface provides a useful assessment of the weaknesses of the 'Cold War' approach to Communist Party history.
28 'Notes', May 1959, 202.
29 J. Klugmann, *History of the Communist Party of Great Britain. Volume One: Formation and Early Years, 1919–1924* (1968); *Volume Two: The General Strike, 1925–1926* (1969). See Thesis, 14–5.
30 N. Branson, *History of the Communist Party of Great Britain 1927–1941* (1985).
31 To give a couple of examples covered by this book, Branson gives no indication that the CP consciously adopted a position more favourable to Nazi Germany than to British imperialism in the early months of the war, nor that at that time it began to denounce the leadership of the Labour movement in terms redolent of the 'Class Against Class' period.
32 P. Bolsover, *DW*, 12.4.39.
33 R. Martin, *Communism and the British Trade Unions 1924–1933: a Study of the National Minority Movement* (1969), 1, vi.
34 S. Macintyre, *A Proletarian Science. Marxism in Britain 1917–1933* (1980).
35 S. Macintyre, *Little Moscows. Communism and Working-Class Militancy in Inter-War Britain* (1980).
36 H. Francis and D. Smith, *The Fed. A History of the South Wales Miners in the Twentieth*

Century (1980); H. Francis, *Miners Against Fascism. Wales and the Spanish Civil War* (1984).
37 R. Croucher, *Engineers at War* (1982).
38 S. Broomfield, 'South Wales during the Second World War: the coal industry and its community' (Ph.D., Wales, 1979).
39 In historical struggles, Marx advised us, we must learn to distinguish 'the phrases and fancies of the parties from their real organism and their real interests, their conception of themselves from their reality'; cited Claudin, *op. cit.*, 11.
40 In his 'Coventry Communism: a study of factory politics in the Second World War' (*History Workshop* no. 10, 1980), Hinton sets out to expose the 'complex interaction between the Party line, contradictory priorities of different sections of the Party membership, rank and file economic grievances and popular attitudes to the bosses, the Russians and the war' during the latter part of the war. Although a short study confined to one locality, this is undoubtedly the best work we have on the CP during its 'Stalinist' period.
41 RPD K4, Dutt to Rust, 13.2.30.
42 RPD K4, autobiographical extract dated Aug. 1935; Dutt to Bernard Shaw, 8.2.49.
43 Dutt's own comment on Paul Einzig in his *World Politics 1918–1936* (1936), 110.
44 Eddie Frow, interview.
45 RPD K4, Dutt to 'Bocca', 7.12.34.
46 Joe O'Reilly, interview.
47 *Marxism Today*, Aug. 1985, 33.
48 *Disc.*, Jan. 1937, editorial, 1–2.
49 For a nostalgic view of earlier efforts, see A. Howkins, 'Class Against Class: the political culture of the Communist Party of Great Britain, 1930–35' in F. Gloversmith (ed.), *Class Culture and Social Change. A New View of the 1930s* (1980).
50 J. Strachey, *What Are We To Do?* (1938), 265.
51 *Ibid.*, p. 308. For 'scientific Socialist' read 'Communist'.
52 W. Rust in *It Can Be Done* (CPGB, report of 14th Congress, 1937), 173.
53 S. Parks of Watford, *DW*, 1.9.38. Commenting that only a third of Party members could be expected at branch meetings, Sparks went on:
> The absentees excuse themselves by saying that they have to attend this or that organisation.
> In the majority of cases members get into these organisations without first consulting the branch committee. Therefore our membership get swallowed up in these organisations and forget their party responsibility.
54 And also neglecting to discuss properly one or two issues – Spain, for example, and the Moscow show trials – which have figured prominently in orthodox accounts of Communist politics in the 1930s. The Spanish issue was, of course, central to Communist politics at this time, but, because it has been so exhaustively covered by a number of other works, it is considered here only in the context of the CP's general conception of international affairs. However, the enduring importance of the Spanish experience will be given its due weight when we consider the Party's decision to oppose the war and its subsequent anti-war policies.
55 V. Gollancz (ed.), *The Betrayal of the Left* (1941). See also *The Politics of Victory* (1941) by the dissident Communist Tom Wintringham. Wintringham, who was expelled from the Party for ostensibly personal reasons in 1938, was a persuasive advocate of a 'People's War' whose ideas seem in retrospect to have been rather closer to the CP's in 1940–41 than he himself argued at the time.
56 *New Leader*, 16.10.42.

57 F. Borkenau, *European Communism* (1953), 235.
58 Claudin, *op. cit.*, 23, 299–300.
59 R. Bourderon, cited in M. Adereth, *The French Communist Party: a Critical History (1920–1984)* (1984), 97.
60 P. Anderson, 'Communist Party history' in R. Samuel (ed.), *People's History and Socialist Theory* (1981), 147–52.

Chapter one
Capitalism's last resort
British Communists and the threat of Fascism, 1934–38

What is Fascism, ask yourselves, what does it stand for? It is capitalism in desperation. Scratch a capitalist and find a Fascist.
(Arthur Horner, May 1936[1])

For more than a decade after its formation in 1920 the British Communist Party, closely supervised by the Comintern, strove with little success to find an effective means of approaching the great mass of British workers and bringing them under revolutionary leadership. Where these workers were organised, it was for the most part as loyal members of the Labour Party and the reformist trade unions which formed its basis; and from the start the decisive question for British Communists was that of their relationship to this overshadowing presence of British Labour. Whereas the establishment of the most important European Communist Parties had defined the lines of a schism from the main body of Social Democracy, the CPGB began life merely as an amalgam of sects and of sections of sects; and if it was to develop into anything more than just another sect, albeit one organised on Bolshevik lines, it had somehow to surmount the towering and deeply entrenched obstacle of Labourism.

For a number of years Communists, both as individuals and working through the Minority and National Left-Wing Movements, chipped away at this obstacle from within. Then in the late 1920s, excommunicated from the Labour Party and subjected to far more stringent discipline by many trade unions, Communists succumbed to the Comintern's latest edicts and mounted a frontal assault not only on the Labour leadership but on their former allies within the Labour movement. The end of capitalism was nigh, Communists insisted with all the intense, irrational fervour of streetcorner evangelists; and there were only two sides to the rising barricades. Those who rejected the leadership of the revolutionary party were, whatever their glib, mendacious phrases, the servile adjutants of the class enemy. This, very crudely, was the thinking behind the characterisation of the whole of the official Labour movement as 'social Fascist' and of its left wing as the spearhead of counter-revolution.[2]

That neither tactic succeeded in weakening the grip of right-wing Labour was but the clearest indication of the unreality of the CP's sanguine and sanguinary expectations and of its consequent failure to make any real impact on British political life. For the first dozen years of its existence the Party's membership fluctuated wildly, but never much above the ten thousand mark and usually far below.[3] By the early 1930s the hard core of Party activists, for the most part out of work, was almost completely isolated from the rest of the Labour movement. Despite one or two pockets of influence and the relative success of the National Unemployed Workers' Movement,[4] the Party's stagnation was a rather bathetic sequel to the high hopes of the immediate post-war period which it had aimed to turn into reality.

An overhaul of the Party's entire strategy was vitally necessary but, so tightly centralised was the Comintern by the 1930s, the initiative for any such change would have necessarily to come from outside Britain, in response to political developments elsewhere. It was in fact the triumph of Nazism in Germany which brought the Comintern down to earth with such force as to jolt it into a dramatic reappraisal of the tasks before it. 'After Hitler, us', the KPD had boasted; but after Hitler came only the consolidation of the Nazi dictatorship and the virtual annihilation of the largest and most prestigious Communist Party outside Russia. After further displays of almost unbelievable complacency, the Comintern came at last to appreciate not only that Fascism stood in the way of Socialist advance in the West but, decisively, that Nazi Germany posed the gravest threat to the Soviet Union since the period of the civil war. Recoiling from the blows of reaction and acknowledging the inability of an isolated Communist movement to stave off the further blows which would surely follow, the Comintern had begun by 1934 to effect a temporary reconciliation with bourgeois democracy. This historic compromise was exemplified by, on the one hand, the united stand of French workers in defence of the Republic and, on the other, the Soviet Union's entry into the League of Nations. The scene was set for Dimitrov's definitive rendition of the new themes in Communist politics at the seventh and last congress of the Comintern in July–August 1935. Dimitrov's report was concerned almost exclusively with the problem of Fascism, in the face of which he urged Communists to rally the broadest possible movement – of social-democratic and unorganised workers, of the peasantry and middle classes, of women and youth – in defence of their immediate interests, of democratic rights, of national independence and their cultural heritage.[5]

The new Popular Front strategy was taken up with vigour and enthusiasm by the British Party, opening up what Communists now regard as 'the most fruitful period in the history of the British left and of the Communist Party in particular'.[6] Such comments require qualification. During this period the National Government tottered from crisis to crisis without facing any serious challenge from the British left, and the decade climaxed not in the triumph of peace and democracy campaigned for by Communists but in war and the extension of Fascist domination to most of mainland Europe. Nevertheless, it is true that the CP emerged from its previous isolation to enjoy a spell of steadily increasing membership figures, ever wider literature sales and pervasive influence on the left of British politics. If this decade of illusions did end in disaster, it was not for want of effort or initiative on the part of Britain's Communists. But what had this effort and initiative to do with the achievement of Communism?

Looking back on the Seventh Congress from the various national roads to Communism which have been laid down since the Second World War, Communists have tended to extrapolate those ideas which prefigure post-Comintern Communist politics, leading inexorably to the Eurocommunism of recent years.[7] It is of course true that the British Party's adoption of a Popular Front strategy was no mere change of line, as transient as the moods of Soviet diplomacy, but a shift of perspective amounting in some respects to a transformation of the character of Communist politics. On the other hand, there is a great deal that is omitted from such teleological accounts of Communist history. So drastic were the tactical changes expounded at the congress and so profound their long-term significance that it is easy to overlook the fact that the Comintern's fundamental conceptions and misconceptions as to the nature of the epoch were not once called into question. The new strategy of defensive alliances did not displace but was grafted onto the Comintern's catastrophic analysis of the general crisis of imperialism as the eve of world proletarian revolution. The Popular Front strategy, it will be seen, rested on an uneasy and ambiguous relationship between immediate defensive struggles on the basis of bourgeois democracy and the conviction that capitalism could no longer satisfy even the most elementary human requirements, including those rights of organisation and agitation permitted under bourgeois democracy.

For this latter reason, Fascism was regarded as the characteristic form of capitalist rule in the period of its general crisis. Communists, following Dimitrov, were certainly aware of the distinctive qualities of Fascism but this distinction did not coincide neatly with state boundaries, with the Maginot Line, for the imperialist bourgeoisie was everywhere drawn towards Fascism as the only solution to its problems. It is generally assumed that, having accepted the primacy of the struggle against Fascism, the British CP was concerned primarily to stifle the growth of the BUF within Britain and resist the advances of the European dictators. From this angle, the Party's subsequent decision to oppose the war against Nazi Germany in October 1939 appears purely and simply as a betrayal of its past struggles, with no obvious mitigating factors. But in fact the CP claimed, both before and after the oubreak of war, that the danger of Fascism in Britain came not exclusively from Hitler and certainly not from Mosley's Blackshirts, but from the frock-coated National Government. Nowadays this view might seem merely curious, but it was central to the Party's understanding of the development of capitalism and lay at the root of the contradictions in Communist policy which would be so forcefully revealed after the outbreak of war. It is therefore essential that we trace the Party's conception of Fascism as it developed from before the Seventh Congress to, in a later chapter, the period in which it opposed the war. The best place to start is Palme Dutt's influential volume on *Fascism and Social Revolution*, first published in 1934.

The key to Dutt's understanding of Fascism was his assumption that 'present society is ripe, is rotten-ripe for the social revolution'.[8] The First World War had inaugurated the '*general crisis of capitalism*, or final phase within imperialism, when the forces of production are in ever more violent conflict with the cramping fetters of the existing property relations of production, when capitalism in more and more obvious decay is faced with the advance to victory of the proletarian social revolution, and . . . is resorting to every device and expedient to maintain its power'.[9] Within this general crisis, cyclical crises took on a new intensity, 'accompanied by growing social and political disturbance and recurrent war'.[10] The bourgeoisie in every imperialist country inevitably turned towards Fascism in a last desperate attempt to suppress these insoluble contradictions. Indeed, Fascism was the form of state corresponding to the decline of capitalism, just as parliamentary democracy had corresponded to its ascendance.[11] In accordance with this approach, Dutt's first three chapters dealt not with the specific question of Fascism – as far as Dutt was concerned there was no specific question of Fascism – but with the global crisis of capitalism of which Fascism was but 'the most complete expression'.[12] His book, as he informed Pollitt, was intended as a sort of sequel to Lenin's *Imperialism*, making it clear why the issue of Fascism inevitably developed at the present 'extreme latest stage of imperialism'.[13]

After this lengthy prologue, Dutt put forward his definition of Fascism as a 'counter-revolutionary mass movement supported by the bourgeoisie, employing weapons of mixed social demagogy and terrorism to defeat the revolution and build up a strengthened capitalist state dictatorship'.[14] The definition was specific inasmuch as it located a particular stage in the downfall of capitalism, but general in that all imperialist countries were held to have reached, or very nearly reached, that stage. Dutt repeatedly stressed the close parallels to be drawn 'between the increasingly dominant tendencies of theory and practice of all modern capitalism . . . and the professedly peculiar theory and practice of Fascism'.[15] It was 'possible to speak of the development towards Fascism of all modern capitalist states', the Roosevelt and Brüning regimes and the National Government in Britain offering 'particular illustrations of near-Fascist or pre-Fascist stages of development towards complete Fascism within the shell of the old forms'.[16]

If Fascism was characterised by its mass basis, Dutt nevertheless denied that this mass movement had any autonomous role to play. Fascism was not, he insisted, 'an independent movement of the middle class and petit-bourgeoisie'. Dutt's interpretation of Fascism was far more instrumental:

> a weapon of finance-capital, utilising the support of the middle class, of the slum proletariat and of demoralised working-class elements against the organised working class, but throughout acting as the instrument and effective representative of the interests of finance-capital.[17]

Reasoning thus could Dutt refer to the 'gigantic, artificial expansion of National Socialism' during the last years of the Weimar Republic as 'a highly organised product of the entire mechanism of the capitalist dictatorship'.[18] Thus too did Dutt entirely discount the spontaneity of the Fascists' populist demagogy. 'Behind the ranting megalomaniacs, bullies, drug-fiends and broken-down bohemians who constitute the outer façade of Fascism', he argued, 'the business heads of finance-capital who pay the costs and pull the strings are perfectly cool, clear and intelligent'.[19] The atavistic ebullitions of a Hitler or a Goebbels were 'as completely rational and calculated, for the present purposes of capitalism, as a machine-gun or a Zinoviev Letter election'.[20] One feature of this approach was that Dutt disputed the significance of the putative conquest of power by the Fascist movement. In every case, he argued, Fascism had been placed in power from above, the bourgeoisie having in practice 'passed power from one hand to the other, and called it a "revolution" '.[21] Whatever the appearances to the contrary, Fascism was nothing but a tool designed to sharpen the existing capitalist dictatorship.

Nevertheless, this purpose-built instrument was central to Dutt's conception of Fascism. As the buttresses of the capitalist order, principally Social Democracy, began to crumble, the bourgeoisie turned to this new mass movement to deflect the growing opposition to capitalism by strident anti-capitalist demagogy. The National Government in Britain was thus not itself a Fascist government, even though it prepared the ground for Fascism by its intensification of the capitalist dictatorship and extension of state regulation of the economy.[22] It was described as ' *"encroaching Fascism"* within the old forms, which precedes and prepares the Full Fascist attack' (hence the analogy with the Brüning Government in pre-Nazi Germany).[23] But when Dutt turned to the future development of Fascism in Britain he concentrated on the openly Fascist parties, and principally the BUF. For, although Fascism grew 'organically' out of bourgeois democracy, its significance lay in the fact that it appeared not to do so:

> On all sides the bankruptcy of the old social, economic and political system becomes recognised, and the demand for a complete change of the social system replaces the old cry for reforms. . . . In this situation capitalism is only able to save its power for one further lease by the final desperate expedient of staging a sham 'revolution' with the nominal aim of 'socialism', but in fact designed to maintain its power – the 'National Socialist Revolution' or Fascism.[24]

Communists should not therefore underestimate Mosley's significance in the drive to Fascism in Britain, as Dutt reminded Pollitt in July 1934:

> You are right about the danger of seeing only Mosley and not NG. But in fact the danger is a double one. The other danger is to see NG as a whole issue and campaign and Mosley as a minor detail. . . . What is essential is for our people to see and explain all the time the twofold character of the fascist offensive, both NG and Mosley, and the effective division of labour and INTERPLAY of both.[25]

The struggle against this dual offensive, it was clear, could not be conducted on the basis of bourgeois democracy, for '*bourgeois democracy breeds Fascism. Fascism grows organically out of bourgeois democracy.*'[26] The mythical alternative of a 'planned capitalism' was in reality 'part of the advance towards Fascism'. 'It will be seen', Dutt noted, 'that the outlook of Keynes has begun to approximate to that of Hitler. This is a valuable measure of capitalism in decay.'[27] Social Democracy too, 'the shadow of capitalism', inevitably went through a 'process of "fascisation" ' as capitalism developed to 'more and more Fascist forms'. And this process of adaptation did not come to an end with the victory of Fascism, but took on 'ever more extreme forms'.[28] The only alternative was the workers' dictatorship which would put an end to the system which inevitably gave rise to Fascism. Even if the revolution did not come soon enough to forestall the Fascist dictatorship, it would come not very long after. For Fascism, in attempting to suppress the contradictions of capitalism by the artificial methods of naked coercion, only succeeded in intensifying them. In its '*laying bare of the civil war at the root of class-society*' and its '*explosion of all the illusions of peace and legality*' lay the 'certainty of its collapse'. The attempted 'organisation of social decay' on 'the basis of *permanent civil war*' would be no more than a passing phenomenon, 'likely to be remembered only as an episode in the long-drawn class-war advancing to the final victory of the socialist revolution'.[29] Fittingly, Dutt concluded his volume with the final rousing couplet from the *Internationale*.

Written in 1933–34, Dutt's book was permeated with the rhetoric and the illusions of 'Class Against Class', but his analysis of Fascism was modified in no significant way before Dimitrov's compelling redefinition of the Comintern's tasks at its Seventh World Congress.[30] Defining Fascism more narrowly than Dutt had as '*the open terrorist dictatorship of the most reactionary, most chauvinistic and most imperialist elements of finance capital*',[31] Dimitrov laid a new emphasis on the distinctiveness of Fascism from other forms of bourgeois rule. The establishment of Fascism, he stressed, was 'not an *ordinary succession* of one bourgeois government by another, but a *substitution* of one state form of class domination of the bourgeoisie – bourgeois democracy – by another form – open terrorist dictatorship'.[32] Fascism usually came to power, not as the result of some dexterous legerdemain by 'some committee or other of finance capital', but 'in the course of a mutual, and at times severe, struggle against the old bourgeois parties, or a definite section of these parties'.[33] More radically still, Dimitrov urged Communists to join forces with definite sections of these bourgeois parties to turn back the Fascist offensive. However, this new-found commitment to defend to the last the democratic rights secured by the working class under capitalism did not entail uncritical support for bourgeois–democratic regimes. On the contrary, if it was a mistake to disregard the qualitative difference between bourgeois democracy and Fascism, it was also 'a mistake, no less serious and dangerous, to *underrate* the importance . . . of the *reactionary measures of the bourgeoisie at present increasingly developing in bourgeois–democratic countries*'. The lesson was of particular relevance to British Communists:

> before the establishment of a fascist dictatorship, bourgeois governments usually pass through a number of preliminary stages and adopt a number of reactionary measures which directly facilitate the accession to power of fascism. Whoever does not fight the reactionary measures of the bourgeoisie and the growth of fascism at these preparatory stages *is not in a position to prevent the victory of fascism, but on the contrary, facilitates that victory*.[34]

Thus did Dimitrov argue that 'at the present stage, fighting the fascist danger in Great Britain means primarily fighting the "National Government" and its reactionary measures'.[35] This was also the position taken by Dutt in his contribution to the Seventh Congress.[36]

In general terms Dutt's thinking had changed little in the previous year, and he continued to regard Fascism as a 'sign of the approaching revolutionary crisis' for which the camps were rapidly forming as Fascism exposed the 'latent civil war in class society'.[37] However, Dutt now attached far more weight to the specific threat posed by Fascism and criticised the previous tendency, so evident in his own writings, 'to use fascism loosely to describe any and every reactionary phenomenon all over the world in the present period, lumping together the whole camp of the bourgeoisie and almost the entire non-Communist camp as "fascist" '. Hitler's accession to power was a 'turning point of decisive importance', but Communists 'had so freely described the previous transitional forms of Bruening, Von Papen and Von Schleicher as already the fascist dictatorship', Dutt admitted, 'that we tended at first . . . to treat the advent of Hitler as . . . merely another stage in an already existing fascist dictatorship'. This unusually frank admission of error was implicit in the whole line of the Seventh Congress, but this refinement of analysis was gradually to be abandoned by British Communists in the coming years. The roots of the CP's later tendency to confuse the reactionary measures of the National Government with Fascism itself can already be discerned in Dutt's depiction of the line of the anti-Fascist struggle in Britain.

In his general comments on the 'process of fascisation' Dutt specified three stages: 'the fascisation of the state apparatus within the old forms'; 'the development of the "reactionary mass movement" '; and the coming together of the two in the 'complete fascism' typified by the Hitler and Mussolini regimes. Dutt did not, then, underestimate the significance of the *special social political mechanism* which sustained this intensified dictatorship of the bourgeoisie. Indeed, he felt that, in neglecting this 'peculiar social basis or mass basis', Dimitrov's definition failed to give 'the whole picture, . . . all the essentials of fascism'; and he therefore recommended that the congress resolution be expanded to cover this point.

However, when Dutt turned to the prospect of Fascism in Britain he was concerned 'first and foremost' with the role of the National Government. True, the BUF posed a threat as 'a reserve weapon of the bourgeoisie'. But Mosley's current significance was as a diversion from 'the main drive of the bourgeoisie towards the preparation for fascism in Britain, as represented by the policy of the National Government':

> Mosley represents at present to some extent a lightning conductor for the National Government . . . . The National Government and the reformist leaders point to Mosley as representing the sole menace of fascism. Meanwhile the National Government is able to get past with its repressive measures of

preparation towards fascism, as a kind of 'lesser evil' compared to Mosley, while the attention of the masses is fixed on Mosley.

Dutt did not as yet suggest that the policies of the National Government were themselves equivalent to Fascism, but only that to avert the threat of Fascism required that Communists '*concentrate the fight against the specific enemy attack at the decisive point of struggle*'. But as Mosley's long-term irrelevance became more apparent, the fight against the National Government became the permanent focus of the CP's anti-Fascism. Of Dutt's 'two characteristic elements' in Fascism, one – the mass movement – came to be overlooked, precisely because it hardly existed in Britain. Of Dutt's three stages of 'fascisation', the last two were largely ignored, leaving just 'the fascisation of the state apparatus within the old forms'. Dutt's first stage of 'fascisation' came to be confused with Fascism itself.

For the moment, however, Communists in many parts of Britain were still very much preoccupied with the BUF. When Mosley's 'travelling circus' tried to penetrate areas of high unemployment like South Wales and the Lancashire cotton towns it encountered fierce resistance led by Communists. The recollection of a Communist from the Cheetham district of Manchester that 'we would physically throw them out as well as politically throw them out' more or less sums up the CP's response to Fascist activities at this time.[38] Especially bitter were the struggles in London's East End, where Mosley came nearest to establishing a mass basis on a 'programme' of crude anti-Semitism. The physical confrontation in the East End climaxed in October 1936 when thousands of Londoners converged on Stepney and successfully prevented a Blackshirt procession from passing along its intended route. This was the legendary 'Battle of Cable Street' which has cropped up in so many works as one of the most compelling and evocative images of the 1930s.[39]

But by 1937 the BUF was visibly in decline, shunned both by the British establishment and by the mass of the British people. The days when it had appeared that Mosley might gain extensive support from Tory MPs, industrialists, press barons and the like were now long gone. The Public Order Act of 1936 had put an end to the provocative, uniformed demonstrations on which Mosley had relied to drum up mass support,[40] while local authorities up and down the country denied the BUF access to public halls for indoor meetings. The BUF's membership dwindled, and outside of the East End it failed to gain even a modicum of electoral support.[41] As Mosley's movement stagnated, the CP increasingly turned its attention away from the Fascists to the more pressing question of how to defeat the National Government. By 1938 the Party tended to regard Mosley as a spent force.[42]

For Communists to have inferred from Mosley's ineffectuality that Britain was, for whatever reason, immune to Fascism would have meant the abandonment of the characterisation of Fascism as the universal product of capitalist decay. But Dutt, at least, did not significantly revise his earlier projection of the development of capitalism.[43] Neither did the Party's other leading theoretician in the 1930s, John Strachey, to whom, writing late in 1937, Fascism represented not the outcome of a specific conjuncture of circumstances but the 'logically necessary and fore-seeable goals' of the 'present line of capitalist development'.[44] But already at the Comintern's Seventh Congress Dimitrov had pronounced that Fascism assumed '*different forms* in different countries' according to their particular circumstances. The illustrations he provided give a good idea of the elasticity of the Comintern's definition of Fascism. In Yugoslavia and Finland, for instance, Fascism had come to power without the support of a 'broad mass base' and had then had to build one up 'by making use of the state apparatus'. And 'embryo American fascism', in marked contrast to German Fascism, came forward 'principally in the guise of an opposition to fascism', portraying itself as 'the custodian of the Constitution and "American democracy" '.[45]

There seems little reason why such an inclusive view of Fascism should not also have taken in the British National Government, which was held to represent exactly those groups – 'a handful of millionaires, big bankers of the City of London, big monopolists and landlords'[46] – whose interests were best served by Fascism. Thus Strachey again:

> Fascism is the most systematic and adequate expression of the needs of capitalism in decline.
>
> Naturally, Fascism will not always be called Fascism. For example, the present policy of the British ruling class appears to be leading towards an attempt to establish its unchecked autocracy . . . without resorting to a special demagogic Fascist movement. The British capitalists appear to intend to use the existing State machinery, and their existing methods of securing mass support, to get rid of the restraints of democracy.[47]

The essence of Fascism lay not in its special mass movement but in the reactionary purposes for which the handful of millionaires made use of this movement; and the CP was coming to adopt the view, held by many on the left, that Britain was susceptible to an indigenous form of 'National Fascism'.[48]

This belief was rooted in the Communist perception of the interrelationship between Fascism and war. Communists had long described Fascism and imperialist war alike as the products of the intensifying contradictions of capitalism and argued that Fascism, by exacerbating these contradictions, inevitably accelerated the drive towards war.[49] This predication was reinforced not only by the undisguisedly belligerent intentions of the Fascist regimes but also by the Comintern's ever-narrower definition of the interests represented by those regimes. 'It is in the emphatic superiority . . . of the arms trusts', a German Communist wrote of the Nazi dictatorship in 1939, 'in comparison with the other financial and capitalist groups, that is expressed the fact of the domination of the most imperialist elements of finance capital . . . at the expense, not only of the proletariat, but also of the greater proportion of the bourgeoisie, such as the textile industry, the foodstuffs industry and so on . . .'[50] At the same time, Communists began to describe Fascism as the form of capitalist state required for the preparation and execution of modern war:

> Fascism appears as the open terroristic dictatorship of capitalism . . . against the rising revolt of the working class. *But Fascism is at the same time the highest expression of organisation for war.* These two aspects of Fascism are inseparably interlinked. On the one hand, modern totalitarian war requires the complete crushing of all popular resistance . . . and the organisation of the entire population and economy for war. . . . On the other hand, Fascism, because it cannot solve the economic contradictions of capitalism which underlie its rise, is driven to foreign adventure and war for its attempted solution.[51]

Imperialist war necessitated Fascism, just as Fascism necessarily led to imperialist war; and as the National Government began to equip itself for war in the late 1930s, its measures were denounced by Communists as the scaffolding for a fully Fascist war economy.

It was with the massive expansion of the government's arms programme in the spring of 1937 that this theme came to occupy a central position in Communist propaganda. Thus Dutt in April of that year:

> The Arms Programme governs henceforth all political issues in Britain. Internally, it prepares the way, in forms corresponding to the present stage of British conditions, towards the same process as the Hitler war machine has prepared in Germany. It is a *stage towards Hitlerisation* in Britain. . . . Its extending scope dominates all internal issues, economic and financial policy, the conditions and livelihood of the people, civil liberties, the relation of parties, the future of the Labour Party, and the existence and rights of trade unionism.[52]

The symbiotic relationship between the government's military preparations and the drive to Fascism at home was frequently stressed in Communist publications. Thus, to pick one example from many, did Wal Hannington depict the government's 'slave camps' for the unemployed as the 'thin end of the wedge for conscription' modelled on 'Hitler's methods of labour service camps and Fascist administration'. Every step in the government's pro-Fascist foreign policy, wrote Hannington, was at the same time a step towards the imposition of Fascism in Britain:

> It is unlikely, unless a very severe crisis suddenly arises, that the British ruling class will attempt to impose the full creed of Fascism all at once. Their policy will be to resort to a series of separate actions, attacking various sections at different times rather than to launch a frontal attack that would call the full power of the working-class movement into defensive action.[53]

As war drew nearer the assertion that Fascism was being introduced into Britain in this curiously Fabian fashion became a commonplace of Communist propaganda. And from about the time of Munich it was stated quite explicitly that the National Government was not simply the forerunner of Fascism but was itself a Fascist regime in embryo.

This and other developments after Munich will be described in a later chapter. But first we must consider the strategy by which Communists hoped to forestall decaying capitalism's inherent tendency towards barbarism.

Notes

1. Cited H. Francis, *Miners Against Fascism. Wales and the Spanish Civil War* (1984), 80.
2. We lack a satisfactory account of the 'Class Against Class' period; see however N. Branson, *op. cit.*, chs 1–7.
3. For figures see H. Pelling, *op. cit.*, 192.
4. See Branson, *op. cit.*, ch. 6.
5. G. Dimitrov, 'The Seventh World Congress of the Communist International' in *Selected Speeches and Articles* (1951), 44 and *passim*. For an account of the Congress, see F. Claudin, *op. cit.*, 182–99.
6. J. Fyrth, 'Introduction: in the thirties' in J. Fyrth (ed.), *Britain, Fascism and the Popular Front* (1985), 15.
7. For an illustrious example see P. Togliatti, 'On the history of the Communist International' in *On Gramsci and Other Writings* (1979), 232–8.
8. Dutt, *Fascism and Social Revolution* (1934), xi.
9. *Ibid.*, 5.
10. *Ibid.*, 9–15.
11. *Ibid.*, 58–9.
12. *Ibid.*, 69.
13. RPD K4, Dutt to Pollitt, 20.7.34.
14. Dutt, *op. cit.*, 75.
15. *Ibid.*, 72.
16. *Ibid.*, 73, 61, 270–1. It is perhaps significant that Dutt was unable to apply his general schemata to specific manifestations of Fascism without repeatedly contradicting himself. Italian Fascism, for example, 'revealed Fascism as a species of *preventive counter-revolution*' which nevertheless occurred 'only after the revolution was already defeated. . . . Fascism was not the weapon of defence of the bourgeoisie against the advancing proletarian

offensive, but the vengeance of the bourgeoisie against the retreating proletariat'; *ibid.*, 93–9.
17 *Ibid.*, 77.
18 *Ibid.*, 117–20.
19 *Ibid.*, 177.
20 *Ibid.*, 57.
21 *Ibid.*, 81.
22 *Ibid.*, 245.
23 *Ibid.*, 247.
24 *Ibid.*, 274.
25 RPD K4, Dutt to Pollitt, 20.7, 34.
26 Dutt, *op. cit.*, 276–9.
27 *Ibid.*, ix–x, 67.
28 *Ibid.*, ch. 8 for Dutt's discussion of Social Democracy and Fascism.
29 Hence the claim that 'Germany is nearer to the final victory of the proletarian revolution than any country in the capitalist world'; *ibid.*, 223, 278, 282, 286.
30 See e.g. RPD K4, 'VI Congress discussion tribune. Some problems of Fascism' (sent CI, 28.2.35) in which Dutt repeated the main arguments of *Fascism and Social Revolution*.
31 Dimitrov, *op. cit.*, 40.
32 *Ibid.*, 42.
33 *Loc. cit.*
34 *Loc. cit.*
35 *Ibid.*, 70.
36 Lecturing in Moscow at this time, Dutt cited the lines of Dimitrov's just quoted and explained at length their particular significance with regard to Britain; RPD K4, 'Lecture JCA', Aug. 1935.
37 This and following quotations from RPD K3, speech to CI Congress, 5.8.35.
38 Benny Rothman, interview. For anti-Fascist activities in Lancashire see M. Jenkins, 'Prelude to better days' (unpublished autobiography, WCML). For South Wales see Francis, *op. cit.*, ch. 4., whence comes the 'travelling circus' phrase used by R. C. Wallhead of the ILP.
39 For the orthodox CP version of anti-Fascist struggles in the East End, see P. Piratin, *Our Flag Stays Red* (1948), ch. 3; Branson, *op. cit.*, ch. 19. For an account by a Stepney Communist criticising the CP for its alleged listlessness in the face of Fascist provocation, see J. Jacobs, *Out of the Ghetto* (1978), chs 6–13.
40 Although there was one last major BUF demonstration, and left-wing counter-demonstration, in Bermondsey in October 1937.
41 See C. Cross, *The Fascists in Britain* (1961), ch. 12; R. Benewick, *The Fascist Movement in Britain* (1972 edn), ch. 12.
42 There was one notable exception to this rule. In the first half of 1939 the NUWM showed grave concern at the possible effects of renewed Fascist propaganda amongst the unemployed; see e.g. W. Hannington, *Fascist Danger and the Unemployed* (NUWM, Jun. 1939). But this emphasis was very rare by this time.
43 See his *The Political and Social Doctrine of Communism* (1942 edn, written 1938), 5–9, 22–32.
44 J. Strachey, *What Are We To Do?* (1938), 252.
45 Dimitrov, *op. cit.*, 41, 119, 68.
46 Pollitt in *It Can Be Done* (CPGB, report of 14th Congress, 1937), 11.
47 Strachey, *op. cit.*, 225. As Strachey wrote in a review of a Left Book Club selection on

German Fascism, 'the forms are German but the content is universal'; *LN*, Sept. 1937, 511.
48 '*National' Fascism in Britain* was the title of a pamphlet by Cripps published in 1935; see also e.g. C. R. Attlee, *The Labour Party in Perspective* (1937), 220–1.
49 See Dutt, *Fascism and Social Revolution*, 70–1.
50 H. Behrend, *The Real Rulers of Germany* (1939), 166–7 and *passim*.
51 Dutt, *World Politics 1918–1936* (1936), 329; see also 107–8 where Dutt argues that this '*process of the increasing adaptation of the entire economy . . . for war . . . is the most characteristic . . . feature of the present latest phase of capitalist economy*', in Britain and the USA as in Germany.
52 'Notes', Apr. 1937, 204–5.
53 W. Hannington, *Beware!! Slave Camps and Conscription* (NUWM, c. March 1939), 4–5, 8–11.

Chapter two
The Communist Party and the Popular Front, 1935–38

the Party is beginning to show itself able, in Dimitrov's words, to act as a real political party of the working class, becoming in actual fact a political factor in the life of the country, pursuing an active, Bolshevik mass policy and not confining itself to propaganda and criticism and bare appeals to struggle for the workers' dictatorship . . .

(Allen Hutt, 1935[1])

As well as establishing that the Comintern's overriding objective was the defeat of Fascism, Dimitrov's Seventh Congress speech provided the clearest delineation of the Popular Front strategy by which the Comintern hoped and expected to realise that objective.[2] The changes enunciated at the congress were not just of ephemeral significance, but amounted in many respects to a redefinition of the style and substance of Communist politics, so far-reaching that Communists today tend almost to regard this as their foundation congress. The Popular Front was not merely the shadow of collective security, an extension of Stalin's attempted *rapprochement* with Western imperialism. It shaped Communist politics in Britain even after the Nazi–Soviet Pact and the Comintern's consequent tergiversations. Its implications went far deeper than the meandering course followed by the Party 'line'.

The Popular Front was conceived as a means of bringing all those threatened by Fascism, and yet in many cases hypnotised by its appeal, under the leadership of a united working class. It would thus at the same time mobilise the forces necessary to defeat Fascism and, in direct proportion as it did so, deprive it of its potential mass basis. The key to building this movement lay, in Dimitrov's words, in taking these masses 'as they are, and not as we should like to have them'. In part this entailed the abandonment of abstract, utopian sloganising and the raising of the issues most directly affecting the masses, but it also meant accepting the legitimacy of the political and industrial organisations in which these masses were to be found, rather than simply of those in which Communists would have liked to have had them. This was to be a united front – and People's Front – from above as well as below.

The essence of Dimitrov's case was that Communists should not attempt 'to leap over those necessary stages of the mass movement in the course of which the working class by its own experience outlives its illusions and passes over to Communism'. For, as these last words implied, the Popular Front was only in its first stages a strategy for the defence of the rights and standards won under bourgeois democracy. Its underlying aim was 'to draw increasingly wide masses into the revolutionary class struggle and lead them to the proletarian revolution, *proceeding from their vital interests and needs as the starting point, and their own experience as the basis*'. The Popular Front was not a temporary diversion from the final aims of Communism, but the surest road towards them: only by means of this strategy, insisted Dimitrov, would the working class *'be able to fulfil its historic mission with certainty – to sweep fascism off the face of the earth and, together with it, capitalism!'*[3] These revolutionary sentiments were echoed by the leaders of the British Party. If the Seventh Congress had made scant mention of the 'coming second wave of wars and revolutions', said Dutt soon afterwards, this was only because 'we are now drawing so close . . . that we need to tackle a whole series of new concrete problems arising from the present stage of gathering world conflict'.[4]

Already at the Seventh Congress, Dimitrov was able to draw on the practical experiences of what was now the leading Communist Party in capitalist Europe, the PCF. By July 1935 the *Rassemblement Populaire* of the republican left had emerged as a vital new factor in French politics, outweighing and overshadowing the Fascist Leagues; and the PCF's decisive contribution to this *rassemblement* was commended by Dimitrov as the exemplar of the correct application of the Comintern's new tactical line.[5] The struggling British Party could not fail to be influenced by the successes of the *Front Populaire* and also of the *Frente Popular* – People's Front governments were elected in both France and Spain in the first half of 1936. However, it was intrinsic to the whole conception of the Popular Front that it could not take the same form in different circumstances. Whereas the policy of 'Class Against Class', proceeding from the universal aim of proletarian revolution common to all Communist Parties, had been carried out without any real regard for national particularities, the Popular Front took as its starting point existing social and political relationships; and British Communists were well aware that in Britain these differed markedly from those obtaining on the continent:

it would be wrong to try to apply to this country in a purely mechanical fashion methods that have been used in France and Spain with their totally different political conditions. . . . In a country like Britain, where the industrial workers are the decisive majority of the population, where the most class-conscious section of the population is already organised industrially and politically, our first job is to bring about unity within the Labour Movement, and when that has been achieved you will have the irresistible magnet that will attract to its side all the progressive forces in this country.[6]

The doctrines of international Communism were thus translated into policies which recognised the peculiarities of Britain's political development. Just as the CP identified the threat of Fascism with the dominant sections of the Conservative Party, so too did it acknowledge the primacy of the established Labour movement in the struggle against Fascism.

Shortly after Hitler's accession to power, the CP made guarded overtures to the Labour Party and began to develop forms of joint activity with the ILP and sympathetic sections of the Labour left. Traces of sectarian vituperation remained, but the CP's attitude to Labour gradually softened and in the 1935 general election it contested only two seats in the interests of returning a Labour government.[7] After the election the CP made its first application for affiliation to the Labour Party since the 1920s. In spite of a spirited campaign lasting the best part of a year, the proposal foundered on the rocks of the trade union block votes at the 1936 Labour conference.[8] Undaunted, the CP tried a different line of approach. Along with the ILP and the Socialist League,[9] it launched a vigorous Unity Campaign at the beginning of 1937, the object being to achieve working-class unity within the framework of the Labour Party and thus open the way to a Labour government truly representative of the working class. 'If this is "disruption" ', commented Dutt, 'words have no meaning';[10] but as far as Transport House was concerned such protestations of loyalty were indeed meaningless. In January 1937 the Socialist League was disaffiliated and in March membership of the League and of the Labour Party were declared incompatible. At this point the CP demonstrated most clearly its determination to consolidate the left wing within the Labour Party. When George Strauss, a prominent Socialist Leaguer, was advised that his appearance on the same platform as Communists would entail his expulsion from the Labour Party, Pollitt withdrew from the scheduled meeting; and at about the same time the League itself was disbanded, with Pollitt's approval, so that its members could continue their work for unity within the Labour Party.[11]

This last episode was indicative of the ineluctable dilemma faced by Communists, whose aspirations to transform the Labour movement from within were constantly thwarted by the wary disciplinarianism of Transport

House. Official Labour's objections to the CP were of the utmost simplicity: it was funded from abroad, received its orders from abroad, and had adopted aims and methods alien to the traditions of British Labour.[12] Its obedience to the dictates of Moscow could not be reconciled with genuine fidelity to the interests of the Labour movement, and its protestations of loyalty were but duplicity concealing disruption. For these reasons Labour activists were informed, as from 1934, that 'united action with the Communist Party or organisations ancillary or subsidiary thereto' was 'incompatible with membership of the Labour Party'.[13]

The guard dogs of traditional Labour values barked threateningly, but they did not often bite and throughout the late 1930s impetuous spirits within the Labour Party discovered and proclaimed their common cause with the Communists. The dividing line between the CP and the Labour left was virtually indefinable, not least because an unquantifiable number of Communists pursued their Popular Front activities within the Labour Party. The extent of this phenomenon varied from area to area, but was of considerable significance in many parts of the Midlands and South which lacked a resilient Labour tradition. In Oxford, one Communist recalled, 'the Labour Party was more or less the Communist Party in a sense because you could hold dual membership then'. Admittedly, Oxford's flagrant disregard for Labour Party rules was somewhat exceptional, but Ted Bramley, the Party's London District Organiser, nevertheless recalled that at this time the CP had members organised in 'almost every divisional Labour Party in London'. It was not a case of Communists being sent into the Labour Party, according to Bramley, but rather of new recruits to the CP being asked to remain within the Labour Party the more effectively to work for unity.[14] This indicates as well as anything the extent to which the CP had become committed, not to superseding the Labour Party, but to transforming it into a vehicle for working-class advance.

More fundamentally still, the CP committed itself irrevocably to work within the existing structures of British trade unionism. 'Held together by mutual solidarity and common principles', John Mahon wrote of the trade union movement in 1937, 'this immense and powerful mass constitutes one of the decisive forces in our time'.[15] Nevertheless, this splendid movement would prove no match for its enemies while constrained by the enervating leadership and ideology of reformism. By their policies of collaboration with the employers and their state, the unions' dominant right-wing leadership were taking the British workers down the same disastrous no-through-road as German Social Democracy. The fate of democracy depended on the speed with which the left was able to revive and extend trade unionism on the basis of militant class struggle. To this end, Communists set themselves the objectives of eradicating non-unionism, strengthening workplace organisation, democratising union structures, overcoming sectional differences and establishing industrial unionism, and winning for themselves positions of responsibility in the movement.[16] In the mid-to-late 1930s the Party made considerable progress in this field, especially in the mining and engineering industries.[17] As evidence of the CP's dedication to strengthening trade unionism, the Central Committee reported to the Party's Fourteenth Congress that over a hundred Communists had been awarded the TUC's Tolpuddle Medal for union recruitment, while scores more were entitled to it; and of the 501 delegates to that congress, more than two hundred held official union positions.[18]

However, Communists did not yet become so entangled in the trade union machinery as to overlook the need for 'unofficial' strike activity and 'unofficial' forms of organisation where that machinery was found wanting. Prominent examples of the latter were the London Busmen's Rank and File Movement and the Aircraft Shop Stewards' National Council, set up in 1932 and 1935 respectively and intimately connected with the CP.[19] The Party portrayed official and unofficial forms of activity as complementary facets of a unified industrial strategy,[20] but some Communists nevertheless perceived a contradiction between the persistence of rank-and-file movements and the turn to official trade union work. Thus did Joe Scott, elected London Divisional Organiser of the AEU in 1935, oppose the formation of the ASSNC as a distraction from the key tasks of winning influence in the union branches and gaining election to official positions of those committed to left-wing policies. His objections were nevertheless overruled on the grounds that it was wrong to counterpose the two forms of activity,[21] and the ASSNC flourished.

But the tension was a real one, if only because so many union leaders were determined to stamp out what they regarded as 'disruptive' activities, even if Communists did not. If the TUC's notorious 'Black Circular' of 1934[22] was ignored by some unions, it nevertheless reflected the state of mind of many union leaders. Bevin's belief that the Communists were 'out to destroy the trade unions' was typical,[23] and he and likeminded union officials were prepared to act on this belief. After the London bus strike of 1937, for example, membership of the Busmen's Rank and File Committee and of the TGWU were declared incompatible and the strike leaders, including the Communists Bert Papworth and Bill Jones, were expelled from the union. Bevin was prepared to counterpose the two forms of activity, even if Communists were not.

Significantly, when this minor purge provoked a number of militants into setting up a breakaway union, the CP dissociated itself from this stratagem.

Instead Papworth and Jones applied for readmission as rule-abiding members of the union.[24] For, while the Communists were certainly out to destroy Ernest Bevin, they were also out to consolidate and extend trade unionism, and their efforts to do so are rarely given their full due except by Communists themselves. They played an especially valuable role in establishing trade unionism in the 'new industries' of the Midlands and South, for which they received no reward, except the odd Tolpuddle Medal and, more often, the sack.[25] Bevin's self-serving calumnies carry less conviction than the more generous and also more accurate testimony of another of the CP's political adversaries, Bob Edwards of the ILP, that 'a good Communist shop steward is the best kind of shop steward you can get with the exception of good left-wing Socialists'.[26] Allowing for Edwards's own political allegiances, this is a fair verdict on the contribution of Communists to industrial struggles in the 1930s.

The established Labour movement thus provided the core of the Communist conception of the Popular Front, and the struggles of industrial workers retained their primacy in the Party's political thinking. However, the CP was acutely aware that the organised workers constituted only a minority of the British population and aimed by its new strategy to draw into political activity the millions hardly yet touched by Labour politics. There were apprehensive churchgoers and disillusioned Liberals and Tories, Pollitt told the CP's 1938 congress. There were the agricultural workers and small farmers, bereft of effective leadership and organisation and mercilessly exploited by the 'big vested interests'. There were the professional and middle classes, eleven million strong, 'ranging from Doctors to Advertising Agents; from Clerks to Teachers; from Artists, Writers, to small Shopkeepers and Businessmen'. And there were the settlers in Priestley's 'third England' of light industry and endless, anonymous semis, which spread its ugliness around so many towns in the inter-war period:

> How are we to capture the imaginations of these people . . . for sustained interest and a hope in a leadership other than the negative dead oppressive bullying of the boss and of Chamberlain? They live in new housing estates, work in new factories, uprooted from the tradition of the Labour and Trade Union Movement. The leadership of a People's Movement would swing them into action and arouse their interest and, as was found in France, rally them to the Labour Movement.

For just as Fascism, and the National Government, represented the interests of only a handful of parasites, so could the vast majority of the population be brought into action against Fascism and against the National Government. The way forward lay in bringing them under the hegemony of a united Labour movement by awakening them to the struggle, not yet for Socialism, but for the needs of which they were already conscious: for 'economic security, peace and democracy'.[27]

In part this could be achieved by building up the Labour movement and working within existing organisations like the Women's Co-operative Guilds. But the period also saw a spate of new broad organisations, usually initiated by Communists or at least subject to a pervasive Communist influence, though subtly enough to avoid alienating potential allies. The prototype for these organisations was the National Unemployed Workers' Movement, ably led by Communists who had remained sensitive to the immediate needs of the unemployed even through the sectarian excesses of 'Class Against Class'.[28] Throughout the 1930s the NUWM continued its invaluable work, for which official Labour apparently felt no inclination, but was now merely one of the stars in what the Labour Party described as the *Communist Solar System*.[29] To list some of the more important of these is in itself to give some idea of the scope of the Popular Front strategy; there were Peace Councils and Aid Spain Committees, the Artists International Association and the National Council for Civil Liberties, the Women's Committee Against War and Fascism and the Left Book Club, with its myriad local and professional groups.

The impact of the new strategy was felt particularly in the youth movement, and first of all in the Young Communist League, which began to regard itself '*not* [as] a Communist Party of the youth, but rather [as] a broad organisation of youth under revolutionary leadership'.[30] In particular areas the new emphasis brought excellent results. In the Cheetham district of Manchester, for example, the YCL emerged both as 'the leading political force in the area', taking the lead in driving the Blackshirts out of Cheetham and supplying close to a dozen recruits for Spain, and as one of the leading social forces, renowned for its dances and its sporting activities. Its membership was many times that of the local Communist Party.[31]

But the YCL was now just one of a number of organisations in which Communists were working to forge links with the main body of 'progressive' youth. By the late 1930s there was a significant Communist presence, though rarely avowedly so, in the Labour League of Youth,[32] the University Labour Federation,[33] the National Union of Students and the League of Nations Union Youth Movement. On the initiative of John Gollan, then secretary of the YCL, these organisations and many others – the Student Christian Movement and the Young Methodists, for example – developed a working political relationship through the British Youth Peace Assembly. The movement was active on a very wide range of issues. Some, like providing homes for German refugees, were basically 'humanitarian' in nature, while others, such as campaigning for collective security, were more overtly political. As a prominent Communist participant recalled, the movement's affiliated bodies contributed only at those levels appropriate to them, while they remained free to carry on their own independent activities:[34] in the YCL's case, for instance, to provide recruits for the International Brigade and organise support for the engineering apprentices' strikes of 1937.[35] Somewhat disrespectful of traditional party dividing lines and relatively unencumbered by traditional party discipline, the youth movement was in many ways a microcosm of how the CP envisaged a Popular Front developing in Britain.

Possibly most successful of the broad mass campaigns organised by Communists were the tenants' struggles of the late 1930s. Tenants' movements were an especially effective means of spreading the ideas of solidarity and struggle among the previously unorganised in cities like Oxford and Birmingham, where housing problems were acute and the Labour movement lacked deep roots.[36] By establishing its presence outside the workplace, the CP was also making possible advances at the point of production. Arthur Exell, who worked at the union blackspot of Oxford Radiators, recalled that 'it was easier to organise outside the factory than inside because you weren't so likely to get the sack'. Exell later became a shop steward at Radiators, but his formative political experience was on the Florence Park Tenants' Committee: 'that was how I got involved in union work, and how I came to join the Communist Party'.[37]

In the East End of London, rent strikes were virtually endemic for a period. Heavily involved was the future Communist MP for Stepney, Mile End, according to whom, in the course of these agitations, 'hundreds of thousands of people learned to understand, through their own experience, the nature of capitalism itself':

> Committees were formed and hundreds of people who had never been on a committee and had no experience of organisation or politics learned these things and learned them well. Outstanding were the women. Every feminist claim was proved. There was nothing that the men could do that could not be equalled by the women, and, in fact, they were mostly more enthusiastic, and hence more reliable.[38]

Those whom official Labour so often treated as voting fodder the CP aimed to stimulate into active rejection of the iniquities which blighted their lives under capitalism; and thus, through their experience of struggle, into the rejection of capitalism itself.

As Communists moved onto the common ground they shared with the millions opposed to Fascism and war, they drew on the traditional lexicon of Marxism–Leninism ever more frugally. Such rebarbative phrases as *Soviet power* and *proletarian dictatorship* were set aside for occasional use only, and their place in Communist speeches and writings was increasingly taken by the rhetoric of radical–democratic patriotism. The new approach had been adumbrated by Dimitrov at the Seventh World Congress. Communists, he said, should no longer give the reactionaries free rein to exploit legitimate patriotic sentiments, but should come forth as the most resolute upholders of national freedom and national culture. Proletarian internationalism had to ' "acclimatize itself" in each country', to adopt appropriate national forms.[39] The trail was again set by the PCF, which began with great adroitness and conviction to revivify its country's republican traditions. In this respect too, however, the new approach could not be transferred mechanically to Britain. As James Klugmann remembered remarking to one French Communist, 'il y a une toute petite différence entre *La Marseillaise* et le *God Save the King*'.[40] Nevertheless, despite this *toute petite différence*, British Communists made a sustained effort to reclaim the language of popular patriotism and democratic struggle as a means of articulating and legitimising the ideals of the Popular Front. 'The revolutionary', wrote Ralph Fox in words which encapsulated the new approach, 'both accepts all that is vital and hopeful in the heritage of the past, and rejects nothing in the present which can be used to build the future'.[41]

The new slant in Communist politics is well illustrated by Jack Lindsay's *England, My England*, a characteristic artefact of the period published in 1939. Lindsay's purpose was to trace the age-long antagonism between two Englands – 'the England of defiant freedom, staunch to death', of 'all the countless unknown who rose in the great insurrections or died in small hopeless outbursts in the lean years of oppression'; and the England of 'the terrified and greed-obsessed rulers and landowners and profit-mongers . . . the invokers of force against all the efforts to create a communal England, an England of brotherhood'. Taking in the Peasants' Revolt, the Diggers and Levellers, Wilkes and Paine, Chartism, syndicalism and the Invergordon Mutiny, Lindsay arrived inexorably at the struggle between Fascism and democracy in Britain in 1939:

> year by year we have witnessed the growth of the police-state, the passing of oppressive legislation which can be used at a moment's notice to wipe out every liberty, the slow intrusion of the governmental executive into every social area – the prelude of the English type of Fascism. And there has appeared a Communist Party which resumes the real tradition of the working class of England, with renewed scientific insight. . . . We can meet the worst that can happen, if we realise our heritage, if we take up again the great English tradition.

Lindsay's patriotism, then, did not call for servile feelings of togetherness with England's rulers, nor for displays of enmity towards the people of other lands:

> What we love in England has nothing to do with profits and parasites. We love England . . . the more we feel in harmony with the producers of other lands. It is only among the classes where profits and parasitism rule – where *Our Country* means the land and wealth which is personally owned – that the need for war and national rivalries can arise.

Thus did Lindsay warn his readers against being misled by cynical appeals to their love of country into fighting wars on behalf of these very same parasites. This was not simply nationalism, but acclimatised internationalism.[42]

On occasion, however, the same note was struck with an uncomfortably chauvinistic flourish. An extreme instance occurred when the CP organised in 1936 a 'March of English History' at which banners bearing the profiles of illustrious democrats through the ages were borne to Hyde Park:

> ENGLAND! A word of power. A name deeply engraved on the minds of men, whether murmured with love, whispered in fear, shouted with hatred. Bringing a picture of green fields and hedges to the soldier stationed beneath burning desert skies. . . .
>
> THE PEOPLE OF ENGLAND! A great nation, . . . desiring above all to live in freedom, in peace and friendship. Proud of their great achievements, whether embodied in the modern construction and technique which makes the 'Queen Mary' the sum of a whole nation's effort, or in those men and women . . . whose endurance, skill and courage conquer nature and space for humanity. A people proud of their instinct for fair play, for the rule of law and justice . . . [etc.]

The *Boy's Own Paper* could hardly have done better; and this England, like that of the *Boy's Own*, was a country worth defending:

> We, the Communists of to-day, remind you of the heritage of England's long struggle in order that you shall join with us in preventing that freedom being trampled under Fascist jackboots . . .[43]

Fascist jackboots says it all, for with this one hackneyed image it was revealed that this England's enemies lay abroad. Where the focus of Lindsay's loyalties was an England of relentless struggle against home-grown despotism, the 'March of English History' celebrated an England of awesome power and fair play and soldiers under desert skies which would not meekly succumb to the foreign tyrants who execrated its achievements. These two documents reveal in an exceptionally acute form the different strands in the CP's concept of patriotism. For the most part, although Lindsay's emphasis was the more common at this time, the two strands were more closely interwoven. But the CP's radical patriotism would leave an ambiguous legacy in the event of a war to defend English fields from trampling jackboots and English parasites from their foreign rivals.

Inevitably, the CP's new orientation brought with it important changes in the organisation and presentation of Communist politics. The Popular Front necessitated the abandonment of 'the old conception of a hole-in-the-corner Party' and the creation of 'a new popular Party of the workers, understandable to all, and speaking in a language that gathers great masses of people around it'.[44] This break with an introverted sectarianism was mainly effected by Communists involving themselves fully in the work of broader Labour and democratic organisations, with the result that relatively few Communists were exclusively occupied with Communist Party work, and many active Communists were hardly occupied with it at all.

At the same time the Party itself became more outward-looking, as Party branches were urged to cut down on 'the interminable inner Party meetings' and concentrate instead on broad mass campaigns on issues directly affecting ordinary people.[45] Moreover, shortly after the Seventh World Congress the CP's internal organisation was modified so as to smooth its entry into the mainstream of British politics. The imported nomenclature of Party *cells* and Party *locals* was dropped in favour of the more familiar-sounding *groups* and *branches*; and where Party membership was insufficient to sustain a viable street group members were organised on a ward basis instead.[46] The aim was to facilitate cooperation with local Labour Party organisations without in any way diluting the CP's basic organisational principles.[47] Some Communists at least were not at all satisfied on this latter point,[48] but there can be no doubt that these formal and informal measures of 'de-Bolshevisation' were a major reason for the steady growth of the Party from 1935 onwards.[49]

During this same period Party propagandists developed a populist style and colourful presentation quite removed from the hortatory declamations of the 'Class Against Class' period. In terms of quantity, content and design, the Party's leaflets and pamphlets made the literature departments of the official Labour movement appear dreadfully staid and unimaginative. The Party prided itself on 'greatly simplifying the language and form of approach in both our written and spoken propaganda, and in keeping it closely related to current events, to the special needs of sections of workers, and to the interests of special areas'.[50] It had at last managed, as one Communist put it, to rid itself 'almost entirely of the old sectarian jargon, the conspiratorial "Marxist" lip-language which no one could understand but Communists',[51] and the benefits were evident in the prolific output of the Party's propaganda department.[52] The *Daily Worker*, too, enjoyed an increasing circulation as it incorporated many of the features of the popular press: murder stories, cocoa adverts,[53] racing tips, workmen's pools, free gifts and beauty hints. The *Worker* could not rest content with preaching to the converted, its editors explained on removing the hammer and sickle from its masthead at the beginning of 1938.[54] The same desire to make an impression on the uninitiated was evident in the use of mass singing, musical turns, theatrical performances and 'surprise items' to enliven Communist meetings, these devices being employed on an epic scale in the Party's historical pageants. 'No more dreary, half-empty halls', said John Mahon. 'No more dull and depressing speeches. Let's have Colour, Energy, Clarity, Confidence.'[55] 'Liveliness and drama', it was argued elsewhere, 'can put us before the masses who are used to wireless, cinemas and mass "American" advertising methods'.[56]

Communists had, in short, become persuaded of the need to work with the grain of popular culture. They were anxious above all to demonstrate that they were not revolutionary pariahs, aloof from the concerns of ordinary working people. Communists in the workplace were advised not to spout endlessly about the class struggle, but to enter into discussions about football and non-stop flights and 'try in a tactful way to use such events to bring home political lessons'.[57] In Fife, Communists made a point of carrying out literature sales on Sunday mornings to show that the CP consisted of 'men who, day after day, are at work in the mines and factories' and was not 'a party of never-works'.[58] Indeed, literature sellers were instructed to make sure that they were 'as well turned out as possible, well shaved, or made up',[59] and demonstrators on the 'March of English History' received similar instructions. One or two Communists at least were discomfited by this determined attempt to court respectability:

> These instructions give the impression that the Party was not seeking on this march to win the proletariat, but to impress more influential allies. It seems to be no longer a question of appearing as comrades of the most indigent, most oppressed strata of the workers, but as the bowler-hatted, Sunday-best allies of Liberals and petty-bourgeois Labourites.[60]

But the objection was overruled. At one time, it was admitted, Party members had contrived to 'appear as disreputable as possible on all public occasions', but as the composition of the Party had become more genuinely working-class these ridiculous affectations had been abandoned by all but an unkempt fringe of collarless bohemians. The average Party member preferred to behave 'like any other normal proletarian and trade unionist who puts on his Sunday best for holidays and celebrations'.[61] Communists had not only to take the normal proletarian masses as they were, but to demonstrate that they too shared their values, their foibles and their aspirations.

The Popular Front, then, as this brief survey has indicated, was not essentially an electoral contrivance designed to erode the National Government's impregnable-looking Parliamentary majority.[62] This point was constantly reiterated by Communists. 'The aim of a People's Front', Dutt insisted in mid-1937, 'is not based primarily on parliamentary or electoral combinations, but on the active union of the mass of the population in struggle for their immediate interests and demands.' Indeed, as late as this Dutt expressed his distaste for any compact between the Liberals and an unreformed Labour Party as a 'reactionary alliance and the opposite of a real People's Front'.[63] The way forward at this time lay in developing forms of cooperation at a grassroots level and, primarily, in the realisation of working-class unity within the Labour Party.[64] Unity could not be manufactured on high, but had to be built up from below.

The following year, with the further deterioration of the international situation, the CP substantially modified its stance. When in March 1938 Sydney Elliott, editor of *Reynold's News*, proposed the formation of a United Peace Alliance – something very akin to a 'Liberal–Labour Coalition' but even broader in scope – the Party gave it an enthusiastic welcome.[65] As Chamberlain's covert alliance with Hitler[66] dragged Europe closer to disaster, the CP seemed prepared to forego the necessary preconditions for a People's Front in the interests of uniting all, including those in the Conservative Party, who stood for collective security. Its new sense of urgency was indicated by its approach to by-elections over the next year: support for non-party 'Popular Front' candidates on three occasions,[67] support for an orthodox Liberal against a Trotskyist Labour candidate on another,[68] and support for an idiosyncratic Tory Duchess on another[69] – in short, support for whoever seemed most likely to defeat Chamberlain's nominee. However, while the Party campaigned for 'an electoral *bloc* of all Labour and anti-fascist democratic forces on a common programme', it insisted that these 'immediate proposals' should not be confused with the People's Front, conceived as a broad popular movement of struggle.[70] Nevertheless, for the majority of historians the Popular Front has come to be identified with exactly this sort of frantic shuffling of the Parliamentary and electoral cards in the hope of putting together a hand to match Chamberlain's.

The spokesmen of official Labour took the same approach. In a running controversy with the Communists and their allies they accused the latter of defeatism and the abandonment of Labour's fundamental Socialist principles, particularly the principle of independence of all ties with capitalist parties.[71] Communists in their turn regarded these arguments with undisguised disdain:

> The reality behind this mock slogan of 'independence' is – *dependence on Chamberlain*. Its exponents are so anxious to be *independent* of the possible *allies* with whose aid they could defeat Chamberlain that they end up by being dependent on the real enemy. . . .
> The real truth is that *the Labour Party has never yet been really independent of capitalism, and we are proposing that the Labour Party should for the first time become independent by leading a People's Front.*[72]

This theme bears further examination, for the CP's analysis of Labourism, or 'British Socialism' as Strachey called it, throws much light on the nature of Communist politics during this period.

The most systematic exposition of the Communist attitude to Labour politics is to be found in John Strachey's *What Are We To Do?*, published as a Left Book Club selection in 1938. Strachey traced the malaise of 'British Socialism' back to its formative Fabian influences, to its belief in the inevitability of gradualness. It had appeared inevitable in the first place that 'the capitalist system should go on developing and expanding' and in the second place that 'the Labour movement would just grow and grow until it dominated the political scene. . . . The idea that something might be happening to capitalism which would impel the capitalists to interrupt the course of this double inevitability never occurred to anyone.' But of course, something *did* happen to cut short this leisurely stroll towards Socialism; with world slump and the rise of Fascism the presuppositions of Fabianism were discredited, and the very existence of the Labour movement was imperilled. There followed, according to Strachey, the 'application of British or Fabian Socialism to the situation of capitalist counter-attack', by which the Labour movement accommodated itself to every essential need of capitalism in decline, even at the expense of 'the gradual debasement of the national standard of life, the emasculation of democracy, and the toleration of war'. In this way, by their craven submission to the will of the National Government on every important issue of foreign and domestic policy, the leaders of 'British Socialism' hoped to 'prevent the appearance of Fascism, by making it unnecessary'. The Labour Party had thus abandoned 'any real attempt to achieve Socialism, whether gradually or rapidly, and by constitutional just as much as by revolutionary means'. Its 'reformism' was a sham; 'the real trouble with the "reformist" leaders of the British Labour movement, in the post-war period, was that they never reformed anything!' The issue was not between revolution and reform but between struggle and accommodation, and into this setting Strachey introduced the Popular Front:

> The purpose of a 'People's Front' movement is to erect an impassable barrier against the capitalists' counter-offensive. Such resistance will undoubtedly involve very severe political struggles. But such struggles are the only alternative to the policy of retreat, surrender and disintegration, down which the British Labour movement has, for the past five years, been propelled.

And the question of whether or not it could be brought round to oppose the National Government along these lines was, literally according to Strachey, a matter of life or death for British Labour.[73]

Strachey's approach and terminology were in some respects distinctive, but his conclusions were an impeccably orthodox statement of the Communist attitude to Labour.[74] However, it is crucial to understand that the Party's outspoken criticisms of the Labour leadership were not based on, nor did they imply, the rejection of the established institutions of the Labour movement ('the historic, irreplaceable creation of the British workers'[75]) or even of the Labour Party's stated programme. The immediate proposals advanced by Strachey were, he admitted, 'almost identical with the official programme of the British Labour Party. But such a programme can be either the rallying cry of millions or a series of lifeless paragraphs . . . according to the spirit in which it is approached.'[76] In short, the issue was 'not to get the Labour Party to scrap its Short Term Programme for a more revolutionary one, but to organise the masses to fight for this programme'.[77] The alternatives were not revolution or reform but militancy or passivity, struggle or accommodation.

This was all very well, but what had the struggles for the Labour Party's Immediate Programme and the similar demands advanced by Communists to do with the fundamental revolutionary aims of the Communist Party, which it still proclaimed as its *raison d'être*? Primarily, of course, the adoption of a Popular Front strategy was an acknowledgement that this revolution was not on the immediate political agenda. The issue facing Europe, Dutt wrote in 1937, 'is no ultimate issue of the future form of society or of final goals . . . the immediate issue is more elementary, and is the condition of further advance'.[78] The immediate issue was, of course, to combat the onslaught of reaction, and Communists were even prone to occasional feelings of uncharacteristic pessimism as to the consequences of failure to win this, the first battle of the campaign. The continuation in office of the National Government, the Party warned in 1938, would mean 'Fascism and war and the destruction of the working-class movement, putting back all hopes of realising Socialism for generations'.[79]

Nevertheless, the Popular Front was never conceived simply as a defensive strategy, 'thrust upon us because of the advent of Fascism'. Rather did it embody the basic principle of 'seeking allies to carry forward the struggle as a whole' which underlay 'the whole theory and practice of Leninism'. It would thus be quite wrong to think that the strategy would have to be abandoned in the event of a revolutionary situation.[80] On the contrary, as it grappled with the evils intrinsic to capitalism, the Popular Front would itself mature into a force for revolutionary change. The movement to defend peace and democracy would be 'raised to a higher level' as the role of monopoly capitalism 'as the enemy of these things' was made clear, and the outlook of the Communists' allies would be 'transformed in the course of the struggle, so that they fight alongside the workers for the Socialist transformation of society'.[81]

One might well wonder, with the benefit of hindsight, how Communists could be so sure that it was not *their* outlook that would be transformed in the course of cooperation with Liberals and reformists. The answer was that history was on the Communists' side. Capitalism, moribund capitalism, could not for long absorb even the mildest pressure and consequently even the most vaporous demands took on a certain revolutionary significance:

> world capitalism, and especially, of course, the crippled, distorted capitalisms of Europe, can now only live by depressing the standards, rights and liberties of the wage-earners. . . . The private ownership of the means of production has now become, in the long run, incompatible with the most elementary interests of the mass of the population. . . . Hence a successful defence of peace, democracy and the national standard of life will make the continued existence of capitalism impossible.

This successful defence would prove 'the decisive engagement of the campaign, after which the road to complete victory is straight and open', not least because those who valued these things for their own sakes would soon come to realise that they were incompatible with the continued existence of capitalism. Strachey likened the positions held by the working class to 'three vital bridgeheads' at which it was necessary 'to mass the very maximum force possible' and thus pen the capitalists 'into a narrow territory on which they cannot live'.[82] There was, therefore, no contradiction between the Communists' commitment to these intermediate goals and their final revolutionary aims. All the Party's partial demands were 'revolutionary in the sense of leading to organised struggle against the ruling class':

> Socialism is not the first stage, but the crowning *achievement* of a long process of social struggle. To refuse the initial stages in the name of devotion to the last stage is not to hasten the last stage, but to prevent it ever being reached.[83]

And it is important to note that the Party devoted little energy to formulating a constructive programme for the Popular Front, but merely latched onto those popular demands which seemed most likely to lead to 'organised struggle against the ruling class'. The main constructive exposition of Communist policy remained its massive 'study of what industry in a Soviet Britain could achieve', *Britain Without Capitalists*. First published in 1936, this volume was reprinted in 1939 with a new preface expressing scepticism that even the finest transitional economic programme to be carried out by a People's Government 'could achieve *permanently* substantial results, or even hold its own for long against the inevitable counter-attack of Big Business-cum-Finance, unless it were prepared to go forward boldly to the expropriation of the large capitalist concerns'.[84] The nature of the epoch ruled out the possibility of measured advance towards Socialism[85] and the underlying purpose of the Party's immediate campaigns was to marshal the forces of progress for the coming struggle for power:

> through all these preliminary and partial struggles a vast process of alignment of the peoples of the world is taking place. . . . On the one side, the camp of socialism, of the Soviet Union, of the international working class, of the colonial peoples and of all the popular anti-fascist forces, striving to save the future of humanity and of human progress. On the other side, the camp of fascism and capitalist reaction, of the barbarous leaders and warmakers of dying capitalism and their supporters in all the imperialist countries. In this way world history is preparing the conditions and mobilizing forces for the near approaching final struggle for the victory of the world socialist revolution.

The issue of the two camps, through all its transitional phases, was 'the issue of the future of the world'.[86]

Everything fitted together nicely in Dutt's pamphlets. However, it is impossible not to see the Popular Front in Britain as essentially an adjustment by a revolutionary party to a situation in which opportunities for revolutionary activity were strictly limited. Inevitably as Communists devoted themselves to immediate, sectional struggles on a broad basis, they tended to lose sight of the relationship of these struggles to Dutt's second wave of revolutions, the more so as these revolutions obstinately failed to materialise. Indeed, the thousands of new recruits to the Party in the late 1930s were attracted primarily by its stance on economic issues, on Fascism and war; conversion to the Party's final aims came afterwards, and not always then. The difficulties of reconciling open revolutionary activity with the exigencies of a broad Popular Front strategy were no more apparent than in the workplace, the decisive locus of the class struggle as far as the CP was concerned.

Ideally, Communists were to go into the unions 'as Communists and remain in as Communists':

> They must set their practical work in relation to the aims of the Party, they must see that their task is not merely to raise the level of wages, but to raise the level of class consciousness, is not only to make the workers see that their interests are opposed to the interests of the capitalists but to make them see that the capitalist system is a menace to the whole human race which must be destroyed.[87]

The need to politicise industrial struggles in this way was one of the fundamental canons of Communist doctrine, but the obstacles to doing so were more considerable than Campbell seemed to appreciate. In a pamphlet describing *How the Communist Party Works* published in 1935, R. W. Robson showed a greater awareness of the problem:

> for members of the Factory Cell to make it public that they are Communists and to carry on agitation openly inside or outside the factory. . . . *is not mass work*. . . . The work of the Factory Cell can only be carried out if its members are *inside* the factory. . . .
>
> Under ordinary circumstances members . . . should not speak at factory-gate meetings, distribute leaflets or sell literature at the factory gate. . . . When necessary to speak at the *factory on issues known only to those working inside*, Party members must speak *not* as Communists, but in their capacity as trade union members, collectors, shop stewards, branch committee members, etc., . . . in a way which conveys the line of the Party. . . .
>
> Even where Communists . . . are already known to the boss as Communists, this does not mean they should give the boss a chance to sack them by working too openly in the factory. . . . The workers will not support anyone victimised for some heroic adventure which does not concern them. *The best defence against victimisation is the mass support of the workers as a result of taking an active part in daily struggles.*[88]

In practice, Communists were not always this cautious; the large number victimised tells us that much. But the extent to which Communists were able to work openly for their political goals depended very heavily on the active sympathy of the workforce, and this obviously varied from place to place. Working at the well-organised and militant Pressed Steel works in Oxford, Norman Brown remembered that 'we used to flog the *Daily Worker*s and *Soviet Britain*, we were in such a position in the section we were in, there was about five or six Party stewards. . . . If ever we got involved in anything, we just went like that and without calling a meeting they'd all down tools'. Nevertheless, Brown was eventually sacked and subsequently took up employment at Oxford Radiators, still unorganised, where he encountered a rather different state of affairs:

> It was like an underground army in the factory if you was in the CP or something, or even wearing a union badge. First time I was in there I thought I'd have my union badge on and they'd say (whispering) 'Take that off, you'll get the bloody sack or something.'[89]

Arthur Exell, who was already working at Radiators, admitted that 'we were very quiet and behind-the-scenes. Well we had to be, otherwise you were out on your neck and that was it.' Exell cited the case of two Communists who entered the factory impatient to build the Party and set about it with such gusto that they were sacked within a week – leaving the Party in the factory two short.[90]

In short, the Party's objective of building a mass base in the factories required that Communists take full account of the attitudes of management, of their fellow workers who provided their best security against victimisation, and, given the CP's aim of permeating the trade unions, of those union leaders who looked askance at Communist activities. Given these pressures, it is not surprising that Party leaders complained that 'our propaganda for Communism is weak':

> We take part, for example, in mass movements for higher wages; we are tireless in our activity and we make our practical proposals to secure the workers' demands, but as a rule we fail to show that the wage struggle is born out of the struggle between the classes, and that so long as capitalism exists the workers will always have to face wage issues, unemployment, reaction and the danger of war.[91]

The issue would crop up in a much sharper form after October 1939 when the Party adopted an immediate policy on the war which the bulk of management and trade unionists alike found intolerable.

So as from about 1935 the CP adopted a more realistic strategy based on taking the masses as they were, and not, as previously, as the revolutionary irreconcilables they ought to have been. Essentially this was a long-term strategy which implicitly acknowledged that the revolutionary struggle could not advance quicker than the readiness of the masses to wage that struggle; and, whatever Dutt's delusions to the contrary, there were few signs of a mass revolutionary consciousness developing in Britain between the wars. But the Popular Front strategy was fraught with tensions and ambiguities. In the first place, the broad lines of Communist policy were determined not by a rational appraisal of what was possible in British conditions but by the erratic directives of the distant heads of world Communism who could not have cared less about the fate of the British working class, nor of the British Communist Party for that matter. Secondly, this pragmatic long-term strategy was at odds with the CP's residing belief in the immanence of revolutionary crisis. Finally, and very much linked with these first two points, the Party's policies and the alliances through which it pursued these policies concealed a number of potentially explosive contradictions. These tensions would be fully exposed after the outbreak of war: first because the Comintern imposed on the Party an anti-war policy repugnant to the mass of British workers; secondly because the Party began to speak not just of the immanence but of the imminence of revolution, in which case a cautious, long-term strategy would appear to be inappropriate for a revolutionary party; and finally because the assumptions underlying the Popular Front had nowhere been so ambiguous, its common platform so fragile, as on the question of war and peace. It is to this last, salient question that we now turn.

Notes

1 A. Hutt, *This Final Crisis* (1935), 279.
2 A note on terminology: in Communist parlance the united front denoted an alliance of working-class bodies, the People's Front a broader anti-Fascist alliance. Here and elsewhere I use the term 'Popular Front' to signify in the broadest sense the political strategy adopted by the CP as from about 1935, i.e. without drawing any distinction between the united front and the People's Front.
3 Dimitrov, 'The Seventh World Congress of the Communist International' in *Selected Speeches and Articles* (1951), 53, 63, 71, 113–14.
4 Dutt, *Decisive Days Ahead* (speech at CPGB Special National Conference, 6.10.35; CPGB, 1935), 3–5.
5 Dimitrov, *op. cit.*, 71–3, 148. For an account of the Popular Front in France, see D. R. Brower, *The New Jacobins* (1968).
6 Pollitt in *It Can Be Done* (CPGB, report of 14th Congress, 1937), 63.
7 Pollitt was defeated at East Rhondda and Gallacher was returned for West Fife. Thereafter the CP did not contest a single by-election until the outbreak of war.
8 The voting was 1,728,000 to 592,000, the bulk of the latter coming from the MFGB.
9 A left-wing ginger group affiliated to the Labour Party.
10 'Notes', Feb. 1937, 69–70. The Unity Manifesto is reprinted in G. D. H. Cole, *The People's Front* (1937), 353–6.
11 See B. Pimlott, *Labour and the Left in the 1930s* (1977), chs 9–10; Pollitt, 'The Communist Party congress and the next stage in the fight for unity, *LM*, July 1937, 397–8.
12 See e.g. the statement 'British Labour and Communism', *Report* of the 36th Annual Conference of the Labour Party (1936), 296–300.
13 Pimlott, *op. cit.*, 83.
14 Norman Brown, Ted Bramley, interviews.
15 J. Mahon, *Trade Unionism* (1938), 7.
16 This paragraph is drawn from *ibid.*, the most comprehensive exposition of the CP's attitude to trade union questions at this time.
17 See pp. 128–45.
18 *It Can Be Done*, 216, 239.
19 See E. and R. Frow, *Engineering Struggles. Episodes in the Story of the Shop Stewards' Movement* (1982), ch. 4; Branson, *op. cit.*, 93–8.
20 See Mahon's comments on unofficial activity, *op. cit.*, 41–2, 73–5.
21 P. Zinkin, *A Man To Be Watched Carefully* (1985), 132–3. See also the debate in *Discussion*

in January 1936.
22 This recommended that affiliated unions declare Communists ineligible for office and prohibited the selection of Communists as delegates to trade councils. It was endorsed by the 1935 TUC.
23 Cited A. Bullock, *The Life and Times of Ernest Bevin. Volume One: Trade Union Leader, 1881–1940* (1960), 596.
24 For these events see *ibid.*, 607–14; Branson, *op. cit.*, 174–7; K. Fuller, *Radical Aristocrats* (1985), pt. 3.
25 See the brief case history of Norman Brown in *Thesis*, 59–60.
26 Interview.
27 Pollitt in *For Peace and Plenty* (CPGB, report of 15th Congress, 1938), 53–5.
28 See Branson, *op. cit.*, ch. 6.
29 The title of a pamphlet published in 1933.
30 G. Patterson (Merseyside YCL organiser), 'The Communist Party and the youth movement', *Disc.*, Jan. 1937, 3–5.
31 Benny Rothman, interview. Cheetham was the main Jewish district of Manchester.
32 See J. Ferris, 'The Labour Party League of Youth, 1924–1940' (MA, Warwick, 1977).
33 A united movement of Labour and Communist students which nevertheless remained affiliated to the Labour Party until 1940.
34 Gabriel Carritt, then national organiser of the LNU youth groups, interview.
35 See R. Croucher, *Engineers at War* (1982), 45–56.
36 For Oxford see A. Exell, *The Politics of the Production Line* (1981), 7–14. For Birmingham see ch. 8 below.
37 Exell, *op. cit.*, 7.
38 P. Piratin, *Our Flag Stays Red* (1948), 45–6.
39 Dimitrov, *op. cit.*, 100–3.
40 'Introduction: the crisis in the thirties: a view from the left' in J. Clark *et al.* (eds), *Culture and Crisis in Britain in the 30s* (1979), 25. See also Campbell, *Disc.*, June 1936, 7.
41 R. Fox, *The Novel and the People* (1944 edn), 111.
42 J. Lindsay, *England, My England* (Key Books, 1939), 4–6, 15, 26, 62 and *passim*.
43 *The March of English History* (held 20.9.36) (CPGB London DC, programme, 1936).
44 William Rust in *It Can Be Done*, 163.
45 P. Devine, 'Fascist votes' in *Disc.*, Apr. 1937, 21.
46 And this comprised the vast majority of cases; see R. W. Robson, 'On Communist organisation', *Disc.*, Mar. 1936, 25. Factory groups remained in existence. A subsequent innovation was the establishment of women's groups within the Party in 1937.
47 Robson, *op. cit.*, 25–7.
48 See 'Building the mass Party', *Disc.*, Apr. 1936, 18.
49 From 7,700 in mid-1935 to 17,756 in mid-1939; see Pelling, *op. cit.*, 192–3.
50 CPGB CC report, *It Can Be Done*, 249.
51 Though not without adopting a different kind of 'cant and cliche', according to this writer. For his entertaining, Orwellian mockery of current 'Daily Workerisms', see E.U.L.W., 'Suggestions for a popular style', *Disc.*, Nov. 1937, 16–17.
52 See e.g. CPGB CC *Report* to 16th Congress (1939, not held), 9–11. In the previous ten months the Party had issued eleven pamphlets with an aggregate sale of 398,000 and 3½ million leaflets – this quite apart from material issued by District Committees and 'ancillary or subsidiary' bodies.
53 And not just cocoa. 'Workers of the World unite in favour of Kleen Blades for Clean Shaves' must surely have flummoxed the *Worker's* older readers; *DW*, 27.4.39.

54 And with it the device *Workers of all lands, unite!*
55 Programme for *1939 on Parade*, St Pancras Town Hall, 26.1.39.
56 *Books and Pamphlets – How to Sell Them* (CPGB, Central Literature Commission, 1938), 24.
57 R. W. Robson, *How the Communist Party Works* (CPGB, 1935), 9.
58 *Books and Pamphlets – How to Sell Them*, 26.
59 *Ibid.*, 28.
60 Lewis Day, 'England expects . . .', *Disc.*, Nov. 1936, 26.
61 Betty Cooper, *Disc.*, Dec. 1936, 31.
62 At least not as far as Communists were concerned. This was, however, the main concern of many others on the non-Communist left; see e.g. R. Acland, *Only One Battle* (1937), chs 7–9.
63 RPD K4, 'For a People's Front – against a Liberal–Labour coalition', article sent *Advance* (unofficial LLY journal), 5.6.37.
64 Pollitt, 'What next for Britain?', *LM*, Oct. 1937, 607; 'Notes', Oct. 1937, 598.
65 CPGB CC statement, *DW*, 19.3.38.
66 So the CP viewed appeasement; see ch. 3 below.
67 A.D. Lindsay at Oxford in October 1938; Vernon Bartlett at Bridgwater in November 1938; Gabriel Carritt (a Communist) at Westminster Abbey in May 1939.
68 At Mid-Bucks in May 1938; see S. Bornstein and A. Richardson, *Two Steps Back* (n.d.), 36–8.
69 The Duchess of Atholl at Perth in December 1938; see *ibid.*, 43–4.
70 'Notes', Oct. 1938, 601; Pollitt in *For Peace and Plenty*, 56–9.
71 See Attlee's fastidious rejection of the Popular Front in *The Labour Party in Perspective* (1937), 123–4.
72 'Notes', May 1938, 278; June 1938, 338.
73 J. Strachey, *What Are We To Do?* (1938), 121–2, 149–50, 171–2, 220, 309, 326.
74 See e.g. Pollitt in *It Can Be Done*, 40–60.
75 Strachey, *op. cit.*, 228.
76 *Ibid.*, 366.
77 J. R. Campbell, *Questions and Answers on Communism* (CPGB, 1938), 30.
78 'Notes', Jan. 1937, 13.
79 CPGB CC statement, *DW*, 11.6.38. More commonly it was argued that Fascism was 'above everything else self-destructive' and that Socialism would inevitably rise phoenix-like from the ashes of Fascism – but as a phoenix scarred and mutilated by mass impoverishment and prolonged international and civil war. Hence the necessity to cut short capitalism's degeneration into barbarism; Strachey, *op. cit.*, 364.
80 Pollitt, speech to CPGB London District Congress, *For Unity in London* (CPGB, 1938), 17–18.
81 Campbell, *op. cit.*, 22.
82 Strachey, *op. cit.*, 145–9, 315–7.
83 Emile Burns, *DW*, 16.6.38; 'Notes', June 1938, 346.
84 'A Group of Scientists, Economists and Technicians', *Britain Without Capitalists* (1939 edn), 2.
85 See the *Draft Programme to be Submitted to the 16th Party Congress* (CPGB, 1939) for a restatement of the Party's fundamental beliefs published the day after war broke out. The assumptions are those of *For Soviet Britain* far more than of *The British Road to Socialism*.
86 Dutt, *The Political and Social Doctrine of Communism* (1942 edn, written 1938), 30–1.
87 Campbell in *It Can Be Done*, 114–5.

88 R. W. Robson, *How the Communist Party Works*, 13–14.
89 Interview.
90 Exell, *op. cit.*, 58–9.
91 Pollitt in *It Can Be Done*, 80–1; see also e.g. Pollitt, 'What is the position?', *Disc.*, Oct. 1937, 3; J. Mahon, 'Our work in the trade unions', *Disc.*, Apr. 1936, 12–13.

Chapter three
Britain: the centre of gravity
1935–38

in world politics, Britain . . . is actually the centre of gravity. . . . The two sides are known, given quantities. On the one hand the forces of Fascism (the Berlin–Tokyo–Rome axis, the states in vassalage to Fascism, the reactionary groups in every land . . .) On the other hand, the forces of peace headed by the USSR, the peoples of Spain, China, Abyssinia, Austria, Czechoslovakia, the supporters of peace and democracy in every country. But the final balance of forces which is also the balance between peace and war is not yet finally established. Everything depends on the shifting of the centre of gravity.

(R. Page Arnot, August 1938[1])

the greatest permanent error in international politics is to under-estimate British policy. The serpent loves to speak like a dove, and the wolf to put on the fleece of a sheep. But it is those who accept the appearance who are the real sheep and deserve their fate.

(Palme Dutt, April 1938[2])

As the suffocating reality of war drew closer in the late 1930s, the spokesmen of virtually every tendency in British politics proclaimed, cynically or ineffectually, their devotion to the cause of peace: Attlee and Cripps, Maxton and Lansbury, Mosley and Chamberlain, and also the Communist Party which campaigned untiringly for the one course of action it felt could advert the 'coming world war'.[3] This was the formation of a 'Peace Front' in which all those states, including Britain, with no immediate interest in war would combine to deter further Fascist aggression.

As presented in the Communist press, this policy would at one and the same time preserve peace and safeguard democracy from its bellicose adversaries on the continent; the potential contradiction between these objectives was barely even admitted. The main ingredient in the Party's recipe for peace was unflinching opposition to Fascist expansionism, and its anti-war propaganda was coupled with fervent expressions of 'proletarian hatred against the fascist tyrants' and 'determination never to relinquish the struggle against Fascism until Fascism is vanquished in Spain and everywhere else'.[4] Such uncompromising attitudes have led many to regard the CP's voluble concern for peace as basically catachrestical. Or, at the very least, the Communists' heroic efforts on behalf of the Spanish republic suggested that their commitment to peace was secondary to their commitment to resist Fascism, even to the point of war. The Party's decision to support war against Germany in September 1939 appears as the logical sequel to its involvement in the war in Spain; and its subsequent reversal of that decision has been presented as the betrayal of the common ideals of the pre-war left.[5] 'No honest anti-Fascist worker cares for them at all', Aneurin Bevan wrote of the Communists in May 1940. 'They shame their own dead in Spain.'[6]

However, the CP's attitude to international affairs was far more complex than is generally made out, and cannot be reduced to support for Britain as a democratic power against Germany as a Fascist power. Certainly, the Party identified the main threat to peace with the open Fascist dictators. But, just as its interpretation of Fascism was based on existing Communist doctrine as to the nature of moribund capitalism, so was its perception of the Fascist war offensive grounded in a traditional Marxist analysis of inter-imperialist antagonisms as the fundamental cause of war. Moreover, if the Party departed from Leninist precedents in adopting a 'peace' policy based on the distinction between those imperialist states with and those without immediate aggressive intentions, it did not automatically follow that Britain fell into the latter, 'peace-loving' camp. On the contrary, Communists argued again and again that *'in the chain of events leading to a new world war, every link in the chain leads back to the National Government'*.[7] Britain was the one major undecided factor in world politics; its leaders pursued a consistent policy of collusion with Fascism, and yet its people still possessed basic democratic rights which could be used to remove those leaders and thus secure world peace. The key to the whole international situation lay in Britain.

In his Left Book Club selection *World Politics*, Palme Dutt located the forces making for war in the context of the general crisis of capitalism as firmly and precisely as he had the phenomenon of Fascism. With the epoch of imperialism, he argued, without pretending to great originality, the colonial question had become the 'central question of foreign politics and war, since each monopolist grouping strives to secure exclusive domination of the maximum area of exploitation, for the control of raw materials and markets, and for the export of capital'. In this way the 'whole available world' had rapidly been colonised by a handful of imperialist powers. The appetite for colonies remained unabated, however, and could now be satisfied only at the expense of rival imperialist powers. The ceaseless and perpetually renewed struggle for the redivision of the world was thus the '*characteristic conflict of imperialism*', of which the first round had begun in 1914 and the second was visibly impending. Currently the 'Fascist revisionist war offensive' dominated the situation in Europe; but, Dutt argued, '*the particular expression of this conflict at any given stage, the struggle between the so-called "satisfied" and "dissatisfied" imperialist Powers . . . is only the reflection of the law of the inequality of capitalist development, and continuously arises anew out of each new "solution"* '. In short, the continued existence of imperialism meant, inevitably, the recurrence of imperialist war:

> The cycle is complete. From the devastation of the world war to the attempted restoration of capitalism. From the restoration of capitalism to the devastation of the world economic crisis. From the world economic crisis to rearmament and renewed war. In this cycle the bankruptcy of imperialism is expressed.

And the cycle could only finally be broken by revolution.[8]

But if imperialism's wheel of misfortune had turned full circle this did not mean, Dutt argued elsewhere, that 'we are repeating 1914, that it is the same thing over again'.[9] Unlike others on the left, notably the ILP, Communists frequently drew attention to the 'profound and fundamental differences' between the situation in 1914 and that in the late 1930s.[10] The decisive new factor, from which all else followed, was the existence of the Soviet Union:

> In 1914 socialism had no country, and it did not matter to us which imperialist powers won. We were simply concerned that the working class should get the maximum fight against all of them. To-day . . . socialists all over the world have got a country.
>
> . . . this at once gives rise to the necessity that we have got to maintain our world base against capitalism . . . and therefore we approach the international situation in a different way from 1914 . . .[11]

And as Communism's world base was imperilled by the Fascist revisionist war offensive Communists were obliged to search out 'those elements in the imperialist camp who for whatever reasons – and the reasons do not matter to us a bit – are prepared to oppose the fascist war-making powers'.[12] For the second crucial difference with 1914, when every major power had had an interest in war, was that it was now possible and necessary to differentiate between those imperialist powers driving towards war and those with no immediate aggressive intentions.[13] A third distinction, keenly appreciated by Communists, was that successful Fascist aggression involved not simply a military victory over an imperialist rival but the imposition of the barbaric rule of Fascism on the conquered people.[14] Communist demands for resistance to Fascist aggression were not phrased primarily in terms of devotion to their world base, but emphasised instead the need to preserve the democratic rights of European workers; it was this latter motive which, for example, impelled so many Communists to take up arms against Fascism in Spain.[15] In time the two motives would conflict, with dramatic repercussions. But for the moment Communists had no need to decide on their priorities. The 'restraining of Hitler' and the 'maintenance of the peace of the world' were the 'paramount duty of the international working-class movement'.[16] 'The mad dogs of Fascism', wrote Pollitt, sounding already the belligerent note that would in different circumstances lead to his removal from the Party leadership, 'will never be hemmed in and prevented from carrying out their devilish work by "olive branches" and "pacifists" prayers', by high-faluting talk about "only concerning oneself with one's own capitalist class", by "revolutionary" phrasemongering.'[17] They would only be hemmed in by a 'peace front' of those powers prepared to stand up to Fascism.

The renunciation of revolutionary phrasemongering and the concern to distinguish and even take sides between aggressive and pacific imperialist powers marked a drastic departure from traditional Communist doctrine. The CP's conversion to the ideals of the League of Nations was, nevertheless, qualified. Quite apart from the continuing Communist emphasis on the independent mass struggle for peace, the 'artificial stabilisation of collective security' was conceived by Dutt simply as a 'temporary device against an immediate menace of war, pending the transition to a new world order'. War was inherent in capitalism and sooner or later the 'dynamic forces of expansion within imperialism' would burst against any system of collective security and overthrow it.[18] Nevertheless, war was not inevitable:

> No passivity! No surrender! No defeatism! No fatalism on this question of war. . . . The mass struggle can defeat the war plans of the imperialists, can delay the drive of capitalism to war.
>
> If we succeed in delaying it what does it mean? Does it mean that we have secure, permanent peace under capitalism? We have no such illusions. It means that we gain time. . . . We weaken capitalism and prepare conditions for the working-class advance to power, to the basic change of relations which finally defeats the war danger. That is the meaning of our peace policy . . .

The fight for collective security was only a 'temporary weapon' in the struggle for power; and if, in spite of the Communists' efforts, the imperialists nevertheless unleashed a new world war, Dutt assured the CP's 1937 congress, this would prove 'the grave of their doomed, dying and damned régime'.[14]

The CP's attitude to international affairs thus combined traditional anti-imperialist themes with the new motif of collective resistance to Fascist aggression. The Party line was, in a phrase, to *'struggle against the supreme offensive of the decaying imperialist reaction, expressed in the fascist war offensive, directly led by the fascist Powers'*.[20] This much is well known, but the CP's perception of Britain's position in this scenario is less well understood. Communists were the most persistent and unyielding critics of the National Government's policy of appeasement, but they did not regard this policy, as so many historians have, as a sign of debility on the part of Britain's rulers. Certainly, they did not view appeasement as 'an affair of the heart . . . close to Christian sentiments of fair play and forgiveness', as 'a desire to make the best of difficult times by offering the hand of friendship'.[21] Early in 1935 Dutt chided the Party's Central Committee for issuing a 'disastrous' manifesto which presented the British imperialists as 'poor innocent babes in the wood deluded and led by the nose' and their policies as 'weak, feeble, kowtowing to the gangsters'. Even if the Soviet press, bound by diplomatic considerations, frequently sounded this note, the British Communist press need feel no such inhibitions:

> On the contrary our job is to FIGHT BRITISH IMPERIALISM and expose its PRIMARY ROLE AND RESPONSIBILITY in the whole war-plot. . . . Our exposure of the BRITISH–GERMAN–JAPANESE WAR ALLIANCE with BRITAIN AS LEADER must be centre of our line, day after day . . .[22]

This would not be the last occasion on which Party propaganda would fail to meet Dutt's exacting standards; but by and large over the next few years the CP portrayed Britain's rulers consistently and undiplomatically as 'the chief bulwark of fascism and of the fascist war offensive throughout the world'.[23]

The Communist thesis that the British ruling class was quite deliberately promoting the expansionist schemes of an imperialist rival which it had so recently and so categorically defeated in the world's bloodiest yet war was a distinctive one. With the knowledge that Britain was shortly to fight a second, even longer war with the same imperialist rival, it might also seem a fantastic one. Indeed, it is remarkable how rarely, in the course of their impassioned reminders of the proximity of the war danger, Communist spokesmen anticipated the war that actually transpired in 1939; and this fact goes some way towards explaining the Party's confusion on the outbreak of that war. On the other hand, the arguments advanced by Communists in support of this thesis, complex and sometimes contradictory as they were, were to re-emerge during the war years in a no less entangled form.

The first set of arguments was predicated on the 'increasingly dominant and primary role of class issues in the present period of extreme weakness of capitalism', in contrast with the supremacy of inter-imperialist antagonisms before the First World War.[24] With the capitalist system itself in jeopardy the world over, the rival imperialist groupings, while remaining bitterly divided amongst themselves, drew closer together in their common concern to maintain their class domination. Especially was this concern felt by 'the biggest, the oldest and the strongest capitalist groups' and pre-eminently by the British ruling class, whose relations with other capitalist states had 'always been influenced by their feelings of responsibility, one can at times almost say, their sense of custodianship towards the capitalist system in general'. Thus, for example, British policy towards Germany was by no means determined simply by imperialist rivalry, for the British capitalists 'deeply appreciated the precariousness of German capitalism'.[25] Indeed, so precarious was German capitalism that it had turned in desperation to a Fascist regime which, unable to resolve the contradictions which had brought it into being and needing continually to divert the German people from their pressing domestic problems, could survive only by constant resort to external aggression.[26] Given its 'paramount class necessity, to avert at all costs the overthrow of Hitler or Mussolini', Communists argued, the National Government could not but give way to Hitler's blustering and blackmail.[27] For Communists, this view, that the British ruling class shunned collective resistance to Fascism out of fear of weakening its class allies abroad, was axiomatic.

The National Government's repugnance to collective security was also explained by its unwillingness to associate with the world's first Socialist state, and here again it was argued that the principle of class solidarity blunted the edge of potentially internecine imperialist antagonisms. 'The issue of socialism or capitalism ultimately dominates every other issue in the world', wrote Dutt; and in the abortive efforts to establish a 'united imperialist front against the Soviet Union' the British ruling class repeatedly took the initiative:

> The leadership of this hostility has throughout lain with the most powerful circles in British imperialism, the most conscious as a world power with extended world interests, with a deep-seated tradition of striking down every revolutionary movement . . . since the struggles against the French Revolution, the centre of world reaction, and now seeing as the basic issue of the post-war period the battle of imperialism against the world socialist revolution.[28]

Again, the designation of British imperialism as the engineer of world counter-revolution was a constant theme in Communist propaganda.

The means by which Britain's rulers hoped to achieve their reactionary aims, Communists regularly pointed out, was the 'Four Power Pact', 'a united front of Western Imperialism under British hegemony, through a strengthened and re-armed Germany to counterbalance the former French predominance . . . and with the ultimate point directed against the Soviet Union'.[29] This, according to Dutt, was the *'real basic continuing line of British policy in post-war Europe through all the apparent vacillations'*. It had surfaced first of all in the Locarno Treaty of 1925 and then again after Hitler's accession to power, though 'this time with the fascist counter-revolution openly dominating the scheme, directly represented by two of the partners and favoured and protected by the third, while France is to be isolated and subjected to the armed preparations of fascism for the overthrow of its régime'.[30] By 1938 Communists were loudly anticipating the consummation of this relationship and Dutt even went so far as to describe the Anglo-Italian pact of April that year as the realisation of the 'British–German–Italian Alliance'.[31]

At times Dutt suggested that this policy of connivance at Fascist aggression was misconceived, even from the point of view of the interests represented by the National Government. 'Only a minority of the more far-sighted imperialists', he wrote in March 1938, had recognised that appeasement might produce not a 'useful ally and instrument against the peoples and ultimately against the Soviet Union, but a powerful and dominating German Imperialism to confront the British Empire'.[32] At other times, however, Dutt supposed that the National Government had no illusions as to 'the ultimate menace of the Triple Pact to the British Empire as the richest world spoils'.[33] The policy of appeasement was an attempt to reconcile general and particular imperialist interests, by which the government aimed simultaneously 'to bolster up the Nazi régime, and to endeavour to ensure that its expansion shall not be in the sphere of British imperialist interests'.[34] To ensure the latter, the National Government embarked on a massive programme of rearmament to encourage Hitler to go east, first by closing the path to the West and secondly by bringing pressure to bear on the beleaguered eastern offspring of Versailles and their French guarantor to yield to Hitler's demands.[35] 'There is little enough vacillation or weakness in a rearmament programme of £1,500 million', as Dutt commented.[36] But if these armaments were intended in the first place to force Hitler away from British interests, they were also a sign that Britain was already preparing for the imperialist war which would inevitably ensue once the Fascist powers had reached 'the fullness of their strength and aggression – either imperialist war of the British Empire for the right to maintain its colonies, or imperialist war in support of fascism against the Soviet Union'.[37] Dutt envisaged no other type of war to which Britain's rulers would commit their augmented military might; and it was this combination of 'collusion with Fascism, alongside intensive isolationist rearmament' that made the National Government 'the real war-criminal behind the Hitlers, Mussolinis and Francos'.[38]

Yes, even behind the Francos, for this same analysis was applied in a modified form to the one protracted episode in which Hitler and Mussolini turned westwards, threatening Britain's strategic domination of the Mediterranean. Fascist intervention in Spain, Communists argued, posed a serious dilemma for Britain's rulers; 'from the class point of view' they welcomed it, but 'from the point of view of imperialist strategy' they were naturally concerned.[39] In this case, the 'class point of view' won hands down, as the British Government pursued a policy of 'continuous conscious assistance by every possible means, at the expense of international law and the Covenant, to the reactionary and invading forces';[40] and also at the expense, of course, of Britain's own strategic interests and of its international prestige.[41] But even Chamberlain's ineffable complacency as British merchant shipping was gunned down in Spanish waters did not betoken helpless capitulation to Fascist warmongering:

> He wants it. It is his policy. His every speech is an incitement to more bombing of British ships. . . .
> The decadent ruling section represented by Chamberlain are not concerned with the national interests of the English people. They have only one concern – their pocket, the interests of their vast capital holdings over the whole world and these interests they identify with Fascism.
> This dominates even their antagonism with their Fascist rivals.[42]

Britain's venal capitalist oligarchy was more anxious about the security of its scattered investments than even the defence of its metropolitan base; and the former it entrusted to the Fascists, even as they threatened the latter. 'An examination of the close association of British and German financial interests in Spain, as well as in other parts of the world', wrote Dutt, 'would show how far the role of Hitler and Mussolini has been in practice the role of the "strong-arm men" of the City financiers (like the Shakespearean First Murderer and Second Murderer, while Macbeth shivers in a palsy in London)'.[43]

In short, the CP's determination to resist Fascist aggression never implied the slightest degree of support for the National Government nor acquiescence in its preparations for war. Dutt upbraided those on the left who rebuked Britain's appeasers for their alleged credulity, their indecisiveness and cowardice. 'Behind this pretty fairy tale', he protested, 'the real role of the reactionary ruling group of British Imperialism . . . as the *leader* of world reaction and main *accomplice* of Fascism is hidden and concealed'. British reaction should not be seen as some vain, doddering old man with an umbrella; it was rather the *'real incendiary of the threatening world war'*:

> *Hitler and Mussolini may be brandishing the lighted torches, but they would be powerless without British support. The directing centre is the inner ruling group of British reaction. . . . Here is the heart of the world situation. Here is the heart of the fight.*[44]

The future of Europe depended 'entirely on the internal fight in Britain'[45] and Dutt decried every tendency to draw back from this fight, as for instance when the PLP abstained on the government's arms estimates for the first time in 1937. 'With this decision the echoes of 1914 sound close', he wrote, for every such move spelt 'surrender to the . . . *extending war of fascist aggression – with British Imperialism in fact on the side of fascism, and with British Labour in the pocket of British Imperialism'*.[46] Just as resistance to Fascism required implacable opposition to the National Government, so did the slightest inclination towards cooperation with the government, under the illusion that it could be pressurised into standing up to Hitler, abet the Fascist onslaught on democracy. And in this respect the leaders of British Labour sinned not just by commission, but by their refusal to provide the leadership need to remove Chamberlain, and with him the danger of war. The Party line hardly wavered on these points; until September 1939, that is, when Chamberlain declared war on his erstwhile bosom companions, the occasion being not a direct threat to the British Empire but the invasion of a backward, almost defenceless country directly *en route* for the Soviet Union. But by that time, of course, Stalin had reached his own *modus vivendi* with the mad dogs of war, under the cover of the same unctuous desire for 'peace' as had lubricated Chamberlain's public utterances.

The fact is that the clearly defined issues of the 1930s – for peace and democracy, against Fascism and war, against Chamberlain and Hitler – were never as straightforward as they sometimes appeared; and under the impact of unforeseen events this solid-looking facade would crumble to reveal a labyrinth of contradictions. Throughout the late 1930s, for example, the CP issued strident calls for peace, and would later recall this fact to legitimise its decision to oppose Britain's war with Germany. But the Party's attitude to peace was ambivalent, and certainly had nothing to do with an absolute renunciation of armed conflict. This was evident above all in its solidarity with the Spanish republic in its war for peace:

> this struggle in Spain is much more than a struggle in defence of democracy, it is a struggle in defence of peace. The defence of democracy to-day becomes the defence of peace. . . . Spain's militia carries on its heroic struggle – and the

British Government denies to the defenders of Peace the right even to buy arms.[47]

Likewise, if Communist propaganda against rearmament occasionally expressed traditional anti-militarist sentiments,[48] the basic objection was 'to *this* re-armament programme of *this* Government' and the uses to which it would be put; a People's Government determined on peace would not be denied the weapons necessary to preserve it.[49] And if the proposed Peace Front did not succeed in restraining Fascism, then war, whether or not by any other name, would be both legitimate and necessary. 'We support collective security', wrote Emile Burns, 'in order to *deter* fascist aggression, and, if necessary, *defeat* it';[50] and no Communist would have quibbled with this. 'Peace', whatever it did mean, did not simply signify the opposite of war.

On the other hand, the defence of democracy, which had apparently 'become' the defence of peace, did not necessarily signify Communist approval if Britain became embroiled in war with Nazi Germany; or, rather, the CP never gave any clear idea of what its attitude to such a war would be. The Party's policies, J. R. Campbell insisted, were intended to preserve peace and would do so if implemented; to conjecture about a hypothetical war with Germany would merely give credence to the calumnies that resistance to Hitler spelt war and thus help 'the pro-Fascist war party in Britain to prevent the building of a peace combination which will restrain the aggressors'.[51] Nevertheless, Campbell was prepared to speculate on, 'in the absence of a Peace Bloc, a war of the Fascist war alliance against the Soviet Union, France and Czechoslovakia' and to recommend that the workers of those countries do their utmost to win such a war.[52] However, Communists did not speculate along these lines with regard to the British workers because of the Party's deep-rooted conviction that the British Government was 'closer to the Fascist bloc than . . . . to democratic countries like France'[53] and would choose sides accordingly. When a Communist from Finsbury wrote that 'the class interests represented by the National Government will never allow huge armaments to be used in defence of democracy',[54] he was only summarising the conclusions of innumerable penny pamphlets and prolix *Labour Monthly* editorials. The first thing was to get rid of the National Government; only then need one address the question of British involvement in a war for democracy.

The CP's commitment to either war or peace was, in fact, conditional, but the fundamental condition was usually obscured by high-flown rhetoric about a Peace Front. Occasionally, however, the basic determinant of Communist policy was frankly admitted:

> Make no mistake about it. If we want the overthrow of capitalism, we must defend

the country that has already overthrown capitalism. . . . It means different tactics according to whether one's capitalist government is in the combination against the Soviet Union or is – for its own purposes – fighting alongside the Soviet Union.[55]

The CP was pledged to the defence of the Soviet Union 'at any cost', wrote Pollitt, who did not even pretend to exercise any autonomy in assessing the best line of defence. On the contrary, he readily accepted that on the CPGB, as on every other section of the Comintern, there fell the obligation to 'support 100 per cent and without reservations everything that the Soviet Union does in its foreign policy'.[56] It was not for British Communists to reason why, and during the years of Litvinov's pre-eminence they felt little inclination to. Whatever the misgivings about the internal affairs of the Soviet Union, surely no anti-Fascist could question the integrity of Soviet foreign policy? No anti-Fascist, at any rate, who read only the *Daily Worker*. Steadfast opposition to Fascist aggression appeared as intrinsic to Communism as febrile threats to eradicate Bolshevism were to Fascism. In time, however, British Communists would have occasion to recall Stalin's declaration that 'our orientation in the past and our orientation in the present is towards the USSR and towards the USSR alone'.[57] The price exacted by Soviet foreign policy would be raised and Pollitt, among others, would prove reluctant to pay the full amount.

The CP, to conclude, campaigned incessantly for peace and against the National Government and its so-called Fascist alliances without formulating a policy appropriate to the sort of war that broke out in 1939. As late as its Fourteenth Congress in 1937, the Party was quite explicit as to its attitude to the coming war, reaffirming the Stuttgart Resolution of the Second International; if war broke out, Communists would 'work for its speedy termination and . . . strive with all their might to utilise the economic and political crisis produced by war to . . . hasten the downfall of capitalist class domination'.[58] However, by the time of the Party's next congress in September 1938 such forthright statements could no longer be countenanced. The Party line, as communicated by Pollitt, was notably evasive, not to say insipid:

> We reject the inevitability of war.
>   We refuse to speculate on this or that tactic if war breaks out.
>   We know if our policy is adopted, peace can be made secure and Fascist aggression brought to an end.[59]

The crisis over Czechoslovakia was at its height and there was, of course, no chance whatsoever of the Communist policy being adopted. As the issues of war drew closer, the position of simply refusing to speculate became less tenable, and in the months after Munich the latent contradictions in Communist policy grew sharper, occasionally even cutting their way through to full public view. Indeed, even as that congress went through the imperturbable motions of Communist Party congresses in those days, the backrooms of Birmingham Town Hall were echoing to the sounds of heated controversy among the Party's leadership.

Notes

1 'Britain the centre of gravity', *LM*, Aug. 1938, 483.
2 'Notes', Apr. 1938, 199.
3 The title of a book by the Communist Tom Wintringham published in 1935.
4 D. Springhall, *It Can Be Done* (CPGB, report of 14th Congress, 1937), 150.
5 Originally and most comprehensively in V. Gollancz (ed.), *The Betrayal of the Left* (1941), written by some of those who had shared these ideals.
6 *Tribune*, 24.5.40.
7 'Notes', Mar. 1937, 132.
8 Dutt, *World Politics 1918–1936* (1936), 28–34, 108–9, 114, 181–3, 244, 361–2 and *passim*.
9 Dutt, *Decisive Days Ahead* (speech to CPGB Special National Conference, 6.10.35; CPGB, 1935), 6.
10 Pollitt, 'A working-class peace policy', *LM*, May 1936, 299.
11 Dutt, *Decisive Days Ahead*, 6–7.
12 *Ibid.*, 12–13.
13 Pollitt, *op. cit.*, 299–300.
14 *Loc. cit.*
15 See the interviews with International Brigaders in D. Corkhill and S. Rawnsley, *The Road to Spain. Anti-Fascists at War 1936–1939* (1981).
16 Pollitt, *op. cit.*, 301.
17 *Ibid.*, 303.
18 *World Politics*, 169–70.
19 Dutt in *It Can Be Done*, 120–1, 142; *World Politics*, 169–70, 323–6.
20 'Notes', Aug. 1936, 459–60.
21 M. Gilbert and R. Gott, *The Appeasers* (1963 edn), 23, 35.
22 RPD K4, Dutt to CPGB Secretariat, n.d. but Mar. 1935. For the manifesto, see *DW*, 21.3.35. It goes without saying that it would have been better for the CP if it had always shown this sort of critical appreciation of the diplomatic constraints which shaped Soviet policy statements and press reports.
23 'Notes', June 1936, 338–9.
24 'Notes', Aug. 1938, 460, 463.
25 G. Graham, 'Notes on British foreign policy', *LM*, Feb. 1936, 115.
26 R. Goodman, 'Hitler means war', *LM*, Mar. 1938, 141–2.
27 I. Montagu, 'The Eden–Hitler Axis', *LM*, July 1937, 409; 'Notes', Aug. 1938, 463–4.
28 *World Politics*, 275, 290–1.
29 'Notes', Feb. 1936, 72. The four powers were the Munich quartet: Britain, Germany, France and Italy.
30 'Notes', Jan. 1938, 8–11. British hostility to France, both because of its Popular Front governments and because of its Eastern commitments, particularly the Franco–Soviet Pact,

was a recurrent theme in Communist propaganda.
31 'Notes', May 1938, 269.
32 'Notes', Mar. 1938, 139–40.
33 'Notes', Dec. 1937, 721.
34 'Notes', Mar. 1937, 138.
35 See e.g. 'Notes', Feb. 1938, 75–6.
36 'Notes', Mar. 1937, 132–3. 'Indeed', Dutt went on, 'the very delay of the programme means that Britain, having had the shrewdness to wait, now comes in to outstrip every other power in the last lap and arrive with the most modernised up-to-date equipment . . .'
37 'Notes', Apr. 1938, 211; June 1937, 347.
38 'Notes', Mar. 1937, 133.
39 R. Goodman, 'The poisoned peace', *LM*, Aug. 1937, 478.
40 'Notes', Apr. 1937, 209.
41 Pollitt in *For Peace and Plenty* (CPGB, report of 15th Congress, 1938), 37.
42 Dutt, *DW*, 2.7.38.
43 'Notes', Jan. 1938, 11. Such an investigation had been carried out by C. Suden, 'Anglo–German interests in Spain', *LM*, July 1937, 426–32.
44 'Notes', Apr. 1938, 197–8, 216. Dutt was not always consistent on this point. At about the same time he warned that Britain under Chamberlain was 'henceforth to be the servile ally and tool of Hitler and Mussolini . . . the fourth wheel in the coach of the Triple Pact', a very different emphasis; *DW*, 22.2.38.
45 'Notes', Apr. 1938, 196.
46 'Notes', Apr. 1937, 203 ff.
47 Editorial, *Disc.*, Feb. 1937, 1–2. This curious usage was common in referring to the Spanish People's Army, the International Brigades and Red Army.
48 See e.g. *Parade of War* (CPGB, 10.4.37), 12.
49 Strachey, *LN*, Apr. 1937, 321. See also e.g. W. Rust, *Labour and Armaments* (CPGB, 8.1.37), 6–7. Rust also argued, however, that the 'collective power of the democratic countries' would be such that not a 'single rifle' extra would be needed (p. 13).
50 E. Burns, *Difficulties Facing Peace* (CPGB, c.1936), 9.
51 *DW*, 23.2.38.
52 *Loc. cit.*
53 Campbell, *DW*, 8.1.38.
54 G. Tucker, *DW*, 6.7.38.
55 Campbell, *Peace – But How? A Workshop Talk* (CPGB, c.1936). 27–8. For workers in countries ranged alongside the USSR Campbell advised a sort of 'war on two fronts' – 'at no stage does it involve co-operation with the capitalist class, neither in peace nor in war'.
56 Pollitt, 'The Seventh Congress of the Communist International', *LM*, Oct. 1935 616–17.
57 Cited by D.N. Pritt, *Light on Moscow* (1939), 3.
58 Resolution on 'The fight for peace', *It Can Be Done*, 282.
59 Pollitt in *For Peace and Plenty*, 40.

Chapter four
The last year of 'peace', 1938–39

> Munich represents the Great Divide of the modern international situation, as decisive in its fashion as 1914. . . . With Munich the entire post-war order . . . is shattered; the peace system, such as it was, is destroyed; the leadership of Britain and France in world affairs is ended for the time being; the immediate initiative has passed to the defeated States, to fascism, which no longer makes any concealment of its aims of world conquest. Fascism's war for the redivision of the world is now in the open . . . 'the second imperialist war has in fact already begun'.
>
> (Palme Dutt, January 1939[1])

The Communist Party 'line' in the late 1930s, as the opening chapters have shown, did not lead directly and unproblematically to certain foregone conclusions in the event of war between Britain and Germany; indeed, it was not so much a line as a tangled web of potentially conflicting assumptions and objectives. Unequivocally opposed to Fascism, the CP advocated military resistance to Fascist aggression; but not, it insisted, in anticipation of war but as the only means of maintaining peace. Moreover, the commitment to resist aggression did not entail automatic support for the strengthening of Britain's defences, for the CP did not identify Fascism simply with external aggression, but also with the reactionary government of democratic Britain. The military preparations on which Britain would shortly rely to withstand Nazi aggression were denounced by Communists as the scaffolding for a Fascist state apparatus at home and as a device for directing the Axis powers through a series of small, unoffending countries towards the Soviet Union. Military resistance as the equivalent of peace, opposition to incipient Fascism within Britain and to the hubristic Fascism abroad which threatened Britain – these were the interwoven strands of Communist politics in the 1930s, and the CP would eventually have to cut through them if it was to make any sense of the approaching war.

But as war drew nearer, the web drew tighter. The CP warned of ever-closer Anglo-Nazi cooperation, even as it acknowledged the imminent likelihood of war between these incestuous imperialist rivals. It opposed with scarcely abated vigour the 'Fascist' war measures of the British Government, even as it argued that the point of Nazi aggression had now been turned westwards, towards the people of Britain. It maintained that by the adoption of its policies peace could yet be preserved, even as it announced that the second imperialist war had already begun, and even as it aligned itself with anti-appeasement Tories long convinced of the necessity of war with Germany. It insisted that its policies *could* still be adopted, that it was 'more than ever *possible* for the united democratic forces to defeat Chamberlain', even as it protested that the 'veiled coalition of the two Front Benches defeats the possibility of expression of the will of the people, robs elections of their reality . . . [and] creates a sense of helplessness and paralysis of the popular will'.[2] In short, it insisted on the achievability of an anti-Fascist peace, even as its own sometimes desperate warnings indicated a far more gloomy prospect ahead. The reality was that Britain was drifting to war with Germany in the most unfavourable circumstances and with Chamberlain firmly ensconced in Downing Street. Of this possibility Communists were increasingly aware, but they rejected its inevitability and thus contrived to postpone the necessary itemisation of their priorities. Nevertheless, as the issues of the coming war grew sharper, the countervailing tendencies in Communist politics began to collide with one another, although the impact was as yet muffled. The first clear sign of the crash ahead came with the Munich crisis of September 1938 during which virtually the whole of Britain, including a number of Communists, became persuaded that the rejection of Hitler's ultimata spelt war.

William Gallacher's lonely protest at Chamberlain's flight to Munich to dismember Czechoslovakia, while his fellow MPs stomped and cheered their approval, is regarded by Communists as one of the proudest moments in their Party's history.[3] However, the Munich war scare was also one of the more trying episodes in the CP's history during which it struggled to maintain an appearance of unity. For the most part the CP presented the issues of the crisis in the by now familiar terms of the Anglo–Nazi war alliance on the one hand and the Peace Front, as the only alternative to this alliance, on the other. Hitler's threats to march on Czechoslovakia had brought Europe to 'the very brink of war'[4] and in this crisis, despite his 'lying "pledges" as the supposed defender of democracy against Fascism', Chamberlain was using 'the whole power of his rearmament . . . to weight the scales on the side of Fascism'.[5] However, this did not mean that either war or the subjugation of the Czechs was inevitable. The task of the British people was to take 'resolute action to force the British Government to abandon concessions to

Fascism',[6] in which case 'Hitler would have no alternative but to abandon his present scheme of aggression'.[7] The choice, as presented by Dutt, was a stark one:

> Either the Alliance of Chamberlain and Hitler . . . will succeed in its plot against democracy and peace in Central Europe and drag the whole world into war.
> Or the Peace Alliance of the democratic peoples, including the British people, can yet bar the way, save Czechoslovakia and save peace.[8]

However, not all Communists saw the issue this clearly. Some there were who were more inclined to take Chamberlain's lying pledges at their face value and who felt, as their rulers intended them to, that the redemption of these pledges meant war.

The issue was fought out backstage at the Party's Fifteenth Congress, held in mid-September. Swayed by the prevalent atmosphere of war hysteria, Dutt recalled many years later, a number of leading Communists felt it the Party's duty to issue a manifesto stating its position on the now-imminent war. Among those who fought tenaciously for such a manifesto were Pollitt, Gallacher and Rust, while Dutt and his wife Salme argued even more tenaciously that the manifesto 'would make the Party a laughing stock as having become a victim of the Government's trick to delude the people'. The issue was still undecided when Dutt was suddenly called to the platform, from which, with 'this controversy still ringing in his head', he settled the matter. Any 'tendencies to defeatism and speculation on the war question', he warned, played right into Chamberlain's hands, for it was the government's intention to spread everywhere the deception that united resistance must inevitably lead to war. Why was this, Dutt asked:

> Is it because they intend to make such a united stand? That is the last thing they mean to do if they can help it. . . . If there were such a united stand that would mean not war but peace. But their aim is on this basis to smash the idea of the peace front by associating it in the minds of the people with war. Their aim is on this basis to put across their policy of breaking the peace front, betraying Czechoslovakia, betraying peace . . . in such a way that it is received as a triumph for peace . . .[9]

And this, despite occasional waverings, was the official Party line until the signing of the Munich agreement which it so astutely predicted. The war scare was simply a public relations exercise meant to disguise the reality of Chamberlain's premeditated alliance with Hitler. Even when the Foreign Office signalled its intention to stand by the Czechs, and even as gas masks were issued, children evacuated and trenches laid in Hyde Park, the CP remained sceptical. 'By Tuesday night, September 27', Charles Mowat tells us, 'almost everyone in Great Britain expected that the country would be at war next day, or at least by the week-end';[10] almost everyone, but not the *Daily Worker*:

> there is no need for panic. The Chamberlain Government is aiming to create a war scare among the civilian population to get people to accept its policy of 'peace at any price' and enable more concessions to be given to Hitler.[11]

The 'supreme betrayal'[12] of the Munich settlement, then, did not take the Communist Party unawares.

Dutt's insistence that Chamberlain would only by the most colossal mischance find himself standing firm against Hitler, and his assurances that if he did so this would bring peace and not war, had apparently had the desired effect. Differences within the Party, however, remained,[13] and on the proclamation of the Munich agreement they received a rare public airing in the *Daily Worker*. The Party's official response to Munich was acidic:

> The victory of peace and democracy seemed certain, and this meant the end of Hitler's threat to Europe.
> But Chamberlain did not want this. He was determined to save the face and prestige of Hitler.
> That was why he went to Munich . . .
> The peace of the world has not been saved. It has been betrayed to the custody of Hitler . . .[14]

But astonishingly a *Daily Worker* editorial two days later painted a very different picture, one based on a sketch by Chamberlain himself:

> Had war broken loose on Saturday as seemed almost certain . . . the corpses of hundreds of thousands of men, women and children, would by now be strewing the streets of Prague, Paris, Berlin and even London.
> Spared from the horrors of this ghastly calamity the whole nation has during the week-end given evidence of its feelings of tremendous relief. In this the British people have shown their passionate desire for peace.
> The Communists who have been, and will continue to be, the foremost fighters for peace, have shared naturally in the general feelings of relief.[15]

The sentiments were those of a Maxton or a Lansbury and were immediately repudiated by the Party's Secretariat as 'directly contrary to the policy of the Communist Party'.[16] This they clearly were; but equally clearly the policy of the Communist Party was such as to create utter confusion as to its position on the pivotal question of war and peace.

The CP had thus manifested 'signs of weakness' first of all by, in Dutt's words, 'tendencies to capitulate to the war scare (speculations on imminent war, "should we support Chamberlain if he fights Hitler?" etc.)' and secondly by 'corresponding subsequent tendencies to capitulate to the "peace-wave" of "relief" at the supposed averting of war'.[17] On this occasion Dutt's judgement had been strikingly vindicated; but sooner or later the question 'should we support Chamberlain if he fights Hitler?' would require an answer.

For the moment, however, Munich appeared to provide clear confirmation that Chamberlain's objective was that of a reactionary alliance with Hitler. 'A preliminary form of reactionary Four Power co-operation, under fascist domination, has been established in Europe', Dutt wrote in November 1938,[18] and until the very outbreak of war he continued to explain the vagaries of British foreign policy by reference to this, Chamberlain's fundamental aim. One new slant to this analysis was that this embryonic bloc was said to be directed not only against the USSR but against the USA as well. Chamberlain's policies thus seemed designed to 'leave Britain a junior partner in the Fascist Axis, clearly and irrevocably aligned against the two greatest powers on earth'.[19] However, if the Communist analysis of appeasement remained essentially unaltered well into 1939, it was nevertheless modified to take into account the unmistakable signs of growing Anglo-German antagonism. By his alacrity to come to terms with Hitler, Dutt argued, Chamberlain had so weakened and isolated Britain that Hitler's policy could 'no longer be calculated in terms of British wishes, but develops as an independent force, capable of turning and leading a very powerful European combination against Britain'. The 'effective domination and initiative' now lay with Fascism.[20]

Soon it was realised that Hitler was not only capable of turning on Britain, but had actually begun to do so. 'The point of fascism's menace is now visibly turned against Britain and France', Dutt wrote in July 1939, even as the *Labour Monthly* featured *exposés* of the interlocking interests of British and German imperialism; and in the face of this menace, 'even the most reactionary crawling bootlickers of fascism were left with no alternative save to take some active steps, not from any desire to oppose Hitler, but if they were to have any hope of even reaching a bargain with Hitler'.[21] And it was in these withering terms that Dutt assessed the more robust-looking policies adopted by Chamberlain after the German annexation of Czechoslovakia in March 1939.

Essentially, Dutt argued that these policies were merely an adaptation of 'the same basic aims as at Munich to a new stage and new conditions'.[22] Chamberlain's system of limited guarantees in the East had nothing to do with collective security, but was rather 'a continuance in new forms of the old policy of endeavouring to canalise fascist aggression on the directions approved by Britain'. Chamberlain blocked up certain rat-holes 'in order to make sure that the rat will break out in other directions'. Likewise, the approach to the Soviet Union was dictated simply by the realisation that, given Hitler's augmented power, rearmament alone was insufficient to push Germany away from British interests and towards Russia. Allies were necessary to force Hitler's hand, and yet the only conceivable ally of real value was Russia itself. Hence Chamberlain's protracted attempt to 'solve the insoluble', to entice Stalin into a *'one-way agreement'* which would block Hitler's path in the West while, just as importantly, leaving it open in the East. The overtures to Moscow were thus only a 'temporary tactical move' in Chamberlain's 'deeper strategy' of the 'counter-revolutionary alliance with fascism', and Britain's rulers betrayed their unmitigated commitment to this objective by their renewed efforts to build up Hitler's strength.[23] In short, Dutt did not accept that Chamberlain had belatedly determined upon resistance to Hitler, and he reproached those on the left who gave credence to the view that he had.[24] NO CONFIDENCE IN CHAMBERLAIN', was the message running through all Dutt's writings, 'NO ILLUSIONS AS TO HIS POLICY'.[25] But Dutt's line of absolute opposition to Chamberlain's war preparations did not always satisfy those Communists whose main preoccupation was with the direct threat to British liberties now posed by German expansionism.

However, it was never Dutt's view, nor officially that of the CP, that the danger of Fascism in Britain came exclusively or even primarily from abroad. Indeed, the CP's apprehensions as to the Fascist tendencies of the National Government became even more pronounced after the Party's Fifteenth Congress in September 1938. Chamberlain's pro-Fascist foreign policy, wrote Dutt:

> is an integral part of a single reactionary policy which is directing its blows against the social and economic interests of all sections of the people, and against working-class rights and democratic liberties; which will inevitably strive to sharpen this reactionary course in the conditions of developing economic crisis and the sharpening international situation; and which must now be definitely characterised as steering towards the realisation of a fascist regime in Britain.[26]

Moreover, it was precisely under the cover of strengthening Britain's defences – 'under the slogans of "national unity", "preparedness", "a truce to party politics", "the nation in danger", "speeding up rearmament", "national service", etc.' – that this process was being carried through.[27] National defence was not, then, a question on which all patriotic Britons of whatever political persuasion should unite. It was, rather, the battleground between Fascism and democracy in Britain, and 'every concession to

Chamberlain's reactionary measures in the name of war-preparedness' only strengthened 'the forces of reaction at home and the armed power on the side of Fascism'.[28]

The CP's alternative to this regime of encroaching Fascism remained a People's Government under Labour leadership, but it is important to note that its warnings of the danger of Fascism in Britain were accompanied by a perceptible hardening of attitude towards the leaders of the Labour movement. These leaders, who remained as resistant as ever to calls for unity, were accused not merely of passivity but of 'positive collaboration in the real policy of the Government', as 'sounding-board', as 'advertising agent', as 'gramophone'.[29] The *'real structure of government'* in Britain, Dutt argued, was the *'tacit alliance'* of the Labour Party leadership and Chamberlain;[30] and it was in this alliance, and the suppression of opposition to this alliance,[31] that Dutt perceived the incubus of Fascism:

> We speak of the menace of fascism in Britain. We speak correctly of the obvious signs of the Chamberlain Government moving in this direction. . . . Do we see the significance of what is happening in that essential pivot of the democratic system in this country, the functioning of parties – this increasing pressure of the machine in the two dominant parties . . . to root out every independent expression of opinion that hampers the domination of Chamberlain? The real palladium of popular liberty in this country is the working class movement. If the freedom of the working-class movement is broken, democracy is broken. . . . For this is the way that the ground is prepared for fascism.[32]

The dualism which had always characterised the CP's attempted reconciliation with Labour was becoming more exaggerated. Communists maintained that a popular movement capable of defeating Chamberlain's Fascist schemes could only be realised under Labour leadership.[33] But so far from rallying such a movement this leadership was itself collaborating quite deliberately in the implementation of these schemes. Moreover, as the decisions of Labour's Southport conference in May–June 1939 demonstrated, the position of this right-wing leadership was virtually unassailable.[34] Not surprisingly, a note of bitter disillusionment with Labour crept into Communist writings.[35] It is perhaps symptomatic of this dualism that the CP decided at this time both to renew its application for affiliation to the Labour Party and to instruct a number of Communists inside the Labour Party to tender their resignations and proclaim to the world their adherence to the Communist Party.[36]

The same ambivalence characterised the CP's extension of its goodwill to embrace Tory opponents of appeasement. The divergences in Conservative opinion which had already been reflected in Eden's resignation from the government in February 1938 became more sharply and publicly defined as a result of Munich.[37] The significance of this development was not lost on Communists, who quickly signalled their readiness to associate even with those who stood 'for the exploitation of man by man' and who for that very reason were 'alarmed at the consequences of the surrender of Empire interests and national interests to Fascism'.[38] The CP had in effect declared a state of emergency in which it was imperative that all those opposed to Chamberlain, for whatever reasons, should unite to defeat him; and over the next few months it was made quite clear that the Communist panacea of a People's Government would necessarily include the Churchillian right.[39]

As usual, however, Dutt sounded a cautionary note. By their outspoken criticisms of appeasement the Tory dissidents undoubtedly performed an 'objectively progressive role', but their related demands that Britain gird itself for war portended more sinister developments:

> the practical points of their programme become: 'national unity', intensified rearmament and conscription. But this policy coincides with the main drive of the pro-fascist policy inside Britain, that is, the course to fascism in Britain. Objectively the present programme of the Conservative Opposition . . . assists the course to fascism inside Britain; and it is even conceivable that under certain circumstances they might become the main pace-makers of such a development.[40]

Subsequently Dutt modified these criticisms,[41] but the lesson was clear. The left should 'beware of allowing the mass fight against Chamberlain to be dragged at the tail of these elements'. The objectively uncertain role played by the Tory malcontents emphasised 'all the more urgently the decisive part which can only be played by the Labour Party in organising and leading any wider democratic combination against Chamberlain'.[42] And yet the Labour Party, of course, was adamant in its refusal to play this part. Thus by 1939 did the CP's broadening conception of a People's Government and its conception of British Fascism overlap. Only a united stand by Attlee and Churchill, and their supporters, could avert the menace of Fascism and war; and yet these leaders showed little predilection for such a stand, and far more for collaboration in the government's war preparations – in other words, those of Dutt, 'collaboration in the development to fascism in Britain'.[43] The balance between democracy and Fascism in Britain was delicately poised, to say the least. Everything depended on shifting the weight of the Labour movement onto the side of democracy.

The tensions within Communist politics were growing sharper with every month as most of the Party's fears, and none of its hopes, were realised. The most crucial unanswered question was whether the international struggle against the aggrandisement of the Axis powers took precedence over the domestic struggle against the National Government. However, the CP's interpretation of appeasement as a policy of deliberately promoting Fascist aggression enabled it to avoid addressing this still hypothetical question. The German people's fight was against Hitler, the British people's against his accomplice Chamberlain;[44] the two went hand in hand. But if appeasement was abandoned, if Chamberlain's Britain found itself at war with Hitler's Germany, then a drastic readjustment of the Party line would be inescapable. For it was in the militarisation of Britain's society and economy that the CP discerned the looming presence of home-grown Fascism; and thus if the CP acquiesced in the government's war measures it abandoned the fight against Fascism in Britain. But if it opposed them, then what of the fight against Hitler?

Not surprisingly, there were one or two indications of the difficulties this dilemma would pose even before September 1939, for the war which broke out that month did not exactly come out of the blue. By 1939 the CP's leaders were referring regularly to the immediate danger to British security, and some Communists became so preoccupied with this threat as to relax their uncompromising resistance to British reaction. The differences of approach to these questions were not consciously publicised in the Party press but nevertheless, just as with Munich, one or two episodes have left their traces for the historian. One such episode was the Party's campaign against conscription in the spring of 1939.

Chamberlain's announcement of a strictly limited measure of compulsory military service some weeks after the German annexation of Czechoslovakia has generally been taken as an indication of his tardy and reluctant realisation of the futility of trying to appease Hitler's insatiable appetite for *lebensraum*. Britain's Communists, however, regarded conscription not as a welcome sign of stiffening resistance to Nazism, but as the sequel to Munich on the domestic front, a calculated step towards 'putting Britain into Fascist fetters'.[45] In his pamphlet outlining the CP's case against conscription, Pollitt recapitulated the Communist view of the origins and nature of Fascism and drew the conclusion that 'Chamberlain represents in Britain that section of monopoly capitalism which wants fascism here' and that his every policy was directed to this end. The aims of conscription were thus to:

> Rob the people of their democratic liberties.
> Break the powers of the trade unions.
> Carry through the plans of industrial conscription.
> Prepare the way for new inroads on the workers' wages and conditions.
> Shackle the democratic movement of the youth.[46]

These points, suitably elaborated, were at the centre of the campaign against conscription, though it was also pointed out, for anybody who felt that such intransigence made a nonsense of the CP's demands for resistance to Nazi aggression, that 'to place compulsory powers in the hands of Chamberlain is not to strengthen the defence of peace, but to strengthen the friends of Hitler and the enemies of peace'.[47]

The CP's case was not at all based on any abstract preference for the 'voluntary' principle to compulsion, but on its appraisal of the government's aims in introducing conscription. 'In general social principle', and in the particular event of a People's Government being formed, the Party made it quite clear that it favoured a system of compulsion – the principle applied in 'all the great struggles of the people' from the English to the Spanish Civil War – as opposed to the 'ruling class system of the so-called "voluntary" army' since incorporated into the 'bourgeois-Labour or "Lib-Lab" tradition'.[48] For these reasons the CP was as disgusted with Labour's stance of opposition to conscription as it had previously been with its decision to cooperate in the government's schemes of voluntary 'National Service'. By accident or design, Labour had obscured the essential point that conscription was 'not simply "unnecessary" [but] a positive and terrible danger to democracy'.[49] Indeed, by lauding the voluntary system and at the same time giving credence to Chamberlain's conversion to collective security, the Labour leadership had succeeded in strengthening Chamberlain in his 'false pose as the promoter of democratic defence against fascism'.[50] This in brief was the official Party line on conscription, a line threading together the main strands in Communist politics: willingness to accept measures of defence against Fascism, but never under the National Government whose Fascist tendencies were disguised by the bogus opposition of the Labour Party.

However, there are indications that the Party's veneer of single-mindedness concealed a certain amount of unease with its unconditional rejection of Chamberlain's preparations for the war that was now so obviously threatening Britain. The most tantalising glimpse of this is to be found in a document prepared by Dutt in January 1940 in which he pronounced that the 'insufficiently serious Marxist–Leninist approach to new political problems' demonstrated by the Party's original decision to support the war in September 1939 had already been revealed in 'the conscription controversy in the spring of 1939'.[51] In the absence of further information on this controversy we can only conclude that some of the Party's leaders felt strongly that the decision to oppose conscription was mistaken, and that it was this wavering attitude to defence under Chamberlain that Dutt felt it pertinent to bring up in the context of the far sharper controversy of September 1939.

No such waverings found their way into the Party press but, significantly, the tendency to voice the diversionary objections to conscription raised by the Labour Party, which Dutt found so pernicious, was very much in evidence. The most notable culprit was John Gollan, Secretary of the YCL. As if oblivious to the Party line, Gollan rejoiced in Britain's 'glorious record for the voluntary system' which he felt was working 'better than ever'. Already, according to this Communist, 'lads are joining the Territorials in their thousands because they wish to resist Hitler', and there was therefore no need for conscription.[52] There can have been no greater contrast than between this spontaneous enthusiasm to join the ranks and the deep-rooted scepticism of the Party's official statements.

A particularly interesting episode was the by-election campaign of Gabriel Carritt, a Communist who resigned as Secretary of the League of Nations Union youth groups to contest the Westminster Abbey division as an independent progressive in May 1939. The campaign was based on one issue, and one issue only: that of uniting 'all elements who passionately desire national unity, whether they be Conservative, Liberal, Labour or Communist, to rally to a movement which would set up a new Cabinet in favour of a real policy of collective defence'.[53] To this call rallied people of all political persuasions: not just Labour and Communist Party members, but 'Tories, Liberals, Church people'[54] – just the sort of alliance, in fact, that the CP proposed as an alternative to Chamberlain. But while such an alliance could be built around the demand for collective security, Carritt's supporters did not share the CP's distinctive perception of the domestic Fascist offensive, nor of conscription as the cutting edge of that offensive. Carritt himself recalled the conflicting pressures:

> You see, the Party itself was confused. I fought that by-election and I started off against conscription at the Party's behest. But it was causing such problems and the Party was already beginning to see that it was really rather an illogical position at that stage, so near to the breakdown of everything, that we switched in the middle and of course created problems; but we switched to supporting. I remember being very embarrassed as the candidate.[55]

Carritt's personal embarrassment was, of course, merely a reflection of the thorough confusion of the Party as a whole.

There were one or two other indications that, now that they could feel the 'hot, foul breath of war' on their own cheeks,[56] some Communists felt that the need to strengthen their country's defences overrode their antipathy to Chamberlain.[57] However, it is impossible to give an adequate impression of the tensions in Communist politics merely by juxtaposing jarring statements from the Communist press, for by and large it was not a case of explicit differences but the more elusive question of tone, of emphasising certain elements of the Party's programme at the expense of others. Such nuances are not easily captured, but Dutt's criticisms of Pollitt's draft of a pamphlet to launch the 'Crusade for the Defence of the People' early in 1939 give a good idea of the very different attitudes which found their expression in different aspects of the Party line.

Pollitt's attitudes at this time were curiously reminiscent of Robert Blatchford's, whose writings had circulated so widely in the Lancashire of his youth, and this strain of Blatchfordian bellicosity elicited a terse response from the astringent Dutt. Thus for example, and very redolent of Blatchford, Pollitt invoked the spectre of Kaiser Wilhelm:

> Why drag in? Looks anti-German merely. Besides the Kaiser didn't say it, it was von Kuhlmann. Omit.

Thus too Pollitt wondered 'how to strike the best blows against Hitler and Mussolini in Germany and Italy':

> This might sound and be quoted as if we meant WAR. We should therefore put what we mean clearly: 'How to help the German and Italian peoples to win their freedom'.

More importantly, Dutt was dissatisfied with Pollitt's treatment of 'the "DOMESTIC versus FOREIGN" question – the main practical problem of our propaganda at present'. Dutt felt that Pollitt's cavalier treatment of domestic issues and his assertion that it was 'because of the foreign policy of Chamberlain that all the domestic questions of work, wages arise' could 'only help those who attack us as a "foreign policy party" ':

> I think the key lies in showing FASCISM as the danger; the ATTACK ON DEMOCRACY (the question of democracy at home and the menace to it isn't covered in the draft). This unites home and abroad. The National Government represents reaction, attacking the people at home, both socially and politically, and linking up with reaction and the enemies of the people abroad, thus bringing direct menace to liberty and independence of the people.
>
> From this follows naturally explanation of what we mean by DEFENCE OF THE PEOPLE – the keynote of the campaign. How we see defence, not only of national independence, but of democracy and social standards; all are united in our conception of defence, and all require defeat of Chamberlain.

Accordingly, Dutt requested that Pollitt give a whole section to social issues,[58] and in his final draft Pollitt duly obliged with a brief section on 'Chamberlain's Home Policy'. But even here, no doubt to Dutt's chagrin, Pollitt was incapable of sticking to the point. Evidently he continued to feel that it was because of Chamberlain's foreign policy that the issues of work and wages arose:

The skilled workers of Lancashire are driven into unemployment or underemployment because the National Government's policy of encouraging Japanese aggression has practically destroyed the China market for British goods.

Chamberlain's policy hands over the markets of Spain and South-East Europe to Nazi Germany, depriving thousands of our workers of employment.

Chamberlain and the big capitalist combines behind him arrange to have ships built in Nazi Germany . . . while our shipyards go to rack and ruin and our shipbuilding workers are unemployed.[59]

Pollitt's emphasis, it goes without saying, was very different from that to be found in Dutt's writings; and within months his overriding concern with the German menace to British interests would lead to his demotion in the Party hierarchy.[60]

Nevertheless, however coherent Dutt's unitary view of politics, the image of the CP as a 'foreign policy party' had less to do with this or that pamphlet by Harry Pollitt than with its broadening of the scope of the progressive alliance to include the likes of Churchill, with whom the CP had nothing in common but an aversion to Nazi Germany. Justifying this unlikely partnership, Pollitt insisted that 'every minute and hour counts if poverty is to be attacked, if constructive schemes for combating employment are to be worked out, if the Peace Front is to be established'.[61] But patently every minute did *not* count in the struggle against the endemic evils of poverty and unemployment; and in any case, it seems unlikely that Churchill was falling over himself to implement the CP's immediate social programme – one of shorter working hours, increased pay, guaranteed trade union rights, a massive expansion of welfare provision ('Make the Rich Pay'), democratic rights for the colonies and independence for India.[62] The only possible rationale for this alliance was the compelling need for a 'Peace Front', and the fact that Pollitt could call on the Labour Party to find common ground with Churchill and simultaneously urge them to organise a vigorous fighting campaign around these social demands[63] was not the least of the incongruities which made up Communist politics.

The policies of the Communist Party were, then, a tangle of potential contradictions, but on one difficult issue at least – whether Communists should support a war against Nazi aggression in the absence of a Peace Front – some Communists were already prepared to voice unmistakable sentiments. One such was J. R. Campbell,[64] and another, expressing an even stronger opinion, was Harry Pollitt:

Our country and our people will never fall victims to fascism. The people of Britain will fight if necessary better than any other people in the world. They stand now unafraid in a land led by capitulators . . . people who are afraid to fight for the right to stand on their own feet, people who will whine about the 'horrors of war', blind to the fact that a real policy of defence means the only sure shield for preventing war. And if it fails, the people of Britain will fight as never before . . .[65]

But the biggest contradiction of all was unsuspected by Pollitt, as by even the most prescient Communist.[66] The Soviet Union, all Communists agreed, was the linchpin of collective security, the irreconcilable foe of Fascist barbarism. 'In the Soviet Union those who were prepared to play the German fascist game were branded as enemies of the people and met their deserts accordingly.'[67] But the last year of 'peace' would climax with the leaders of world Communism shaking hands with Nazis and smiling their goodwill. Stalin had decided to play the German Fascist game, and for British Communists there lay a difficult time ahead.

Notes

1 'Notes', Jan. 1939, 4.
2 'Notes', Apr. 1939, 209; June 1939, 334.
3 For the Munich crisis see C. L. Mowat, *Britain Between the Wars 1918–1940* (1956 edn), 604–19. For a Communist account citing Gallacher's intervention see N. Branson, *op. cit.*, 253–9.
4 *DW*, 12.9.38.
5 Dutt, *DW*, 10.9.38.
6 CPGB statement, *DW*, 14.9.38.
7 *DW*, 12.9.38.
8 Dutt, *DW*, 17.9.38.
9 'Notes', Apr. 1971, 180–1; Dutt in *For Peace and Plenty* (CPGB, report of 15th Congress, 1938), 90–1. Note that Pollitt and Gallacher were two of the three Central Committee members who voted against the Party's anti-war manifesto a year later (although Gallacher later asked that his vote be rescinded); see ch. 5. below.
10 *Op. cit.*, 615.
11 *DW*, 28.9.38.
12 Dutt, *DW*, 1.10.38.
13 See *Thesis*, 133 n. 16.
14 CPGB CC statement, *DW*, 1.10.38.
15 *DW*, 3.10.38.
16 CPGB Secretariat statement, *DW*, 5.10.38.
17 RPD K3, 'The new situation and the next stage of the fight', post-congress report, Oct. 1938.
18 'Notes', Nov. 1938, 654.
19 J. Strachey, 'Mr Chamberlain's Anti-Americanism', *LM*, May 1939, 278–83. On this point see *Thesis*, 117.
20 'Notes', Nov. 1938, 654–5, 666.
21 'Notes', July 1939, 391–3.
22 *Loc. cit.*

23 'Notes', May 1939, 271; July 1939, 388–98.
24 E.g. 'Notes', July 1939, 388.
25 RPD K4, 'Situation notes', 23.2.39.
26 'Notes', Oct. 1938, 600.
27 'Notes', Nov. 1938, 672.
28 RPD K3, 'The new situation and the next stage of the fight'.
29 'Notes', July 1939, 399–400.
30 'Notes', May 1939, 263–5.
31 Three of Labour's most prominent advocates of a People's Front, Cripps, Bevan and Strauss, were expelled early in 1939.
32 'Notes', Apr. 1939, 215.
33 See CPGB CC statement on 'The Cripps memorandum', Feb. 1939, in CPGB CC *Report* to 16th Congress (1939, not held), 49.
34 At this conference Cripps's expulsion was ratified and a People's Front resolution defeated, both by large majorities.
35 See e.g. Pollitt, 'After Southport', *LM*, July 1939 and also Dutt's private expression of disillusionment in RPD K4, 'LM article', sent to Pollitt 16.6.39.
36 CPGB CC statement on 'The Southport Conference', 28.6.39, in CPGB CC *Report* to 16th Congress, 66–7. The public resignations of crypto-Communists in the Labour Party continued well into the war. Perhaps it was intended as a temporary tactic to tie in with the campaign for affiliation and was then prolonged when the CP came out in open opposition to the Labour Party over the issue of the war. Alternatively, it might have reflected a long-term change of emphasis from the start. Either way, the continuity in CP policy before and after October 1939 is striking.
37 About thirty Tory MPs abstained when Labour divided the House over the Munich issue, and Duff Cooper resigned from the government; see Mowat, *op. cit.*, 620–1.
38 Pollitt, *Defence of the People* (CPGB, 7.2.39), 12; 'Notes', Jan. 1939, p. 18.
39 For a notable example see Pollitt's 'Communist appeal to Attlee, Sinclair and Churchill', *DW*, 30.3.39.
40 'Notes', Dec. 1938, 728–9.
41 'Notes', Jan. 1939, 16–17.
42 RPD K3, 'The new situation and the next stage of the fight'; CPGB CC 'Political letter to the Communist Party membership', 9.11.38.
43 'Notes', Dec. 1938, 725. It was a recurrent fear of the Communists that a number of Labour leaders and Tory dissidents were about to join an extended National Government.
44 These being Pollitt's words after the German occupation of Danzig, which he described as 'the responsibility of both the Nazi and Chamberlain Governments'; *DW*, 3.7.39.
45 Dutt, *DW*, 3.4.39; *DW*, 27.4.39.
46 Pollitt, *Can Conscription Save Peace?* (CPGB, 6.5.39), 7, 12.
47 Dutt, *DW*, 3.4.39.
48 *Loc. cit.*; CPGB CC statement, *DW*, 24.5.39; Dutt, *DW*, 12.6.39. Rather confusingly, it was also stated that, given the existence of a Peace Bloc, conscription would not be necessary; e.g. Pollitt, *op. cit.*, p. 29.
49 *DW*, 29.4.39.
50 'Notes', June 1939, 336–7.
51 RPD K4, 'Draft supplementary report of the Central Committee', 8.1.40.
52 *DW*, 28.4.39, 29.4.39.
53 M-O TC 46/2, cutting from *Star* interview with Carritt, 12.4.39; Gabriel Carritt, interview. Social issues, Carritt recalled, were 'absolutely secondary'.

54 Carritt, interview. The campaign was instigated by Richard Acland, the Liberal MP, and Carritt received the support of the local Liberal and Labour Parties. He was even led to believe, though he could not swear by this, that not only Churchill but also one or two disenchanted Cabinet ministers contributed to his campaign fund.
55 Interview.
56 Pollitt's phrase, *op. cit.*, 4.
57 See *Thesis*, 128–9.
58 Interestingly, Dutt's comments on Campbell's earlier pamphlet on Munich (*How Chamberlain Helped Hitler*, CPGB, 10.10.38) also regretted the absence of a section on the offensive against democracy in Britain; interestingly, because Pollitt and Campbell were the Central Committee members whose preoccupation with the fight against Hitler would lead them to resist the CP's later decision to oppose the war; RPD K4, Dutt to Campbell, 11.10.38.
59 Pollitt, *Defence of the People* (CPGB, 7.2.39), 7. For Dutt's comments on the draft see RPD K4, 'Basic points (general consideration)', 13.1.39.
60 It might be objected that Pollitt's pamphlet on conscription was to strike a very different note, so it should be pointed out that, as General Secretary, Pollitt's writings were not necessarily all his own work. The pamphlet on conscription was based on and incorporated the relevant Political Bureau statement, *DW*, 28.4.39. Ted Bramley (interview) could not recall Pollitt's exact role in the conscription controversy but went on:

> You can take it for granted that Pollitt was very much to the fore in broadening the approach of the Communist Party, recognising the changes that had to be faced because of Fascism. There were others who were more inclined to stick rather rigidly to Marxist theoretical propositions until they were absolutely certain that this was not wrong. I can tell you this quite definitely: there was a terrible fear that we might be caught in a trap. On the one hand we wanted to resist Fascism, but on the other hand we didn't want to land the British working class, bound hand and foot, into a war machine that could get switched against the Soviet Union.

61 'After Southport', *LM*, July 1939, 402.
62 Amongst other things; *ibid.*, 412–13.
63 Pollitt, *op. cit.*, 402–16. The incompatibility of these demands is perhaps suggested by Carritt's concentration on foreign policy issues in his Westminster election campaign.
64 *DW*, 19.7.39.
65 *Will It Be War?* (CPGB, 7.7.39), 29.
66 Although Dutt came closest with the warning that Stalin would not willingly become involved in a war between Britain and Germany consequent on the rejection of the 'Peace Front'; *DW*, 22.5.39.
67 Campbell, *DW*, 5.7.39. The reference is, of course, to the victims of the Moscow show trials.

Chapter five

For or against?
The Communist Party and the outbreak of war

I said yesterday that I stand for the speedy and effective defeat of the Nazi régime as a sure way of bringing about hope for a lasting peace for the peoples of the world. In taking that stand I want to declare here with the utmost confidence, from experience and from knowledge, that I will not come into conflict with the policy of my working-class comrades of the Soviet Union.

(William Gallacher, 3 September 1939[1])

Undoubtedly every party makes mistakes. But there are mistakes and mistakes.

(Palme Dutt, April 1936[2])

Through the long, heavy summer of 1939 the British Communist Party's hopes of peace were expressed in one insistent demand: for the signing of an Anglo–Soviet pact of mutual assistance. Convinced by appeasement that the Western powers were a 'far easier nut to crack' than the Soviet Union, Hitler was increasingly drawn by the idea of 'settling accounts with the West ... *before* seeking to destroy the USSR'. Thus, in two books and numerous articles, Communists explained that to reach an agreement with the Soviet Union was a matter of immediate self-preservation for the British people.[3] This much was apparently becoming clear even to Chamberlain, who had begun in a dilatory fashion to negotiate the terms of such an agreement, while yet hoping that a reactionary settlement with Hitler would still prove possible.[4] The Soviet leaders, on the other hand, were irreconcilably opposed to Fascism, for they understood that peace was indivisible:

> knowing what Fascism is, the Soviet Government is the last government in the world to be lured into a false sense of security by promises from Hitler that he would only move towards the West ... Therefore such a rapprochement as is sometimes forecast is a mirage. Fascist aggression and the Soviet policy of resisting aggression have been, and must be, fundamentally opposed to each other.[5]

Weeks later the mirage became a reality. On 23 August, under the heading 'SOVIETS' DRAMATIC PEACE MOVE TO HALT AGGRESSORS', the *Daily Worker* reported the signing of a Nazi–Soviet Non-Aggression Pact. Unknown to the *Worker*, the Pact included a secret protocol allocating the signatories their respective spheres of influence in north-eastern Europe. The way was open for the German invasion of Poland on 1 September. The war which ensued was inexplicable in the terms which Communists had used to describe world politics. The Peace Front was dead, though British Communists were slow to realise it.

Conditioned by years of its own propaganda, the CP could not but see the Pact as a 'master stroke of Soviet peace policy . . . a genuine stand against aggression'. A Central Committee statement warned that, now that Hitler had been forced to abandon his anti-Soviet aims, there was an immediate danger that he would turn his offensive westwards. Given the unquestioned assumption that the Soviet Union would still 'help any country that fights against Fascist aggression', the signing of an Anglo–Soviet pact was thus 'more urgently necessary than ever before'.[6] For a few days this urgent necessity dominated Communist propaganda. All over the country rallies were organised around the slogan SIGN THE ANGLO–SOVIET PACT NOW! and evidently this slogan had a certain appeal. 'It is a complete mistake', wrote one Communist, 'to imagine that the public are hostile and that Russia is being denounced':

> I have been to dozens of street meetings and have been selling Daily Workers every night. In this way one gets into immediate contact with the ordinary people. Sales are enormous – about 135 copies in less than two hours is my average – double the usual sale. Our meetings are crowded, with huge collections and lots of questions, but not violent denunciation of Russia.[7]

Such a meeting was the Chenies Street rally on 28 August which attracted 10,000 people, 8,000 of whom bought copies of the *Worker* with 51 reportedly joining the Party and a collection of £65.[8]

The Party line was apparently going down well. Of the reception given the CP's official explanation of the Pact, the *Worker* reported that 'people were standing at street corners, under lamp-posts, devouring the statement issued by the Central Committee'.[9] This was probably the best thing to do with it. Given the understanding between the Soviet Union and Germany that neither power was to take part in any combination directly or indirectly aligned against the other, the campaign for an Anglo–Soviet Pact was a waste of time and Gallacher's assurances that the Franco–Soviet Pact remained operative were worthless.[10] This discrepancy between the CPGB's conception of international politics and the new Soviet policy would not be cleared up until the end of September.

For the time being there was no change in Communist policy. There remained the suspicion of Chamberlain's complicity – 'the Tory–Nazi conspiracy against peace and democracy'.[11] Thus there remained the fear of a repeat of Munich; war measures were seen as 'part of a war of nerves directed against the people of Great Britain, preparing them for sweeping concessions to Fascist aggression'.[12] Thus did the CP continue to oppose such war measures as the Emergency Powers Act, which was allegedly introduced to crush opposition to appeasement and 'suppress those democratic rights which the people must have if democracy is successfully to resist the Fascist aggressors'.[13] There remained too the suspicions of inter-party collusion at Westminster with the object of 'keeping up the façade of the war crisis, while the real job of preparing the betrayal of Poland was going on behind the scenes'.[14] Finally, there remained the belief, expressed by Pollitt as late as 27 August, that war 'need never take place, and it can be prevented even now', and this without pandering to Hitler.[15]

However, by this time Pollitt was well aware that the chances of halting Fascist aggression and simultaneously preserving peace were slim indeed. In the same speech he outlined the policy of a 'war on two fronts' with which the CP would answer the German invasion of Poland:

> If Britain takes its place in any common front, with no open or secret imperialist aims or intentions, against a Fascist attack, then the Communist Party will do everything in its power to bring about the defeat of Fascism.
>
> But the Communist Party openly declares that it is not possible to do it with any guarantee of success so long as the Chamberlain Government is in power. . . .
>
> You cannot fight the foul menace of Fascism . . . if your country is led by a man whose sympathies are with the Fascist enemy . . . [and] who proposed at the very start of a war with Fascism to himself impose Fascist methods on the British people.[16]

Pollitt's main worry by this time was not that war might break out, but rather that Chamberlain might perpetrate another betrayal of democracy in the name of peace. On 2 September he emerged from the House of Commons complaining that 'that old bastard Chamberlain refuses to declare war!'[17] It was in this frame of mind that Communists tuned in to Chamberlain's fateful wireless broadcast the following morning.

The CP's original line on the war was expressed in a Central Committee statement. 'War! Communist policy', and a piece by Pollitt which were published together as the pamphlet *How to Win the War*. Pollitt's commitment to the defeat of Nazism was unmistakable:

> To stand aside from this conflict, to contribute only revolutionary-sounding

phrases while the fascist beasts ride roughshod over Europe, would be a betrayal of everything our forbears have fought to achieve in the course of long years of struggle against capitalism.[18]

But if the CP was committed to the 'support of all necessary measures to secure the victory of democracy over Fascism',[19] this did not imply support for the government conducting the war, but rather the opposite. According to Communists the war was being waged for both imperialist and legitimate anti-Fascist motives, and the course of the war depended on the outcome of the struggle between these two tendencies. The British ruling class, wrote Pollitt, 'would never do anything except for its own imperialist interests',[20] and these interests would not be served by the restoration of democracy on the Continent:

> They are not out to get rid of the fascist system but to secure a change in the governing personalities of the fascist system – a change that will install people who are willing to co-operate with reaction in Britain.[21]

But the British people were fighting for very different reasons. There was no jingoism, none of the flag-waving that had greeted war in 1914, for they were resolved that this was to be a '*different kind of war*':

> Whatever may be the aims, or the opinions, of a certain section of people in Britain, the common people . . . have one aim and one aim only: THE DESTRUCTION OF FASCISM AND THE REPULSE OF ALL ATTACKS UPON DEMOCRACY.[22]

Whether the war was pursued for reactionary purposes or whether it led to the destruction of Fascism depended on the assertion of their conception of the war by the common people. 'The essence of the present situation', according to the CP's Central Committee, 'is that the people have now to wage a struggle on two fronts. First, to secure the military victory over Fascism; and second, in order to achieve this, the political victory over Chamberlain and the enemies of democracy in this country.' These two aims, the statement went on, were 'inseparable'.[23] Thus it was that Communists continued to denounce the National Government and all its works, not just because it was attacking the liberties of the British people but because, by doing so, it made impossible the waging of an effective, democratic war against Fascism. 'Those who propose political or industrial truces with the pro-Fascist Junkers and financiers of Britain', warned the *Daily Worker*, 'are opening the way to a Fascist victory in Europe.'[24]

The most important themes in Communist propaganda were brought together in a spirited *Tribune* article in which Don Renton, the leading NUWM activist, argued that 'the gulf which separates the British people from their masters and underlines the separate objectives they possess in the present conflict has become wider and more clearly marked'. The outstanding feature of the developing situation three weeks into the war, Renton felt, was 'an unparalleled offensive against the rights and standards of the British working class':

> The smashing of trade union agreements, the beginnings of dilution, the unprecedented volume of overtime, the spreadover of work, the mass dismissals, the treatment the unemployed are receiving, the foul conditions imposed upon evacuated women, the complete lack of preparation made in safe areas for their reception, the tragic conditions of aged and crippled people not yet evacuated, the never-ending rise in prices, the absence of adequate protection for the teeming millions in the big industrial towns, the absence of any real effort to wage a determined war against Germany on the Western Front – all of this, when brought together and made part of one picture, seems suspiciously like a deliberate effort on the part of the Chamberlain Government and the employing class to spread demoralisation, to play into the hands of the Nazi enemies of the British people by creating conceptions that 'peace at any price' is better than a continuation of the present situation.[25]

On both fronts the Party line was unequivocal: no confidence in Chamberlain and his accomplices, 'All the men of Munich Must Go'.[26]

The Party's proposed alternative to the Men of Munich remained a People's Government that would 'transform Britain into an effective democracy in war-time . . . put before the German people the terms for a real democratic peace . . . control industry, stop profiteering, levy great fortunes and assure the British people that they will not emerge from the war as the bond slaves of the great financiers'.[27] The war, said J. R. Campbell, 'would only be a war to defend democracy if the Governments of England and France were converted into truly democratic governments'.[28] It was because they appeared oblivious to the need to oust the Men of Munich that the leaders of the Labour movement were as bitterly castigated by the Communists as before the war. Their 'complete paralysis and self-effacement' was likened to that of their predecessors in 1914, and the Labour Party's posture of independence of the government was dismissed as 'an empty formality'.[29] In this respect as in so many others, the line of a 'war on two fronts' had a good deal in common not only with the Party's pre-war policy but with the policies with which it was to oppose the war.[30]

Communists in Britain received their first inkling that such a line of opposition to the war might be necessary on 14 September, when a Moscow radio broadcast described the war as 'an imperialist and predatory war for a new redivision of the world . . . kindled from all sides by the two imperialist groups of powers'. Dutt at least took the hint and the following day began to canvass support among the Party leadership for a new line of opposition to the war. He later claimed to have had 'several supporters in the Politburo' at this stage but that at the next Central Committee meeting (24 September) they 'all ran away' leaving him in 'absolute isolation'. However, the same evening David Springhall returned with new instructions from Moscow and a 'correction' of the CP's original manifesto became inevitable. Although the Central Committee adjourned for several days before making up its mind, a new emphasis was immediately apparent in the *Daily Worker*. Already on 27 September the *Worker* denounced the government's first war budget without suggesting any alternative means of financing the war effort or indeed making any mention of the need to defeat Nazism.[31] Three days later a Political Bureau statement on the suppression of the PCF stated that the war was 'now being conducted against the interests of the peoples of Europe', and in the same issue came the news of the Soviet–German peace offer, to which the *Worker* responded predictably:

> To talk of war to the end, which means the wholesale slaughter of the youth of Europe, would be sheer madness.

When the Central Committee reassembled on 2 October it was now Dutt rather than Pollitt who presented the Political Bureau report, and this report was eventually accepted with only Pollitt and Campbell dissenting.[32] The new line was then given formal expression in a Central Committee manifesto which described the war as a 'fight between imperialist powers over profits, colonies and world domination' which would bring 'only great suffering and boundless misery to millions of working-class homes'. It only remained for Pollitt and Campbell to be removed from their positions in the Party leadership and for the Party as a whole to endorse the new policy, which it did at a series of district meetings at which, according to official reports, there were anything between nought and three dissentients. This, then, was the 'betrayal of the left'.[33]

The premises for the new line were laid down by Dutt in his report to the Central Committee. Dutt argued that the CP's mistake had been to apply the conceptions of the Peace Front to an altogether new situation in which there was no longer any possibility of Britain and France playing a 'temporarily progressive role'. Citing the *History of the CPSU*, Dutt pointed out that ' "qualitative changes occur not gradually, but rapidly and abruptly, taking the form of a leap from one state to another". We were very late in noting the signs of the change and we clung to the old estimations, even after the historical leap had taken place.' Moreover, experience had shown that a 'struggle on two fronts' was a 'contradiction in terms':

The only way of carrying on the struggle on the front against Hitler was by supporting the military measures of the Chamberlain–Churchill Government. How could we support these measures and at the same time fight Chamberlain?

The Party had to fight on one front or the other, and in the new situation created by the Nazi–Soviet Pact this had to be the anti-Chamberlain front. The Anti-Comintern bloc had broken up and Germany had retreated from leadership of the 'Anti-Soviet Front' at the same time as Britain and France had begun 'to move more and more openly in this direction'. Apprehensive at the growing strength of Communism, it was now Hitler who sought peace, while the Western powers, far from drawing back, were 'loudly proclaiming their intention to wage war to the bitter end'. Roles had been reversed, and 'the significance of the distinction between the fascist and so-called democratic states *in respect of their world political role* (*not* in respect of the difference of their internal régime for the working class in each country) becomes transformed by these changes'.[34] Already Dutt was suggesting that the responsibility for the war did not rest equally on all warring powers. The Party's task, he argued, was 'to *unmask the character of this imperialist war . . . and to show that British and French imperialism have become the spearhead of international reaction, against which our main fire must be directed*'. Finally, Dutt outlined the main issues on which Communists were to campaign over the coming months:

(a) *The Fight for Peace . . .* We demand the ending of the war and the starting of immediate peace negotiations. (The question of peace *terms* is not the issue. The terms will depend upon the kind of government that we have in this country and the extent of its co-operation with the Soviet Union. But the immediate issue is the stopping of the war.)
(b) The Fight on Immediate Mass Issues Affecting the Workers and the widest sections of People.

What this all boiled down to was that Stalin had signed a pact with Hitler and that the CP had to adjust its line accordingly; that was the real historical leap, however well obscured by Dutt's sophistries.[35]

So far in this chapter we have portrayed the Communist Party rather as it portrayed itself: as 'a monolithic organisation hewed from a single block, possessing a single will'.[36] However, it would be wrong to regard the transition to the new line as simply an exercise in Bolshevik discipline. Far from possessing a single will, the reaction of Communists to the Nazi–Soviet Pact and Chamberlain's declaration of war was confused and heterogeneous, for the war shattered the Party's whole conception of international politics. Britain had at last stood up to Fascist aggression, but with the pro-Fascist Men of Munich still in power, while the Soviet Union stood on the sidelines shouting for Germany. It is hardly surprising, then, that Communists reacted to the Party's decision to support the war and its subsequent revocation of that decision in diverse ways. Some were never happy with the policy of a 'war on two fronts', while others were loath to accept the reversal of this line; and if the majority of Party members accepted both the original line and its successor, their motivations were complex. In the second part of this chapter we will attempt to demonstrate this complexity with the oral and written testimony of a number of those Communists – the majority – who stood by their Party through this difficult period.

When William Rust made a lightning tour of Party districts in mid-September he found general assent to the Party's position on the war but noted that 'individual members put forward opposing points of view in the course of the discussion on policy and tactics'.[37] Rust did not elaborate on this, but it would appear that a number of Communists already had qualms about supporting a war under Chamberlain's leadership. Ernie Trory later claimed that 'many members of the Communist Party had doubts right from the beginning'. Trory himself, Sussex District Organiser of the Party, felt 'a bit uncomfortable about the situation' and recalled the decision to oppose the war as a 'moment of clarification . . . comparable to the conversion of Saul because I immediately saw that this resolved all the doubts that I'd had in my mind'.[38] The Party intellectual Alick West also felt that the Party's second line made better sense than its original manifesto, which, he recalled:

> seemed to me another voice in the air. To say that the war was against fascism was to deceive ourselves. The war was being fought by the state, not by us; and the state, being the imperialist state, was not opposed to fascism.[39]

Likewise, Douglas Hyde doubted the validity of the Party line for the first time in several years of Party membership and spent that September 'finding excuses for dropping almost all my political activity'. His reservations, he recalled, were widely shared:

> The rank and file . . . although maintaining an outward appearance of unity, on this occasion tended to be privately divided. Those who had fought in Spain or had been in direct conflict with fascism in Britain tended to welcome the chance of 'having a go at the Nazis' under any banner, even that of Chamberlain.
> Others distrusted Chamberlain to a point where they could not believe that any war fought under his leadership could be of any use to the workers . . .[40]

Hyde's suggestion that the division within the Party reflected the different priorities and experiences of Communists before the war is an important one, for these differences had acquired a new significance now that the question of what the Party should do if Chamberlain fought Hitler could no longer be dismissed as speculation.

Some Communists had long been preoccupied with the struggle for peace. One such was Bill Moore, who had been raised by his grandparents in an intensely anti-war atmosphere, his father and two uncles having been killed in the First World War while 'a third uncle died a few years later because his guts had been rotted with mustard gas'. His mind filled with such impressions, Moore's first real political activity was to assist with the Peace Ballot in his native Sheffield. Shortly afterwards he became a Communist, and within a month or two of the Party's having initiated the broadly-based Sheffield Peace Council in November 1935 Moore became the Council's Secretary. It was in this capacity that in 1937 he wrote a hard-hitting pamphlet describing and denouncing in their entirety the British Government's preparations for war. Until the outbreak of war Moore felt no misgivings about the Party's political pronouncements, which seemed fully to confirm his own deep distrust of British imperialism; but the Party's decision to support the war, with Chamberlain and his accomplices still in the saddle, left him feeling 'stunned and very worried'. It was only with the announcement of the new line at the beginning of October that he 'breathed a sigh of relief . . . because of its continuity with the whole experience of the previous ten years'.[41]

Other Communists, on the other hand, had been heavily involved in the struggle against international Fascism through their various activities on behalf of the Spanish republic. The most prominent of these, who had long been itching to 'have a go at the Nazis', was Harry Pollitt.[42] Pollitt's resistance to the line of opposition to the war stemmed from his deep commitment to the struggle against the dictators in the 1930s, as his subsequent recantation made clear:

> My hatred of fascism had developed by five years' intensive anti-fascist propaganda, which led to a position where I did not see in time the true role of British imperialism. . . .
>
> The influence of the fascist war of invasion on Republican Spain also affected my outlook because of the strong personal feelings which had been aroused by what I had witnessed in Spain, and the responsibility I felt I had in regard to the sacrifice made by the British Battalion of the International Brigade.[43]

So too Charlotte Haldane, who had played a key role in the ferrying of volunteers to Spain through Paris and in raising funds for their dependants, recalled that 'all those who had fought in Spain, or taken part in the anti-Nazi struggle in any way, responded with enthusiasm to Pollitt's declaration. I know I did.'[44] One such enthusiast was Jack Edwards, an International Brigader from Liverpool:

> actually the Party at that period of time at the first break out of the war said that we shouldn't go into the Army. I was opposed to this. I've always said the fight against fascism irrespective was the fight against fascism. When you're fighting for an imperialist power like England, if this is Germany and it's a fascist – we must fight it. . . . I remember having a run in with McGree on it see. Then after that I volunteered and went in the RAF.[45]

However, it would be wrong to oversimplify matters. Some Communists who had fought in Spain fully accepted the need to oppose the war, while Benny Rothman was eager to support the war effort precisely because he had *not* fought in Spain:

> I went to volunteer and I joined the Home Guard and that. I was particularly very anti-Hitler because, among other things, I was still smarting at the fact that I'd never done anything in Spain for a whole number of reasons. As much as anything, I was just beginning to get involved in the trade unions for the first time and playing quite an important part and, rightly or wrongly, the feeling was that that was where I should be making the effort, not in Spain. I felt, to an extent, that Pollitt was right at the time.

Among the other things influencing Rothman was the fact that he had been heavily involved in anti-Fascist struggles in Cheetham, the main Jewish district in Manchester.[46]

If recent memories of Spain led many Communists to welcome any opportunity to take up arms against Fascism, the very different image of the First World War could be taken as a warning that Communists should not fall into the trap of furthering the imperialist designs of their rulers, as Harry McShane recalled:

> Our declaration in favour of war led to even more confusion in the Communist Party. There was a tremendous hatred of fascism; but there was also the old anti-war attitude, and a fear of repetition of 1914 when the entire socialist movement collapsed.[47]

Among those Communists inclined to stand firm against Hitler who were swayed by the recollection of this, the first betrayal of the left, were Ted Bramley, the Party's London District Organiser, and the *Daily Worker's* 'Frank Pitcairn'. Thus Pitcairn:

> gripped by memories of 1914, I could not feel the Comintern was necessarily wrong, although not to be encouraging one and all to go for Hitler seemed hopelessly wrong too. But then, I would reflect, sincere Socialists like Blatchford

had felt, in 1914, that that war, too, was an exception to the rules he had been brought up on.[48]

Bramley's reflections went deeper than this. His father had been a lifelong Socialist, owing particular allegiance to the SDF; and yet in 1915 he had been so affected by the anti-British feeling among the German community in Detroit, where he was then living, that he sailed back to Britain to enlist against the German peril. 'I was loyal to the International', Bramley recalled. 'I was not going to be caught like my father was caught when he served in the Dardanelles and in France in the imperialist war and then bitterly regretted it afterwards.'[49]

Of course, while some Communists, like Harry McShane, had their own personal memories of 1914, far more were acquainted with the issue of imperialist war by their study of the Leninist texts distributed by the Party. For some of these, like Dave Priscott, opposition to imperialist war was a fundamental tenet of their Communism:

> My Party education had been to a large extent a self-education based on reading the classics, especially Lenin. Burned deeply into my mind was the awful warning of 1914 and the treachery of the Social Democrats on that occasion. This led me to feel that war was a touchstone for a real revolutionary, and that one had to be on guard against taking what might appear to be the 'easy' course . . .

That September Priscott regarded the 'Pollitt line' as the 'easy' course and thus experienced his 'first ever serious disagreement with the policy of the leadership'. Indeed, Priscott succeeded in winning the Portsmouth Party branch to his point of view, while at the same time he willingly publicised the pro-war manifesto with which he 'so violently disagreed'.[50] Priscott's close study of the 'classics' was no doubt exceptional, but it is worth remembering that in 1939 the Communist analysis of the First World War had been very widely disseminated by means of the official *History of the CPSU (B)*, around which many Party courses and educational classes were organised.

But for some, the study of basic Communist doctrine, far from disposing them to accept the Party's revival of the Leninist analysis of imperialist war, merely engendered scepticism about the policies of the Soviet Union and of the British Party. Back in the mid-1930s, Bernard MacKenna had been 'an enthusiastic Young Communist Leaguer, keen on probing and studying Marxism and relating this to known Communist policy':

> Even then I was conscious of a deep schism between what I had read historically about the development of the Russian revolution and the (then) present attitude of Russia. . . .
> If questions came up, as they frequently did, that seemingly contradicted the

'party line' many members, I remember, would stall until they read the 'party line' on it in the *Daily Worker* maybe a few days or even a week or two later. Even the D.W. leaders were sometimes contradicted by Palme Dutt in *Labour Monthly*.

It became a bit of a cynical joke with some members. 'Bugger the Party line, I'll sit back and wait for it to catch up with me' was often raised.

However, the Party's general perspective of a 'united front against fascism' conformed pretty well to MacKenna's own political priorities, so much so that he went to fight in Spain. When war between Britain and Germany 'inevitably ensued' MacKenna regarded it very much as a continuation of the battle he had fought in Spain and once more volunteered to take up arms against Fascism:

> there was, in my recollection, a *unanimous* reaction in favour of fighting Hitler . . . I never was aware of a jot of opposition to this view. I and many others joined the forces right away. Wherever I was posted I contacted local party members for political and social contact, again hearing no criticisms.

The Party's subsequent decision that Britain should sue for peace thus caused 'bewilderment among us but an almost united refusal to accept this line. It was still an anti-fascist war!':

> When I returned home on leave later I was dumbfounded to hear many party people (civilians) trying to tell me that I was now 'wrong'. I had many rows, failing to convince them that Hitler was still a baddy and I got the feeling that I was being shunned as a political innocent. Not one tittle of what was now advanced as argument had been deployed before so it went off my back uselessly.

And MacKenna was not the only Communist who in October 1939 said, in effect, 'bugger the Party line' and yet remained in the Party.[51]

In Ipswich, for example, according to the official history of the local CP, 'there was very little campaigning for the line of the International. . . . In the main our Branch considered Pollitt's analysis to be correct, and it was not long before events confirmed their view'.[52] In Oxford, Communists were thrown into consternation by the events of that autumn, as Arthur Exell recalled:

> Now, we had awful ups and downs in Oxford alone with different members of the Party who didn't think we were doing the right thing. Some of them went rushing off into the forces to go and fight Hitler and some said, 'No, you shouldn't go'. We were all at sixes and sevens because of the attitude of Russia. At the time we were surprised how Russia could even agree with Hitler to carve Poland in half. We couldn't understand it at all, how they could do that. We lost loads of members and fell out with one another, we had fights with one another – awful really.

A special problem in Oxford was that Communists had developed very close working relations with Labour activists, for the most part from within the Labour Party. As Exell recalled, the CP's left-wing allies were disenchanted by the Party's sudden change of tack:

> Well, they were critical of us, of the Party line which was not to fight at that time. But you see the point was there was those of us who agreed with fighting, you see, and therefore the Labour Party didn't know which way to turn then; we were agreeing with fighting. It was only the Party, top Party people, who were against it at the time. We thought the top Party line was wrong and we still think so.[53]

Exell's account was borne out by the more cautious testimony of his close friend, Norman Brown, who, like Exell, tried to join up at the beginning of the war.[54] Another indication that opposition to the new Party line may have persisted in the Oxford area was a report that after the South Midlands District congress of the Party early in 1940 'the careful re-election of every Branch Committee was carried through'.[55] No reasons were given for this purge, but in the light of Exell's testimony they are not hard to guess.

It would seem, then, that most but by no means all Communists accepted the original 'Pollitt line', some with such fervour that they rushed to join the forces, just as Communists had enlisted in the struggle of the Spanish people against Fascism. And yet when the CP's leaders overturned the Pollitt line at the end of September, the Party did not disintegrate; few Communists left the Party for political reasons, and most were prepared to stand by the line of opposition to the war.[56] This was not simply a case of mechanical obedience to instructions from Moscow, of Communists putting their loyalty to the 'Workers' Fatherland' before the interests of their country, or their class. There were in fact a variety of reasons for their general acceptance of the new line.

The first was, of course, loyalty to the Party, a sentiment well expressed by Exell:

> I always believed in the principle that if the Party had made a decision then you tried to keep in with what the Party had said; and they'd made that decision [to oppose the war], so therefore I was going against the Party decision and it was so difficult because I was so firmly convinced that Communism was the right thing, and I didn't want to fall out with them in any shape or form.[57]

Hyman Levy, the mathematician, was another Communist who had reservations about the Party's policies at this time, but his support for the Party was based on considerations which were 'very little concerned with detailed changes in line etc of the CP'. In 1941 Levy was informed of rumours that at various times since the outbreak of war he had been 'violently opposed to the CP line':

> Both *violent* and *opposed* are the wrong words; but I am always critical and hope to remain so. I will always speak my mind, but at a time like this I will not rush into print. Class solidarity is much more vital to me than intellectual differences within the class.[58]

Claud Cockburn – the *Daily Worker*'s 'Frank Pitcairn' – even had an impulse to throw in his lot with the 'Churchillian Tories' but was 'dominated by the feeling that I had, of my own free will, joined, so to speak, a regiment and that I had better soldier along with it, particularly at a moment when it was obviously going to come under pretty heavy fire'.[59] And if any Communists were thinking of deserting the regiment, Harry Pollitt provided an example of the selfless devotion to the cause expected of the true Communist, as Gabriel Carritt remembered:

> At the time I followed the Party line. Looking back on it, I think it was probably wrong but very difficult. But you see, if Harry Pollitt, who wanted to fight the war and believed it was possible to swing the whole thing into an anti-Fascist position, if he accepts that the Party is right and gives up being General Secretary and goes back to work in the docks, well, once you have a leader who sets an example of loyalty to the majority decisions of your leadership, your elected leadership, what can you do? You must follow. You must.[60]

Given Pollitt's unequalled stature in the Party,[61] his decision to abide by the decision to oppose the war must have carried a great deal of weight with wavering Party members. A combination of political and personal loyalties disposed most Communists to accept the decision of the Party.

There was, of course, an international dimension to this sense of loyalty, this sense of discipline. Communists felt themselves part of a world movement, 'the only international organisation . . . with sections in every country and corner of the globe following a single leadership and a single policy', as Dutt was to describe it;[62] and they accepted that the British Party had to stand by its decisions. 'What you have to remember', Betty Reid pointed out, 'is that the Communist International had enormous weight in the Party and there was a tremendous acceptance of discipline in the Party',[63] and Peter Kerrigan too felt that 'the dominant thing that influenced was this sense of loyalty and discipline also to the international movement'.[64] Here again Communists were 'subtly or crudely' influenced by the recollection of how the parties of the Second International had 'retired to their national fastnesses' in 1914.[65] And just as Pollitt personified the British Party's hatred of Fascism, so was Dimitrov an international symbol of unyielding resistance to Nazi tyranny, and so did his statement that the war was simply an imperialist war help reconcile Communists to a policy which seemed to discount the threat that tyranny posed to humanity.[66]

Bound up with this sense of international obligations was a deep-rooted commitment to the Soviet Union. For some Communists, like Patrick Curry, the principle that all other issues were subordinate to that of defending the Soviet Union was decisive. Curry, it should be noted, had previously fought in Spain:

> as far as we were concerned one imperialist power was as bad as another. And the thing that had to be prevented at all costs was a ganging up of all imperialist powers against the Soviet Union. So it didn't really matter how the division took place as long as there was a division . . . as I saw it we would support any move that would preserve the Soviet Union.[67]

Lon Elliott, another ex-International Brigader, did not even believe that all imperialist powers were as bad as each other. He accepted that 'from the local interest of Britain, and above all France, it was tragic that one had to take this "Imperialist War" line'; tragic, but nevertheless unavoidable given that 'the defence of the one and only socialist state was an absolutely paramount question at that time'.[68]

The shape taken by the war in its first month, the shape outlined by Don Renton in the passage quoted earlier, was another factor which lent plausibility to the anti-war line. While Chamberlain and Daladier sat and watched Hitler overrun Poland, they waged the war on the home front with martial vigour. Thus for example did George Matthews explain his acceptance of the Comintern line:

> The original Pollitt line fitted in very well with the whole emphasis that the Party, and myself in the University Labour Federation, had been pursuing. But there was enough happening to make the change of line seem reasonable and plausible, because of the fact that it was clear that the Chamberlain Government certainly was not really keen on an anti-Fascist war and it was dragging its feet, and in France the Communists were being arrested and so on and so forth. I mean, looking back I think that the original policy was right and the change of policy was wrong, but at the time it was acceptable.[69]

One Young Communist Leaguer in London even felt that the Party 'had been right all along; they had been right to support the war at first and then not to'.[70] This might seem eccentric, but it should be noted that the YCL paper *Challenge* presented the Party's demand for peace simply as a sensible response to the Soviet-German peace offer. It did not publicly repudiate the YCL's original statement of support for the war but merely stressed that 'the new situation which has arisen in recent days has opened up great possibilities for peace and security'. 'The Soviet Union is working for a peace that is in the interests of the peoples', proclaimed *Challenge*, and to many Communists the fact that the Soviet Union had supposedly checked Nazi aggression and would be a party to any peace settlement suggested that a peace without appeasement was possible.[71]

Another problem for those who might have thought of breaking with the Party was, as Philip Toynbee pointed out on leaving the Party early in 1940, the lack of any viable alternative to the CP on the extra-parliamentary left, and certainly of one offering such a scope of activities.[72] This might explain why some Communists who were unhappy with the developments of that autumn bottled up their feelings, for the time being at least. John Strachey, for example, wrote in that last week of August that if 'the Soviet Union were to go into benevolent neutrality to Germany, my whole political position would be shattered' and eighteen months later he reaffirmed that 'my world picture . . . fell to bits with the signing of the Nazi–Soviet Pact, in spite of all efforts to deny to myself that it had'. However, at the time he did nothing more decisive than sell his £1,000 worth of Five Year Plan Bonds and invest his money with General Motors instead.[73] He proceeded to publicise the Party's anti-war line and did not break with the CP until the following spring. Ted Willis too argued that 'the seeds of my leaving the Communist Party were sown then, as I'm sure they were sown for others. For the very first time you questioned the wisdom of the Party.' He did not, however, leave the Party till after the war.[74]

For Willis, as for many other Communists, the period of opposition to the war was less traumatic than it might have been because they were not greatly involved in promoting the Party's anti-war policies. Willis for instance was conscripted in 1940:

> It was a very convoluted blurb and how anybody could have swallowed it, I don't know. Had I not been in the army I don't think I could have done it. But being cut off, as it were, in the army and only seeing people on leave and getting the odd letter from time to time – I mean, they tried to involve me in work for the Party in Glasgow while I was stationed up there (in Kirkintilloch) but it was impossible. I didn't want to be involved anyway; it was hard enough being a bloody soldier.
>
> *So you think that if you'd still been in civilian life and had had to be putting the line over at meetings . . .*
> I think I would have quit, or at least I would have moved back to the Labour Party.[75]

A similar case was that of Charlotte Haldane, a Communist inside the South-West St Pancras Labour Party who was co-opted as a councillor early in 1940. That May she was appointed to the local ARP Emergency Committee which enabled her 'to remain a loyal Party supporter, without having actively to outrage my deeply patriotic feelings, and to canalise my endeavours in a direction which put neither allegiance to the ultimate test'.[76]

Most importantly of all, perhaps, the work of Communists active in the unions or other mass organisations was only tangentially affected by the Party's decision to oppose the war. Winnie Lowe, a Communist so preoccupied with her work for Birmingham Trades Council that she could not recall being 'very much concerned or interested' in the Party's discussions on the war, provides an extreme example of the fragmentation of Communist politics which arose from Party members specialising in particular fields of activity.[77] But if this was obviously an exceptional case, Eddie Frow, a leading AEU shop steward in Manchester, also felt that whichever line the Party had taken it would not have made 'a terrific lot of difference to what we did in the engineering industry'.[78] The fact is that the CP's attitude to the main issues of domestic politics remained much the same as before the war. These issues were generally kept separate from the question of the war itself, and the fact that it did not have an appreciable effect on their day-to-day activities no doubt made the line of opposition to the war more palatable to most Communist militants. The result was the 'economism' we describe in our next chapter.

The overall picture of the CP at this juncture is thus one of confusion. This is hardly surprising, seeing that its political stance had been based on unresolved ambiguities about peace and anti-Fascism, Chamberlain and Hitler, and these ambiguities were cruelly exposed on the outbreak of war. Even the Party's most unequivocal commitment, to an immaculate conception of the Soviet Union, had been put to the test by the vagaries of Stalin's foreign policy. In a sense the CP's original policy of a war on two fronts was an evasion of the need to face up to these realities, as the policies of the People's Convention would be a year later. Given the impossibility of mounting an effective challenge to the British ruling class, in view of the Labour Party's aversion to leading such a challenge, then the only options were to support a war led by the representatives of British imperialism – and thus, of course, of incipient British Fascism – or to sanction yet another act of Nazi aggression. The Party eventually made its choice along the lines laid down by Moscow, just as it would reverse this choice when the Soviet Union was invaded in June 1941. But in October 1939 there were, as we have seen, a number of other factors which led most Communists to accept the verdict of the Comintern, and in any case the CP's approach to many political questions and its basic political strategy remained virtually unaltered. This is perhaps surprising, as in Communist theory imperialist war provided revolutionaries with new opportunities and new responsibilities to bring capitalism to an end. But British Communists entered the new period unready and unwilling, or perhaps just unable, to face the revolutionary implications of opposition to imperialist war.

Notes

1. 351 *H. C. Deb.*, 301–2, 3.9.39.
2. 'Notes', Apr. 1936, 202.
3. R. Goodman, *Britain's Best Ally* (Key Books, 1939), 8–9; P. Sloan, *Russia – Friend or Foe?* (1939), 17, 176.
4. See e.g. Pollitt, *Will It Be War?* (CPGB, 7.7.39), 25–6.
5. Sloan, *op. cit.*, 112. Campbell made the same point just as confidently on three occasions; *DW*, 14.6.39, 5.7.39, 9.8.39.
6. *DW*, 23.8.39.
7. VG MSS.157/3/DOC/1, Betty Reid to Gollancz, n.d. but late Aug. 1939. Following the Pact the *Worker* apparently broke its mid-week sales records; *DW*, 26.8.39.
8. *DW*, 29.8.39.
9. *DW*, 24.8.39.
10. *DW*, 25.8.39; Gallacher in the Commons, *Parliament and the War* (CPGB, 15.9.39), 5.
11. *DW*, 30.8.39.
12. *DW*, 1.9.39.
13. CPGB statement, *DW*, 25.8.39.
14. Pollitt, speech, *DW*, 31.8.39.
15. Speech, *DW*, 28.8.39.
16. *Loc. cit.*
17. H. McShane, *No Mean Fighter* (1978), 231.
18. Pollitt, *How to Win the War* (CPGB, 14.9.39), 4.
19. CPGB CC manifesto, DW, 2.9.39 (reprinted in *ibid.*).
20. Pollitt, *op. cit.*, 6.
21. Campbell, 'War – and the new phase in Britain', *WNV*, 23.9.39, 988.
22. *DW*, 5.9.39.
23. CPGB CC manifesto, *DW*, 2.9.39.
24. *DW*, 8.9.39, 16.9.39.
25. *Tribune*, 29.9.39 (written a few days earlier; *Tribune's* 'War Diary' for that week ends on 26 September and presumably copy had to be submitted by that date).
26. CPGB CC manifesto, *DW*, 2.9.39.
27. Campbell, *loc. cit.*
28. Note 'converted' and not 'replaced'; Campbell at *DW* conference of trade unionists, *DW*, 4.9.39.
29. 'The Soviet Union and the war', *LM*, Oct. 1939, 611–12; J. R. Campbell and Finlay Hart, 'The Labour movement and the war', *LM*, Oct. 1939, 622. Dutt's 'Notes' for this issue were completed by 25 September, as presumably were these articles.
30. In this respect a comparison with the very different stance adopted by French Communists can be instructive. In the Communist picture of a Europe divided into 'peace-loving' and 'aggressor' states, Britain had been the one uncertain factor, its pivotal role in world politics depending on the outcome of the popular struggle against its reactionary government. France, on the other hand, was emphatically one of the 'peace-loving' democracies and the

policies of the PCF were set in the framework of broad national resistance to what it came to regard as the inevitable German assault on France. Even the suppression of the French Communist press in August 1939 did nothing to dampen its ardour for national unity, and on the outbreak of war it rallied to the tricolour with battlecries reminiscent of the *union sacrée* of 1914, using just those 'moral platitudes designed to cover aims of vested interests' ('national honour', 'national unity', etc.) which the British party categorically spurned. For this point see *Thesis*, 144–5, and for the CPGB's attitude see *DW* editorial, 5.9.39.
31 Previously the CP had demanded that the war be financed by taxing the rich; e.g. *DW*, 9.9.39.
32 Gallacher originally voted with them but at the end of the meeting asked that his vote be registered in favour of the resolution.
33 RPD K4, 'Amendment to resolution endorsing declaration of September 2', 22.8.39; 'Draft supplementary report of the Central Committee', 8.1.40; J. Mahon, *Harry Pollitt: a Biography* (1976), 250–3; M. Johnstone and Appendix IV in J. Attfield and S. Williams, *1939. The Communist Party and the War* (1984; hereafter *1939*), 26–8, 160–8; 'Notes', Apr. 1971, 184; Dutt interviewed in *Sunday Times Magazine*, 30.8.70; *DW*, 27.9.39, 30.9.39; CPGB CC manifesto, *DW*, 7.10.39; *PO*, Nov. 1939, 5–6. Pollitt and Campbell subsequently recanted; *DW*, 23.11.39.
34 This distinction between a regime's internal and external policy was, of course, an artificial one and incompatible with a serious Communist analysis of either imperialist war or Fascism. Dutt himself had previously stated quite bluntly that '*the foreign policy of a given State is a function of its inner system of class relations*'; *World Politics 1918–1936* (1936), 181, 311.
35 RPD K3, 'Notes for report on CC manifesto and resolution', 5.10.39.
36 Stalin cited by M. MacEwen, 'The day the party had to stop' in R. Miliband and J. Saville (eds), *The Socialist Register* 1976, 38.
37 *DW*, 13.9.39.
38 Interview, Imperial War Museum.
39 A. West, *One Man in His Time* (1969), 175.
40 D. Hyde, *I Believed* (1951), 69.
41 Bill Moore, interview and in *1939*, 55–6; *Sheffield and Rearmament: An Exposure of the 'Defence' Programme* (Sheffield Peace Council, 1937). I am indebted to Bill Moore for giving me a copy of this pamphlet.
42 See Gollancz's recollection of Pollitt returning from a visit to Spain possessed by a 'passion of fury against Hitler'; *The Betrayal of the Left*, p. 135.
43 *DW*, 23.11.39. For Pollitt's deep involvement in the Spanish war see Mahon, *op. cit.*, ch. 16.
44 C. Haldane, *Truth Will Out* (1949), 180.
45 Interview, Imperial War Museum. Leo McGree was the local Party Organiser.
46 Interview.
47 McShane, *op. cit.*, 231.
48 C. Cockburn, *Crossing the Line* (1958), 53–4.
49 Interview; see also *1939*, 85.
50 *1939*, 103–4.
51 Letter to author.
52 R. Pipe, *History of the Ipswich Branch of the Communist Party* (CPGB, Ipswich branch, 1982), 13–14.
53 Interview.
54 Interview.
55 *PO*, Mar. 1940, 12–13.

56 See *Thesis*, ch. 9:2.
57 Interview.
58 VG MSS.157/3/DOC/1, Levy to Gollancz, c. Mar. 1941, 30.4.41.
59 Cockburn, *op. cit.*, 49–50.
60 Interview.
61 Betty Reid (interview) recalled that Pollitt's tribulations caused 'enormous distress. Pollitt was a tremendously loved and revered figure in the Party because of his strength and his integrity and his humanity.'
62 'Notes', Aug. 1940, 424.
63 Interview.
64 Interview, Imperial War Museum.
65 Cockburn, *op. cit.*, 45.
66 See *ibid.*, 54.
67 Interview, Imperial War Museum. Logically, of course, this way of thinking should have led to support for a war which was so obviously dividing the imperialist powers. The fact that the anti-war line was not in the long-term interests of the Soviet Union need hardly be stressed. Subject to the constraints of Soviet diplomacy, the Comintern was an inefficient instrument of Soviet foreign policy.
68 *1939*, 68–9.
69 Interview.
70 M-O, Diarist B5036, Oct. 1939.
71 *Challenge*, 9.9.39, 7.10.39.
72 *New Statesman and Nation*, 16.3.40, 365.
73 H. Thomas, *John Strachey* (1973), 183–5, 206.
74 Interview.
75 Interview. In fact, Willis did publicise the anti-war line during the phoney war, before he was conscripted; e.g. *Our Youth*, Jan. 1940, 9–11.
76 Haldane *op. cit.*, 182–3. A similar case was that of Phil Piratin, whose misgivings about the Party line in the summer of 1940 (see p. 245, note 7) were mitigated to some extent by the fact that 'to a large degree the talking was limited because we then got so immersed [in practical issues]. At that particular time, for example, no-one could have done more to help the people in the war as an organisation, outside of the official organisations, than sections of the Communist Party did in connection with the shelter conditions' (interview).
77 Interview.
78 Interview; see pp. 132–3.

Chapter six
From the Soviet–German peace offer to the Blitzkrieg
the CPGB, 1939–40

The Party had publicly stated that it was an imperialist war. Every well-instructed Marxist knew what that meant.

(Douglas Hyde[1])

In October 1939 the British Communist Party did not suddenly have to improvise a political strategy appropriate to the conditions of imperialist war. It had only to turn to the classic Leninist texts which stated with devastating clarity the ideas which came to be labelled 'revolutionary defeatism' and which were encapsulated in the slogan *A revolutionary class in a reactionary war cannot but desire the defeat of its own government*.[2] And evidently Communists did turn to these texts. The 'classics' began to sell in record numbers,[3] and according to Douglas Hyde were read 'no longer [as] merely of purely academic interest or just a question of acquiring knowledge which might possibly some day be useful' but as guides to action directly relevant to the 'events of the moment'.[4]

In as far as the CP existed to follow the trail set by the Bolsheviks, these texts were indeed of immediate relevance, for the Party described the war as a continuation of that analysed by Lenin, a product of the same general crisis which could only end in revolution.[5] Some of the CP's pre-war allies concluded, most tellingly in a Left Book Club selection called *The Betrayal of the Left*, that Communists were following Lenin's recommendations 'without an iota of change' in the qualitatively different circumstances brought about by the rise of Fascism.[6] Moreover, Victor Gollancz, the editor of that volume, claimed to have had private confirmation of this 'direct from the Pope himself':

> At Palme Dutt's invitation I spent four hours with him in the early part of this year . . . for the express purpose of hearing him expound CP policy. He was absolutely explicit.[7]

Publicly too, while cavilling at the term 'revolutionary defeatism' as 'the drivel of a spy-maniac', Dutt fully accepted the authority of Lenin's teachings on imperialist war, the question of defeat included. These, he felt, were simply 'robust revolutionary common sense which can be understood by every militant worker'.[8] It is therefore worth beginning our account of the 'imperialist war' period with a brief consideration of this revolutionary common sense of Leninism, if only to underline the dichotomy between the practice of the Communist Party and the ideology which it claimed to embody.

6.1 Revolutionary defeatism

Transform the present imperialist war into civil war – is the only correct proletarian slogan . . . and logically follows from all the conditions of an imperialist war among highly developed bourgeois countries. However difficult such a transformation may appear at any given time, Socialists will never relinquish systematic, persistent, undeviating, preparatory work in this direction . . .

(Lenin, October 1914[9])

In August 1914 the Second International reneged on every principle of international Socialism. Everywhere, the stinking corpse of Social Democracy, shrouded in the banners of the warring nations, was reincarnated as apologist and recruiting agent for imperialist war. The Bolsheviks alone, and of the Bolsheviks principally Lenin, expressed revolutionary opposition to the war and the system which had engendered it. Thus was opened the crack which, widening as dissident Socialists throughout Europe asserted their independence of their leaders, led to the eventual cleavage between Social Democracy and Communism. For those who saw imperialist war as the precursor of great revolutionary developments, it was now clear that the leaders of Social Democracy would always be content to plod along the road of gradualism, patiently awaiting the maturation of the crisis which would bring down capitalism while the fires of war and revolution raged on either side. Disillusioned Socialists sought an organisation which would make a revolutionary intervention in history, not accommodate itself to the murderous status quo. In short, the Leninist strategy of revolutionary opposition to the war and to the role of Social Democracy in the war was of crucial importance in the establishment of a Communist International, and a hundred times more so in that it left the example of a successful revolution as well as a series of trenchant pamphlets.

Lenin's understanding of the war which was to end all wars was based on the famous axiom of Clausewitz that 'war is nothing but a continuation of political relations by other means'.[10] This led to two conclusions. The first was that Marxists, unlike pacifists who oppose war *per se*, 'deem it necessary historically . . . to study each war separately'. The second, more pertinent here, was that the struggle against the war could not be divorced from the struggle against the political realities underlying the war. The errors of 'bourgeois pacifists and their "Socialist" imitators' arose from their abstract conception of peace as 'something in principle distinct from war'. The peace that succeeded any war was nothing but 'a summing up and registration of the changes in the relation of forces brought about in the course of, and in consequence of, the given war'. If the imperialist war was to be followed by anything but a reactionary imperialist peace, the 'relation of forces' would have to be transformed by revolution, and propaganda for peace which suggested otherwise was capable only of deluding and demoralising the proletariat. Appeals to international law and arguments about who 'started' this or any war were completely irrelevant, except in so far as such irrelevancies spread confusion where revolutionary clarity was required. It was because they obscured the need for revolutionary class struggle with the platitudes of bourgeois debating societies that Lenin so vehemently denounced the 'centrist' trend in the Second International who had turned Marxism into 'the most filthy clerical mush'.[11] For Lenin, the question of peace was inseparable from that of revolution, for 'without revolutionary actions on the part of the proletariat there can be neither a democratic peace nor disarmament' but only an imperialist truce leading to 'years and even decades of armed struggle between the "great" powers for the artificial preservation of capitalism'.

This then was the theory underlying 'revolutionary defeatism', a phrase which is virtually self-explanatory. The 'general, meaningless, non-committal, goody-goody desires of pacifism' had to be countered with the slogan 'convert the imperialist war into civil war', for not only was the problem of imperialist war insoluble without revolution; it also furnished conditions conducive to this outcome, to the violent overthrow of the 'artificial' system of capitalism. Lenin argued that the war had brought about in most of Europe an ever-deepening revolutionary situation and that it was therefore the task of revolutionary Socialists to imbue the proletariat with the consciousness and determination necessary to bring this situation to a head. The paradox of imperialist war was that it required the mobilisation, militarily and industrially, of entire populations merely to fight for the interests of a parasitical clique. 'All governments live on a volcano', wrote Lenin; 'all appeal, *of their own accord*, to the initiative and heroism of the masses'. In the most uncompromising terms Lenin exhorted revolutionaries to exploit this contradiction, to recognise that the bourgeoisie was placing splendid weapons in the hands of the workers and prepare to turn these 'so useful weapons of death and destruction' on their own bourgeoisie. For, as one side of the coin showed revolution, the other as clearly denoted defeatism. Revolutionary activity 'undoubtedly and incontrovertibly' hindered the war effort of one's 'own' imperialists, but this was to be welcomed:

> Revolution in wartime is civil war; and the *transformation* of war between governments into civil war is, on the one hand, facilitated by military reverses ('defeats') of governments; on the other hand, it is *impossible* really to strive for such a transformation without thereby facilitating defeat.

Thus the slogan of defeat *alone* implied a 'consistent appeal for revolutionary action against one's own government' and to shy away from this slogan inevitably meant 'reducing one's revolutionary action to an empty phrase or to mere hypocrisy'.

That, in brief, was the robust common sense which, according to Dutt, Gollancz and many others, guided the activities of the Communist Party after September 1939. The first imperialist war, wrote Dutt, had led only to 'the first step, the re-awakening and organisational separation of revolutionary Marxism in preparation for what was to follow. It remains for the second imperialist war to complete the process in the realm of action.'[12] The reality was very different. The CP's attitude to the issues raised by the war did not remain constant, but it is nevertheless possible to make the following general points:

1 Despite the occasional use of apocalyptic language, the CP's activities were not shaped by the belief that the war had created or was in the process of creating a revolutionary situation. While it continued to express the idea of an epoch of revolutions, it showed little optimism about the prospects for immediate revolutionary advance except at a purely verbal, even ritualistic, level.
2 It therefore confined its activities to the defensive struggle against the effects of Fascism and war, without seriously envisaging the ending of the system which gave rise to these phenomena.
3 As the best strategy for waging such defensive struggles, the CP continued to attempt to build alliances with those who shared these limited aims.
4 The exigencies of such alliances – as well as the desire of Communists to hold on to the political and organisational gains they had made in the 1930s, threatened as these were by popular sentiment in favour of the war and a government armed with emergency powers – meant that Communists were often unwilling openly to oppose the war, let alone work towards its revolutionary conclusion.

5 In line with the current direction of Soviet foreign policy, the CP did not consistently take the Leninist line that all the belligerent powers were equally responsible for the war. Rather, for several months it portrayed Britain as the instigator of the war and the leader of world reaction.
6 However, the CP was reluctant to admit that the persistence of domestic class struggle facilitated a German victory. Indeed, at times of the greatest threat to national security Communists expressed no opposition to the war at all, but rather accused the ruling class of treachery to the nation. And throughout, Communist politics continued to be defined in anti-Fascist terms, even though the main danger of Fascism coming in Britain was seen to lie with the British ruling class.
7 Because it did not get entangled with the war effort, the CP was able, with a degree of success, to promote the sort of immediate mass struggles with which it had been so concerned before the war. Indeed, the social upheaval brought about by the war, and also the political truce observed by the Labour Party, provided new opportunities in this respect. But if these immediate issues were related too closely to the question of ending the war, advances were unlikely, and this reinforced the disjunction between the stated policies of the Party and the mass activities of its members.
8 By effectively renouncing revolutionary defeatism and by maintaining their often exemplary record in trade union and mass work, and by the very ambiguity of their Party's political line after June 1940, Communists laid the basis for the remarkable expansion of their influence which occurred after the attack on the Soviet Union.

Inasmuch as it opposed the war at all, the Communist Party's politics were characterised by economism – the failure to relate immediate struggles to the question of ending the war – and pacifism – the failure to relate the question of ending the war to the question of ending capitalism.[13] If the CP revived a few old slogans, it also retained most of its more recent ones and its opposition to the war was very much a piece with the political stance it had adopted in the 1930s. Admittedly, the CP was something of a political chameleon, but a chameleon only changes the colour of its skin: it cannot transform itself into a tiger when it finds itself in a 'new situation'. Of the three trends which Lenin had discerned in the Socialist movement, the CP most closely resembled neither the chauvinists nor the revolutionaries but the centrists whom Lenin found so contemptible. The analogy is an artificial one. Lenin also pointed out that 'it is the method of all the sophists of all times to quote examples obviously relating to basically dissimilar cases', and clearly the establishment of a Fascist dictatorship in Germany provided at least one basic dissimilarity between the situation in 1940 and that in 1914. However, it was the CP itself which maintained that the distinction between 'democratic' and Fascist states was no longer of significance and so frequently likened the second imperialist war to the first. And it was the CP itself which in 1940 told its supporters that they would find in Lenin's writings on imperialist war a 'gold-mine of information . . . on all aspects of the question [of] war, peace and revolution'.[14] The CP developed a quasi-Leninist analysis of the war while, as we shall discover if we bear the Leninist perspective in mind, its political practice was very far removed from that of the Bolsheviks. The real illusion was and is to imagine that it could have been otherwise.

6.2 The British precedent

> Revolt was seething everywhere. . . . We had within our hands the possibility of giving actual expression and leadership to it, but it never entered our heads to do so. We were carrying on a strike when we ought to have been making a revolution.
> (William Gallacher on the Clydeside strike of January–February 1919[15])

This 'economism' and this 'pacifism' might be taken as proof of the degeneration of Communism in the era of Stalin, evidence that, faced with imperialist war, the CP was too atrophied, ideologically and organisationally, to respond to it after the fashion of Lenin. This would be far too simplistic. The CP was not simply the product of an ideology called Leninism, but grew out of and continued Britain's existing revolutionary traditions. Indeed, a whole generation of Communist leaders – Pollitt, Gallacher, Campbell, Dutt – was drawn from the left-wing opposition to the First World War. It is therefore worth considering how Lenin's British contemporaries dealt with the problem of imperialist war.

The First World War and its immediate aftermath have often been portrayed as the golden age of the British left, on the verge of attaining revolutionary maturity when suddenly its growth was stunted by the rigidities of the Comintern. Perhaps, but the challenge to class collaboration, the emergence of new organisational forms, and all the potent myths of Red Clydeside cannot disguise the fact that the tempestuous wartime industrial struggles took place wholly within the framework set by the war, by capitalism. The many stirring accounts of these events are accounts of a heroic militancy, not of a frustrated revolution.

We need not chronicle these events here. Suffice it to say that when Wal Hannington did so in 1940 his failure to mention any revolutionary intent on the part of the first shop stewards' movement reflected the current position of the Communist Party without doing any great disservice to the protagonists of the earlier struggles.[16] Industrial action over conscription, dilution and wage rates was not broadened out to encompass the wider political implications of these sectional issues. The struggles on Clydeside were led by a number of exceptionally talented individuals, some of them committed to the principles of international Socialism; and yet the vision of the Clyde Workers' Committee remained constricted, perhaps because its industrial might rested on the unity of both supporters and opponents of the war. Thus the CWC's rejection of conscription, for example, was expressed in phrases which ignored the war which necessitated it:

> This delegate meeting of the Clyde Workers' Committee, recognising that the purport of the conscription is not a fuller supply of soldiers but the cheapening of soldiers and the military control of industry and consequently the abolition of the function of our trade unions, resolves to take such action as is necessary to prevent conscription.[17]

No cheapening of soldiers. We shall come across exactly this sort of mentality when we consider the Communist Party twenty-five years later. While workers on the Clyde and elsewhere made their stand on industrial issues, organisations like the British Socialist Party issued inspiring, if naive, calls for peace; and yet when members of the BSP, like Gallacher, threw themselves into industrial struggles they seemed to leave their political consciousness behind them. The Workers' and Soldiers' Councils movement, which might have brought the two agitations together, foundered, according to James Hinton, because the shop stewards were 'more concerned with sectional wage claims than with peace'.[18] Likewise, according to the same author, the one serious attempt to precipitate direct action against the war, in 1918, came to nothing because 'despite the wave of revolutionary resolutions, militancy still ... posed itself as an alternative to class politics'.[19] The industrial and political agitations were not brought together, and working-class militancy never transcended its immediate economic objectives.

The explanation given for this by R. Page Arnot during the 'second imperialist war' was that 'there was no co-ordination of the struggle of the working class, no lead such as a political party working consciously for a Socialist aim could give. The fusion of the Labour Movement with revolutionary Socialism had not yet been achieved in Britain.'[20] This fusion – of the industrial with the political, of mass struggles with revolutionary consciousness – was the purpose for which the Communist Party was formed in 1920 and then reorganised on Bolshevik lines in 1922. Unfortunately, though, the obstacles to the British revolution could not be conjured away by the formation of a 'party of a new type'. The immiscibility of the industrial objectives of the Clyde Workers' Committee and the political objectives of the various Socialist groupings during the First World War would be just as evident during the 'second imperialist war', only now this disjunction manifested itself *within* the Communist Party. Revolutionary opposition to the Second World War was certainly no more effective or cohesive than that to the First, and was arguably far less so.[21] Like their predecessors, Communists proved more adept at carrying on strikes than making revolutions, the main reason being that there was no revolution to be made.

6.3 Why this war?

THE COMMUNIST PARTY DECLARES THAT

This war is a fight between Imperialist Powers over profits, colonies and world domination. All warring Powers are equally responsible.

The Soviet Union is leading the world fight for peace. The immediate issue is the cessation of hostilities and the calling of a peace conference.

If you agree with this you will JOIN the Communist Party today.

(CP application form, October 1939[22])

The first months of the war have gone down in history as the 'bore war' or the 'phoney war'. The unconvincingly belligerent Chamberlain and his ally Daladier had lifted scarcely a finger to help Poland, ostensibly the cause of the war. Now Poland was no more. 'One swift blow to Poland, first by the German Army and then by the Red Army, and nothing was left of this ugly offspring of the Versailles Treaty', said Molotov, offering an important insight into the workings of non-aggression pacts.[23] With this *fait accompli*, Europe settled uneasily down to a war not so very different from the uneasy peace which had preceded it. In Britain, the children of the urban poor were herded out to the safety of the countryside, and then straggled back to the familiar squalor of the still-standing cities. The long-expected, bomb-heavy German aeroplanes stayed put in their aerodromes, though the bombs remained, ready for use the following summer. Germans stared at Frenchmen across the Maginot Line, and Frenchmen stared back again in a grim parody of the entrenched immobility of their last confrontation, apparently without purpose enough for an exchange of gunfire. Chamberlain's declaration of war seemed no more than a symbolic renunciation of appeasement, the restoration of Poland an unattainable objective which would now require the defeat of Russia as well as Germany. Neither could the war be credibly portrayed as an anti-Fascist crusade, as wary British statesmen refrained from stating such war aims as might antagonise the neutral Fascist powers. They were noticeably less conciliatory towards the neutral Soviet

Union, on the other hand, and at one point a *de facto* alliance of European reaction, including Britain but excluding Germany, seemed poised to intervene in the Soviet–Finnish war. In the end nothing came of this. The Finns capitulated, the reports of offensive and counter-offensive in the North having served mainly to reinforce the impression that all was unnaturally quiet on the Western Front. As the days grew shorter, and then longer again, it remained unclear what the war was meant to achieve. Meanwhile, at the end of September Britain and France had received an offer of peace from Hitler, backed up by the Soviet Government. This declaration of peaceful intent lay at the centre of the British Communist Party's campaign against the war that winter.

In urging acceptance of this offer, the CP was faced with a crisis of political credibility, for its prescriptions for peace bore a marked resemblance to those so recently and half-heartedly abandoned by Chamberlain and so eloquently denounced by Communists. To condone one act of Nazi aggression, Communists had argued, was merely to invite another; the road to peace lay not through conciliation but through the promise of resistance. And yet by October 1939 the CP was calling for a 'peace conference' with Germany, rather as Chamberlain had flown to just such a conference to secure 'peace' a year earlier. Communists, however, argued that the Soviet Union's determination and ability to enforce the terms of any settlement offered an 'absolute guarantee for a lasting peace in Europe', a peace qualitatively different from that which had followed Munich.[24] For Stalin and Hitler had revealed nothing of their prior agreement to partition Poland and so British Communists were able at first, however implausibly, to describe this sordid piece of secret diplomacy as a decisive check to Nazi expansion.[25] Thwarted by the Soviet Union in the East, Hitler was 'suing for peace' in the West.[26] Paradoxically, a month after the outbreak of war the CP claimed to regard the prospects for a lasting peace as more favourable than for years past.

Such a settlement between the belligerent powers, needless to say, would hardly constitute a 'democratic' peace. The Communists' immediate objective was, rather, to pressurise the British Government into a 'temporary accommodation', a 'patched-up peace', for in their view an imperialist peace was to be preferred to imperialist war in much the same way that bourgeois democracy was to be preferred to Fascism – not as an end in itself but as providing the best conditions for progress towards Socialism.[27] Moreover, in the course of their struggle for peace, as against Fascism, the workers equipped themselves for the decisive battles of the future. In a key pamphlet elaborating the Party's new line, Dutt admitted that any imperialist peace was necessarily full of injustices and sources of future conflict, but nevertheless argued that 'the victory of the mass struggle for the immediate ending of the war would enormously strengthen the working-class and democratic movement for further advance'.[28] Intrinsic to such an argument was the assumption that the British Government at least would not curtail the war of its own accord, but only in response to pressure from below. This indeed was how British Communists seemed to interpret Dimitrov's ambiguous call on the world's workers to end the war in their own fashion.[29]

The various points in the CP's case for an armistice were brought together in a *Left News* article in which John Strachey attempted to demonstrate that any peace settlement would automatically include the advance to Socialism as one of its hidden clauses:

> The truth is that all sorts of things unexpected and undesired by the Hitler, Chamberlain and Daladier Governments alike would in all probability emerge from an armistice. . . . Peace would mean that none of the capitalist Governments were strong enough to go on with the war. Peace now would confront the rulers of Britain, France and Germany alike with an insoluble economic problem which could not even be tackled by anything but a drastic modification of capitalism in a Socialist direction . . . these are exactly the reasons why we demand that the war shall be stopped now.[30]

But these were also the reasons why Strachey's demands were hopelessly misguided. According to the traditional Leninist schema, imperialist wars occurred precisely because they provided capitalist regimes with a last hope of escaping from their insoluble problems. Although they feared the consequences of war, wrote Dutt, the 'handful of sharks and vultures' were irresistibly impelled towards it continuation and extension by 'the driving force of their conflicting imperialist interests'.[31] And yet Strachey demanded, not that these compulsive warmongers be divested of their power to make war, but that the sharks and vultures should get together to negotiate a peace settlement which would lead inevitably to the extinction of these disagreeable species. Just as before the war, Strachey argued that capitalism and peace were incompatible; and, just as if war had not already broken out, he deduced from this not that Socialism was the only guarantee of peace, but that through peace lay the certain road to Socialism. In the event of capitalism being strong enough or desperate enough to continue with the war, there was no hint in this article of what Communists should do about it.

With such arguments as these, the CP came close to a pacifist standpoint, referring to 'war' and 'peace' as separate entities in a way that obscured the political realities underlying these issues. One advantage of this approach was that the word 'peace' gave an appearance of consistency, of coherence, to Communist policy; but this was, nevertheless, only an appearance. The CP's pre-war agitation for a 'Peace Front' had been imbued with a clear political purpose, that of deterring further Fascist aggression. The Party's declaration of qualified support for the war at its outbreak was, in one sense, an affirmation that the political task of stopping the spread of Fascism took precedence over an abstraction, 'peace', no longer coincident with the anti-Fascist aims of the British people. The Party's endorsement of the Soviet–German peace offer a month later implied the opposite, and retrospectively the Party's earlier campaigns were divested of much of their political content:

> We fought for a Peace Front, not in order to launch a world war, but in order to prevent a world war. Now that the war has followed through the refusal of the Peace Front, the fight for peace necessarily goes forward as the fight to end the war by the mass action and victory of the working class.[32]

Dutt's revolutionary turn of phrase cannot hide the fact that what Communists meant by 'peace' at the time of Munich and what they meant during the first winter of the war were two rather different things. To suggest otherwise in an attempt to demonstrate the undeviating rectitude of Communist policy required that the word 'peace' be robbed of many of its previous connotations.[33]

The result of this was what Dutt described and repeatedly criticised as an 'abstract propagandist approach to the fight against the war' which tended to 'fall into the trap of . . . encouraging pacifist illusions of a just and democratic peace under imperialism'.[34] His admonishments might have carried more weight had the Party leadership not itself been so prone to the 'Pacifist Distortion', as for example when, on the ending of the Soviet–Finnish war, it called on 'all sections of British peace opinion' to demand an 'honourable policy of peace and friendship with the Soviet Union', the 'sending of an ambassador to Moscow as a proof of good faith' and the 'ending of the war'.[35] The wooing of 'all sections of British peace opinion' was as characteristic as the demand for 'an honourable policy of peace'. In fact the two were inseparable. Because it defined its conception of peace only in the most general terms the CP felt it possible and worthwhile to construct a 'peace alliance' incorporating political tendencies quite opposed to Communism; or perhaps it was in the interests of such an alliance that Communists were so vague about the nature of the peace they desired and so reluctant to address the real problems involved in achieving it. Either way, the CP found itself in some rather unlikely company during these months.

For a short while Communist propagandists seemed indecently eager to commend just about anybody with a good word to say about Hitler's peace offer, and that included Tory MPs and that past master of imperialist war, Lloyd George.[36] This tone was subsequently moderated, but the CP's priority nevertheless remained that of establishing a 'broad political movement of opposition to the war on a common platform',[37] without insisting that this platform include the revolutionary political demands which alone could transform hopes of a lasting peace into reality. Thus did the Party express its approval of those sections of the Labour movement, pacifists and others, who were critical of official Labour policy on the war. Thus did it twice approach the ILP with a view to mounting joint anti-war by-election campaigns, only to be rebuffed by the ILP on the grounds that the CP functioned 'not as a genuine British Working-Class Party, but simply as the agent in Britain of the foreign policy of the Russian Government'.[38] Thus too did Communist delegates at a Scottish Peace Council convention in April 1940 align themselves *with* the sizeable pacifist contingent who stood for a negotiated peace and *against* those ILPers who sought to disrupt this unlikely coalition by means of 'revolutionary phrasemongering'.[39]

The paradox was that the Communist Party's own interpretation of the war frequently gave rise to phrasemongering as revolutionary as anything the ILP could manage. In the mass struggle to end the war, according to a Communist pamphlet published that same month, 'the whole question of Socialism and the fight for Socialism as the way out becomes an immediate issue'.[40] If this was the immediate issue, then one might have thought that the Party's immediate task was to dispel, not propagate, pacifist and reformist illusions and point out the revolutionary way out of the crisis. In reality, although Communist pamphleteers occasionally articulated a quasi-Leninist analysis of the war, this did not form the basis of the Party's political activity, but rather provided a rousing counter-melody to it, in a different key and at a different tempo. The CP's basic strategy remained that of the 1930s, even though its allies were not always the same. Fundamental political differences were blurred in the interests of building broad movements on immediate issues, the rationale being that these movements would become transformed through struggle and thus come to tackle the roots of class power. But for the moment the Party's decision to immerse itself in a broad 'peace' movement, rather than attempt to lead a revolutionary one, merely reinforced its tendency to divorce the will for peace from the means of attaining it.

That the Party adopted this pragmatic, even opportunist, approach, might seem to indicate that a realistic appraisal of the British political situation underlay its more dogmatic assessments of the crisis of imperialism as revealed by the war. But if the CP was unquestionably a genuine British working-class party responsive to the British political situation, it was also, from another aspect, an 'agent' of Soviet foreign policy: possibly the main problem in writing Communist Party history is to comprehend the sometimes complex relationship between the two. During this period Soviet professions of eternal friendship with Germany were reflected in the willingness of the CP almost to absolve Hitler of any responsibility for the war. By April 1940 this British agent of the Russian Government was evincing ever more blatant signs of a pro-Nazi interpretation of the war; and from this genuine British working-class party murmurings of disquiet began to be heard.

The beginnings of this tendency can be discerned in the CP's original anti-war manifesto. Typically, the manifesto incorporated traditional Leninist themes at a general level, arguing that responsibility for the war lay equally on all the warring powers. However, the most important of the manifesto's specific proposals – that calling for a positive response to the Soviet–German peace offer – gave rise to a less balanced judgement, for in accepting the *bona fides* of Hitler's peace offensive the CP suggested that only the bellicosity of the Western powers stood in the way of a settlement.[41] The war 'could be stopped tomorrow' and went on 'only because the ruling classes, British and French, are opposed to the conclusion of Peace':

> End the war. Do not allow yourselves to be muddled with old formulae about 'the aggressor'. . . . The stigma of aggression belongs to those Powers that want to continue the war . . .[42]

But the CP was adopting all the old formulae about aggression, merely applying them differently. The classic Leninist texts stressed the complete irrelevance of which side actually 'started' an imperialist war. Lenin did not seek to apportion blame between the warring powers, for the 'responsibility' lay with imperialism itself, which stood condemned by its endemic wars. In the 1930s the CP had gradually abandoned this perspective, motivated by its belief in the qualitative difference between bourgeois democracy and Fascism. Fascist aggression was condemned not merely in abstract, League of Nations terms, but also because of its all too tangible effects on hopes of working-class advance. The fact of aggression mattered less than its political connotations, although this was never spelt out as there occurred no conflict between the two; Fascism was aggression, and vice versa.

With the Party's decision to oppose the war, the old liberal attitude to aggression remained, but was neatly reversed as the Allied powers were stigmatised as the aggressors. Thus the notorious *Daily Worker* editorial 'Hitler Speaks' employed all the vacuous phrases of international morality, but in a new and perverse way:

> Hitler repeated once again his claim that the war was thrust upon him by Britain.
> Against this historical fact there is no reply. Britain declared war, not Germany. Attempts were made to end the war, but the Soviet–German peace overtures were rejected by Britain. All through these months the British and French Governments have had the power to end the war. They have chosen to extend it.[43]

For by this time, as the last of these fatuous sentences indicates, not only was the war as a whole seen as the responsibility of the Allies, but virtually every single development in that war was portrayed as an act of Allied aggression.

Well before the end of 1939 the incipient crisis of Soviet–Finnish relations was blamed on the British Government pressurising the Finns into rejecting legitimate Soviet demands.[44] By the time of the Soviet invasion at the end of November, 'semi-Fascist' Finland was seen as no more than a client state, 'the outer tentacle of an octopus whose vital centres are London and New York', while the Soviet invasion, poorly camouflaged by an agreement with Kuusinen's farcical People's Government, was celebrated as a blow for Finnish independence.[45] Despite this charade, the invasion reflected understandable fears for Soviet security on Stalin's part,[46] and the sanctimonious and pugnacious over-reaction of the Western powers had more to do with hatred for Communism than with respect for international law. But while Soviet actions showed an undiminished awareness of the Nazi threat, Soviet explanations of these actions were couched in the diplomatically inhibited language required by the pact with Germany. The CPGB, to whom these words spoke louder than actions, thus attempted to fit the Finnish events into an unconvincing pattern of Anglo–French aggression. And when these aggressive designs were thwarted by the Soviet–Finnish peace settlement, Communists concluded that the British and French Governments would now turn elsewhere 'to strike with even greater fury and desperation':

> The Chamberlain–Citrine gang is feverishly searching for new battlefields. The air of London and Paris is thick with talk about new theatres of war, the sweeping aside of moral and juridical considerations, the coercion of the neutrals.[47]

The threat of Allied aggression was by now a major theme in Communist propaganda, and the one or two incidents between Britain and Germany which interrupted the Bore War – notably the *Altmark* incident – were interpreted in this light.[48] Consequently, when the war was extended to Denmark and Norway the Communist Party – with impeccable logic and admirable consistency – pointed the finger of accusation at Britain and France.

On 8 April the British navy mined Norwegian territorial waters in contravention of international law. The following day Germany invaded Norway and, incidentally, Denmark. The day after that – in an issue of the *Daily Worker* of which it was 'literally true that someone who . . . took no other newspaper . . . would have been unable to discover that on the previous day the German Army had invaded Denmark and Norway'[49] – the CP issued a statement which blamed the British and French exclusively for these new developments. Not coincidentally, the statement was phrased in all the familiar jargon of the rights of small nations and international morality:

> Peaceful peoples, who have no wish save to remain at peace are dragged into war against their will. . . .
>
> The Chamberlain Government and the Reynaud Goverment had deliberately provoked this extension of the war . . . by their violation of Norwegian neutrality. With cynical disregard of international law they deliberately laid minefields in Norwegian territorial waters in order to extend the war.[50]

As if this pious nonsense were not bad enough, the *Worker* featured equally grotesque statements from the Soviet press, presumably as definitive interpretations of the affair, warning against 'cheap lamentations regarding the legitimacy or non-legitimacy of German actions in Scandinavia'. The gist of all this was that 'Germany's actions were forced upon it', and forced upon it by Britain.[51]

On the most charitable reading, this analysis was infantile. Hitler's decision to deal with Norway had been taken by the end of 1939 and his formal directive for an invasion had been issued on 1 March.[52] Even without hindsight it was obvious that simultaneous attacks over the length of Norway, from Oslo to Narvik, had not been prepared in a day! But in a way this is all beside the point. If the war was an imperialist one in which the working class was equally opposed to both sides, then it did not matter which side instigated a particular incident. If the war was a necessary anti-Fascist war which Britain was justified in fighting, then British 'acts of aggression' would be judged according to their contribution to the defeat of Fascism, not by legalistic criteria. Evidently, the *Daily Worker* did not interpret the war as one in which neither side was justified, nor as one in which Britain was justified. The suspicion arose that it had hit upon a third, unspeakable interpretation.

This suspicion was voiced most eloquently by the Left Book Club selectors, Victor Gollancz and John Strachey. Gollancz felt compelled to publish a lengthy pamphlet in which, citing both British and German Communist sources, he argued that the Comintern was keener to see Britain lose than Germany.[53] Strachey took a similar view and publicly broke all ties with the Party.[54] Equally disconcerted were those Communists who, invoking their Party's long and honourable traditions of internationalism, protested that the *Daily Worker*'s failure to condemn German aggression gave a pro-Nazi impression. Apparently such criticisms were voiced as high up in the Party as its London Secretariat.[55] Particularly interesting is the record we have of a conversation between two London Communists which indicates that some Party members at least were beginning to feel impatient with the crudities of the Party's peace propaganda by this time and took a view of the war quite different from that of their leaders:

> 'I do feel this stop the war slogan is a bad one. . . .'
> 'Down with the war would be better.'
> 'No, what I mean is you can explain about the war bringing profit to the rich and nothing for the workers, capitalist racket and all that, and they agree with every word. . . . But what they say is if we do stop the war why won't Hitler come here?'
> 'Well, you tell them.'
> 'Yes, yes, I know. But I mean our line is we get a real Socialist Government here and in France to appeal to the German workers on the "we have got rid of our capitalists why don't you" ground. But the point is we *don't know* that that would have immediate effect – in fact it is very unlikely. Almost certainly we should have to intervene against Hitler on behalf of some movement inside Germany. The intervention would be successful, of course . . . but it's not what any ordinary man means by stopping the war.'
> 'It is stopping *this* war.'
> 'Yes, but that is just a quibble. I mean so long as we have the Army out and everyone in uniform, you aren't going to have any working man thinking that you have stopped the war. Turn it into the right sort of war, yes, but that is not what the slogan says.'[56]

It was not what the slogan said, and the views expressed here were not those officially held by the Party although they would become so within a month or two. The conversation is a useful reminder that we cannot take it for granted that all Communists necessarily understood or accepted the full implications of Party policy. But for a definitive statement of the official Party line at this time we must turn to the draft of a 'Political Letter' in which Dutt attempted to deflect the criticisms of those who were unhappy with the Party's abandonment of any sort of anti-Nazi perspective.

As far as Dutt was concerned, the feeling that the Party should have condemned German as well as British aggression was 'a survival of the conception of the "War on two fronts" – that is the conception of the simultaneous struggle of the British working class against British and German imperialism'. To echo 'jingo denunciations of German imperialism' was to 'strengthen jingoism and incite to war'. Just as in 1914, the working class in each individual country directed its fire against its own imperialists; this was the 'Liebknecht principle'. But in one crucial respect the second imperialist war differed from the first, for in the background there now stood the first Socialist state. 'This main issue of Socialism and Imperialism governs every alignment', Dutt went on, and 'the world historical role of the two camps thus differs in this situation. The main aggressive world reactionary role is that of British and French imperialism.' Put more plainly, the signing of the Nazi–Soviet Pact imposed on British Communists a special duty to defeat the plans of their own imperialists:

> to apply the theory of equal responsibility would be an incorrect analysis of the objective facts. . . . We have a special responsibility in this country to expose this aggressive role of British Imperialism and to defeat the myth of Imperialist propaganda which seeks to lay the blame on the enemy Imperialism.

Inevitably, this repudiation of 'the official theory of German responsibility or any theory of equal responsibility' would be 'interpreted by enemies or luke-warm friends as equivalent to "White-washing" Germany'. And, of course, such 'luke-warm friends' apparently existed even within the Communist Party.

Clearly, Dutt's conception of 'aggression' had little to do with an objective analysis of developments in the war, but merely reflected the transient interests of Soviet foreign policy. For this reason Dutt's reassurance that the KPD had not abandoned the Liebknecht principle, that it was 'carrying forward the fight against . . . German imperialism', was untenable. And in fact statements printed in the British Communist press reveal that German Communists, while continuing in their fashion to oppose Hitler, also echoed Nazi denunciations of British imperialism, also fought just 'as pitilessly against those who want to rob us of the fruits of our struggle, who want to instal the rule of Vickers-Armstrong, Nuffield, the City of London and their servants, Chamberlain and Churchill instead'.[57] Within Britain the main enemy was British imperialism; and internationally too, despite Dutt's disingenuous allusion to the Liebknecht principle, the main enemy was British imperialism. The *Daily Worker*'s preoccupation with British reaction was not 'an error in presentation. . . . What is here involved is the whole international line.' Moreover, British aggression in Norway was 'only a beginning. If the plans for the extension of war are allowed to go forward there may be attempts to involve the Balkans and the Near East, possibly also Holland.'[58]

As the international situation deteriorated, the *Daily Worker*'s warnings of the imminence of further acts of Allied aggression appeared ever more absurd. One illustration will suffice:

> We want to invade Holland and Belgium. We are frightened of the possible international consequences. We therefore declare in advance that the Germans are about to do so. Thus we shall be in a position to extend the war there first.

And the same day 'grave tension in Berlin' was reported 'in anticipation of an Allied move at any moment'.[59] One almost expects to read of German fears of an Anglo–French invasion of France, justified on the specious pretext that the Germans were about to do so. To put it in these terms is enough to suggest that the CP's perception of the war would have sooner or later to give way to the pressure of events, and fortunately it did so. Because of the pace of international developments Dutt's statement was never printed[60] and by the time the Party eventually issued its next 'Political Letter' in June it had, in Dutt's terms, revived the conception of a war on two fronts. Just as our Communist in Battersea had hoped, the CP dropped the 'stop the war slogan' and belatedly accepted the fact that German aggression had not come to an end with the Nazi–Soviet Pact.

These developments will be described in the next chapter. For the moment we must conclude that the CP offered no revolutionary opposition to the war, but campaigned for an immediate peace with Hitler; that it argued that Britain and France bore full responsibility for the war; and that it not only restricted its analysis of the war to one of individual acts of aggression but, viewing events through the prism of Soviet diplomacy, invariably described these as acts of Allied aggression. In their general aspect and in every detail the CP's policies bore no resemblance to those of Lenin.

In charting this uncongenial territory we have been concerned chiefly with the highest levels of the Party, with the official Party line on the war. In the pages that follow we shall consider the implications of this line for the wider activities of the Party, and most crucially of all its activities in industry.

6.4 The rich man's luxury[61]

> THE COMMUNIST PARTY DECLARES THAT
> The rulers of Britain and France are using this war to declare heavy blows against their own peoples ... employers have launched a sweeping attack on workers' standards and conditions.
>
> The workers must organise to resist the combined attack of the employers and the Government.
>
> If you agree with this you will JOIN the Communist Party today.
>
> (CP application form, October 1939[62])

It was claimed by both Communists and their opponents that the CP's involvement in industrial struggles during this period formed an integral part of its strategy for ending the war, and, with it, capitalism. By their militant defence of their economic interests, Peter Kerrigan claimed, the workers were creating 'a movement which, as it swells and expands, will shatter this rotten system of monopoly capitalism and on its ruins build the new Socialist order which must come out of our success in ending the war'.[63] Victor Gollancz took such statements at their face value and more. In an imperialist war, he argued, 'Communists *want* industrial conflict, *want* strikes, *want* stoppages . . . irrespective of the immediate issues on which they are fought'; and the reasons they wanted these things were 'to slow down production with the object of "embarrassing the Government" in its war effort, and to lay the foundations for launching civil war in the moment of the defeat which the slowing down of production had helped to produce'.[64] Common to both views was the conception of the Communist Party as an organisation whose 'every policy and action' was 'aimed at the winning of power by the workers for construction of Socialism in Britain'.[65] But this conception was always and inevitably a chimerical one; this at least is the conclusion suggested by a study of Communist industrial militancy during the war. Whatever the relationship between political and industrial struggles at a theoretical level, Communists were generally reluctant to express their opposition to the war in the mass organisations in which they were active and made little attempt to use their influence in the most important of these organisations, the trade unions, for either revolutionary or anti-war purposes. In its failure to connect the localised struggles of shopfloor politics with the wider, determinant issue of the war, the CP placed itself very firmly in the tradition of Red Clydeside.

To some extent this tendency to isolate the economic effects of the war from their political context was dictated by the pattern of international events. Periodically, leading Communists would try to dispel the popular belief that the war was being waged half-heartedly, if that, with evidence of frenetic diplomatic activity, naval skirmishes, the blockade and Allied attempts to extend the area of hostilities.[66] However, propaganda against the sanguinary aspects of the war was bound to be unconvincing, especially as these isolated naval tussles and diplomatic manoeuvrings bore no comparison with the aerial annihilation of entire cities with which so many people, including Communists, had expected the war to commence. One suspects that many Communists had noticed, like William Gallacher, that it was 'All Quiet on the Western Front', but less tranquil at home:

> The Home Front – your Front, reader – the Front of wages; trade union conditions; of one Friday night after another – not so quiet. On this Front there have been ceaseless bombardment, constant raids, incessant attacks. No sparring for position, no reconnaissance flights.

> But war – and war.
> Unceasing, deadly, and carried through by the ruthless general staff of British capitalism.[67]

Moreover, before very long the Soviet–Finnish war began to provide a stark and eventful contrast with the undeclared truce in the West. The CP thus found itself in the unenviable position of demanding peace at a time when the only bloodshed in Europe flowed from an act of aggression which every Communist was obliged to condone if not celebrate. Its predicament was summed up in the sceptical retort 'Which war?' when Communist speakers exhorted their audiences to 'stop the war'.[68] Regardless of any more fundamental explanations of 'economism', the absence of military activity in the West and the surfeit of it in the North might well have inclined Communists to make what they could out of the domestic hardships arising from the war.

A major Communist campaign on the economic issues raised by the war took place early in 1940. 'The greatest war offensive ever organised is now being launched', announced the manifesto which opened this campaign. 'Not in France, or on the high seas, or in the air, but on the wages and conditions of living of the whole of the working people of Britain.' The key demand in this defensive, economistic manifesto was that the rich should be made to pay for the 'rich man's war'. The war was not in the interests of the British people and it was essential to limit the hardships which resulted from it. However, neither the manifesto nor the accompanying literature raised the question of stopping the war; rather, they took it for granted that the war would continue:

> The working class – young and old – must pay for this war, say the rich. Pay in blood or hunger.
> But the Communist Party says the rich must pay.

The war was apparently regarded as the unyielding framework *within* which the class struggle took place; and while it was theoretically possible for the rich to bear the economic costs of the war, it was ludicrous to suggest that they could also be made to pay 'in blood'. But this campaign ignored the blood-letting aspects of modern war, as its reminder of the 1914–18 war made clear:

> Remember the lies the Government told you in the last war, their broken promises and pledges. The unemployment crisis after the war. The wage cuts. The slashing of social services. The driving down of the miners, engineers and railwaymen.
> But that war made many millionaires . . . Let us say – Never again shall this happen in Britain. . . .
> BETTER TIMES FOR THE PEOPLE. MAKE THE RICH PAY.

NO BLOCKADE ON WAGES. NO PROFITEERING. NO TIGHTENING OF BELTS FOR THE POOR.

There was no mention of the necessity or even the possibility of ending the rich man's war.[69]

Of course, Party leaders frequently stressed that the fight to end the war and the fight to deflect its economic consequences were not alternatives, but that the one was implied by the other. Just as the waging of imperialist war involved an attack on living standards, on working-class rights, on personal consumption, so did the defence of these things involve the ending of the imperialist war. Thus did David Springhall argue that 'every social and economic struggle was now a struggle against the war policy of the Government'[70] and Dutt point out that 'to fight for the needs of the people means at the same time a fight for the end of the war. The needs of the people are incompatible with the continuance of the war.'[71] One might well agree that the maintenance of living standards was incompatible with the continuation of the war. In that case, it might be argued that the fight for the 'needs of the people' was itself weakened to the extent that Communists made no adequate response to the war propaganda which justified working-class sacrifices by invoking the danger of Fascism. When the 'capitalist offensive' was being waged by political means, a successful 'workers' counter-offensive' could hardly be organised around purely economic demands. In other words, the failure to address firmly and openly the problem of the war, the 'tendency to separate the immediate economic and joint issues from the anti-war fight',[72] impaired the fight on immediate issues as well as, obviously, that against the war. This much was acknowledged by Dutt himself.

In April 1940 Dutt complained that the 'main weakness' of Communist propaganda had been the failure 'to link up our day-to-day fight against the war and war policy of the Government, and our day-to-day fight for the immediate economic and social demands of the workers, with the basic aims of our struggle against capitalism and for socialism'. Party propaganda, he argued, had tended to fall into 'two compartments'. On the one hand there was the demand that the war be stopped, and on the other the demand for higher wages and better social services; and both were 'commonly presented in isolation from our basic struggle against capitalism' resulting in the 'distortion and misunderstanding of our line':

1 *Pacifist distortion* – presentation of our line so that it becomes misunderstood as the pacifist line of the call for 'Peace at any price', 'Surrender to Hitler', etc. . . .
2 *Reformist distortion* – the tendency to treat the immediate economic and

social issues in separation from the issues of the war; to present the slogan 'Make the Rich Pay' in such a way as to give the impression that the war could proceed smoothly without imposing burdens on the workers; hesitation to raise the basic issues of the war, etc.

As Dutt appreciated, these 'distortions', both of which reflected more than they distorted the 'Party line', were closely connected. They would only be corrected, Dutt wrote, 'to the extent that we can present every issue of our fight as a part of the fight of the working class against capitalism'.[73] The truth of this remark was evident from the attempt to develop a comprehensive strategy for ending the war before the London District congress of the Party three months earlier.

The congress discussion statement posited a revolutionary interpretation of the war as the 'opening of a new period of great revolutionary class battles and prospects of new socialist victories' to which the workers should respond 'by taking the offensive, not only against the effects of the war, but against the continuation of the war itself, against the Government, and against the capitalist system'. From this perspective the relation of immediate struggles to the final goal of Socialism was clear enough, and the statement did not fail to point it out:

> Every hardship created by the war must be exposed and shown to be inseparable from the rule of the capitalist class and its imperialist war. . . . At this stage we must concentrate on continuous and patient explanation of the nature of the war. The way to end the war must be shown to be through the activity of the workers themselves in struggle for better immediate conditions, and as the forces become powerful enough, through the ending of capitalist power.

The only problem was that this superficially plausible strategy could only be put into practice by those Communists in industry who knew from their own experience that this attractive scenario was also an illusory one and that patient explanation of the nature of the imperialist war would most likely lead to an impatient rejection of Communist leadership. This at least is the most likely explanation for the 'wrong tendency . . . to accept formally the policy of opposition to the war, but in practice to carry forward the conceptions of the past period':

> This was shown by a marked reluctance by leading comrades to raise openly the issue of opposition to the war in the mass organisations. Only after several weeks and considerable discussions were efforts made to put resolutions, the good support often causing surprise. Even now there are hundreds of organisations in which the issue has not been raised.
>
> Often the raising of other issues, the economic issues, the effects of the war, is made a substitute for raising the issue of ending the war.[74]

Accordingly, the delegates to the conference endorsed a resolution preaching vigilance 'against all tendencies to shirk the fight against the war itself [and] against failure to see the struggle on economic issues as an essential part of this fight'.[75] But we have already seen that the record of the Party leadership was hardly exemplary in this respect. With the exception of one or two ambiguous headlines,[76] one would scour the files of the *Daily Worker* in vain for a report on an industrial dispute bringing out its relationship to the war. Is it any wonder that those Communists actually involved in the struggle on economic issues, alongside workers who generally supported the war, should occasionally 'shirk the fight against the war itself'?

Of course, there were apparent exceptions to this trend, notably a *Labour Monthly* conference on 'Labour and the War' attended by delegates from 379 working-class organisations in February 1940. The resolution approved by these delegates constituted one of the clearest formulations of revolutionary opposition to the war to be found in the CP literature for this period. It explicitly linked the struggle to defend living standards with that against the war, explicitly linked the struggles of British workers with those of the oppressed peoples of Europe and the Empire and explicitly linked the ending of the war with the question of class power by invoking the famous Basle anti-war resolution of 1912. Its concluding slogans left no room for misunderstandings:

DOWN WITH THE WAR! DOWN WITH CAPITALISM! FORWARD TO SOCIALISM![77]

But if there were occasions when the war was seen as the harbinger of revolutionary developments, the sort of ideas expressed at this conference did not shape the activities of most Communists. The delegates at the conference did not, by and large, take its grandiloquent message back to the organisations they represented. To raise the question of ending the war and proceeding to Socialism in circles in which Communist views predominated was one thing; to raise the same questions in mass organisations with limited aims and functions was quite another, and could easily jeopardise the important advances that Communists had made in these organisations in the 1930s. And yet only if these mass organisations somehow transcended their limited aims and functions could an effective opposition to the war be built up.

The Communist Party as an organisation and its individual members had therefore to reach some decision as to their priorities. Either they could risk their laboriously accumulated assets in a determined effort to end the imperialist war which – it was asserted from time to time – was hastening capitalism to its doom; or they could treat these revolutionary prognostications as merely the ideological dues owed the Comintern, and commit their assets only to the less controversial, day-to-day struggles in which they had been involved long before the war. The speakers at the 'Labour and the War' conference, for example, included figures prominently identified with the two movements in which the CP had before the war most successfully developed a coherent industrial strategy with pronounced political overtones: the engineering shop stewards' movement and the South Wales Miners' Federation. And, in a sense, their industrial activities were transformed by the anti-war policies to which they subscribed. For, so divisive and perhaps so unrealistic were the CP's latest pronouncements, that Communists in these movements largely abandoned the political perspectives which they had opened up in the 1930s and retreated into the sort of stolid economism which the Communist Party had been formed to overcome.

6.5 Engineers in the front line

All the brave drilled men, willing to rush towards death, all the flags and national anthems, all the patriotic speeches, cannot rescue a people now. Without such factories as this, they are lost or dependent. Where these factories are, there is power.
(J. B. Priestley describing a Midlands aircraft factory, 1943[78])

machines make war; machines, in industry and in war, develop; this development brings about a change in the nature of war; in the new form of war, power to make war and to end war is mainly in the hands of the industrial working class.
(Tom Wintringham, 1935[79])

The Aircraft Shop Stewards' National Council (ASSNC) was set up by Communists in 1935 in the favourable circumstances of the pre-war armaments boom and made rapid headway in organising a shop stewards' movement in that industry.[80] Its progress was reflected in the steadily expanding circulation of its lively paper, the *New Propellor*, edited by the Communist Peter Zinkin.[81] Naturally, the *New Propellor* was primarily concerned with industrial matters, but Zinkin did not fail to encourage its readers to lift their eyes from their lathes and their pay packets to the wider horizons of national and international politics. This was very much in line with the internationalist, anti-Fascist perspective adopted by the ASSNC.[82] The *Propellor's* strength lay not just in its expressing its opinion on political questions, as many trade union journals did, but in its perception of the interrelationship between industry and politics, and the benefits of projecting this sort of unitary view of politics were demonstrated by the tremendous efforts made by engineers on behalf of Spain.[83] During the late 1930s, the CP's line on international affairs was one that could be effectively and uninhibitedly related to the activities of shop stewards.[84] Moreover, the aircraft workers at least demonstrated a consciousness not merely that they were producers, but of what they produced and of the uses to which the product might be put. As early as 1937 De Havilland's shop stewards threatened a strike if the planes they produced were sent to the rebels in Spain.[85] On this occasion their resolve was not put to the test, but eighteen months later there came from five of the biggest aircraft factories in London the encouraging news of the 'first political strike the aircraft industry has known'. The purpose of the stoppage was to add weight to the strikers' demand that the planes produced by their labour should be sent to the Spanish Government.[86] Led by Communists, aircraft workers were beginning to show an awareness that the power to make and end wars lay with the working class.

In articulating the line of a 'war on two fronts' in its first wartime issue, the *New Propellor* maintained its pre-war perspective, juxtaposing the political with the industrial and addressing its readers as both workers and citizens:

> As Britishers, we value our freedom, we value the democratic rights we enjoy. Therefore we swear an end to Hitlerism so that we can again build a 'new and better world', from which Fascism has been banished as surely as the Dark Ages.
> . . . as trade unionists we shall see that no barriers are put in the way of a victory over the Nazis. . . .
> Everything must be done to ensure maximum production of munitions, but we must insist on *full trade union control*.[87]

Then all of a sudden, when the CP changed its line on the war, references to international politics became taboo. Where the *Propellor* had imparted political enlightenment about Spain's war, it now maintained a gloomy silence about Britain's. The sympathies of its editor might have been deduced from his apparent readiness to put the barrier of industrial militancy in the way of a victory over the Nazis. However, no connection was drawn between the two, and the obmutescent *Propellor* did not even take the trouble to modify or repudiate its initial commitment to a British victory. The CP's line on the war corresponded badly with the National Council's long-term aims of building up the shop stewards' movement, of broadening its scope (it became the Engineering and Allied Trades Shop Stewards' National Council in the spring of 1940) and of expanding the *New Propellor*'s circulation (a figure of around 45,000 was claimed in May 1940[88]). Therefore the Council and its organ opted to steer well clear of the issue of the war and retreated into the purest form of economism. Significantly, when Herbert Morrison banned the *Daily Worker* in January 1941 he thought it unnecessary to extend the ban to the *New Propellor* – the paper through which the CP spoke directly to workers in war industry *as* workers in war industry. The *Propellor*, Morrison pointed out, was 'devoted entirely to the exploitation of industrial grievances and contains no direct references to the war'.[89]

Typical of the new emphasis was the national conference of the EATSSNC held in Birmingham in April 1940. At this conference delegates representing over 200,000 of those key engineering workers whose labours made the war possible formulated a detailed, coherent set of industrial policies without ever addressing the issue of the war which had created so many of the problems discussed. Apparently, the analysis of the war expressed in the 'Labour and the War' conference was not to be allowed to interfere with the Party's industrial work.[90]

In the AEU at least there was an additional reason for treading carefully. In the late 1930s the CP had moved decisively towards work within the established Labour movement, adopting a far more positive attitude towards work within the trade unions. During the 'imperialist war' period its strategy remained that of working through existing union channels, while at the same time building up unofficial movements unrestricted by union rules.[91] Communists insisted that their unofficial activities could only strengthen the official movement, but there was nevertheless an implicit tension between the two, and this tension was heightened during the early part of the war. In the late 1930s the leftward-moving AEU leadership had shown little antagonism towards the rightward-moving Communist element in the union, and the AEU had adopted progressive policies towards such questions as Communist affiliation and Spain. But after the CP's decision to oppose the war there was renewed hostility towards what Fred Smith, the AEU's General Secretary, described as the Communists' 'disruptive and mischief-making methods'. 'Disturbing incidents have occurred', Smith wrote early in 1940, 'to show that the old "union smashing" tactics are again being employed by Moscow's agents in promoting unofficial strikes and intensifying local discontent'. Thus it was that, rather than permit 'a few mendacious whitewashers to undermine the power and prestige of our union',[92] the AEU's leaders decided that it was high time to curtail the various unofficial activities organised by Communists.

In December 1939 AEU stewards were given a formal warning against participation in *Daily Worker* conferences discussing issues such as dilution and overtime for which the union felt it bore exclusive responsibility.[93] However, the Birmingham conference of the EATSSNC was concerned with exactly this sort of issue and consequently a number of Communist delegates to the conference, all prominent figures in the AEU, were threatened with expulsion from the union.[94] In the end they were let off with a caution when one of them, Joe Scott who had been forewarned of the Executive's intentions, produced evidence that he had been attending to official union business at the time. Nevertheless, the episode was a warning to Communists in the sense that it set limits to their 'unofficial' activities if they wished at the same time to make headway within the AEU. However harmonious the relationship between official and unofficial activity in theory, in practice Communists had to strike a delicate balance between the two. Their predicament was epitomised by the case of Edmund Frow, one of the stewards involved in the episode recounted above.

Frow was a well-known figure in the Manchester AEU; he was shop stewards' representative on the union's District Committee and in 1940 he stood for its national Executive for the No. 4 Division (the North West and Midlands) gaining a respectable level of support.[95] The CP had no intention of squandering this sort of influence and took heed of the abortive attempt to expel Frow. Thus, although a signatory to the People's Convention manifesto,[96] Frow did not attend the Convention:

> I was trying to keep my head down a bit because of this expulsion business and I'd got orders; the Party told me, 'You've not got to get yourself expelled from the union because we don't want to lose people that have influence in the union just by them sticking their necks out.'

Accordingly, when subsequently the union wrote to Frow to ask him if he had attended the Convention, and if so why, he was able to write straight back with written evidence that, like Scott previously, he had on that very day been attending to official union business![97]

Frow's experiences were indicative of the dilemma faced by the Party as a whole. Communists in engineering had developed a long-term industrial strategy combining official and unofficial activities which had achieved a measure of success by the time that war broke out. As Frow recalled, the effectiveness of this strategy depended on Communists not going 'so far in the unofficial sense that you stepped completely out of line',[98] and this obviously precluded a sustained effort to develop a factory-based movement of revolutionary opposition to the war. Had Communists striven to build such a movement they would in all probability have forfeited the confidence of the union rank and file, faced disciplinary action by the union leadership and been subjected to stringent government measures, even to the point of making the Party illegal. Instead of securing an ever wider distribution, the *New Propellor* might well have suffered from plummeting circulation figures or suppression by the Home Office. The Party's industrial militants did not resist the Party line; the vast majority of them no doubt accepted it as a *political* perspective, but they made little attempt to relate it to their industrial work. However, it would be wrong to exaggerate the spontaneity of this retreat into economism, when the Party leadership itself so often failed to draw the connection between industrial struggles and the fundamental political issue of the war. It would be absurd to imagine that the *New Propellor* had worked out its new stance independently of King Street; its glorification of trade union consciousness was an extension, as much as an evasion, of the Party line.

The priorities of 'industrial Communists' and the sort of pressures they faced especially during this period were lucidly described by Eddie Frow. Discussing the impact of the Party's change of line at the beginning of the war, he revealed that there were practical as well as political obstacles to the full implementation of the new line, obstacles which are poorly indicated by written sources from the period:

> I don't think either policy would have made a terrific lot of difference to what we did in the engineering industry. The things we were arguing about, whatever the political policy had been, would have been basically the same. I mean, rightly or wrongly we were fundamentally trade unionists who were dealing with industrial issues on a day-to-day basis as we were confronted with them. We were political animals inasmuch as we were a small circle of people who were able and willing to explain our political case. But what we were doing on the industrial side wouldn't have been a great deal different, in my opinion, whichever policy we'd had.
>
> The blackout was really murderous. I mean, I was living in Droylsden and I was working in Salford. I was cycling down to work; it took me fifty minutes in the blackout. It was absolutely bloody murder. You were working overtime, you were operating in the blackout. I would say right from the outbreak of war to the end of the war Communist Party members had enough to do to get to work and back home and attend a limited number of meetings.

So would this lead to something of a division between Communists' industrial and their political activities?

> I'm afraid there always was some division in that regard. I don't want to exaggerate this, but unfortunately there was a tendency to be what you called 'industrial Communists', and a main body of political activists who were involved. Traditionally in Manchester there were a lot of engineering workers and a lot of teachers in the Party; and teachers were the sort of people who could take on as secretary of a branch or something like that and have the time to do it. There were a lot of industrial workers in the Communist Party who didn't really get involved to a tremendous degree in general Communist Party work. I mean, if you were a member of the District Committee of the AEU as a branch representative, you had five meetings a fortnight. You had three branch meetings to attend every fortnight and two District Committee – one District Committee and one subcommittee. So that's five nights, and if you were delegate to the Trades Council

that's one more a month, and there you go on. It was more or less inevitable that you weren't as much involved in what you might call general Communist Party activity.

Was that reinforced by the conditions in the war?
It was worse in the war in some respects. To give you an illustration of this, before the war I was Chairman of the Manchester Area Committee of the Communist Party; and I was Chairman of the Manchester Area Committee after the war. But during the war I didn't sit on any Communist Party committees at District or Area level. We were pushed out of some aspects of Communist Party work because we were just working too many hours.[99]

Norman Brown, a shop steward at Oxford Radiators, did not entirely agree when Frow's arguments were put to him; in Oxford there was a 'pretty fair division' and during the war Brown himself held official positions in both the Party and the industrial movement. However, he did agree that there were difficulties in maintaining such a level of activity:

Well in a way you just had too much to do. I mean I had a bloody nervous breakdown really because when I was on nights during the war I never used to go to bloody bed for a week. I'd be going to something in the afternoon, back up the factory in the afternoon and slacking an hour and then going off to work at night and all that sort of stuff; and there'd be Party meetings, Party conferences and going down to High Wycombe and God knows what. I nearly collapsed in the end, you know, I had a bloody nervous breakdown.[100]

So, during the war at least, some sort of separation between the political and industrial 'wings' of the Communist movement was enforced by the finite capacities of the individual Communist. For the sort of reasons described by Frow, the specialisation and fragmentation of Communist politics inherent in a Popular Front strategy became more marked.

However, during this early part of the war these practical problems were reinforced by the unwillingness of Communists to relate their industrial activities to the political line of the Party. Less than at any other time did they strive to overcome this divarication. Dutt's predictions of imminent revolutionary developments were not, it would seem, taken so seriously as to risk throwing away years of work in industry. The power both to wage and to end the war lay in the munitions factories, but the workers in those factories did not want to end the war, and the Communists in those factories opted to remain with the workers. A similar picture emerges when we turn to consider the South Wales Miners' Federation.

6.6 War! and the Welsh miner: Hornerism resurgent

It has often been said of me that I was a miner and trade unionist first and a communist second. . . . It was true, too, of Arthur Horner and of most leaders who have lived and worked in the mining valleys of South Wales. . . . Politics take second place to the trade union job, and if and when they conflict, as they did on occasions for Horner and myself, loyalty to the trade union and its decisions came first. . . . I think the process of development is from thinking and acting purely as a communist, to thinking and acting as a communist who has accepted that his primary obligation is to the interest of the union and its members. There are occasions when these two positions do not coincide. . . . the point is that the communist with these responsibilities will think and react to situations in a somewhat different way from the communist without which can result in opposing stands being taken in given situations.

(Will Paynter[101])

Uniquely among British Communists, Arthur Horner, President of the South Wales Miners' Federation, had given his name to an *ism*. During the 'Class Against Class' period the assumption behind the Party line had been that the revolution was on its way and that, as the proven agent of counter-revolution, Social Democracy was Communism's main enemy. Industrially, this implied a rupture with existing, non-Communist trade unions and led to unrealistic demands for unofficial strike activity in unpropitious circumstances.[102] In South Wales, misgivings about the Party's extravagant fantasies were such that the CP's Political Bureau coined the expression 'Hornerism' to signify its disapproval of the 'opportunism' prevalent in the Rhondda and elsewhere. Horner himself was indicted for his 'complete lack of confidence in the fighting power of the masses', his 'faith in the Social Fascists' bureaucracy and their trade union apparatus', his 'failure to understand the depth of capitalist crisis' and his 'anarchistic flaunting [sic] of Communist discipline'.[103] Moreover, this was not just a personal failing. A disgruntled Communist from Blaenclydach complained that in the Rhondda 'trade union legalism is rampant; nothing can be done unless it has first of all been discussed by the Lodge Committee'.[104]

The roots of 'Hornerism' went right back to the syndicalism of *The Miner's Next Step* and the refusal of militant miners after the First World War to be tempted by the unofficial organisational forms which flourished in the engineering industry. With some justification, miners insisted that the lodges were as comprehensive and as effective a form of organisation as any they might build up from scratch.[105] For, just as the economic life of the valleys was dominated by coal, so were the industrial and political activities of the mining communities dominated by the 'Fed':

The 'Fed' was the single decisive union operating in the pits, the communities existed around the pit, the union branches were based upon it, hence the integration of pit, people and union into a unified social organism.[106]

The same writer, Will Paynter, had in 1931 defended 'Hornerism' as 'merely a recognition of the dominating influence of the SWMF'.[107] Seen in these terms, Hornerism was not so much a fleeting deviation from a reckless Communist policy as the defining characteristic of South Walian Communism.

If the strength of their allegiance to the Fed pitted a number of South Wales Communists against their Party in the early 1930s, the CP's conversion to a Popular Front strategy seemed to rule out any such conflict of loyalties, for the Federation provided the ideal framework for a non-sectarian political and industrial strategy which recognised the legitimacy of existing working-class institutions. Although the emergent united front of all working-class political organisations would soon be stifled by the arid orthodoxies of the Labour Party,[108] the united front of the different political tendencies continued to find its expression in the Federation. The SWMF was, perhaps, the most political of British unions, and during the Spanish Civil War – the Colliers' Crusade – the South Wales miners demonstrated a sense of urgency and an internationalist commitment unequalled elsewhere in Britain.[109] Thus could Communists express their solidarity with the Spanish republic through official union channels, through its rank-and-file Executive Council and through the lodges. Indeed, by 1939 Communists had won for themselves positions of influence at all levels of the union,[110] their greatest success being Horner's election as President in 1936.

However, even at the dizzy heights of its achievement the Party in South Wales did not escape mild rebukes from the CP's national leadership. While William Rust applauded the advances made in the Federation at the CP's 1937 congress, he also deprecated the tendency of South Wales Communists to 'look upon themselves as militants rather than as revolutionary leaders of the working-class'.[111] From within South Wales too came criticisms of 'the belief among many Party members that it is only necessary to be active trade unionists to become good Communists'[112] and of 'the defect termed "hiding the face of the Party" ' which was attributed to the persistence of a 'syndicalist outlook' in the valleys.[113] However, if this was syndicalism, it was an exceptionally politicised form of syndicalism, just as the SWMF was an exceptionally politicised trade union. It was a 'syndicalist outlook' which, for many Communists, led straight to the battlefields of Spain.

Although the pertinence of this type of criticism would become apparent after the outbreak of war, for the time being the political and industrial perspectives of union and Party were so nearly the same that any drawbacks in such total commitment to the Fed were far less obvious than the benefits. By the late 1930s the Party in South Wales had developed an acute perception of the international dimension of the class struggle and, inseparable from this, an irrevocable commitment to non-sectarian work within the established structures of the SWMF. Then, in October 1939, these Communists were saddled with an anti-war policy which seemed to shatter the anti-Fascist consensus which had virtually defined the politics of the South Wales miners; and worse still there were sporadic instructions to wage the anti-war struggle by the relentless pursuit of the workers' industrial objectives, and the linking of these objectives with the political fight against the war. The Communists of South Wales were not averse to raising political issues in an industrial context, except where the issue was such as to divide the miners. The war was precisely such an issue, and the new Party line was therefore implemented with a degree of discretion that suggested that Hornerism was far from dead.

No more than in the 1930s did Horner's wartime activities bear any trace of 'adventurism', one indication of this being the respect in which he was held by those who did not share his political beliefs. Early in 1941, a Liberal journalist and sometime war correspondent for the coalowners' organ, the *Western Mail*, wrote of him:

> He has a good reputation – a Welsh editor said the owners trust him as much as the men do, that he has kept peace in the coalfields for five or six years – a feat an ordinary Labour leader would probably have failed to achieve.[114]

This is hardly the description of a man anxious to use his considerable influence to foment industrial unrest as a contribution to ending the war. In his own way Horner was certainly committed to industrial struggle, but the object of this struggle was not to end capitalism and its wars but to better the lot of the workers under capitalism. In April 1940 he expounded his philosophy of trade unionism to the annual conference of the SWMF:

> So long as society is composed of buyers of labour energy on the one hand, and sellers on the other, so long must the conflict of interests exist, the buyer must always endeavour to buy cheaply, i.e., by paying the lowest wages possible, just as the seller must always aim to secure the highest wages possible. This conflict of aims is within the nature of the system under which we live, and obtains during periods of war, as well as in times of peace.[115]

The exploitation of the miners, then, was not a wartime phenomenon but the very condition of their employment in capitalist Britain; and to lessen the degree of this exploitation was therefore an aim which could unite all miners, irrespective of their views on the war.[116] However, if Horner rejected the notion of an industrial ceasefire this did not mean that he intended to wage the class war by indiscriminate displays of industrial militancy. Long years of dogged resistance to the encroachments of capital had left him with a keen sense of what the miners could hope to achieve in given circumstances, and what was just wishful thinking. Turning to the writings of Clausewitz when confined in Cardiff jail in 1932, it had dawned on Horner that the miners were involved in a protracted war of attrition. No longer, as after the First World War, were there sweeping victories to be had. On the contrary, if the miners were to realise their potential strength, Horner reflected, 'we had to mobilise our forces with the same care as a successful general. We had to use the strike weapon carefully.'[117] In the long term, as Horner well knew, exploitation in the pits would be resisted only to the extent that the miners, in South Wales and nationally, were united.[118] The successful general had first of all to be able to deploy his troops, and 'to mobilise our forces' meant, in South Wales in the 1930s, to eradicate non-unionism and company unionism in the coalfield.[119]

However, the steady pursuit of Horner's aims, avoiding strikes if possible, was seemingly incompatible with the fundamental tenets of Communism: that capitalism had entered its final crisis; that war would bring this crisis to a head; that the only long-term goal of Communists was the conquest of power; and that their immediate task was to build up the mass movement of struggle which would, as the 'forces of the working class' grew stronger, achieve this goal. The greatest degree of damage that could be inflicted on capitalism was its overthrow, not the imposition of constraints on profitability. In Horner's philosophy, on the other hand, trade union and labour disputes appeared not as a potentially revolutionary force but simply as an aspect of capitalist industrial relations. In adapting his long-term strategy to the conditions of imperialist war, Horner evinced not the slightest belief in the capacity of Communists to end either that war or capitalism; and within weeks of the war's outbreak the tension between his conduct of union affairs and Communist Party dogma became apparent.

It was Horner's deep-rooted commitment to miners' unity that determined his attitude to the wage negotiations of September–October 1939. The significance of these talks was that, for the first time since the General Strike, they were conducted at a national level, a step towards Horner's long-term aim of one national miners' union.[120] Although the talks resulted in the offer of a flat-rate increase a third less than that demanded by the miners,[121] the SWMF EC unanimously recommended acceptance and its position was endorsed by a special conference of the Federation.[122] The matter then went to the lodges which overwhelmingly – by a nine to one majority – rejected the advice of their leaders.[123] At the MFGB conference called to decide the issue the SWMF delegation was accordingly mandated to reject the settlement, and so one can imagine the surprise of the other delegations when the SWMF's Communist President stood up to make a judicious case for acceptance of the owners' terms:

> I believe in using every possible situation to unify the conditions of the miners of this country. . . . Our national policy has been to try to secure the maximum national control. Someone may say, 'Yes, you have got it, but it is only for the period of the war.' I put this to you, that if it is good to get it for ever, it must be good to get it for three years or whatever the war period may be . . . if we can establish national control for the period of the war we have gained a stronger position for the miners of this country than we will have as districts for the period of the war.
>
> . . . this conference is not deciding 8*d*. and 4*d*. It is deciding whether . . . there is the basis and the possibility for national uniform control of our wages for the course of the war.[124]

Thus are we presented with the unlikely spectacle of this incorrigible Communist urging restraint on the restive elements in the coalfields. Horner's speech was remarkable for the absence of any hint that the war might not have to drag out its course ('three years or whatever the war period may be') or that the miners – some, like the SWMF, formally committed to the establishment of Socialism – could aspire to anything greater than ameliorating their condition as wage slaves ('it is good to get it for ever'). Horner envisaged an indefinitely lengthy struggle against the coalowners in which temporary concessions were justified if they left the miners better equipped to wage that struggle. His priorities were not in this case those of the CP, which repudiated the stance taken by Communists on the SWMF EC in a leaflet distributed in 50,000 copies to South Wales miners. National unity, it argued, should have been built not around this compromise with the coalowners but around the demand for a bigger increase.[125] The question of the war was not mentioned, but the real issue at stake was not, to paraphrase Horner, 8*d* or 1*s* but whether the perceived long-term interests of the mining unions took precedence over the immediate task of developing a movement of industrial struggle against the war.

If Horner and the other Communists on the miners' Executive in South Wales were not prepared to allow the implementation of the 'new line' to interfere with their conception of the miners' industrial interests, they were no more willing to throw away the positions they had won in articulating those interests. In their practical effects these two motivations cannot be separated, for they led to the same conclusion: that the miners should not be divided along the lines of those who supported and those who opposed the war. Thus it was that Horner meticulously avoided addressing the issue of the war itself. His speeches and writings dealt almost exclusively with the 'war on the home front'[126] and he insisted that his attitude to this 'war' was in no way determined by the CP's opposition to the 'other' war.[127] He did not disavow the Party line, but steered clear of it and, where this was not possible, maintained that his views on the war had no bearing on his conduct of union affairs. Horner's reluctance to propagate the Party's anti-war policy was due also, no doubt, to the fact that it was 'against [his] personal convictions'. He later wrote that he 'did not accept the thesis that it was an Imperialist war like the First World War'[128] and this statement is borne out by the recent oral testimony of those who knew him.[129] For whatever combination of reasons, the most important Communist trade unionist in the Party's history carried on his activities much as if the Party line did not exist. Horner was both the President of the SWMF and a member of the CP's Central Committee, and yet these two roles seem during this period to have been mutually autonomous, a symbol of the Party's inability to transform defensive economic struggles into a political challenge to imperialism, and of the indisposition of some leading Communists even to make the attempt. The dichotomy personified by Horner is best illustrated by the one episode where it appears to have been overcome in South Wales: the debate over the character of the war in February and March 1940.

With a view to clarifying the Federation's attitude to the war, early in 1940 two resolutions expressing the 'pro-war' and the 'anti-war' positions were drawn up and put to the judgement of the lodges. The coalfield-wide debate which followed gave the CP a valuable opportunity to secure, and demonstrate, mass support for its policies. The Party attached considerable importance to the passing of Communist-inspired resolutions by Labour movement organisations, largely because of their publicity value;[130] and in terms of publicity the CP could not hope for a more resounding success than to secure the backing of such a major union as the SWMF. However, there were were deficiencies in the Party's resolutionary strategy, as the debate in South Wales was to reveal.

The first of these shortcomings was that, according to the *Western Mail*, the Communists were able to disguise their lack of mass support 'by snap votes at small meetings, wholly unrepresentative and by other dubious methods'. Of the examples given, the most farcical was that of Treharris where twenty-two votes had apparently been sufficient to commit a lodge of 2,000 miners to support for the Communist resolution.[131] Of course, as the *Western Mail* omitted to point out, this worked both ways, and twenty-three votes would have been enough to have committed the same lodge to a pro-war position. The likelihood is that only a small minority of South Wales miners expressed their preference for either resolution and that, whichever was passed, the decision would be that of this minority, not of the miners as a whole. The political significance of such resolutions was therefore limited, not just in this case but in hundreds of others in different organisations and different parts of the country. If the SWMF declared its opposition to the war, this would be a propaganda coup for the CP but not necessarily much else.

This was all the more so given the efforts of the SWMF's Communist President to distance himself from the debate and play down its significance. Horner made no attempt to throw his weight behind the Communist resolution, saying next to nothing in its favour and presiding over the special conferences with the impartiality and taciturnity of a cricket umpire. Moreover, voicing the view of the Executive, Horner insisted that the stance taken on the war would have no industrial repercussions, that 'the question of a person's attitude towards the war is his personal affair' and that 'nothing would happen beyond recording an expression of opinion of the miners of South Wales as a body'.[132] In no sense was this an attempt to bring together political and industrial forms of struggle, to relate the miners' economic grievances to the need to end the war. On the contrary, said Horner, 'whatever resolution is passed the general attitude of the Federation towards its basic industrial problems will not be influenced'. In that case, asked a *Western Mail* reporter, would the Federation be taking any steps to implement the anti-war resolution, if carried? 'Certainly not', replied Horner. 'Never under any circumstances has any member contemplated taking such a step.'[133] But what Horner's leadership lacked in Dantonesque audacity was made up for in sagacity, as the proceedings of the special conference would demonstrate.

By more than three votes to one the SWMF rejected the orthodox Communist line in favour of a resolution supporting the war 'so long as it is fought against Fascist aggression and for the achievement of a permanent peace'. The size of the majority was an indication of how much more effectively the successful resolution conjured up the spirited anti-Fascism which had united the Federation before the war. It made no concession to national unity, but rather called for a war on two fronts, against Chamberlain and Hitler, in stirring phrases very like those used by the CP at the beginning of the war:

> We realise that our rights and liberties were never won in a battle with a foreign power, but that, on the contrary, they are the fruit of centuries of struggle against oppression in our own land. Nevertheless, these rights and liberties can be lost by foreign aggression.

These ideals, so recently abandoned by the CP, having carried the day, the expediency of Horner's detachment from the issue became clear. Straight away he urged the delegates to forget about the war and get back to what he regarded as 'the fundamental task of the Federation, which is to safeguard and improve the wages and working conditions of the members of the organisation'.[134] On these matters Horner could serve the miners as well as anybody, and he did not believe that his political differences with majority opinion in the coalfield constituted an obstacle to his doing so.[135] And neither, apparently, did the Federation's membership, for at the SWMF's annual conference that April Horner was re-elected President almost unanimously. This was not simply an acknowledgement of Horner's personal qualities, for his Communist colleagues retained their seats on the Executive throughout this period.[136] Likewise, there were few reported cases of Communists being turfed out of their positions in the lodges at this time. Interestingly, of these instances one occurred just as the lodges were deliberating on the war; perhaps it was the intrusion of this divisive question that led to an apparently untypical anti-Communist backlash in this Rhondda lodge.[137] For the most part Communists remained embedded in the Federation.

It should perhaps be added that Horner soon came to regard the Federation's declaration of support for the war not merely as an expression of opinion but as a determinant of its industrial policy. By the end of May he was frankly concerned to raise production 'to meet the needs of the country in its present dangerous situation', explaining that the terms of the pro-war resolution 'did not entitle any encouragement to be given to actions which might reduce output and thus contract-out the burden and the sacrifices of the war to the men who are suffering and dying'.[138] Again this was not an isolated stance: in mid-June a scheme devised by the Federation and the Coalowners' Association to increase production was unanimously approved by an SWMF conference.[139] This only confirms the view that Communists in South Wales were quite aware of the connection between political and industrial questions, but were not prepared to integrate divisive, revolutionary, anti-war politics into their basic industrial strategy.

One consequence of the failure of Horner and his comrades to translate their influence in the Federation into support for the current policy of the Communist Party was to provoke an outburst of criticism from the Party leadership. Such criticisms had been uttered *sotto voce* throughout the 1930s but after the triumph of the pro-war elements in the coalfield they took on a more strident note. Idris Cox, for example, complained that the 'winning of official union positions' had become a substitute for 'Communist mass activity among the workers':

> The result is that the Communist leaders in the SWMF tend to isolate themselves from the political mass work of the Party. They are respected by the miners as good individual leaders, but not regarded as representatives of an organised political Party which leads the fight of the workers against capitalism on all fronts.[140]

Pollitt himself joined the attack, bemoaning the 'increase in previous tendencies to regard the SWMF as the main field through which the Party expresses its policy, and as the substitute for the Party' and the 'really striking inactivity on the part of the majority of the Branches in connection with the day-to-day questions that affect the masses'.[141]

There was a good deal of truth in these accusations, but they overlooked the fact that, in the early months of 1940, it was precisely because Horner was not regarded primarily as the representative of the Communist Party that he maintained his ascendancy over the SWMF. It was impossible, and not just in South Wales, to lead mass struggles against the war; Communists had either to lead mass struggles, if and when they developed, or concentrate on opposition to the war. The temper of the British working class, indicated by the pro-war sentiments of the South Wales miners, permitted of no other option. Moreover, Cox was possibly mistaken to emphasise 'the dangerous separation . . . between the mass work of the Party and leading members in the trade unions', for the spirit of 'Hornerism' pervaded the Party in South Wales. To substantiate these arguments it is worth considering the 'All-In Movement' by which the Communists of the Rhondda attempted to resurrect the pre-war popular front early in 1940.

The purpose of the All-In Movement was to bring together all sections of the Rhondda community to wage 'an immediate campaign on the widest possible basis' in defence of living standards.[142] The moving force behind the movement, and its Secretary, was George Thomas, formerly a Rhondda councillor and South Wales correspondent for the *Daily Worker*. Characteristically, although the initiative came from the Communists, they chose to work through official union channels: the movement was instigated by the Rhondda Area of the SWMF and subsequently received the backing of the union's Executive. Although local CP branches provided some financial support, it was decided at the movement's inaugural conference that 'the lodges should be responsible for calling the local conferences to establish local committees'. Within a month Thomas was able to report that 'we are making headway in various parts of the valley and the initiative everywhere is being taken by the Miners' Lodges'. However, the movement did not long flourish and its grand finale, though not intended as such, was the appearance of Willie Gallacher at two meetings attended by about a thousand people towards the end of April.

Corresponding with Gallacher before the meetings, Thomas indicated the sort of political self-restraint which the building of such a broad movement necessitated of Communists:

> Please note the meetings are organised by the All-In Movement to deal with pensions, compensation, allowances to dependants of those in the forces, unemployed etc. The war is excluded and you will need to be careful if you bring it in at all when speaking. It is difficult not to do so, but please remember we are united on the issues mentioned above but not on the war.

The Communists, then, were determinedly non-sectarian. They 'hid the face of the Party' and worked through the lodges instead. They welcomed the participation of any organisation, 'irrespective of character' – and that included the Rhondda Allotments Association – and to facilitate this were prepared to remain silent about the war.

The problem was that too many of those approached by Thomas knew that the Communists were behind the All-In Movement and knew that the Communists opposed the war, and they were not prepared to overlook these facts. Gallacher was not, for instance, automatically chosen as the movement's Parliamentary figurehead. An assortment of pro-war and pacifist Labour MPs were invited to address meetings, but none accepted. The Rhondda Borough Labour Party was no keener to associate with Communists and, according to Thomas, did its utmost to stifle the movement, 'possibly because a repetition of the mass movement of 1935 is feared'. Even the movement's Chairman had regretfully to abandon his post out of loyalty to his lodge, which was of the opinion that the official movement was quite capable of waging any necessary immediate campaigns.

The episode, slight in itself, highlights the dilemma faced by Communists. In the Rhondda at least they were still zealots for unity but, no matter how amenable they were, their Party's policies and Labour's prohibition of any association with Communists deterred many potential allies. Those who had always disliked and feared the Communists were now joined by those who would not cooperate with opponents of the war, on however innocuous an issue. The All-In Movement gained a measure of support, but its sponsors were fighting against heavy odds and there is no evidence that it existed for more than two or three months. The imperatives which led Communists to concentrate their efforts on work within the SWMF are clear. But at least the Communists of the Rhondda tried to adapt to the reality of which those in King Street were, or at least affected to be, unaware: that a mass movement against the war was impossible while the 'mass' supported the war. Like many others all over Britain, the Rhondda Communists tried to maintain their links with the masses rather than isolate themselves by steadfast, uncompromising opposition to the war.

Exception may be taken to this concentration on South Wales, where the CP had long exhibited certain distinctive characteristics; and it is true that a study of a different coalfield might reveal different features. Nevertheless, this emphasis is amply justified by the fact that South Wales was a notable, and rare, stronghold of Communism and that Horner was the Party's leading trade unionist. Moreover, whatever the rumours of 'Bolshevik discipline', there appears to have been little central interference with the activities of Horner and his associates and there was never any question, as there had been in 1931, of recantations or even expulsions. Whether the Party leadership shared Horner's pragmatism, or whether it disapproved but was pragmatic enough to avoid antagonising such a key figure in the Party, is immaterial. No doubt the Party's leaders appreciated that the constraints felt by Horner were experienced by all those who had attained a degree of influence in the outside world; the failure to relate the Party's opposition to the war to the questions 'directly affecting' the miners and other workers was by no means confined to South Wales.

So the issue raised here is more fundamental than any personal idiosyncrasy on Horner's part. In earlier days of revolutionary optimism and organisational creativity, Communist thinkers, in Britain as elsewhere, had been acutely aware of the inherent limitations of trade unionism:

> They simply bolster up or modify part of the capitalist system itself. The trade unionist thinks in terms of wages, of employer and employee . . . and approaches the management or a set of employers simply for the modification of a particular condition. So long as the trade unions do that . . . they are simply pillars of the capitalist order of things.[143]

In a series of contemporaneous articles Gramsci expressed views similar to Murphy's in words strangely akin to Horner's own stated philosophy of trade unionism;[144] for Horner, of course, thought very much in terms of wages, of employer and employee. But during the whole of the Popular Front period, during which it turned decisively towards work within the unions, the CP never really addressed the question of whether the functions of a trade union official were incompatible with revolutionary activity, were inherently 'reformist'. Or rather the CP tended to assume that the existence of a disciplined vanguard party was sufficient to overcome this tension. Communists were to go into the unions as Communists and remain Communists, owing their primary allegiance to the revolutionary party of the working class and thus transcending sectionalism and legalism. In reality, as Paynter recognised, the Communist trade union leader was very often, and perhaps even necessarily, a trade unionist first and a Communist only second; and this was never more apparent than when the Party appeared to veer to the left. But in a sense, the Party's concern to maintain its positions in the trade union apparatus at this time indicates that its revolutionary rhetoric concealed more limited, defensive aims which presupposed the continuation of capitalism for the foreseeable future. By 1939, 'Hornerism', in its various forms all over the country, was accepted in the Party, imperialist war or no imperialist war.

National Union of Students; Artists International Association
Although we have focused on the problems which the 'new line' posed for Communists in industry, it should be emphasised that, wherever Communists were committed to a movement broader than that which would oppose the war, there was a tendency to steer clear of this difficult issue. Two brief illustrations will give some indication of this.

In June 1940 Margot Gale was appointed Secretary of the National Union of Students, an organisation in which Communists played a leading role; indeed, a British Student Congress organised by the NUS had only just passed a resolution against the continuation of the war.[145] Gale, a member of the CP, though not publicly, saw it as her task as Secretary to heal the divisions which such a resolution seemed designed to accentuate:

> When I became Secretary of the NUS my real brief was: 'We've got to hold the NUS together, we've got to do things which are appropriate for students in wartime to do and at the same time make people think about the issues behind it.' So at the next congress we discussed why we studied our particular subject; it was called 'The Student, His Subject and Society'. You see, we left the war alone for a bit and that had the effect of healing some of the awful rifts that we had.
>
> I used to define the word *political* as something which would split the NUS. In those days you could say fighting Fascism was political, but it was a unifying thing. Everybody was on the same side basically, as with all sorts of things like refugees and ARP and so on.[146]

The imperialist war, of course, was not a unifying thing.

A similar philosophy seems to have guided the organisers of the Artists International Association, an organisation which had played a conspicuous role in the struggle against Fascism and war since 1933. The AIA's first wartime bulletin in September 1939 adopted what was in essence the CP's original line. However, by January the Association's Communist Chairman, Misha Black, had become persuaded of the inadvisability of issuing forthright statements on the war:

> I cannot believe that we shall be best serving the cause of peace or democracy or

culture by splitting our membership on the political issues which are now troubling all of us. . . .

When we have felt that the great majority of our membership was in almost complete agreement, as was the case over the Spain issue, the question of helping artist refugees from Czechoslovakia and the question of retaining our civil liberties in England – then I think we had every justification, and in fact a duty to state openly and clearly what we felt about these issues. . . .

But to-day I do not think that there is a general consensus of opinion amongst our members.[147]

Significantly, once the CP had swung round to support for the war, both the AIA and the NUS reverted to more overtly political stances. Whether active among students, progressive artists or industrial workers, Communists were more reluctant during this period to address 'openly and clearly' the burning questions of the moment than either before the war or after the invasion of the Soviet Union.

6.7 Imperialist war, anti-Soviet war

the Finnish conflict has thrown into fierce light all the forces of the world situation. The masks are thrown aside. All the forces of imperialism . . . on the one side, and of socialism on the other, are revealed in their true alignment. . . .

The present war is, in short, an imperialist war of a peculiar type, or rather, set against a peculiar background; and the background is more important than the war.

(Palme Dutt, January 1940[148])

The inevitable concomitant of the Communist Party's failure to politicise economic struggles was its paucity of ideas as to how the war might be stopped. While the political truce excluded any possibility of dramatic political changes by constitutional means, the CP itself seems to have ruled out the use of industrial action in the interests of peace and Socialism. The Party press recorded only one exception to this rule, a resolution passed by the Executive of the Fife Miners' Union in January 1940 calling on the MFGB to 'use its organised strength, even to the extent of withdrawing labour, in order to compel the National Government to call a truce to hostilities'.[149] Ironically, of course, any such proposals to exert industrial pressure on the government for overtly political ends would certainly have been resisted by the leading Communist in the MFGB.[150] And in general, there was confusion as to the tactics most likely to bring about an end to the war, although this confusion was artfully concealed by the simple device of ignoring the problem.[151] When it wanted to, however, the CP could be quite explicit as to the means of achieving anti-war ends, as became apparent with the prospect of war on the Soviet Union.

To historians, the Anglo–French plans to send military aid to Finland seem 'wholly irrational', 'the product of a madhouse'.[152] To Communists at the time, on the other hand, this was a calculated, if desperate, move to 'form a new front of the imperialist world against the Soviet Union', proof that British imperialism's most fundamental antagonism was towards Communism.[153] 'The capitalist sharks would like to fight to the last Finn', warned William Rust, one trusts with a dry sense of humour, 'but they are going to get a rude shock.'[154] In part, this shock was to come from the British working class. This was no mere inter-imperialist war, but a threat to the one haven of Socialism in a world of ravenous capitalism which, just as in 1920, called for direct action:

> Workers in the aeroplane and munitions factories, in the shipyards, docks, railway centres and ports, be on your guard! Demand to know where the armaments you are making and transporting are being sent! Be vigilant! Remember that all war material sent to Finland is in reality to be used against the working class, against Socialism, against your own liberation from poverty, unemployment and war.
>
> Show by your actions that you stand by the Soviet Union. . . . The real power is in your hands. It is a mighty power. Nothing in Britain can withstand it, once you decide to use it. Use it now. Use it on behalf of yourselves, and of the people of the Soviet Union, and of Finland . . .
> STOP ALL WAR MATERIAL TO FINLAND![155]

Here at last was an awareness of where lay the power to end wars! The CP encouraged workers to exercise their power at the points of production and distribution in blunt terms not heard in other contexts. It would seem that the war in Finland was being waged 'against the working class' in a qualitatively different way from that against Germany; and that, as a result, the CP's opposition to this war was also qualitatively different.

How far this industrial solidarity with the Soviet Union might have materialised is impossible to tell, for the Finns capitulated before the Allied war plan got off the ground. The Soviet invasion seems to have earned Communists more public hostility than anything else before the Cold War and there is some evidence that, as Dutt chose to put it, 'the weakness and confusion among considerable sections of the working class found an echo even among some elements of the Party membership'.[156] Nevertheless, the CP's explicit instructions to sabotage the abortive Allied intervention in Finland contrasted markedly with its patient, non-committal opposition to the other war. This brief flirtation with direct action was the exception which proved the rule that the CP made little attempt to use industrial militancy as a weapon against imperialist war.

6.8 May Day 1940

Whereas our fathers lived and laboured, scattered over the country,
We are organised in mine, workshop and factory,
and huge town. Think of the difficulty the peasant had
to collect an army. We, as quick as the word,
can turn out in millions, possess the streets,
bring industry to a standstill, are disciplined . . .

(Clive Branson, *May Day 1940*[157])

I think if somebody wrote the history of the Communist Party or the Labour Party from the standpoint of the sort of pronouncements they made and all the rest of it, it would be very unrealistic because in reality, when it comes down to local level, it's a question of what the members of that organisation decide they can do in regard to all the practical realities they're confronted with. There are times when a policy has been enunciated and the activists have looked at it and just shrugged their shoulders.

(Edmund Frow, interview)

By 1940 May Day had been established for half a century as the occasion for the workers of all countries to assert their solidarity. In the midst of imperialist war, a demonstration of proletarian internationalism was more necessary than ever. Every marching worker, every scarlet banner and anti-war slogan, would be a blow struck for Socialism, an indication that, in war as in peace, the call of one's class took precedence over the demands of capitalist production.[158]

In Britain, 1 May was identified above all with the CP. As Communists saw it, the significance of May Day could never be realised by docile processions on the nearest day off allowed by the bosses. May Day was 'a day of challenge' when 'the bondage that capitalism exercises over the masses of the people is defied' and 'the wage-slave asserts the right to his own time and energy'.[159] The official Labour demonstrations, on the other hand, were always held on the first Sunday of May and so 1 May had become the occasion for a manifestation of working-class militancy independent of the Labour and TUC leadership. Especially conspicuous were the annual demonstrations in Hyde Park organised by the London First of May Committee, nominally a non-Party organisation but run by Communists. The presence of Labour speakers like Bevan (1936) and Strauss (1937) had legitimised these rallies as expressions of working-class unity, but at no time were London's Communists prepared to sacrifice this annual gesture of independence in the interests of unity with Transport House[160] for the essence of May Day was the organisation of a 'mass political strike':

> The workers generalise their demands, direct them against the Government and the State, and show that they mean what they say by going on strike.
>
> In other words, May First raises economic and sectional demands to the plane of political struggle by uniting the workers in action against the whole employing class and its Government. The failure of the British Labour Movement ever officially to organise a real May First strike and demonstration is a reflection of its failure to organise a political struggle against capitalism.[161]

May Day 1940 therefore provided Communists with the perfect opportunity to politicise economic struggles and back up their demands that the war be ended with industrial action. However, even before the war the difficulties of organising a 'mass political strike' had been such that Communists outside London had generally had to be content with adding their numbers to the officially organised processions. Even in London the affiliation of a number of important trade union district committees to the First of May Committee had in practice involved 'nothing but an affiliation fee or a resolution'. This failure to try to mobilise the mass of trade union members for decisive action, the Party's London DC complained in 1939, raised once again 'the old question of Communists not finding their way to break through the Union routine and to use their posts constitutionally but effectively in making a change'.[162] Not surprisingly, then, the Party's grandiose predictions in 1940 of a 'red letter day in the history of the British workers . . . when masses will surge on to the streets proclaiming their determination . . . to achieve peace'[163] were not, and could not have been, fulfilled. And this despite the fact that the two major Communist proclamations for May Day 1940 made it crystal-clear that the responsibility for ending the 'millionaires' war' fell primarily on the British working class.

If the 'May Day Appeal' of the ECCI[164] did not actually condone Nazism, this was only because it did not trouble to mention it – surely, in the spring of 1940, an indication of complete ideological bankruptcy. Instead it called for 'relentless struggle' against 'the British and French warmongers and their social-democratic lick-spittles' who bore full responsibility for the 'orgy of reaction and terror'. It seemed thus to assign to the CPGB a pre-eminent role as the Communist Party best placed to thwart the war plans of British imperialism, and accordingly the CP's own May Day manifesto acknowledged that 'the heaviest responsibility falls on the British working class to take the lead in the fight to end this war'. Moreover, the same manifesto pointed out in the stirring phrases that were kept by for such special occasions, to fulfil this responsibility required *revolutionary* actions:

> This war is the mortal crisis of capitalism. This war has shown that capitalism is

completely outworn and has become a fetter on the progress of humanity. This war is the signal for all working people to utilise the crisis it has set loose in order to advance against their real enemies, the ruling capitalist class, and throw off the chains of slavery.[165]

As befitted this dramatic scenario, the CP insisted that May Day activities should constitute a conscious interruption of war production 'during the daytime of Wednesday, May 1, i.e. during working hours':

> Whatever activity is organised during the evening of May 1 should be regarded only as secondary and supplementary. . . . The main point is that, considered politically, the activities carried out during the daytime assume a far greater importance as the demonstration of the militant working class.
>
> Wherever possible, the call for such May 1 demonstrations should be made on the widest basis. . . . Nevertheless, where we have not succeeded in this, the Party itself must accept responsibility for the May 1 call.[166]

The stage was set for nationwide demonstrations during working hours directed exclusively against the British warmongers – the very stuff of revolutionary defeatism. The parts were all written, but would the Communists on whom these peremptory demands fell be able to play them? As May Day approached, John Mahon evinced a more realistic appraisal of the possibilities open to militant workers, merely expressing the hope that they would mark the occasion in whatever way they felt able – 'some by holding Trade Union Card Inspections, some by sending deputations demanding higher wages and improved conditions to their management, some by holding factory meetings, and wherever they feel it possible to do so, by laying down their tools and joining our demonstration in Hyde Park'.[167] And as it turned out, very few workers did feel it possible to down tools, and for most of them there were no demonstrations to go on, even had they wanted to.

Of the May Day meetings listed in the *Daily Worker*, the vast majority – those in Edinburgh, Greenock, Sheffield, Newcastle, Liverpool and Wigan, for example – were to take place in the evening, outside working hours.[168] Such daytime meetings as were organised did not really break this pattern. In Bristol, for instance, the slogan 'All out on May Day!' heralded an evening rally at the Horsefair which was presumably 'secondary and supplementary' to the one in the afternoon – of 'housewives, shop assistants and unemployed'. The same sort of thing happened at Leeds, while in Southampton nothing at all had been arranged and local Communists were merely urged to take part in the official demonstration the following Sunday. In South Wales, where May Day was traditionally a workers' holiday but had been postponed with the consent of the Federation,[169] government investigators kept their eyes open for Communist activities but 'failed to find any evidence of meetings and processions organised on May Day'.[170] In Glasgow too, where the Trades Council was subject to a strong Communist influence and had issued a May Day statement pledging itself 'to intensify the struggle against Capitalist oppression, poverty and war', the Labour Day activities took place, with full and prominent Communist participation, on the Sunday.[171] In most towns and cities the Party's instructions to come out during working hours, alone if necessary, were ignored.

There were a couple of exceptions to the general trend. Heavily publicised in the *Daily Worker* was the refusal of the Lanarkshire Miners' Union, unlike the SWMF, to abandon the tradition of holding its Gala Day on 1 May. In London, too, Communists held their customary rally in Hyde Park, despite the Home Office ban on political processions in the metropolis. About three thousand Communists and sympathisers (the *Worker*'s figure) assembled in Chenies Street and made their way to Hyde Park in groups, thereby sidestepping government restrictions. It is impossible to say how many of the demonstrators were industrial workers, but whatever the figure it was a minute proportion of the 98,000 workers officially represented on the First of May Committee.[172] Surreptitiously, the Party leadership itself had consigned its May Day instructions to a King Street wastepaper bin. Pollitt, Gallacher and Campbell, three great crowd-drawing orators, went up to Scotland to address mass meetings for May Day; but these meetings took place on the evening of 30 April and the evening of 1 May. In between, the crowds they pulled in were free to go about their normal jobs of work.

The only British demonstration to attract widespread notice was that in Oxford, where the marchers were assailed by hooligan students, many of them stationed in the colleges that overlook the streets in that town. One is glad to report that the students did not escape entirely unscathed:

> All the right-wing students had bloody great big boiling pots and rotten tomatoes and Christ knows what. Murder it was. Never seen so much food in my life. That was because we had a May Day march in the town while the war was on. I'll never forget, we'd told everybody not to break the ranks and we was going past Longwall and somebody threw a ruddy apple or something and it hit old Jock Villiamuir. He was a stocky Scotch lad and it hit him in the eye and he went across and hit this bloke and damn near killed him. Once or twice there was almost a break in the ranks. People like Pat Mills were involved in it. He fought a world championship, eliminators, boxing and that you know. Pat got involved in one or two things there.[173]

It was, of course, the students' behaviour which aroused such interest in the national press. Of greater concern to us here is the fact that the demonstration, although labelled 'Communist' by the press, was organised by the local Trades Council and took place in the evening. Oxford Communists preferred to march along with the rest of the local Labour movement, as they had done in previous years, than to strike out on their own during the day. Moreover, in following this course they were quite prepared to play down their opposition to the war. Presumably with the objective of allowing Communist and Labour Party speakers to mingle amicably on the same platform, the Oxford Trades Council had laid it down that speeches at the demonstration should 'be kept to one subject (May Day as it affects Industrial Workers)'.[174] The Communists showed their commitment to this sort of unity with social-democratic lick-spittles by withdrawing those of their banners 'which might be provocative' at the behest of Labour Party officials.[175] Rather than jeopardise their political alliances and mass contacts by the flamboyant gesture recommended in the *Party Organiser*, Oxford Communists played – or at least tried to play – a relatively inconspicuous part in the activities of the wider Labour movement.

Clearly, the events of May Day 1940 show that Communists were unable to 'raise economic and sectional demands to the plane of political struggle'; and, because they knew they were unable to do this, most Communists did not even try. This failure to attempt the impossible revealed the huge divide between the extravagant formulae which the Party photocopied from Comintern pronouncements and the down-to-earth political analysis which guided, if only implicitly, its day-to-day activities. This in itself was just a reflection of the discrepancy between the realities of British politics and revolutionary hopes and expectations which bore little relationship to reality. The politics of the Communist Party can only be understood in terms of the tension between the two sides of this divide, the thesis and antithesis which failed to produce a synthesis. But it would be too easy to picture this divide as one between the deracinated ideologues of King Street, on the one hand, and the mass of unprofessional revolutionaries rooted in the working class on the other. If the Party leadership seriously envisaged May Day 1940 as a 'red letter day in the history of the British workers', then why was Pollitt not billed to speak at demonstrations in Birmingham or Manchester that Wednesday afternoon? And why not Gallacher on Glasgow Green, and J. R. Campbell or Isabel Brown in some other great industrial centre? May Day 1940 revealed the complexity of the interrelationship between myth and reality in Communist Party politics.

6.9 Electoral contests

> seven hundred or a thousand votes in a by-election, cast in war-time for a clear anti-imperialist programme, bear the same relation to ten thousand votes cast for a turgid mass of hypocritical phrases about fighting Hitlerism or a war for a new world, that gold bears to lead . . .
>
> (E. M. Winterton, June 1940[176])

Fortunately for its self-respect, the CP has never made a fetish of electoral success. Nevertheless, it regarded electoral contests as an important, if dispensable, means of taking its political message to the great mass of the population whose political curiosity is briefly awakened by the fleeting exercise of popular sovereignty. Following its decision to oppose the war, the CP abandoned the tactic of supporting Labour candidates in Parliamentary elections and resolved instead to promote its own candidates and support acceptable 'progressive' candidates.[177] To the campaigns which resulted from this decision, the Party devoted considerable time, effort and money with indifferent results. An attempt at a psephological analysis of this handful of results would be futile, but, thanks largely to the extensive Mass-Observation files on four of these campaigns, a study of these by-elections provides us with a fascinating glimpse of Communist Party politics at this time.[178] Most striking, perhaps, is the way in which the Party presented its anti-war policies not in Leninist terms, but as the authentic expression of the traditions of British Labour.

The first wartime election in which the Party was involved was that at Stretford in December 1939.[179] Because of the failure of the CP and the ILP to reach agreement on a joint candidature, two anti-war Socialists – Eric Gower for the CP and Bob Edwards for the ILP – entered the contest. However, these rivals for the anti-government vote wasted little time attacking each other. Instead, each staked his claim as the legitimate representative of Labour in a contest from which official Labour was excluded by the electoral truce. Gower was well chosen for his part for, as his election address pointed out, he stood as a 'lifelong Trade Unionist, Co-operator and worker in the Labour Movement'. His local experience included his Labour candidature for the Exchange division of Manchester in 1931 and a spell as full-time Secretary of the Manchester Borough Labour Party. As recently as July 1939 he had been the prospective Labour candidate for Stretford, and made no secret of the fact:

> I stand not only as a Communist, but as the candidate selected by the Labour Party and endorsed by the National Executive Committee.
>
> It is not so much that I have changed my views; it is the Labour Party leaders who have thrown Socialism overboard.[180]

Declarations of support from the local Labour movement were sought to substantiate Gower's claim to represent 'the whole Labour and progressive movement in the Stretford constituency',[181] while on his election bills he apparently presented himself not as the candidate of the Communist Party but as 'Labour Candidate for Stretford, 1938-39'.[182]

The drawback of this slightly disingenuous approach to the electorate was that the distinctiveness of the Communist Party and its policies seldom emerged. Gower's aim was to gloss over political differences and thereby capitalise on the absence of a Labour candidate and popular discontent with the government. His election address contained nothing which might have alienated non-Communist opponents of the war, but merely listed traditional demands for peace and better living standards. Socialism was briefly mentioned, not as the way out of the war but as the vague aspiration common to many political tendencies, including the 'Labourism' of Transport House. His campaign was addressed to all those who, 'whatever their political faith', wished for 'peace and a better life for the common people'. However, two sizeable obstacles stood in the way of Gower's being accepted as the non-partisan representative of democratic opinion.

The first was the candidature of Bob Edwards, a forceful speaker with a long record of activity for the ILP in Lancashire. Like Gower, Edwards claimed the support of many members of the Labour Party, like Gower he dwelt heavily on domestic and social issues, and like Gower too he presented his decision to fight the election as a stand against the drift towards totalitarianism exemplified by the electoral truce. Indeed, the two candidates initially differed only in that Edwards advocated a 'Socialist peace' while Gower favoured the acceptance of Hitler's peace offer. However, halfway through the campaign there arose an issue which set the two candidates apart and presented a second impediment to Gower's electoral strategy: as if indifferent to the result in Stretford, Stalin ordered the invasion of Finland.

Prior to the Finnish crisis, Gower had chosen not to make an issue of Soviet policy, mentioning it only incidentally in his address. Presumably it was felt that a discussion of recent Soviet actions would kindle the sort of political differences which Gower was more inclined to ignore than overcome. But with the invasion of Finland these questions could no longer be avoided. Like some buffoon, William Rust rejoiced that 'from Northern Europe there comes a freshening wind which blows sharply through the constituency, wiping away the cobwebs of apathy and whipping up a rosy confidence on the faces of the campaigners'.[183] In reality, of course, the Communists were confronted with a popular mood of Russophobia unknown in years, and rosy-cheeked Communist campaigners were greeted with cries of 'you bloody bastards!'[184] Gower and his helpers attempted to stem this torrent of criticism by circulating a leaflet in which Dutt gave the Communist version of events in Finland, but the breeze from the North proved too bracing for many of Gower's supporters, as a 'prominent Communist worker' admitted after the poll:

> Until the Russian–Finnish situation developed we had crowded meetings and support was promised from every direction. When the Russian–Finnish trouble broke we were deserted.

This comment requires some qualification. There were very few crowded meetings because of the blackout, while Gower was not completely deserted but obtained just over fifteen hundred votes. The result was nevertheless a disappointment, not least because Bob Edwards polled three times as well as the Communist.[185] This disparity was even more striking given the very great imbalance of resources, human and financial, at the two candidates' disposal.[186] The CP later acknowledged that Finland had been an electoral liability, but it tended to see the problem in purely organisational terms.[187] In fact, it was basically political. Little separated Gower and Edwards except the word *Communist*; and, no matter how sparingly Gower used the word, nor how temperate his pronouncements, this was enough to deter potential supporters as the Red Army advanced clumsily into Finland. Perhaps this was appreciated in King Street, for at its next electoral contest the Party took its anonymity a stage further.

In February 1940 the people of Central Southwark were offered an intriguing choice of candidates for the right to represent them in Parliament.[188] The least interesting of them was J. H. Martin, a local Labour councillor of orthodox views. Against him stood Mrs Violet Van der Elst, an Independent National candidate of independent means and, very emphatically, 'a thorough Englishwoman' with 'no foreign blood'. Smothered in furs and bedecked with jewels, this gifted lady – 'a composer of 60 pieces of music – preludes, symphonies, nocturnes, etc., an author and portrait painter' – presented herself as the 'WORKERS' CHAMPION' to this overwhelmingly working-class constituency. The third claimant to this title was another Labour councillor, Charlie Searson, who stood in defiance of Transport House as a Labour Anti-War candidate. It was to Searson that the CP gave its enthusiastic backing.

For a few weeks, the *Daily Worker* almost took on the appearance of a Searson Election Special. On several occasions, Communists in London were instructed to 'set aside other jobs that they may have in order to give the maximum assistance to Councillor Searson'.[189] In response, they descended on Southwark in hordes; at one of Searson's three committee rooms the number of helpers rose from six at the beginning of the campaign to over three hundred at the end. Messages of support arrived from a number of leading Communists as well as the CP's Central Committee. Searson himself, though, was not a Communist, and some of his helpers expressed doubts as to his political reliability, though without showing much concern. 'Anyway', said one, 'all his canvassers are party, so what they're really getting is the party line. A victory will mean a victory for the Party line.'

The Party's aim in concealing its identity behind the bespectacled façade of Councillor Searson was to build up a broad anti-war movement encompassing left-wingers within the Labour Party as well as without:

> In his support have rallied two Labour Councillors, ex-Mayors of Southwark; eight prominent clergymen; 12 trade union branches, the Bermondsey Trades Council, the local Communist Party, influential members of the Bermondsey Labour Party, the Labour League of Youth, and Young Communist League.
> This is the beginning of a real united front of the working-class movement against the war.[190]

Such claims played a prominent part in the contest between Searson and Martin as to which of them should be accepted as the genuine voice of Labour. Martin, predictably, derided Searson as 'one of Stalin's stooges', a mere tool of the Communists. Indignantly, Searson denounced the 'conspiracy to tie a red label' on him, claiming to draw support not just from the Communists but from the Labour rank and file, ten of whom had signed his nomination papers. Searson's canvassers were instructed to tell voters that they were campaigning for 'the official candidate of the local Labour organisations which have condemned the war as an imperialist war', a trade unionist of forty-nine years standing and a Labour councillor for eleven. It was, said Dutt, the Transport House candidate who sought to disrupt the Labour movement, while Searson stood for 'working-class unity against those who are seeking to split the workers' ranks for the sake of the alliance with capitalism and war'.[191] One of Searson's leaflets made the same point more pithily:

> Central Southwark is a Labour Seat. Then why give it to Chamberlain's Candidate?
> Keep it LABOUR by Voting SEARSON ON FEB. 10th 1940.

One consequence of this rivalry between avowedly Labour candidates was that the war emerged as the main issue separating them, the question on which the electorate were invited to pass judgement. This was certainly the emphasis put forward by Searson's canvassers, as this typical doorstep encounter shows:

there's Martin, the Labour chap put up by Transport House, and Searson, the official Labour stop-the-war candidate. It rests with you whether you want to stop the war or not.

Not surprisingly, Mass-Observers found that Searson's supporters were attracted primarily by his opposition to the war: 'anything to stop the war', as one said. And indeed, 'anything to stop the war' was about the sum total of Searson's ideas on the subject.

In the attempt to build up an anti-war movement so extensive that the leaders of the Labour Party would appear as disruptive elements, the CP chose to harness vaguely pacifist sentiments rather than insist on a distinctive Communist solution to the crisis. Thus, for example, Searson's election literature included a warning from twenty-four preachers that the war was 'God's judgement on the nations for their refusal to order their economic and political life according to His just laws' and urging an immediate peace. In another leaflet, an 'old soldier' depicted the horrors of the trenches in graphic, indeed lurid, terms. 'I am not concerned with the political side of the Election', he went on, 'but only with what is likely to happen to you and your lads who are, or will be, compelled to go into the armed forces. . . . Don't be misled by the politicians and politics. *USE YOUR COMMON SENSE AND VOTE FOR SEARSON the Labour "STOP-THE-WAR" CANDIDATE.*' Searson himself, although he occasionally invoked the 'International Solidarity of the workers of Germany and Britain' as the guarantee of Socialism and a lasting peace, seems to have held similar beliefs. From a platform shared by leading London Communists, he introduced a seasonal note into his campaign:

> Spring is usually a time we look to with the flowers and the trees, but now we have to look for a rain of bombs that will make our homes a shambles . . . the time to talk of peace is now. . . . I do not go all the way with Sir Arthur Salter but I do agree with him when he says that a Round Table in which America and the Pope helped would bring peace by negotiation.

The war is God's judgement, don't be misled by politics, the Pope and America, the trees and flowers of Southwark. . . . Thus was the message of the Communist Party submerged in a welter of pacifism. The Party's own statements on the war were ambiguous enough, but the decision to link arms with such a disparate collection of anti-war elements meant that even these were lost in a cacophony of discontent from which only one word stood out: peace.

Whether in spite or because of this, Searson secured a respectable level of support – a fifth of a low poll as against two-thirds for Martin.[192] Although only just enough to beat the inimitable Mrs Van der Elst into third place, this was a big improvement on Stretford, for which a number of reasons might be suggested. Searson himself was well known locally, having even given his name to a block of council flats, and he obtained some of his support from personal sympathisers. However, this was possibly offset by the rumours going round the constituency that Searson had not only made a mint out of the First World War but ran a local firm which, even as he campaigned, was eagerly tendering for war work. No more helpful to Searson's case was the revelation in Martin's literature that he had applied unsuccessfully for the Labour nomination before his ambition lured him 'clean into the arms of the Communists'. Perhaps Searson's reasonable showing owed something to the resources the CP threw into the campaign; it provided hundreds of canvassers and 127,500 copies of election literature were distributed.[193] However, it was the plausible view of the Labour agent that the Communists' enthusiastic, intensive and sometimes untimely campaigning aggravated more people than it converted. A more likely explanation is that, despite the efforts of the Labour Party, the Finnish question played an insignificant part in the campaign. Searson himself said little on the subject, although he did warn against British intervention, while some of his Communist supporters were just as fastidious:

> 'Still, we don't want to bring up Finland any more than – I mean, if they start themselves it's different. But most of them just aren't interested. There's no point in going out looking for trouble. . . .'
> 'Of course not.'

Probably most importantly, Searson's call for peace was not related to the question of Communism, as Gower's necessarily had been, if only implicitly. The appeal to loyalty to the principles of the Labour movement came more convincingly from an unofficial Labour candidate than from a Communist; and this, along with the fact that Searson faced no rival for the anti-war vote, probably explains why Gower was unable to profit from the absence of a Labour candidate at Stretford, and yet Searson polled well in opposition to Labour at Southwark.

An especially interesting campaign pitted Harry Pollitt against a Labour candidate and a Fascist at West Ham, Silvertown, in February 1940. As probably the best known Communist in Britain, Pollitt obviously made no secret that his policies were those of the CP. But in presenting these policies Pollitt had first to overcome the deep-rooted loyalty to Labour which prevailed in this dockland seat[194] and was well described by one constituent after the result of the election was announced:

> Well, mate, it's a Labour sort of place, and a working-man is proud to see a Labour MP get so many votes. All a working-man wants to see at an election is a huge Labour majority and a sock in the eye for the outsiders.[195]

In these circumstances, Pollitt chose to present the Communist Party, not as the historically necessary revolutionary party which would supersede the reformist traditions of British Labour, but as the contemporary embodiment of those traditions, long since abandoned by the Labour leadership.

Several times during the campaign Pollitt cast himself in the mould of the 'Labour pioneers'. He respected Silvertown's loyalty to the Labour Party, he said, but true loyalty to the 'grand old fighters who built up the Labour movement' required that a stand be taken against Labour's current policy 'of being hand in glove with the boss class'. Certainly, the most significant accomplishment of the grand old fighters – the assertion of Labour's political and electoral independence – appeared to be in jeopardy in 1940 and Pollitt unblushingly exploited the aura of sanctity surrounding the pioneers to legitimise his own claims to the constituency:

> When in 1895 the first fight for independent Labour representation was made in West Ham, and Keir Hardie was returned as Member, those who fought for Labour never dreamed that the independence of Labour would be thrown away at the very moment it was needed most.
>
> This is why I fight for the policy of the Communist Party – the policy that represents the interests of true Labour.
>
> That is in keeping with what the pioneers had in mind.[196]

Like the Labour candidate, who paraded Ben Tillett on his platform, Pollitt tried to associate himself with the past struggles of the dockers by distributing a leaflet in which the veteran Communist, Tom Mann, recalled his role in the fight for 'the Dockers' Tanner, the building of Trade Unions and the formation of the workers' political Party'. For those whose memories did not stretch as far back as the Dockers' Tanner, Pollitt also made much of his own involvement in the Thames-side Shop Stewards' Movement and the *Jolly George* affair.[197] However, such claims did little to erode Silvertown's fidelity to Labour and Pollitt obtained a paltry 966 votes. Over 14,000 voters felt that Alderman Hollins, a councillor for the past twenty-six years and the Labour election agent for more than twenty, spoke with the authentic voice of Labour.[198]

The other interesting feature of Pollitt's campaign was his failure to address the issue of the war directly. So acute an observer as Tom Harrisson felt that 'Pollitt did not *in fact* run on a stop-the-war policy', and he produced statistical evidence to support this claim: 'while the Fascist devoted 17% of his space to stop-the-war, the Communist had only 3% stop-the-war material'.[199] Pollitt's line of opposition to the war was more oblique than, say, Searson's in three ways. First, insofar as he discussed international issues, he tended to concentrate on the imminent danger of British intervention in Finland; this was the significance of his harking back to the *Jolly George* episode. Secondly, Pollitt took an emphatically anti-Fascist stance, arguing that the German people, not Chamberlain, were Hitler's real enemies: *'Chamberlain will no more hang Hitler than Lloyd George hanged the Kaiser.'* His literature, notably a message of support from the International Brigade, made much of Chamberlain's collusion with Fascism in Spain, against which it set Pollitt's consistent anti-Fascism.[200] Lastly, Pollitt exhibited the trait we have characterised as 'economism'; he deplored the social hardships arising from the war without relating them to the war itself. Thus did Pollitt produce a remarkable leaflet on the *Altmark* incident which managed to reduce one of the very few acts of belligerency during the Phoney War to a question of wage rates and working conditions in the shipping industry.[201] No doubt Pollitt felt it impolitic to repeat the pro-Nazi interpretations of the incident which were being expounded in the *Daily Worker*. It was because Pollitt's opposition to the war was so muted, thought Harrisson, that he failed to poll as well as Searson in Southwark.

Whatever the explanation, and Harrisson's seems unlikely, Pollitt's poor showing was a great disappointment. Not only was Pollitt the CP's most charismatic spokesman, but the Party had been preparing to fight the seat 'over a long period' in anticipation of a by-election. Indeed, Ted Bramley had been nursing the constituency for five years and Communists had previously polled well in local council elections.[202] Moreover, Pollitt distributed a staggering amount of election material: 257,500 copies of twelve pieces of literature, or 266 copies for each vote he received. This was money down the drain. On polling day, Mass-Observation asked 100 voters which leaflet they liked best: 27 didn't remember any leaflet, 19 weren't interested in any leaflet, 17 didn't look at any leaflet and 10 didn't know or couldn't think. Four of them thought Pollitt's leaflets the best.[203] The personal touch was not necessarily more effective. While 'our strongest points were the energy and devotion of our comrades', David Springhall reflected, 'our weakness was lack of ability to talk to the ordinary men and women in the way that would reach them'.[204] In fact, the comrades' energy and devotion were probably excessive, for there was a point at which intensive canvassing became counter-productive:

> You're Communist, aren't you? It's always the Communists round worrying about something. It don't help anybody. Who d'you think I am, the Government? Go and tell *them* to stop the war; *I* didn't start it.

Impervious to any such moods of fatalism, Communists acted as if the movement against the government would be built up in proportion to the effort they put into the task.²⁰⁵ In fact, as Pollitt's meagre poll showed, the working class was largely unresponsive to Communist propaganda, no matter how much of it was stuffed through their letter boxes.

Eric Joyce's campaign as Labour Stop-the-War candidate in Battersea North in April 1940 shared many of the features of the campaigns already described.²⁰⁶ Joyce's election machine was basically that of Searson and Pollitt, so poorly concealed that the second 'T' in Pollitt was left exposed when Joyce's name was superimposed on his election posters. Joyce's policies were those of the CP and, echoing Pollitt, he claimed to 'carry on Battersea's Labour traditions' and called on the shades of John Burns and of Saklatvala, one-time Communist MP for the constituency. Similarly, he distributed a clerical message of support of almost identical wording to that used by Searson. However, Joyce laboured under several disadvantages not shared by Searson and Pollitt.

More serious even than the lack of sufficient time and helpers to mount an effective campaign were the widespread doubts as to Joyce's personal and political integrity. Joyce, the Assistant Secretary of the local Labour Party, had actually signed his Labour opponent's nomination papers before deciding to stand himself less than a fortnight before polling day. Worse still, Joyce passed his army medical only the weekend before the election and presented himself as a 'young man of 24 years of age, who is liable for military service in a few weeks time'. Already in Silvertown, Mass-Observers had noted a degree of resentment at the youthfulness of Communist speakers and canvassers, but in Battersea the candidate himself appeared little more than a stripling and, moreover, seemed to many to be seeking a career in Parliament as a way of evading his call-up:

> Joyce ought to be fighting for his country. He's just out to dodge conscription. I heard him the other night talking about 'our experience of the last war' – 'our' experience indeed! (Man of 70.)

> Why should my son fight and Joyce get off because he can talk himself into Parliament? (Woman of 40.)

Matters were aggravated by the extension of the war to Denmark and Norway during the campaign. Although this seemed only to confirm the CP's forebodings and predictions, the intensification of the war was felt by his agent to harm Joyce's chances. The extension of the war had two effects, equally damaging to Joyce's hopes. Among many it engendered a mood of fatalism, a belief that the war could not now be stopped and that it was futile for Joyce to wish to do so. In other cases it exacerbated the resentment felt at Joyce's candidature, and manifestations of public hostility ensued; angry constituents slapped his face and on at least one occasion his platform was broken up by abusive women denouncing him as a malingerer. Given all this, it is perhaps surprising that Joyce polled as well as he did: 791 votes, as against nearly 10,000 for the official Labour candidate.[207]

The last of the by-elections saw Isabel Brown challenge the Labour nominee at Bow and Bromley in June 1940. The vacancy had arisen on the death of George Lansbury, the revered Socialist who had represented the constituency for eighteen years.[208] Lansbury's artless pacifism, which had led him into well-meaning dialogues with the likes of Hitler, had at one time been anathema to the CP. However, there was no sense in letting the late Member's constituents know this for, according to a Labour canvasser, 'they were all very fond of G.L. You've only got to mention George Lansbury to them, and you've got them.' It was on this principle that Brown ran her campaign.

At the very beginning of the campaign Brown was advertised as 'a candidate who personifies all the peace principles of the late member' and thenceforth Lansbury's name was continually on the tongues and nibs of Communists.[209] To give flesh and blood to her claims, Brown enlisted the support of Lansbury's daughter, Violet, wife of Clemens Dutt and organiser of the *Daily Worker* Fighting Fund, who 'as a supporter of the Communist Party and its struggle for peace to the peoples . . . carries on the finest traditions of her father'.[210] Apparently, Lansbury might even have stood herself but for the fear of gaining an unfair personal vote and confusing the issue with pacifism. She might just as well have stood. At one meeting to which she addressed 'a short and very emotional speech about her aims and her father's aims' the audience soon became divided between 'whole-hearted sympathy and whole-hearted antagonism' until, such was the commotion, Lansbury had to leave the platform 'amid violent cheers and shouting'. Meanwhile, 'George Lansbury and what he might have done, and what he would say if he were brought out of the grave were discussed over and over again'. In Brown's election literature, too, the younger Lansbury made every effort to provide Brown's candidature with the posthumous endorsement of her father.

The irony was that by this time the CP's policies bore little resemblance to the woolly-minded pacifism of Lansbury, or of Searson for that matter; so much so that one Labour canvasser assumed that the CP no longer opposed the war at all and was now simply 'squabbling over little things that could be much more easily fought out a different way'. The CP's new stance will be described in the following chapter. Here we need only point out that the Party no longer favoured an immediate peace. At one meeting Brown was asked whether she adhered to the 'Communist policy of Stop-the-war':

When in all my speeches have I said 'stop-the-war' – like that. . . . Who in this audience has heard me say 'stop the war' (in a very feeble and meaningless tone)? (Laughter, 'you didn't'. 'It isn't true.')

Lenin has said, once you have got into an Imperialist war it is difficult to get out of – we can't promise we could get out of it at once – First step to getting out of it is by the formation of a workers govt. Have never suggested just down arms and appeal to Hitler. No surrender to Fascism of any country, either German or British. Workers govt. could appeal over heads of Hitler and Co, to German workers (loud applause). Not immediately successful of course – but would make great impression. . . . Help from Soviet Union would be certain (applause). Find a people's way out of the war (applause).

(Questioner) Then you don't agree with the Communist Party 'Stop the war' . . .

Significantly, Brown's supporters at the polls appear to have had no desire that the war be stopped. One, asked about possible conditions for ending the war, replied 'Let it go on.' Another was asked what his main grumble was:

Well, I've got quite a few. Most important, why don't we go out there and have a go at them?

Such evidence cannot be conclusive because there were so few of Brown's supporters to be interviewed – she polled only 506 votes. One problem was again the lack of helpers, but this can only be a very partial explanation for Brown's poll was less than a twentieth of that of her Labour opponent.[211] Despite Communist efforts to the contrary, the people of Bow and Bromley preferred to see Lansbury's red flag in the hands of a Labour man.

These elections tell us a good deal about how the CP presented itself to the British people during these months. Most noticeable, perhaps, is the way in which the Party related itself to the traditions of British Labour, rather than of international Communism, in accordance with its aims of building a broad left movement against the government and the political truce. Also noteworthy was the Party's vacillating attitude towards the war; at times this issue was at the forefront of Communist campaigns, yet at others it was very much subordinate to economic issues or the threat of British intervention in Finland. Even when the issue of the war was faced head-on, the Party's policy of the *main tendue* led it to align itself with near-pacifists, so that the revolutionary way out of the war remained poorly marked. Finally, it is clear that the Party failed to appeal to the majority of the British people, and failed abysmally when it came out in its own colours. Of course, the Party's aim in fighting these elections was not merely to amass the greatest possible number of votes. Signs of electoral pragmatism were not entirely absent, but significantly, whereas Labour canvassers were instructed simply to record voting intentions ('Do not argue with opponents. Politely pass on.'), Communist canvassers were given detailed lists of points to put across on the doorstep.[212] But however much effort was put into this task of mass conversion, the electorates of these constituencies remained largely unresponsive to appeals to stop the war.

However, by the time Isabel Brown came to contest Bow and Bromley, things were beginning to look up, as a conversation between two of her helpers indicates:

> 'It's much easier canvassing here. . . . We haven't got that awful stop the war slogan to put across. . . . It always was a mistake. I thought so at the time . . .'
> 'It was all right at the time . . .'
> 'No, I don't think it was all right at the time. People thought at once that you just meant give in to Hitler . . .'
> 'Well, comrade, you have to explain it of course . . .'
> 'A slogan that needs explaining is a bad slogan. You can take that as a principle. You ought to have had "Workers must end the war". That's quite different, and it's what we really meant. Then we couldn't have got mixed up in people's minds with the Fascists and the pacifists. . . . Anybody who has had to do street work will tell you how much the slogan was worth. . . . It's just been a mill-stone round our necks . . .'

It is to the lifting of this millstone that we turn in the next chapter.

Notes

1. D. Hyde, *I Believed* (1951), 72.
2. Lenin, 'Defeat of one's own government in the imperialist war' (July 1915) in *Selected Works*, vol. 5 (1936), 142.
3. See *Thesis*, 169–70.
4. Hyde, *op. cit.*, 72–8.
5. See e.g. Dutt, *We Fight For Life* (CPGB, 14.11.40), 5–11.
6. V. Gollancz, 'Revolutionary defeatism and its development in CP policy' in Gollancz (ed.), *The Betrayal of the Left* (1941), 115.
7. VG, Gollancz to Hyman Levy, 17.1.41.
8. 'Notes', April 1941, 163.
9. 'The war and Russian Social-Democracy' in *Selected Works*, vol. 5 (1936), 130.
10. Works by Lenin cited in this section are: 'The collapse of the Second International' (1915) in *The War and the Second International* (1934 edn); 'Socialism and war' (1915) in *Lenin on War and Peace* (1970 edn); 'English pacifism and English dislike of theory' (1915) in *Lenin on Britain* (1934); 'Bourgeois pacifism and socialist pacifism' (1917), 'Proposals submitted by the Central Committee of the Russian Social-Democratic Labour Party to the Second Socialist Conference' (1916), 'Conference of the RSDLP abroad' (1915) and 'Defeat of one's own government in the imperialist war' (1915), all in *Selected Works*, vol. 5.
11. The centrist trend consisted of those who stopped short of outright chauvinism, while failing to express a revolutionary policy towards the war or admit the bankruptcy of the Second International.

12 'Notes', Aug. 1940, 420.
13 Dutt himself used these very words; see RPD K4, 'Main Issues for political report to the congress' (i.e. of CPGB London District), 20.1.40.
14 *Our Youth*, Jan. 1940, 18.
15 W. Gallacher, *The Revolt on the Clyde* (1941 edn), 221.
16 W. Hannington, *Industrial History in Wartime* (1940).
17 Gallacher, *op. cit.*, 116.
18 J. Hinton, *The First Shop Stewards' Movement* (1973), 241.
19 *Ibid.*, 263.
20 R. P. Arnot, *Twenty Years. The Policy of the Communist Party of Great Britain from its Foundation July 31st 1920* (1940), 9.
21 For which a number of reasons may be suggested. The most obvious is that, during the period in which the CP opposed the war, revolt was clearly not seething everywhere, even though it seethed extensively within the covers of Communist Party pamphlets. Another possible reason is that the CP's industrial militants were more closely integrated into the official trade union movement than were the left-wing stewards of the First World War.
22 *DW*, 17.10.39.
23 *WNV*, 4.11.39, 1,057.
24 Gallacher in the Commons, 3.10.39; 351 *H. C. Deb.*, 1896–1901.
25 E.g. CPGB CC manifesto, *DW*, 7.10.39; Dutt, *Why This War?* (CPGB, 1.11.39), 18.
26 CPGB CC manifesto, *DW*, 7.10.39.
27 Ivor Montagu, *DW*, 18.1.40.
28 Dutt, *op. cit.*, 22–3.
29 See Montagu, *DW*, 18.1.40.
30 *LN*, Dec. 1939, 1,411.
31 Dutt, *op. cit.*, 17.
32 Dutt, speech at *Labour Monthly* conference, 25.2.40, *LM*, Mar. 1940, 138.
33 And very often without even bothering with a revolutionary turn of phrase; see e.g. Pat Sloan's particularly insipid exegesis of Communist policy, and contrast with the ILP's robust case for 'revolutionary socialism', in *LN*, May 1940, 1,487–90.
34 Report to CPGB CC, *DW*, 23.11.39; RPD K4, 'Main issues for political report to the congress', i.e. of CPGB London District, 20.1.40.
35 CPGB PB statement, *DW*, 16.3.40.
36 This paragraph is drawn from *Thesis*, 188–93.
37 Rust, report to CPGB CC, *DW*, 20.12.39.
38 Statement by Scottish ILP, *New Leader*, 4.4.40.
39 Report by R. Goodman, *WNV*, 13.4.40, 224–5.
40 P. Kerrigan, *The New Stage of the War* (CPGB, 19.4.40), 12.
41 CPGB CC manifesto, *DW*, 7.10.39.
42 *DW*, 2.11.39, echoing a statement by Molotov reported in the same issue.
43 *DW*, 1.2.40.
44 E.g. *DW*, 14.11.39.
45 Dutt, *DW*, 1.12.39; I. Montagu, *WNV*, 20.1.40, 36–7.
46 Leningrad lay less than twenty miles from the Soviet border with Finland. Subsequently the Finnish armed forces took part in the German attack on the USSR.
47 CPGB PB statement, *DW*, 16.3.40.
48 See e.g. *DW*, 19.2.40.
49 John Strachey in *New Statesman and Nation*, 27.4.40, 559.
50 CPGB PB statement, *DW*, 10.4.40.

51 *DW*, 12.4.40. For a presentation of some of the more offensive material appearing in the *Worker* at this time, see V. Gollancz, 'Where are you going?' in Gollancz, *op. cit.*, 27–34.
52 P. Calvocoressi and G. Wint, *Total War* (1974 edn), 107.
53 Gollancz, *op. cit.*
54 *New Statesman and Nation*, 27.4.40, 559.
55 *DW*, 11.4.40, 13.4.40, 22.4.40; RPD K4, CPGB Secretariat to Ted Bramley, 12.4.40; 'The new stage of the war and the campaign against the Party', 23.4.40.
56 M-O TC 46/6, report from committee rooms of Eric Joyce, Labour Anti-War candidate in the Battersea North by-election, 14.4.40.
57 German YCL statement, *DW*, 20.4.40. Gollancz made some telling points about this inconsistency, *op. cit.*, 17–26, 37–9, 302–10.
58 RPD K4, 'The new stage of the war . . .'; CP Secretariat to Bramley, 12.4.40; Dutt to W. H. Thompson, 19.5.40.
59 Frank Pitcairn, *DW*, 13.4.40.
60 RPD K4, Dutt to Thompson, 19.5.40.
61 'The capitalists are the cause of this war, let them pay for it. It's their luxury not the working man's'; Notts miner's letter to *DW*, 26.3.40.
62 *DW*, 30.10.39.
63 P. Kerrigan, 'The workers' counter-offensive', *LM*, Mar. 1940, 157.
64 'Revolutionary defeatism and its development in CP policy' in Gollancz (ed.), *The Betrayal of the Left* (1941), 137, 141–2.
65 R. P. Arnot, *Twenty Years* (1940), 16.
66 E.g. Rust, *DW*, 13.11.39; 'Notes', Dec. 1939, 711–12.
67 Gallacher, *The War and the Workers* (CPGB, 1.11.39), 4–5.
68 E.g. during the Stretford by-election; *Manchester Guardian*, 7.12.39.
69 *DW*, 24.1.40, 25.1.40. *Wages are in Peril!*, CPGB leaflet, Jan. 1940 (WCML). It should be pointed out that in the Party's theoretical journal Peter Kerrigan (*op. cit.*) put the campaign in a much broader perspective.
70 Report to CPGB CC, *DW*, 23.1.40.
71 Speech to CPGB London District congress, *DW*, 29.1.40.
72 Dutt, report to CPGB CC, *DW*, 16.2.40.
73 RPD K4, draft political letter, 'The new stage of the war and the campaign against the Party', 23.4.40.
74 'Draft discussion statement' for CPGB London District congress, 26.1.40–28.1.40, 4–5, 7, 15 (WCML).
75 *DW*, 7.2.40.
76 Gollancz read a lot into such headlines, *op. cit.*, 137–8.
77 Conference report, *LM*, Mar. 1940, 131–49.
78 *Daylight on Saturday* (1943), 3.
79 T. Wintringham, *The Coming World War* (1936 edn), 212.
80 See R. Croucher, *Engineers at War* (1982), 40–2; E. and R. Frow, *Engineering Struggles. Episodes in the Story of the Shop Stewards' Movement* (1982), ch. 4.
81 Croucher gives figures of 14,000 in August 1937 and 20,000 in October 1938; *op. cit.*, 41. By April 1939 a figure of 27,000 was claimed; *NP*, May 1939, 1.
82 See Thesis, 216–17.
83 See e.g. J. Fyrth, *The Signal was Spain* (1986), ch. 17.
84 This was in fact much less true of some issues, like rearmament, than of others, like Spain; see Thesis, 128–9 for confirmation.
85 Croucher, *op. cit.*, 43–5.

86 *DW*, 27.1.39; see Fyrth, *loc. cit.*
87 *NP*, Sept. 1939, 1, 11.
88 *NP*, May 1940, 1.
89 PRO CAB. 98.18, Memorandum by Home Secretary, 17.1.41. In fact by this time it would have been more accurate to say that the *Propellor* contained no direct references to *opposition* to the war; see pp. 225–36.
90 The conference resolution can be found in *LM*, May 1940, 316–18.
91 See pp. 199–200.
92 *AEU Monthly Journal*, Feb. 1940, 50–1.
93 Circular letter from Fred Smith, AEU General Secretary, 6.12.39 (WCML).
94 They included Joe Scott, Charlie Wellard, George Crane and Eddie Frow; for an account of this episode, see Frow, *op. cit.*, 147–8.
95 Almost a third of the votes on the second ballot; *AEU Monthly Journal*, July 1940, 217.
96 For the Convention, see pp. 201–13.
97 Interview.
98 Interview.
99 Interview.
100 Interview.
101 W. Paynter, *My Generation* (1972), 109.
102 Two 'red' unions were formed at this time, the United Mineworkers of Scotland and the United Clothing Workers' Union.
103 CPGB PB statement on Horner, *Communist Review*, Apr. 1931, 146–8, 155.
104 *DW*, 23.2.32.
105 See J. T. Murphy, *Preparing for Power* (1972 edn), 156–7.
106 Paynter cited by H. Francis and D. Smith, *The Fed. A History of the South Wales Miners in the Twentieth Century* (1980), 34.
107 *DW*, 30.4.31.
108 Francis and Smith, *op. cit.*, 261–2, 273; H. Francis, *Miners Against Fascism* (1984), 113–15.
109 *Ibid.*, ch. 7 and *passim*.
110 Including the Executive Council on which there sat 'several' Communists, while 'several other ... members, who were in the Labour Party, had sympathies that lay in that direction'; S. Broomfield, 'South Wales during the Second World War. The coal industry and its community' (Ph.D., Wales, 1979), 90. This should be borne in mind when we consider the war period.
111 *It Can Be Done* (CPGB, report of 14th Congress, 1937), 166–8.
112 C. Parry, letter, *DW*, 17.8.38.
113 Howell D. Williams of Aberdare, letter, *DW*, 3.8.38.
114 J. L. Hodson, *Towards the Morning* (1941), 90.
115 Horner, *Address* to SWMF annual conference, Apr. 1940 (SWMF, 1940), 3–4.
116 Horner, speech at *Daily Worker* conference at Pontypridd, *DW*, 4.12.39.
117 Horner, *Incorrigible Rebel* (1960), 125–6. Horner, as a matter of fact, opposed the call for a token strike in support of Spain; Francis, *op. cit.*, 148–52.
118 Horner, *Incorrigible Rebel*, 125–6.
119 See Francis and Smith, *op. cit.*, especially ch. 9.
120 For these negotiations see R. P. Arnot, *The Miners: One Union, One Industry* (1979), 16–24.
121 8*d* (men) and 4*d* (boys) instead of 1*s* and 6*d*.
122 SWMF EC minutes 20.10.39, special conference minutes, 21.10.39.

123 *Manchester Guardian*, 26.10.39.
124 *Special National Conference on Wages. Speech by Mr Arthur Horner* (SWMF, 1939), 3–4.
125 *DW*, 28.10.39.
126 The title of an article of his, *LM*, Nov. 1939, 655–65.
127 See Horner's *Address* to 1940 SWMF conference, 6.
128 Horner, *Incorrigible Rebel*, 162.
129 Broomfield, *op. cit.*, 581.
130 See RPD K5, CPGB CC, letter 'To all districts' on the Paris trial, 29.3.40, cited *Thesis*, 246.
131 *Western Mail*, 24.2.40, 27.2.40, 29.2.40.
132 *Western Mail*, 24.2.40.
133 *Western Mail*, 28.2.40.
134 SWMF special conference minutes, 17.2.40, 2.3.40; *Western Mail*, 4.3.40.
135 *DW*, 26.4.40.
136 Broomfield, *op. cit.*, 607.
137 *Loc. cit.*; *Western Mail*, 24.2.40.
138 *Western Mail*, 30.5.40, 1.6.40.
139 *Western Mail*, 17.6.40.
140 *PO*, May 1940, 8–9.
141 *PO*, June 1940, 8–10.
142 The following paragraphs are based on material in the George Thomas papers (SWCA). Detailed references are provided in *Thesis*, 247.
143 J. T. Murphy in 1919 in K. Coates and T. Topham, *Workers' Control* (1970), 81–2.
144 See A. Gramsci, *Selections from Political Writings 1910–1920* (1977), 98–102, 109–13, 265–8.
145 See G. Matthews, 'British students on the move', *LM*, May 1940, 307–11. The resolution was not binding on the NUS.
146 Margot Kettle, interview.
147 L. Morris and R. Radford, *The Story of the Artists International Association 1933–1953* (1983), 55–67.
148 'Notes', Jan. 1940, 3, 6.
149 *DW*, 29.1.40.
150 I.e. Horner.
151 One occasion when this was not possible was the *Daily Worker* libel case of April–May 1940. See especially the evasive and inconsistent testimony of Ben Francis; *Citrine and Others v. Pountney. The Daily Worker Libel Case* (Modern Books, 1940), 38.
152 P. Addison, *The Road to 1945* (1977 edn), 70; A. J. P. Taylor, *English History 1914–1945* (1970 edn), 571.
153 Quaestor, 'New fronts for old', *LM*, Feb. 1940, 83–8; I. Montagu, 'The truth about Finland', *LM*, Jan. 1940, 15–28.
154 *DW*, 8.12.39.
155 E. Burns, *The Soviet Union and Finland* (CPGB, 5.1.40), 15–16; see also e.g. CPGB PB resolution, *DW*, 24.2.40.
156 RPD K4, 'Draft supplementary report of the Central Committee', 8.1.40.
157 *Poetry and the People*, May 1940, 2–3.
158 See Pollitt, 'After six months – what now?', *LM*, Apr. 1940, 217.
159 J. Ellerbe, 'May First. A day of challenge' in *May Day 1936* (All-London First of May Demonstration Committee, 1936), 3.
160 Although they marched with the official procession in 1938, when 1 May fell on a Sunday.

161 J. Mahon, 'May First, 1938', *Disc.*, Mar. 1938, 26–7; see also his *The Meaning of May Day* (First of May Demonstration Committee, 1940), 5–6. Mahon was the committee's secretary and main spokesman.
162 CPGB London DC letter on 'preparations for May First 1940 based on the experiences of 1939' to 'all DPC Members and Industrial Leaderships', n.d. (MML).
163 CPGB PB statement, *DW*, 16.3.40.
164 *DW*, 1.5.40; *WNV*, 4.5.40, 261–3; Dimitrov, *ibid.*, 264–5.
165 CPGB CC manifesto, *DW*, 27.4.40.
166 CPGB Secretariat, *PO*, Apr. 1940, 3–6.
167 J. Mahon, *The Meaning of May Day* (written after 7 April); see also *DW*, 13.4.40.
168 Subsequent references to *DW*, 1.5.40, 2.5.40, 3.5.40 unless stated.
169 Broomfield, *op. cit.*, 53–4.
170 PRO INF 1/319, Welsh RIO to Home Intelligence, 7.5.40. Apparently, even the meetings held in South Wales the following Sunday 'were not markedly communistic in character; only Mr. Harry Pollitt . . . seems to have expressed anti-war views. Mr. Arthur Horner, another communist . . . was more general and non-committal than Mr. Pollitt.'
171 *Glasgow Labour Day 1940* (Glasgow Trades Council programme, 1940), 1–3. The CP itself organised a meeting in Glasgow on the evening of 1 May.
172 'Memorandum of the First of May Committee to the Home Office', 29.4.40 (MML).
173 Norman Brown, interview.
174 Oxford Trades Council minutes, 11.4.40.
175 Oxford City Labour Party General Council minutes, organiser's statement, 9.5.40.
176 ' "Left" intellectuals and the war', *LM*, June 1940, 359.
177 CPGB CC statement on 'The Communist Party and the Labour Party', *LM*, Dec. 1939, 759–60.
178 Except where otherwise stated, this section is based on material to be found in M-O TC 46/3 (Central Southwark), 46/4 (Silvertown), 46/6 (Battersea North) and 46/8 (Bow and Bromley). These fascinating files comprise election literature, press cuttings, canvassers' reports, interviews with candidates, agents, helpers, constituents etc. The account of the Stretford election, on which there is no M-O file, is drawn from the local press, the CP and ILP press and an interview with Bob Edwards. Full references will be found in *Thesis*, 282–6. The one relevant by-election not discussed here is that in Kettering in March 1940 at which Councillor William Ross, standing as a 'Workers' and Pensioners' Anti-War Candidate', polled over a quarter of the vote against a Tory opponent.
179 Stretford was a scattered and diverse constituency on the west side of Manchester which included Trafford Park, where the CP was firmly established, and a number of pits. Labour had never won the seat. In 1935 it gained 35.6% of the poll in a straight fight against a Tory.
180 *DW*, 27.11.39.
181 *DW*, 7.12.39.
182 J. McNair, *New Leader*, 1.12.39.
183 *DW*, 4.12.39.
184 Bill Keable in Attfield and Williams, *op. cit.*, 70.
185 Etherton (Cons.) 23,408
    Edwards (ILP) 4,424
    Gower (CP) 1,519 (turnout 36.6%).
186 See *Thesis*, 266–7.
187 See E. Gower and resolution of CPGB Secretariat and Lancashire DC, *PO*, Jan. 1940, 2–5.
188 This was a Labour-held seat in inner London.

189 E.g. *DW*, 4.1.40, 18.1.40, 22.1.40, 25.1.40, 1.2.40, 3.2.40.
190 Ted Bramley, *DW*, 22.1.40.
191 *DW*, 3.2.40.
192 Martin   (Lab.)   5,285
    Searson   (Ind.)   1,550
    Van der Elst (Ind.) 1,382   (turnout 24.7%).
193 M-O FR 39 on Silvertown by-election, 17.
194 Even in 1931 the Labour candidate had obtained 77.8% of the vote, and he improved on this in 1935.
195 Other respondents made similar points: 'We don't want stunt people coming in here. It's a Labour place and we was all brought up Labour.'
196 *DW*, 19.2.40. In fact Hardie was first returned in 1892.
197 See J. Mahon, *Harry Pollitt* (1976), ch. 7.
198 Hollins (Lab.)   14,343
    Pollitt (CP)   966
    Moran (BUF)   151   (turnout 40.1%)
199 M-O FR 39, 20.
200 See also the leaflet reproduced in Attfield and Williams, *op. cit.*, 183.
201 Leaflet reproduced in *Thesis*, 275.
202 *DW*, 9.2.40; Bramley in Attfield and Williams, *op. cit.*, 88.
203 M-O FR 39, 17; *DW*, 24.2.40. The Labour candidate distributed less than a quarter as much literature.
204 *PO*, Mar. 1940, 2.
205 The reasoning was apparently that of the American Communist recalled by Jessica Mitford who 'tended to see everything, causes and results, in simple mathematical terms. If 1,000 leaflets could be said to influence, say, 10 votes in an election campaign, then 100,000 leaflets would bring a corresponding 1,000 votes; by the same reasoning, if we could muster the funds to print a million campaign leaflets . . . the election would be in the bag'; *A Fine Old Conflict* (1977), 73.
206 This constituency returned a Labour MP with 58.7% of the vote in 1935. In the 1920s it had twice been represented by S. Saklatvala, the only Communist MP to be returned at the 1924 election.
207 Douglas (Lab.)   9,947
    Joyce   (Ind.)   791   (turnout 25.1%)
208 In 1935 he had been re-elected with 77% of the poll.
209 E.g. Pat Devine, *DW*, 30.5.40; *DW*, 31.5.40, 8.6.40; Dutt, *DW*, 10.6.40; Brown, *DW*, 14.6.40.
210 *DW*, 31.5.40.
211 Key   (Lab.)   11,594
    Brown (CP)   506   (turnout 32.4%).
212 M-O FR 81 on Battersea North by-election, 23–5.

Chapter seven

From the fall of France to the invasion of the Soviet Union

the CPGB, 1940–41, and some general themes from the 'imperialist war' period

7.1 The 'Party line' turns a circle[1]

> The communist party doesn't seem to have been able to make up its mind, lately.
> (Romford woman's reaction to the CP leaflet *The People Must Act*, 1 July 1940[2])

For the British politicians who evicted Chamberlain from Downing Street, for the British public which generally welcomed the more defiant posture adopted by his successor, and for subsequent historians, the 'phoney war' ended with the German occupation of Denmark and Norway. For British Communists, the decisive turning point came a month or so later, when the Nazi Blitzkrieg swiftly overcame the feeble resistance of France and the Low Countries, leaving thousands of Britons stranded on the shores of Dunkirk.

Even before this, in mid-May, Dutt had acknowledged that Party statements represented 'definitely a new stage in the presentation of our line' and had had the gall to claim that the 'stop-the-war' slogan 'was never at any time the correct presentation of our viewpoint, and only became a label fixed by outsiders to our campaign'.[3] The crucial factor, however, was the ignominious collapse of France which, unlike Denmark and Norway, had previously been portrayed as a vicious predator, not the innocent prey of imperialist war. The CP's depiction of Britain and France as the aggressor powers could not satisfactorily explain the rapidity of the French capitulation to the patently aggressive Germans, while Britain itself, the main promoter of world war, was now faced with the imminent prospect of invasion. Only the width of the English Channel separated Hitler from almost total domination of the West, aggressor powers included. British Communists had no alternative but to re-evaluate the war. This they did in a confused and contradictory fashion.

In June 1941 Dutt argued that the war to that date had consisted of 'two main phases', during the first of which there existed the possibility of a 'general peace' but during the second of which, after the extension of the war to Western Europe, there was no longer available any 'easy temporary solution within the framework of imperialism'.[4] Thus it was that after June 1940 the CP issued no more simplistic demands that the war be ended. Instead it stressed that it found the prospect of a German victory abhorrent and denounced whomsoever it felt favoured a compromise, or capitulatory, peace. Just as unattractive was the thought of a victory for the British ruling class. Over the coming months Britain's rulers were damned both as imperialist warmongers and as traitors who put the interests of their class before those of their country, thereby undermining the popular will to resist Fascism. The CP advocated a struggle against the threat of Fascism both from within Britain and from without, a reversion to a modified policy of a 'war on two fronts' in which, as until September 1939, class issues were tightly intertwined with inter-imperialist antagonisms. Previously the Party had characterised the war as an uncomplicated struggle between rival imperialisms, combined with the threat of an Anglo–French counter-revolutionary war of intervention against the Soviet Union. By mid-1940, however, the talk of the moment was not about whether Britain should go to war with the Soviet Union but about how Soviet support might be enlisted against Germany. Moreover, if the war remained an imperialist war, the CP now incorporated the legitimate anti-Fascist struggle of the British people into a more plausible analysis of international politics.

There was, however, a crucial difference between the 'new line' of June 1940 and the Party's original attitude to the war. In September 1939, while the CP was pledged to fight the Chamberlain Government, it was ready to support the war until the issues of domestic politics were resolved satisfactorily. This was not the Party's position after June 1940. The formation of a 'People's Government' was given as the necessary precondition for a 'People's War' which Communists would support. Meanwhile, on the premise that the nature of the war was determined by the class nature of the government which waged it, the war remained imperialist. But if the Churchill Government was incapable of waging a 'People's War', it was no more able to achieve a 'People's Peace'. For this, too, a People's Government was required, and Communists no longer suggested that peace could or should be obtained merely by stopping the war and coming to terms with Hitler. To sum up rather crudely, the CP supported neither war nor peace under Britain's present government, but put forward the alternative of a 'People's Government' which would if necessary fight a 'People's War' with a view to securing a 'People's Peace'.

It should be stated at the outset that the CP did not repudiate its earlier analysis of the war, nor did it accept that the Party line had 'turned a circle'. The defence of the people from their enemies within and without Britain was not to be confused with a 'war on two fronts', though at this point the subtlety of Communist dialectics was enough to deceive even a trained Marxist like Strachey, who believed that the CP had reverted to the original 'Pollitt line'.[5] It is no tribute to the clarity of Communist propaganda that George Strauss, another of the CP's recent associates, should share this view, or that ordinary Londoners interviewed by Mass-Observation should feel that the distinctiveness of this propaganda from that of supporters of the war lay mainly in the terminology that it used.[6] Indeed, even within the Party's own ranks the confusion was such that the Political Bureau felt compelled to warn Party members 'not [to] allow illusions spread by other elements to creep into our propaganda'. In this respect, the campaign against the Men of Munich had been marred by 'concessions to national defencism', 'speculation on "capitulation" as the main danger' and similar 'serious shortcomings':

> These mistakes cropping up in the current propaganda . . . have led to speculation inside the Party whether the Party has changed its estimation of the war or has changed its line. Such speculations are without foundation. So long as the monopoly capitalists remain in power, the characterisation of the war remains, whatever the military situation.[7]

As was so often the case, the Party leadership itself bore the main responsibility for the 'mistakes' it criticised, for its propaganda was full of such 'mistakes'. Indeed, it is hard to see how the Party could have thrown its energies into a campaign against the 'Men of Munich' without thereby suggesting that the main danger was capitulation.

Nevertheless, whatever the appearances to the contrary, the CP's characterisation of the war remained unchanged. But just as, according to Dutt, the war went through two distinct phases before June 1941, so too did the CP's attitude to the war. The difference between these phases cannot be regarded as simply 'tactical', unless one regards all the Party's activities as tactics leading to the same goal – Communist revolution. This was basically the position taken by such as Gollancz and, in theory at least, by the Party itself. A more disinterested examination reveals that the CP was a long way from leading a revolution, and well aware of the fact.[8] It shaped its policies accordingly.

7.2 A summer of discontent

> unless the reactionary imperialist cliques and capitulators in one's own country are curbed, it is impossible to curb the unbridled Fascist brigands, it is impossible to conduct a successful struggle in defence of the liberty and independence of the people . . .
>
> (Dimitrov in 1938, cited *Daily Worker*, 3 September 1940)

On 22 June 1940 the representatives of France and Germany met in a railway carriage at Compiègne to bring to an end the Third Republic and ratify the most dramatic military and political triumph of Hitler's Third Reich. The same day the British Communist Party issued the definitive statement of its reaction to the French débâcle. This manifesto, *The People Must Act*, provides the best introduction to the main themes in Communist propaganda that summer.

'The appalling catastrophe that has befallen the French people is a final warning to us', the manifesto began. 'We must learn the lesson or go under', for Britain's leaders had 'the same record, policy and aims as those who are responsible for Hitler's victory over France'. The lesson was that Britain's rulers, who dared falsely 'to identify the real defence of the people with the maintenance of Empire possessions and the dominance of the ruling class', were incapable of organising effective resistance to Nazism. This required the mobilisation of the workers, for the 'independence and militancy of the working-class movement' were 'the life-blood of the people's defence'. This reawakened commitment to the struggle against the foreign aggressor was awkwardly combined with the Party's peace rhetoric. The manifesto demanded 'the speediest ending of the war', not by 'surrender to Fascism', however, but by the 'unity and unbreakable will to victory' of 'a free people organising their own defence'. Only by the formation of a 'People's Government' could 'the danger of Fascist invasion and tyranny be successfully withstood' and the British people, in unity with the working people of all countries, 'find the way to a peace that is not a peace of subjection'.

The CP's alternative to the imperialist war was thus no longer an imperialist peace, nor even apparently a 'people's peace' in the short term, but a form of people's war. The nine demands on which the people were exhorted to act could be taken as a succinct programme for a popular war effort:

1 Clearing out of all friends of Fascism from the Government, the Services or the control of industry.
2 Conscription of wealth and nationalisation of the principal industries without compensation.

3 Election of Workers' Control Committees in every factory to safeguard the workers' conditions and end the corruption in the production of armaments and of necessities of life.
4 Arming of the workers in the factories.
5 Increased pay for the men in the armed forces, adequate allowances and pensions for their dependants, and the breaking down of the class system in the appointment of officers.
6 Adequate air raid precautions and evacuation schemes.
7 Withdrawal of all regulations that take away the right of free speech, Press, meeting and organisation.
8 Independence for a united Ireland and for India.
9 Close relations with the Socialist Soviet Union.

Over the following weeks these demands formed the basis of an energetic Communist campaign against the threat of Fascism from within and without. With one eye cast on Churchill and the other on Hitler, the manifesto ended on a rousing but still somewhat equivocal note:

FORWARD TO MAINTAIN A FREE AND DEMOCRATIC BRITAIN!
FORWARD TO A PEOPLE'S PEACE![9]

The Communist case against the Men of Munich and their allies in government comprised a number of related charges. The first was that they looked favourably on Fascism, and had long done so. Every insistent call to throw out the Men of Munich raised the spectre of appeasement and, sometimes implicitly, sometimes quite bluntly, Communists attributed the fragility of the Western democracies to a foreign policy based on cordial relations with the Axis powers and hostility to the forces of democracy the world over. In this revival of the themes of the People's Front, Communists reserved their most bitter indignation for the fraud of 'non-intervention' by which Britain's rulers had 'betrayed not only the Spanish Republic, but also the interests of their own peoples'. Conversely, the International Brigades had been fighting for British democracy as much as Spanish, and quite deliberately the International Brigades Association described its current political stance as a continuation of these earlier battles:

> For 32 months of the struggle we denounced the assassins of the Spanish people with the demand that 'Chamberlain Must Go'. In the present grave situation we repeat the demand. Chamberlain Must Go! and with him all the friends of Franco and supporters of Fascism in Britain.[10]

Thus Franco's declaration of non-belligerency, which was perceived as 'an intensification of the grave threat to British sea power in the Mediterranean and the Atlantic', was blamed on 'the representatives of Tory imperialism who allowed their hatred of democracy to blind themselves to the security of Britain'.[11] Similar arguments were resurrected when Italy entered the war.[12] Moreover, the CP felt that this ruling-class hatred for democracy was still giving rise to policies which jeopardised British interests. Thus, the government's antipathy towards Communism was seen as the main obstacle to the establishment of good relations with the USSR at a time when Britain faced the threat of invasion without a single ally.[13] Likewise, Communists decried efforts to remain on cordial terms with Franco, while the closing of the Burma Road was interpreted as a sign of anxiety to appease Japanese Fascism.[14] However, their greatest fear was that a large section of the British ruling class would be as willing to collaborate with the German representatives of their class as their French counterparts had been. The French betrayal demonstrated that the bourgeoisie would never subordinate its sectional interests to those of the nation, that the Fifth Column was to be found 'exclusively in the ranks of the upper classes, those whose love of capital knows no national boundaries and whose patriotism is conditional on the rate of profit'.[15] This brings us to a second major theme in Communist propaganda: not only were Britain's rulers bound by the ties of class solidarity to their country's enemies, but they unscrupulously exploited the war crisis in their private interests and neglected vital measures of defence where they conflicted with those interests.

According to this new line of argument, the ruling-class offensive at home endangered not only the people's living standards but also national security, and it was therefore suicidal to entrust the country's fate to 'those whose first concern is the safeguarding of their own property rights'.[16] 'Even in the hour of greatest crisis', the *Daily Worker* complained of Britain's decadent ruling class, '[it] thinks only of its gilded luxury and purpled ease and will not forgo a single privilege';[17] and of course, the bourgeoisie only maintained itself in gilded luxury by continuing and extending its exploitation and subjection of working people, as if oblivious to the national emergency. Unwavering in its pursuit of its domestic class interests, this clique could not begin to tap the material resources and enthusiasm of the nation in its struggle against foreign subjection:

> the dead hand of the capitalist profitmakers will continue to disorganise production. The workers in the factories know what this means with a million examples of wasted labour and effort.
>
> The same deadly path of the suppression of the independence of the working class and of democratic liberties will still be pursued. The old imperialist aims and the iron hand in the colonies will remain.

The example of France showed clearly where this path led unless 'big changes' were carried out.[18]

If the experience of France taught that the rule of the bourgeoisie spelt disaster, the very different experience of Spain demonstrated that Fascism was not invincible, nor was resistance to Fascism necessarily ineffectual. The key to this, 'the greatest war yet fought against Fascism', was that it was fought by 'a democratic Government, a democratic people and a democratic army. . . . Had they been oppressed by Anderson regulations, they would have been defeated before they started.'[19] The British soldier was no less capable of defending his country than was the Spanish, but his courage and resolution were of no avail while the British army remained subject to orders from incompetent and sometimes treacherous Blimps.[20] 'Only the working class can do the things the Spanish people did', said Sam Wild on opening a deliberately topical exhibition of photographs from the Spanish war, 'and form a People's Army capable of producing men like Modesto, Lister and Campesino, who stand in such striking contrast to Ironside, Pétain and Gort.'[21] The message was encapsulated in the slogans for an IBA rally that July:

The People Defended Spain!
Only the People can Defend Britain![22]

A People's Government was not simply the key to greater military effectiveness. The very idea of a 'People's War' was a response to the way in which the whole population, military and civilian, was drawn into modern, total war; and yet a government which represented only the anti-social interests of an exploitative minority was in no position to arouse the fighting enthusiasm of the millions required to sustain the war effort. A truly representative government prepared to challenge vested interests, on the other hand, would be able to 'use all the resources of the country for the welfare and defence of the people' and, by restoring freedom at home, 'release all the tremendous power of the working class for defence against fascism'.[23] Communists seemed to agree with the pro-war left that British liberties would be best defended by an upsurge of the democratic initiative of the British people, by a 'People's War' in fact, if only rarely in name at this stage. However, Communists did not accept that such a war was being or could be led by 'the imperialists Chamberlain, Churchill or Attlee'. Thus arose the demand for a People's Government 'which could alone make this a just war'.[24]

Communists further argued that a People's Government, and a People's Government alone, could count on the support or at least sympathy of the forces of progress throughout the world: the peoples of the Empire, the downtrodden workers of Europe, and the Socialist Soviet Union. The question of Anglo–Soviet relations especially was the subject of much public concern and, due partly to exaggerated hopes in Cripps's Moscow ambassadorship, optimism at this time. Communists were not impervious to this mood. Indeed, it has recently been revealed how leading Communists were anxiously and naively imploring the government to allow them to go to Moscow and have a comradely word in the ears of the Soviet leaders.[25] However, in this area of policy as in others, it was generally stressed that, while there was room for an improvement in Anglo-Soviet relations even under Churchill, it was 'to a workers' Government and only to a workers' Government that real help on any scale would come'.[26] The same sort of argument applied to the peoples of the Empire and of Nazi-occupied Europe.[27]

An interesting accompaniment to the CP's new line of simultaneously opposing the government and demanding popular resistance to Nazism was the revival of the 'popular patriotism' which had been so characteristic of its propaganda in the late 1930s. In 1940, as in earlier years, the CP's espousal of the interests of the nation was counterposed with the abandonment of these interests by the ruling class. International proletarian solidarity was mirrored by international bourgeois solidarity. Even as imperialist rivalries were being settled by force of arms, the bourgeoisie was bound by stronger ties to its class allies abroad than to its own people. For the workers, on the other hand, there was no contradiction between their class interests and their national interests, for their national independence was always threatened by their class adversaries, never by the workers of other lands. Only the people had the indomitable will, though not always the means, to defend their country. This set of ideas both explained and was confirmed by the surrender of national honour and national rights by the French bourgeoisie in June 1940. The tension between this portrayal of a ruling class too decadent to defend itself and the classical Leninist analysis of imperialist war goes a long way towards explaining some of the ambiguities which characterised the CP's pronouncements at this time.

The recrudescence of radical–patriotic themes is well illustrated by the *Daily Worker*'s 'The Voice of History', an eclectic series of featured quotations culled from that archetypal product of Popular Front culture, Lindsay's and Rickword's *Handbook of Freedom*.[28] Strangely enough, the flavour of these extracts is captured best not by Bacon or Byron, Cobbett or Gladstone, but by an Irish Marxist:

> I make no war on patriotism, never have done. But against the patriotism of capitalism . . . I place the patriotism of the working class. . . . That which is good for the working class I esteem patriotic.

The voice of history was generally invoked in support of this concept of a patriotism grounded in the well-being of the working people. An eighteenth-century Tory aristocrat was quoted in justification of the campaign to remove the Churchill Government:

> If you ask who hath the right and means to resist the supreme legislative power, I answer, the whole nation hath the right, and the people who deserve to enjoy liberty will find the means.

But the voice of the past was equally concerned that free-born Englishmen should stand firm against the foreign aggressor:

> We must be free or die, who speak the tongue
> That Shakespeare spake – the faith and morals hold
> That Milton held. In everything we're sprung
> Of earth's first blood, have titles manifold.[29]

Of course, one cannot present romantic sonnets as definitive statements of Communist policy. The change of tone was nevertheless important, if only because it was the influential view of Victor Gollancz that the primary aim of Communist propaganda was to create a mood of despondency and defeatism, and that anybody who thought otherwise was a 'dolt', 'innocent to the point of criminality'.[30] In fact, the tone of the CP's propaganda during the national emergency aptly reflected its policies – hardly defeatist, yet never committed to support for the war. Communists felt they must be free or die, and saw Hitler as a threat to their freedom; but they did not regard Churchill as the champion of British liberties.

These then were the main themes of Communist propaganda that summer. The underlying motif was that resistance to the Nazis was vitally necessary, but could not be organised by a capitalist government. The CP therefore remained undeceived by the emollient pleas that Britons were all in it together and that political differences should be submerged in the common struggle. Instead, when the various points in its propaganda were assembled together, the Party put forward a convincing case for a popular government to lead a popular war effort.[31] Although superficially plausible, these arguments were flawed. The view, based on the French collapse, that a dictatorial imperialist government would necessarily wage war ineffectively was belied by the conspicuous military achievements of Germany. More fundamental was the question of how a People's Government would come to power without a drawn-out internal struggle during which the way would be open for a German invasion. Communists rarely addressed this topic at this time, partly because their immediate, more feasible objective was the removal of the Men of Munich; but partly also, as would later become apparent, because they had no convincing answer to this question. But at this point we need only conclude that during the summer of 1940 Communists never suggested that a British defeat would be anything but a disaster. What they did say was that the Churchill Government had little chance of defeating Germany, and none at all of achieving a victory of benefit to the people of Britain.

7.3 One step back?

INVASION IS AWAITED AT ANY MOMENT
(*Daily Worker*, 16 September 1940)

... a political scare like the great Munich War Scare ...
(Palme Dutt, December 1940, on the expectations of a German invasion in the summer of that year[32])

In his useful introduction to this period, Monty Johnstone argues that, after the immediate threat of invasion had been fended off, 'there was to be a tacit shift away from the line of the 22 June manifesto, or at least from the emphasis and implications of it, for a certain time'.[33] Two suggestive episodes from the latter half of 1940 seem to bear out this statement. The first was Dutt's insistence that there had never been any real danger of a German invasion of Britain. The second, mentioned by Johnstone, was William Rust's highly critical review of Ivor Montagu's *The Traitor Class*, a book which summed up very well the 'defencist' tendencies in Communist politics. The significance of these episodes will be considered in the following pages, for they raise the question of whether the Party line had, once again, changed by November 1940. They also throw light on the unresolved tension between two distinct conceptions of the war which dragged the Party in different directions: was the war to be regarded as a European war in which Britain stood alone against Hitler, or as a world war of clashing empires in which Britain was fighting, not for its independence, but to maintain its rule over half a billion colonial subjects.

In his scornful dismissals of the 'invasion scare' in November 1940, Dutt took the latter approach. Amazingly, he had come to regard 'the months between May and October' as 'an interlude in the war' and claimed that the invasion scare, like the Munich war scare before it,[34] had been manufactured for internal consumption. Faced with 'a very difficult home situation', the government had cynically conjured up a non-existent threat to national security in order to 'rally home opinion to the Government and to the acceptance of all reactionary measures in the name of "the nation in danger" '. Dutt further alleged German complicity in this bluff in order to 'immobilise a certain proportion of British forces by a legitimate strategic feint, while both sides concentrated their main preparations in other directions with less publicity'.[35]

This was not, of course, the view of Communists at the time. On 13 September the *Daily Worker* saw fit to print twenty-six lines penned by Coleridge 'during the alarm of an invasion', while a couple of months earlier Dutt himself had warned that 'the question of the invasion of Britain is on the order of the day'.[36] However, the point is more than just to exhibit an example of Dutt's inconsistency. The threat of national annihilation, of subjection to Nazi tyranny with the consent of at least some sections of the British ruling class, had provided the motive and the driving force for the CP's campaign to oust the Men of Munich and install a People's Government untainted by sympathy with Fascism. The burning issue was the survival of Britain. But now Dutt insisted that Britain's surivival had never been at stake and reverted to a more straightforward analysis of imperialist war, the outcome of which was of no concern to the working class:

> The British imperialist rulers knew very well that this was not a war for the defence of an island, but for the possession of an Empire. They knew that the control of the island was only one strategic element, and its people a pawn, in this battle for world domination. They knew that the question of invasion of the island . . . could only arise as a practical possibility at a later stage . . . if the capitalist rulers, having sucked the orange dry and completely disorganised its economy, should find it no longer worth defending and find it more advantageous to transfer their Empire base elsewhere.

'This was a war, not for national existence, but for colonial exploitation', wrote Dutt, but these sordid aims had to be dressed up in a more attractive guise:

> Neither set of rulers could inform their peoples that they must die in order to win for the big banks and trusts spheres of profitable exploitation in distant Asiatic countries. . . . While the British world conquerors of one quarter of the world might be orating to their home public, with the dramatic heroism of a gallant little nation making its last stand for existence . . . they were busily engaged in planning dashing strokes at Dakar on the West African coast, or in dispatching troops and supplies out of the island to Rhodesia, Egypt, the Middle East and India.

The war was, then, simply a product of the same imperialist antagonisms that had underlain the First World War, and Dutt concluded his article with an appropriately old-fashioned call on the workers of the world to take 'the path of the October Revolution'.[37]

The same change of perspective is evident from Rust's critique of *The*

Traitor Class. Written in the summer of 1940, this volume, which enjoyed wide sales and enthusiastic reviews in the Communist press, was basically a compilation of material to support the CP's allegations of ruling-class treachery. Drawing heavily on the experiences of France, Spain and China, Montagu set himself the question: 'How can the liberties of our people, which we cherish and would die to preserve, be rescued from betrayal?' He was quite certain that nothing would be gained by burying one's differences with Britain's rulers for these, of course, were the 'traitor class' of the book's title, the 'Fifth Column' which, 'bound by class solidarity even to the ruling class of the state with which it is in conflict, inevitably follows policies which tend to increase the menace to the freedom and national independence of the peoples of both'. But, if those who claimed to represent the nation were bound by ties stronger than those with their homeland, if 'the British ruling class acted, objectively, as German agents', then who *could* be trusted to remain 'inflexible and indefatigable in the struggle for national independence'? Montagu answered by identifying the nation with the sovereign people:

> It is the people themselves . . . who are vitally concerned in their own bodies with preservation from enslavement. . . . *They* cannot make terms to conserve a part of privilege in return for service as puppet viceroys, as factory overseers. It is the fruit of *their* sweat that the conqueror seeks as prize.

The contrast with the article of Dutt's just quoted is immediately apparent. Whereas Dutt argued that the war was being fought for the spoils of empire, Montagu saw the British people itself as the prize. Dutt's perspective was that of an imperialist redivision of the world, any outcome of which was inimical to the interests of the working class; Montagu's perspective was that of the possible subjection of the British people to Nazism and he stressed that Communists 'would die' to prevent this. In Dutt's article Fascism appeared only as an element in ruling-class propaganda seeking to legitimise imperialist aggrandisement. In Montagu's book, on the other hand, the colonies were mentioned only as a factor in Britain's struggle against Fascism: a liberated India, he wrote, would energetically resist conquest by Germany and thus 'instead of troops and resources which could defend the British people being used to maintain that rule [in India], the British people in a defensive struggle would be able themselves to use those resources and to receive collaboration from those now ruled'. *The Traitor Class* epitomised the resurgent anti-Fascist strain in Communist propaganda. Essentially, it did no more than elaborate the theme that the bourgeoisie betrays democracy, and with it the nation, and must therefore be cast aside if these are to be defended:

Everybody knows that . . . conscription of material resources, mobilisation of the initiative of the people, purging of the friends of Fascism . . . would infinitely fortify the defensive power of the British people, infinitely weaken the power for conquest of Hitler.

Hence, anyone who obstructs these measures, is working against these aims, is a traitor to the interest of the people and the independence of the nation.

But the ruling class, because of their class interests, cannot fail to oppose these measures.[38]

By November 1940, these arguments could not go unchallenged, and so Rust's belated critique of *The Traitor Class* appeared in the *Labour Monthly*. Rust's main objection was to Montagu's 'mechanical transference of the lessons of France to the different situation prevailing in Britain', giving rise to the assumption that the ruling class constituted Britain's Fifth Column. The specific dilemma of the French bourgeoisie had arisen from France's position as a subordinate power caught between two stronger imperialist blocs under one of whose hegemony it had necessarily to fall. Britain faced no such dilemma; it was 'struggling for world domination' and so its rulers were unlikely to hoist the white flag with the unseemly haste of the French. Rust further censured Montagu for suggesting that Britain's international policies remained those of appeasement. In reality, 'the war marked a turning point in international relationships, as a result of which the division of states into Fascist and "democratic" lost its former sense and the rival imperialisms entered the path of open conflict in the struggle for world domination'. Like the writings by Dutt which appeared at the same time, Rust's critique analysed the war in the simple 'imperialist' terms used at the beginning of the war.[39] Moreover, the review was to be taken as 'a considered expression of the party's viewpoint' published 'by special decision of the Secretariat after a careful consideration of the issues'.[40] It would seem, then, that by November the Party had once more altered its stance. The war was presented by Dutt and Rust as a worldwide crisis of capitalism in which the question of British independence was of only secondary importance. However, authoritative as they were, these expositions of Communist policy did not represent a decisive break in the CP's attitude to the war. Indeed, in one crucial respect they were at odds with the dominant trend in Communist propaganda, which, for the most part, maintained a precarious balance between the 'imperialist' and the 'anti-Fascist' interpretations of the war.

Rust had argued that to draw too close a parallel between Britain and France was to obscure the vital distinction between a subordinate imperialism, France, and the stronger imperialisms of Britain and Germany. The capitulation of the French ruling class, in this analysis, indicated that it had bowed to the might of German imperialism and abandoned its ailing

British ally. But British imperialism, however it was presented by Dutt or Rust, was, in 1940, so visibly ailing that Communists began to doubt whether it was one of the dominant powers at all. Already in May Dutt had described the war as 'especially a crisis of the British Empire and British capitalism':

> Not only German, Italian and Japanese imperialism, but also American imperialism openly calculate on the demise of the British Empire and their share of the spoils.[41]

But whereas Germany aimed at the direct military subjection of its fading imperialist rival, the United States, exploiting Britain's desperate shortage of resources in the face of the German onslaught, connived at Britain's subordination in an Anglo–American bloc. As the glib phrases of amity and mutual respect crossed and recrossed the Atlantic in the latter part of 1940, it appeared to Communists that the British imperialists faced the same stark choice as had the French:

> The French capitalist class had the alternative of surrender to German imperialism, of union with German finance-capital, or of surrender to and union with British finance-capital. They chose the former.
> The British capitalist class, faced with the alternative of a deal with German finance-capital or of union as a junior partner with US imperialism, chose the latter.[42]

But the choice had not been easily made, nor was it settled once and for all. The CP, which fulminated at one and the same time against the capitulationist and the warmongering tendencies of Britain's rulers, explained this duality by reference to the deep divisions between the pro-German and pro-American sections of the ruling class.[43] From this view of world politics, it was evident that Britain's rulers could not but act as a 'traitor class'; for, even as it stood firm against Germany, the 'corrupt bourgeoisie' subjected the British people to 'the crude, brutal domination of the Dollar Imperialists of America'.[44] The possibility of a 'reactionary settlement with German imperialism' was certainly not ruled out and at the time of the Hess mission in May 1941 fears of a move in this direction mounted. However, it was now more commonly argued that the dominant sections of British capital favoured an arrangement with US imperialism.[45]

In developing this theme, the CP frequently sounded a note of aggrieved nationalism while, quite consistently, denouncing the war aims of British imperialism. The British people were being cajoled into fighting not in the interests of their own homeland but on behalf of American Big Business. By the provisions of Lease-Lend they would be required 'first, to spend their blood to win the war for the ultimate hegemony of the United States, and then to labour after the war, for nothing, in order to provide American capitalism with the arms to complete its hegemony and finally absorb the British Empire'.[46] Interestingly, and perhaps appropriately, this strain of anti-Americanism, which in some writings foreshadowed the darkest years of the Cold War, found its fullest and most virulent expression in a pamphlet by Ivor Montagu, *Roll on, Mississippi!*[47]

America's increasing intervention in the war thus reinforced the prevailing view in the CP that the Churchill Government could not protect the interests of the British people. On this issue the 'imperialist' and the 'defencist' interpretations of the war coincided, for a global, Marxist view of international politics suggested that Britain was fighting not so much for world domination as for the right to dominion status in an American bloc. Whether Britain guarded its coasts like a bulldog, or whether it begged terms off Germany, the only prospect offered by this senescent imperialism was foreign domination.

From this premise one could deduce either revolutionary opportunities and obligations or the need for a democratic war for national independence. But another, probably more decisive, factor led the CP to adhere to a political line approximating to that of a 'war on two fronts'. This was the belief that Britain was threatened by Fascism from both within and without; and that those who were beguiled by the persuasive demand for national unity against the external foe thereby neglected the equally important struggle against the Fascist enemy at home. It was this conception of indigenous Fascism, rather than the role of British imperialism in world politics, that figured most prominently in the CP's campaigns against the Churchill Government. This we shall try to demonstrate, later on by bringing up to date our account of the CP's perception of British Fascism, but before that by examining how far and with what consequences Communists lifted their eyes to take in the totality of the crisis of imperialism.

7.4 A war for empire

So the robbers have fallen out again. In the sharpening crisis of world capitalism they look with greedy eyes upon one another's property, they itch to lay hold on the huge imperial preserves which are the foundation rock of the big monopolies; the conflicts deepen; someone lets off a pistol; there is a general dive for the booty.

. . . the colonial people now begin to occupy the centre of the world stage, not simply as peoples fighting for their national freedom, but as the front-line fighters in the struggle of all the exploited and oppressed to end the capitalist system and to advance towards Socialist peace and prosperity.

(Communist Party pamphlet, June 1940[48])

In October 1939 the Communist Party had defined the war as simply an imperialist conflict for world domination which rendered invalid the former distinction between democratic and Fascist powers. 'Fascism is only one expression of the basic world conflict of capitalism and Socialism', Dutt reminded Communists in 1940, and the forces of Socialism would be weakened 'if the fight against fascism is falsely isolated from this world conflict'. For, according to Leninist orthodoxy, imperialist war provided the opportunity for 'the camp of the rising world of Socialism' to resolve this basic world conflict by means of proletarian revolution. If the road to Communism lay open, it would be nonsensical for Communists to be diverted by the side issue of bourgeois democracy or Fascism. And Dutt at least was sure that this road did lie open. The war brought with it, he insisted time and time again, the 'visibly developing new world revolutionary wave which bears on its crest the issue of capitalism or socialism for the leading countries of the world'.[49]

In this scenario the colonies, the 'chief cause of the war',[50] loomed large. India especially was seen as the pivot of the whole imperialist system. According to Dutt the struggle to dominate this sub-continent had been the root question of international politics for centuries. Behind Britain's successive rivalries with Spain, Portugal, Holland, France and Russia lay 'the issue of the route to India and the domination of India';[51] and so too were the Anglo–German struggles of the twentieth century reduced somewhat mechanistically to this same issue:

> The seizure of Poland implied a direct threat to Rumania i.e. the possibility of Germany emerging on to the Black Sea. Once there, Germany would begin to threaten Britain's road to India – through Turkey and Palestine, or through Turkey and Irak as the case might be. Hitler began to threaten the Empire . . . that was what precipitated the pledge of Poland.[52]

'Politically, strategically and economically', India was 'the foundation rock of a ruling class which is the most reactionary enemy of the international working class',[53] and therefore that ruling class had unleashed war as soon as it perceived even the most oblique threat to this, the jewel in its sack of imperialist plunder. Economically, India was a prized source of super-profits, while strategically it provided the foundations for Britain's Middle Eastern Empire and a possible base for operations against the Soviet Union.[54] Within Britain, the domination of India had underlain the structure of politics since the accession of George III, or thereabouts; 'behind the inner course of politics in England, and directly under-propping the whole social and political structure laboriously and precariously built up in England, may be traced the role of this same domination'.[55] In brief, India, and the colonies generally, were central to the CP's understanding of British imperialism, its crises and its wars. Moreover, the Indian people were not the passive objects of imperialist rivalry, but were rising to challenge the system which enslaved them. So crucial was India to the imperialist system that its demand for freedom raised 'in its sharpest form the question of the modern colonial system, which is an integral part of modern imperialism and at the root of the issues of imperialist war . . . the liberation of India will strike a decisive blow at the whole colonial system, which is inseparably bound up with modern capitalist society'. Hence the 'profound world significance' of India's liberation struggle, and its significance especially for the British people.[56]

Here was the answer to those who claimed that Britain was fighting for democracy! 'Failure to understand the imperialist character of the war is above all failure to understand the Colonial question';[57] and therefore to expose the character of the war it was necessary above all to spread an understanding of the colonial question, not as a side issue but as an integral part of the Communist case against the war:

> In all forms of propaganda engaged in on behalf of the colonial peoples, comrades should avoid isolating this question from the general Party work. Instead of falling into the mistake at meetings of holding separate platforms for the colonial issue, speakers, in exposing the imperialist character of the war, and explaining to the masses the true nature of imperialism, should in the course of their speeches, deal with the colonial struggles and link them up with the fight of the working class at home.[58]

But if the colonial question was apparently the key to understanding the war and an indispensable component of any revolutionary strategy for ending the war, it nevertheless remained of fairly marginal concern to most British Communists.

This assertion is perhaps most clearly borne out by the lack of interest aroused by the periodical, *Inside the Empire*. At the beginning of 1940 the duplicated sheet which the Party's Colonial Information Bureau had been circularising since 1937 was replaced by a monthly printed journal, an initiative most certainly in keeping with the Party's stated aims and perception of the war. However, the journal's circulation, initially around 2,000 and possibly falling sharply when an export ban was imposed on Communist periodicals in mid-1940, was insufficient to sustain publication. At the end of 1940 *Inside the Empire* therefore shut up shop and recommended its readers to subscribe to *World News and Views*, just as that journal had decided to concentrate more closely on the issues of domestic politics. The failure of this venture was all the more striking at a time of stable or increasing sales for most other Communist publications.[59]

Of course, as the writings cited earlier indicate, it would be wrong to infer from such evidence that the CP made no attempt to elucidate the colonial question; and it would be wronger still to imply that Communists lacked sympathy with the struggle of the colonial peoples. At a succession of People's Convention meetings, for example, Mass-Observers remarked on the great enthusiasm displayed by audiences whenever internationalist sentiments were voiced or a black speaker rose to the microphone.[60] However, these displays of solidarity were not signs of a revolutionary commitment to the dissolution of imperialism but of a democratic commitment to the right of all peoples to self-determination. This might appear a casuistical distinction, but it offers us a real insight into the way the CP approached the issues raised by the war. The Empire was merely one of a range of democratic issues addressed by the Party; it was not the essential basis on which it built its case against the imperialist war. Indeed, in the programme drawn up for thePeople's Convention the demand for colonial freedom at first found no place, although it was later added with the excuse that it had, in any case, been implicit in the demand for a People's Peace.[61] Communists tended to take up or leave imperialism rather as if it was a certain reactionary policy adopted by the government, like its policies on food or ARP, and not the system that had produced the war and for the preservation of which the government existed.

As befitted components of an essentially democratic programme, the Party's demands for the colonies were not usually presented as leading to or arising from the revolutionary break-up of British imperialism. On India, Communists supported the broad national front embodied in Congress and demanded, just as they had before the war, the calling of a constituent assembly to determine India's form of government.[62] On Ireland, Communists advocated the ending of partition and respect for Irish neutrality, but in the terms of British self-interest in which Montagu had discussed the Indian question: a friendly, neutral Ireland would provide Britain with such benefits as the provision of essential foodstuffs and a refuge for women and children. Moreover, just as Communists remained sympathetic to the forces of bourgeois nationalism in India, in supporting Irish neutrality they made little attempt to distinguish their policies from those of the socially reactionary de Valera Government.[63]

To summarise, then, the CP only rarely addressed the question of imperialism and when it did so it was as part of a set of democratic demands far removed from Dutt's eschatological fantasies. By and large, the colonial peoples were presented 'simply as peoples fighting for their national freedom' and not as 'the front-line fighters in the struggle . . . to end the capitalist system'. This conclusion enhances our understanding of the rationale behind the CP's political stance. From the global perspective intermittently adopted by Dutt and others, the CP's opposition to the Chamberlain and Churchill Governments appeared as the British counterpart to the struggles of the peoples of Europe and the Empire, the practical application of Liebknecht's dictum that the enemy is at home. Seen in a worldwide context of crumbling empires, the struggles of British Communists could be described as part of an international revolutionary movement against a war which was 'more and more clearly laying bare its final decisive character as the struggle of the dying capitalist order and the new socialist order for the future of the world'.[64] The view that the 1914–18 war had inaugurated an epoch of wars and revolutions which would only end with the victory of Communism had always been an unquestioned tenet of Communist ideology, but these triumphalist assertions had long coexisted with a less ambitious, defensive political strategy. Communists continued to believe in a revolutionary day of judgement but, as is generally the case with days of judgement, they did not expect it just yet; their chiliastic prognostications did not determine their immediate political objectives. Communists set themselves more limited tasks which would not end capitalism but which would make the road towards that inevitable destination somewhat easier. After October 1939, Communist politics continued to be dominated by the need to preserve the rights won by the working class under bourgeois democracy, rights which were threatened not only by foreign aggressors but, more directly, by Britain's own ruling class. To put the case in a deliberately contentious nutshell, in opposing the policies of the British Government the CP stood for the maintenance of bourgeois democracy, not its overthrow. Its immediate objective was not to end capitalism but to preserve the elementary rights and living standards of the British people from the encroachments of domestic Fascism. It was the offensive of British imperialism at home, rather than its decline internationally, which preoccupied Britain's Communists. Their political vision remained Eurocentric, at times even Anglocentric. Above all, their political priorities were defensive ones, for the issue of the day remained that of combating Fascism.

7.5 The 'new order' in Britain

the question before the Labour movement to-day is not whether Fascism is a loathsome thing or not, but the question 'from whence comes the danger of Fascism to the British people?'

(J. R. Campbell, February 1940[65])

According to the sort of criteria adopted in most interpretations of Fascism, the claim that Britain in 1940 was threatened by the imposition of Fascism from within is untenable. This was not, however, the view of Britain's Communists at the time, whose policies in the first year or two of the war were continually justified by reference to the quickening development of Fascism within Britain. Even if the distinction between the bourgeois democracies and the Fascist states was no longer thought relevant, the distinction between bourgeois democracy and Fascism was as crucial as ever; and as democratic Britain came increasingly, in the Communist perception, to resemble Fascist Germany, the CP's primary task was to build up the movement which could arrest this development. During the first couple of years of the war the Party added little that was new to the analysis of Fascism it had developed in the 1930s, but merely applied it to new political circumstances. It is with the application of this theory that we are concerned here.

Communists had long regarded Fascism as a product of the general crisis of capitalism, but during the war they tended to concentrate on the specific relationship between Fascism and the imperialist war economy.[66] Their belief that the British ruling class was inevitably drawn towards Fascist economic methods as the most effective way of waging total war under capitalism was based on empirical observation as well as well-worn theory. From the very beginning of the war Communists detected an extension of state control over the economy. Unlike the more credulous theoreticians of the Labour Party, they did not conclude from this that big business, like the rest of society, was meekly subordinating its sectional interests to the wider national interests as determined by a neutral state. Increasingly, Communists argued, big business *was* the state: observe how quickly every branch of economic life had been equipped with a controller 'drawn from the board of directors of the principal monopoly concerned'.[67] Communists discerned both an increase in the power of the executive and a growing domination of the executive by the monopolies; in other words, a trend towards that dictatorship of finance capital which Communists called Fascism.[68] This dictatorship concentrated ever more power in the hands of the trusts 'by squeezing the workers and the smaller capitalists, by reducing non-war imports and cutting consumption to the bone, by concentrating a larger share of profits in their own hands, by monopolising and trustifying industry'.[69] The government's proposals for the cotton industry – 'clearing out the smaller firms, concentrating production in the more highly rationalised concerns and "revising out-of-date wage systems" ' – were typical and, according to Emile Burns, 'remarkably like the so-called "National Socialist Revolution" in its economic aspects'.[70]

The dictatorship of finance capital found its expression not just in the trustification of industry but in an intensification of the offensive against popular living and working conditions. To ensure the production of war goods at an ever faster rate, the workers in the factories which produced them were driven ever harder, while the need to divert labour and resources into the production of these goods, and to reserve shipping space for military supplies, required that levels of working-class consumption be restricted. The result was, according to one Communist statistician, a steady decline in the standard of living of the British worker.[71]

The paradox was that, as unemployment fell and the forces swallowed up able-bodied young men, the potential strength of organised labour increased. The state of the labour market grew objectively more favourable to the working class at precisely the time that it was required to work harder and eat less. And how could workers be induced to work longer and more intensively when there was a shortage of goods on which increased earnings might be spent, when they had to eat less no matter how hard they worked? These were exactly the sort of contradictions which Fascist methods alone could resolve in favour of capital:

> Civil consumption must be ruthlessly cut down to a minimum; and in a class society this means of course that the consumption, not of the rich and luxurious, but of the poor and needy must be cut down to a minimum.
>
> But how are the new measures . . . to be imposed, in view of the war-scarcity of labour and the consequent enhanced bargaining power of the workers [?]. . . . It is not enough to have drawn the leading trade union officials to the side of the war machine, if the workers still go forward with their demands, with the looming possibilities of action. The formal prohibition of strikes is not enough, if strikes still continue. . . . The whole question of wages requires to be taken into the hands of the State. A compulsory labour system must be imposed. The Nazi system begins to be seen clearly by the ruling class, not merely as the ideal, but as the immediately necessary system.[72]

From this perspective, collaboration in industry appeared not as a genuine partnership but as 'Fascism by consent'.[73] While trade union officials flattered themselves on their new-found importance, the real effect of this collaboration was to emasculate the unions by entangling them in a form of corporate state manned at every key point by the nominees of big business.[74] In August 1940, for example, Peter Kerrigan argued that the integration of Labour into the state through various advisory councils and supply committees, coinciding as it did with restrictions on the movement of labour and the right to strike, meant that a 'Labour Front' now existed in Britain.[75] Similarly, when Ernest Bevin first mooted the idea of factory councils on which workers and management would have equal representation, it was denounced as 'Bevin's Labour Front', an attempt to undermine the position of shop stewards by methods *'closely resembling the Nazi system of factory organisation'*.[76] Driven by the logic of the imperialist war economy, Britain's rulers were developing the forms of economic and industrial organisation already tried and trusted by the Nazis.

Moreover, according to the rather mechanistic Marxism taught by the Communist Party, this concentration of economic power could not go unaccompanied by a comparable concentration of political power. The alleged suppression of independent trade unionism showed just how artificial was any dividing line between economic and political dictatorship. According to a leading Communist theoretician, 'the greater concentration of production and distribution in the hands of the big trusts, and their closer association with the State through the system of Controllers and Committees, is the economic background to the casting aside of democratic methods and the spread of compulsion. As the economic structure grows more "totalitarian" so also do the political methods come closer to fascism.'[77]

This line of argument stemmed from the belief, held by Communists before the war, that the British ruling class was in a position to create an essentially Fascist state without any of the upheaval or calculated exhibitionism that had marked this process on the continent. To many people, D. N. Pritt explained, with just a hint of condescension towards those nations less civilised than Britain, Fascism appeared to be a matter of castor oil and rubber truncheons and 'a particular form of salute, accompanied by such cries as "Heil!" or "Duce!" ' However, these 'rather unamiable or even ridiculous' habits of continental Fascists were no more likely to be imitated in Britain than the liquid Italian vowels and German gutturals which characterised their speech:

> The more serious ways in which Fascism has been encroaching in Britain have not been by means of such bodies as the Blackshirts or by any spectacular changes in constitution. One reason for this is that there is no written constitution requiring to be changed, amended or abrogated . . . it should be possible to advance towards Fascism without constitutional changes . . .[78]

As far as Pritt was concerned, the ritual and demagogy of Fascism, its mass movement and illegal violence, were incidental. This was essentially the position of the Communist Party, although interestingly on a couple of occasions Dutt did warn that the objective conditions for a reactionary mass movement – inchoate discontent with the government and the war which could be 'drawn towards fascist channels' – were developing in Britain.[79] But this emphasis was rare and the CP was far from reassured by the government's efforts to block up these Fascist channels:

those who have interned Mosley are the very people who have introduced Mosleyism into this country. The totalitarian system, the corporate State, industrial conscription and the abolition of democratic rights, all of this has been done, not by avowed Fascists, but by a much more dangerous combination, the coalition of Tory, Labour and Liberal leaders.[80]

The traditional British parties were allegedly introducing Fascism without even the semblance of a revolution.

It is certainly true that the flexibility of Britain's political arrangements allowed its rulers to accord themselves potentially despotic powers with a modicum of political upheaval and that the government's Emergency Powers Acts were undeniably 'totalitarian' measures. In presenting the second Emergency Powers Bill in May 1940, Attlee demanded that 'the Government should be given complete control over persons and property' and to effect this control should be empowered to make whatever Defence Regulations it deemed fit.[81] Communists were convinced that it was against persons and not property that the government was likely to wield these powers.[82] Of particular concern to the CP was the granting to the Minister of Labour of the power to do with labour just as he pleased, and it expressed its concern in extravagant terms. 'The liberties of a thousand years have been destroyed in a single afternoon', the *Daily Worker* protested. 'Britain is being Nazified', it had ' "gone totalitarian" '. Thus had powers 'unsurpassed even in Nazi Germany' been vested in a practically unaccountable government of the ruling class.[83] Theoretically, of course, the government was still subject to the will of Parliament, but this was little consolation at a time when Britain had 'reached the stage not only of totalitarian warfare with a totalitarian war machine but of what are the beginnings of a single totalitarian party'.[84] Moreover, this 'single totalitarian governmental bloc'[85] immunised itself against popular pressures by the simple device of not holding elections – another indication of the unhealthy malleability of the British constitution. As the CP saw it, Britain's democratic institutions were being reduced to a façade behind which the ruling class accumulated ever more tyrannical powers.

Of the various uses to which these powers were put, two were of special concern to the CP. The first was the internment of John Mason, a Communist shop steward, under Defence Regulation 18B in July 1940, by which the fiction that that state was playing the role of disinterested arbiter in industrial affairs was disproved once and for all. Mason's internment, without any specific charge having been brought against him, seemed to portend a general attack on militant, independent trade unionism and thus provoked widespread and vociferous protest, coordinated by a John Mason Defence

Committee. In the course of this campaign, Communists frequently alluded to the onset of Fascist methods of pacifying trade unionists which his internment seemed to signify. More than once they referred to 'a policy of concentration camps for Shop Stewards', which was a ludicrous overstatement of the case as it stood but expressed the legitimate fear that Mason's case might prove the first of many.[86]

The second instance of the use of emergency powers against Communists was the suppression of the *Daily Worker* and *The Week* in January 1941, which finally confirmed the CP's fears that Britain was proceeding rapidly towards open Fascism.[87] The *Worker*'s editor, William Rust, explained that, just as coalition government 'signified' one party, so did one party signify one press; and Dutt too portrayed the mainstream press as one reactionary mass of war propaganda. The ban on the *Worker* thus amounted to 'the suppression of the only opposition press', leaving 'only a Government daily press, like the BBC – the same system as the Nazi totalitarian system'. The campaign against the ban was therefore not just a fight for the particular interests of the Communist Party but the 'undying fight of the people through the ages' for democracy. 'The crisis of democracy', wrote Dutt, 'has always opened with an attack on Communism and the militant working class vanguard . . . led by Social-Democratic Ministers in Coalition with Big Capital'. The attack could not stop there, as the experiences of Italy, Germany, Austria and France showed, but would proceed to 'the destruction of the legal working-class and democratic movement and the victory of fascism'. And the *Worker* itself, boasted Rust, was a worthy champion of freedom of thought and the liberty of the press, and it was on these principles, rather than specifically Socialist ones, that Communists demanded that the ban be lifted:

> The Communist Party fights for democracy . . . Marx, Engels, Lenin and Stalin have always made clear that within capitalism democracy, even though limited by capitalism, provides the best conditions for the advance and organisation of the working class in order to end capitalism . . .

There could be no better summary of the reasons given by the CP for opposing the Churchill Government.[88]

The theme of a British road to Fascism was a leitmotiv running through Communist Party propaganda throughout this period. However, it was not until after the ban on the *Worker* that the definitive rendition of this theme was given, by Palme Dutt needless to say. In his 'Notes of the Month' for March 1941, entitled 'The "New Order" in Britain', Dutt recapitulated his analysis of the historical development of Fascism and demonstrated its relevance to wartime politics in Britain, thus bringing together many of the ideas we have just been discussing. The concept of Fascism, wrote Dutt, should not be employed indiscriminately to denote merely violence and reaction, but neither should it be 'identified with a specific imperialism'. Rather, it arose in all imperialist countries during the general crisis of capitalism when the preservation of capitalist rule could only be preserved by a Fascist state, fused with the banks and trusts and resorting to naked oppression to overcome the contradictions which threatened to bring down the whole edifice of imperialism. Parliament was divested of its powers, and the working-class and democratic movement eliminated; all forms of political expression and organisation were subjected to 'unified governmental control'. Whatever the appearances to the contrary, this was not a revolutionary political transformation but 'only a change in the form of the continuous bourgeois dictatorship . . . always introduced under the protection of the higher military and official authorities'. The foundations for open Fascist dictatorship were always laid within the existing state forms, and in Britain this stage had already been completed 'within the shell of inoperative democracy'. For, just as the concentration of economic power was common to all imperialist states, so was the parallel concentration of political power signified by Fascism:

> Once this class character of Fascism is clearly and firmly understood, the fantastic and suicidal folly of seeing Fascism as the peculiar invention and system of one or another imperialist country, instead of the common tendency towards which all monopoly capital increasingly drives, with varying degrees of success according to the relations of class forces within each country, becomes manifest.

But if the progression towards Fascism was economically determined and therefore inevitable, its outcome was not; this depended on 'the relations of class forces', which Dutt assessed in political terms. 'The victory of the onslaught is not inevitable. The struggle is in front', and the march towards Fascism could still be arrested by 'the strength and independence of the working-class front, in unity with all democratic forces against monopoly capital'. Dutt did not insist that this united front rest on a revolutionary basis with revolutionary objectives as the only alternative to this expression of capitalism in decay. The 'essential condition of victory' was the unity of all those, 'irrespective of their views on other issues', who would struggle to defend the 'elementary democratic rights' which struggle had won. Dutt's caustic attacks on the Labour leadership were prompted not by its disavowal of revolution but by its refusal to make any sort of stand for these elementary rights. Worse than this, it was actually collaborating in the subjection of the British people to Fascism, for Fascism could come to power only when the 'superior strength of the workers is sapped and destroyed by the agents of reaction at the head of the working-class organisations'. The lesson was of special relevance to Britain where, in the absence of an indigenous Fascist movement, it was the leaders of Social Democracy who produced the demagogic phrases about 'community of interests', 'replacement of the profit motive by social service', 'recognition of the rights of labour' and so on, which were the characteristic and necessary camouflage under which the Fascist dictatorship was imposed. The workers would have to cast aside this leadership or else 'see their organisations handed over to a capitalist totalitarian system, their rights and freedom destroyed in the name of the battle for freedom, and the "new order" finally blossoming in its full glory as the British version of "national socialism" '.[89]

The continuities with Dutt's pre-war writings are manifest, even if the tone was more extreme. A collaborationist Labour movement was being used to introduce Fascism in Britain; and yet at the same time an independent Labour movement was the essential basis of a successful struggle against the introduction of Fascism. The question of the Labour movement was pivotal.

7.6 Labour movement or Labour Front?

> Is the Labour movement an independent movement of the working class or is it not? Is it opposed to capitalism and the political parties of capitalism or not? Is it opposed to a régime of Big Business that is bringing the mass of the people to ruin and threatens their young men with decimation or is it not?
>
> (Allen Hutt, April 1940[90])

Not since the days of 'Class Against Class' had the CP made the mistake of treating the Labour movement as an undifferentiated monolith labelled Social Democracy. Far from it, in the late 1930s Communists had developed multifarious forms of common action with other left-wingers, worked energetically within the Labour and trade union movement and campaigned for Communist affiliation to the Labour Party.[91] However, the dominant Labour leadership remained steadfastly opposed to any form of association with Communists and to the CP's strategy for defeating Chamberlain, and so the CP in its turn had maintained, with varying degrees of acerbity, its criticisms of this leadership, or lack of it. The tactic officially recommended by the Comintern, and implemented in those countries where the Socialist leadership proved more amenable, was the united front from above, even to the point of amalgamating Communist and social-democratic organisations. In Britain, however, through no desire of the Communists, the embryonic Popular Front had perforce to be built up 'from below', in opposition to the Labour leadership. Consequently, when Dimitrov at the beginning of the war called on European Communists to forge 'working-class unity from below' by 'a most resolute struggle against the Social-Democratic flunkeys of imperialism',[92] this did not require quite the *volte-face* in Britain as in some other countries.

In one respect, the Communist analysis of the role of Social Democracy in the war closely resembled the earlier formulations of 'Social Fascism'. The CP literally portrayed the Labour leadership as the left wing of Fascism which used its influence over the working class, its control of its basic organisations and its familiarity with anti-capitalist phraseology in the interests of a totalitarian capitalist dictatorship. Frequently the role of the Labour Party was likened to that of the Nazis. Within the 'single totalitarian party' which sustained the government each section had its own particular function. That of the 'Labour detachment of the Government Party' was 'to keep the workers quiet', 'to curb the unrest of the people, to hold them down, while they are fleeced and exploited, robbed of their rights and sacrificed to the war machine'. It was therefore no accident that the likes of Bevin, Morrison and Wilkinson were given responsibility for such sensitive issues as industrial conscription, ARP and the suppression of the Communist press. A Fascist state apparatus was being erected in Britain, while Labour propagandists distracted their supporters with specious talk of 'revolutionary changes' and 'War Socialism'. The Labour movement itself was being integrated into this Fascist state as the British counterpart to the Labour Front. This theme, of Labour's complicity in the advance to Fascism, was a persistent refrain in the Communist press.[93]

The Labour leadership's positive contribution to the establishment of Fascism had its equally disastrous negative corollary: by these policies of class collaboration it was destroying the Labour movement, without which no effective resistance to Fascism was possible. Here lay the crucial difference between this period and that of 'Class Against Class'. Although the CP described Social Democracy in terms very like those of a decade earlier, it did not, as it once had, demand a decisive break with the traditional ideology and organisations of British Labour, nor did it present Communism as the only, necessarily revolutionary, alternative to an obsolescent Labour movement.[94] On the contrary, the Party claimed to stand for the integrity and independence of Labour at a time when Attlee and Bevin were attempting to deliver their organisations to the class enemy. Long accused of disruption, the CP now reversed the charges. It fought against the 'splitters and disrupters' of the 'capitalist Fifth Column' for the 'unity of the working class, in their basic organisations . . ., on the programme of the class struggle'.[95] For in such a programme lay the only alternative to the demoralisation and disintegration of the Labour movement.

The evidence for the decline of the Labour Party was striking enough and others on the left than Communists had come to the conclusion that it was 'dying, and soon it may be dead':

> All over the country its death-throes are apparent. Hundreds of local parties 'have a name to live but are dead'. Active membership has slumped enormously. . . . In scores of constituencies the Labour Party – as a living, breathing, functioning organism – is wrapped in the grave-clothes of the mausoleum.[96]

There were three sides to the problem. The first was that wartime dislocation constituted a formidable hindrance to organised political activity, no matter what the organisation. This problem was accentuated for the Labour Party by the absence of elections. Unlike the CP, the Labour Party had long been strong on electoral politics and weak on just about everything else, and where local Labour parties had been geared towards winning periodic elections they now risked falling into disrepair. This problem was in its turn accentuated by an exodus from the Labour Party of a number of those of its members – mostly Communists or their very close allies – who had been keenest to broaden the scope of its activities.

As from July 1939, a number of Communists inside the Labour Party declared their revulsion from Labour's official policies, announced their membership of the Communist Party and encouraged like-minded members of the Labour Party to do the same.[97] The trickle of resignations continued throughout the early part of the war. By June 1940 the CP's position, as laid down by Dutt, was that 'comrades in the Labour Party should come out in open fight for the policy outlined in the PB manifesto.[98] Any passing over to the Communist Party should take place first on the basis of an open fight within the Labour Party, with a view to winning and bringing over the maximum support in any break that takes place.'[99] The effect of these resignations was quite disproportionate to the relatively small numbers involved, for they were drawn from the active minority whose efforts kept the Labour Party going at a grassroots level. Many of those who went over to the CP held positions of responsibility in the Labour Party, especially in 'backward' areas, and a number were councillors or prospective Parliamentary candidates.[100] The departure of such left-wingers was further hastened by the disciplinary actions of Transport House and a number of local Labour Parties, especially once their public adhesion to the People's Convention movement had made the identification of the CP's 'comrades in the Labour Party' so much easier.[101] The end result of these three factors – dislocation, the absence of elections, and the departure of a number of those left-wing activists best fitted to cope with the absence of elections – was the *rigor mortis* of the Labour Party as described above. According to official figures, Labour's individual membership virtually halved within a year.[102] Its local activities, circumscribed as these were by the edicts of Transport House, declined at least proportionately.

According to Communists, the industrial wing of the movement was in no better health. True, membership figures were rising, union recognition was spreading and union officials were being consulted on a whole range of issues: the partnership dreamt of since the days of Mondism was at last being realised. Communists, however, protested that this leap in status was not worth the price of relinquishing the independence of organised Labour, without which the defence of working-class interests was impossible. One historian has remarked that during this period 'the annual reports of the TUC General Council began to read like the records of some special government department responsible for coordinating policy in the social and industrial spheres'.[103] For Communists, as we have seen, when trade unions became indistinguishable from government departments, then Fascism was just around the corner. Moreover, by pursuing their goals of consultation and conciliation, union officials discredited trade unionism in the eyes of ordinary workers. Communists argued that the traditional functions of the unions were being undermined by enforced arbitration, the compulsory allocation of essential labour and other interferences with free collective bargaining, 'so that men and women begin to wonder what is the use of the trade unions after all'.[104] 'Once the Trade Union leadership has succeeded in committing the Trade Unions to support for the war', wrote Peter Kerrigan, 'really serious obstacles arise in endeavouring to utilise the Unions as instruments for defending the workers' economic interests'.[105] Like the Labour Party, the trade unions were faced with a crisis of justifying their very existence.

Communists, so they claimed, obtained no sectarian satisfaction from this situation. Pollitt, for example, deplored the 'sorry state of affairs' prevailing in the Labour Party in much the same terms as the Labour spokesmen quoted earlier, arguing that the leadership's collaborationist policies had 'so corroded the Labour movement that it becomes easier for the Tories to impose Fascism on the working class'. To retrieve the Labour movement for the class struggle, 'to end the present disastrous policy and leadership, and work for the restoration of Labour's independence from capitalist politics', was thus the first condition for the defeat of the Tory Fascists, 'for there can be no success in the fight against capitalism, fascism or war unless it is on the basis of a powerful, united and independent working class movement'.[106]

Even more did Communists regret the 'tragic decline in Trade Union branch life' and call for a revival of the 'real spirit of militant trade unionism'. This, they insisted, would be achieved, not by left-wingers devoting themselves exclusively to unfettered workshop activity, but by their showing a willingness to take on official positions and use them to challenge the policies of collaboration.[107] In other words, Communists in industry were to fight against particular reactionary officials, not officialdom as such. In 1940 Jack Owen related the case of a group of AEU workers who proposed to tear up their union cards and pay their dues into a fund to maintain a full-time shop steward. If others followed suit, they suggested, this could form the basis of a national shop stewards' movement based on the class struggle. To Owen, such attitudes, however understandable in the circumstances, were unadulterated 'Leftism':

> Should I tear up my card of membership in an organisation half a million strong, built up in struggle against the boss, and which has proved itself adaptable to changing conditions just because its present leaders are reactionary? The question, looked at in this light, answers itself. . . . We can and must work to bring the AEU in the vanguard of the fight again.[108]

The same applied to each and every trade union. The struggle against the putative Labour Front required not that the existing institutions of the Labour movement be replaced but that they be transformed. The contest for the leadership of the working class was intensified, but the legitimacy of the basic organisations of the workers was not called into question.

This strategy rested on an abiding faith in the militant temper of the Labour rank and file. During the war, as before it, the issue between the Communist Party and the Labour leadership was not revolution or reform but struggle or submission, militancy or conciliation. By this token, those members of the Labour Party who, whether of revolutionary outlook or not, were prepared to struggle for working-class interests remained the CP's natural allies. Thus, late in 1939, did the CP renew its application for affiliation to the Labour Party, not as 'a demand for a united front with the upper leadership' but as 'a lever of struggle against the official leadership and policy in order to promote the development of the united struggle of the workers in the factories and local organisations'.[109] Thus too did the CP attach such importance to the passing of coordinated resolutions by these local organisations.[110] For the CP, the activists who passed these resolutions, and who assisted in the unofficial election campaigns described earlier, constituted the incorruptible core of the Labour movement. The distinction between these militant activists and their timid, place-seeking leaders was axiomatic. Discussions of the 1940 Labour Party conference hinged on this supposed cleavage within the ranks of Labour[111] and, although this conference endorsed the policy of coalition under Churchill by an overwhelming majority, Communists remained as hopeful as any Micawber on the grounds that 'such a policy is too bad to carry much of the movement for long, and the great mass must soon react and return to active militant Socialism'.[112] The problem, as diagnosed by D. N. Pritt, was simply one of leadership and organisation:

> Who is to gather and unite the growing opposition? At the very moment when the need for leadership is greatest . . . the great organisations of Transport House . . . have abdicated. . . . Other ways must be found to unite the mass of the people, including of course large sections of the rank and file of the Labour Party, and develop a definite programme of opposition. How is this invaluable and urgent work being done, or to be done?

Pritt answered his own question:

> I appeal for the widest support of the People's Convention. Only the people can save themselves by their own action.[113]

7.7 The People's Convention

> the Convention and the People's movement behind it are not intended to take the place of, or in any way weaken, the existing industrial, co-operative or political organisations of the working class. On the contrary, its purpose is to *strengthen* these organisations, to help them to establish their independence of the ruling class, and in this way to help them to carry out the job which is the purpose for which they were founded . . .
>
> (D. N. Pritt, 1940[114])

Although the programme of the People's Convention merely echoed the latest demands of the Communist Party, the thinking behind the Convention was not entirely new. Back in the mid-1920s, while MacDonald and Henderson insisted on the severance of all links between Labour and Communism, Communists attempted to reinforce these links with a loosely organised National Left Wing Movement. Consisting of 'sympathetic Labour Parties and Left Wing Groups who are pledged to work for a left-wing programme', this organisation aimed 'not to supersede the Labour Party, but to "remould it nearer to the heart's desire" of the rank and file'.[115] A decade later, after the triumph of inertia and anti-Communism at the 1936 Labour conference, the CP and its allies tried to regroup the left around the Unity Campaign in order to rescue the Labour movement 'from the consequences of the disruptive policies which are being pursued with incredible light-mindedness by the present leadership'.[116] During the imperialist war period, too, Communists believed that the independence and effectiveness of Labour required that the Labour leadership be challenged by a united front of Socialists, both within the Labour Party and without. The specific forms of this united front were worked out by Palme Dutt.

In February 1940, Dutt mooted the idea of a Socialist Labour Alliance to carry forward the struggle against the war. Such an alliance would bring together Communists and those 'sincere socialists in the Labour Party' who were coming increasingly into conflict with the 'counter-revolutionary' Labour leadership. Only a minority of these 'manifold and scattered elements' had attained sufficient political consciousness to join the Communist Party and yet, said Dutt, 'the issue raised for the Labour Party membership . . . cannot be met by hopes of the future reform of the Labour Party, alongside submission to existing discipline and official policy in the name of unity'. Already there existed 'various forms of local association and common activity' but these were 'still only passing forms, sporadically appearing and not closely knit together'. The way forward lay in a national 'Socialist Labour Alliance, with corresponding local groupings, uniting equally organisations and individual members' sections'. The first step in this direction would be the calling of a 'National Conference of all working class organisations and sections on the basis of the common struggle against the Government, the war and capitalism and for the aims of the working class and socialism'. Ideally, this call would come not from the CP but from 'leading representative bodies which have already taken decisions of opposition to the war' – the Glasgow Trades Council, for example, or the SWMF if it came down against the war. This conference would not at first establish a national organisation but merely 'adopt a common platform of struggle, issue a call to all socialists, trade unionists and working class organisations to rally on the basis of this platform of struggle, and elect a Provisional Co-ordinating Committee to guide the further development of the movement'.

Dutt was already thinking along the lines that would lead to the People's Convention, although these early proposals would be modified in crucial ways. In the first place, their objective was a 'united front from below' based on the local organisations of the working class; the People's Convention, on the other hand, was a sort of 'People's Front from below' encompassing a diversity of elements. Secondly, while Dutt warned that the Socialist Labour Alliance should not be built at the expense of splitting the trade union movement, he advised the 'withholding of payment of the political levy until such time as the political fund is used for socialist labour purposes'.[117] At this point Dutt had no faith in the regeneration of the Labour Party and felt that a clean break was necessary. He conceived the Socialist Labour Alliance as a stage in the development of a 'United Socialist Labour Party . . . on a basis of revolutionary socialism'.[118]

These proposals were not made public and were in some ways an aberration on Dutt's part. By June, while still urging 'the political independence of the mass of the membership from the reactionary leadership', Dutt acknowledged that 'the organised membership of the Labour Party is not yet ready for a decisive break. Not only the illusions on the war and the instincts of national defencism, but the deep loyalty to Labour, as the expression of the principle of class solidarity and unity, still hold the mass of the workers in disciplined submission to the leadership . . .' Dutt still insisted that left-wingers in the Labour Party should express their opposition to 'the policy of war and coalition', despite possible disciplinary measures, but now recommended that they 'direct their appeal and propaganda to the Labour organisations, and not regard themselves as the nucleus of a new party'. In keeping with this regained awareness of the centrality of the official Labour movement, Dutt acknowledged that 'the continued payment of the political levy is essential. Refusal of payment . . . by militant trade unionists isolates from the political fight in the trade unions.' Indeed, Dutt saw the fight in the unions as the key to winning the fight within the Labour Party:

> Most of our work in the past has been done through the individual members' sections and the delegate bodies. What is vital now is to pay far more attention to the affiliated organisations. . . . The trade union branches can fight Transport House far more effectively than individual sections, and the attitude of the local Labour parties and local trades councils depends very largely on the feeling and strength expressed by the local trade union branches.[119]

At the same time, Dutt argued that 'the main task continues to be the development of united activity in the localities'. 'Sustained and serious efforts' were required, but no longer with the aim of building an alliance against capitalism and war. On the contrary, particular care needed to be taken 'in choosing the types of demand that have the widest form of appeal, e.g., in the mining districts questions of compensation, silicosis and tuberculosis, etc; in all cases questions arising out of the conditions of the dependants of men in the Forces'.[120] Dutt had come to realise that a Labour Alliance based on revolutionary Socialism was not yet feasible.

By August, Dutt's thinking had moved a stage further. He now sketched the precise lines along which the People's Convention would develop as 'a wide coming together of all types of organisations and mass elements', adding that 'participation in this campaign is now the main task before the Party and all forces need to be thrown into it' and that 'the Political Bureau as a whole should be continuously and actively guiding the work of the campaign, and its main members participating in it'.[121] It is to this campaign, with the knowledge that Dutt's guiding hand lay behind it, that we now turn.

The Convention movement originated in July 1940 when an all-London conference convened by the Hammersmith Labour Party and Trades Council set up a People's Vigilance Committee to mount campaigns on what were in effect the current demands of the Communist Party.[122] By September it had been decided to organise a national convention of interested parties in January 1941 towards which end a People's Convention manifesto was issued with more than five hundred signatures appended. Henceforth, the 'main task' of Communists was to publicise and win support for the six-point programme on which the Convention was to be based:

1. Defence of the people's living standards.
2. Defence of the people's democratic and trade union rights.
3. Adequate air raid precautions, deep bomb-proof shelters, rehousing and relief of victims.
4. Friendship with the Soviet Union.
5. A People's Government, truly representative of the whole people and able to inspire the confidence of the working people of the world.
6. A people's peace that gets rid of the causes of war.[123]

So attractive was this platform that when the Convention assembled in London the following January three halls were filled by 2,234 delegates purporting to represent 1,200,000 people.[124]

There can, of course, be no real doubt that the vast majority of these million or so people had had little say in the mandating of their 'delegates', some of whom were apparently repudiated in subsequent weeks.[125] However, this was not always the case. From London, for example, J. T. Murphy reported that the Convention aroused 'much discussion both in the workshop and in the trade union branches' and estimated that it could count on three hundred supporters in his factory alone.[126] Moreover, even if the report of the Convention's Credentials Committee undoubtedly exaggerated the level of popular support for the campaign,[127] it also indicated that the 'call to the people' had been answered by a considerable number of Labour movement activists. In her Mass-Observation report on the Convention, Celia Fremlin described the delegates as follows:

> There was, of course, a liberal sprinkling of CP and extreme left-wingers – particularly among helpers, bookstall assistants, etc. The vast majority of the rank and file were, however, ordinary trade unionists, etc., of very varying shades of left-ish opinion.[128]

These were exactly the sort of people to whom the CP looked for the reinvigoration of the Labour movement. As one Convention delegate recalled, 'we took the view in those days that if you got two or three people from each of the key factories, then it was more important than mere numbers'.[129] Whatever the extent of its mass support, the representation at the Convention demonstrated the enduring ties between the Communist Party and large numbers of working-class activists.

The Convention provided these delegates with little opportunity to engage in vigorous debate on the issues which had brought them to London. The *Daily Herald* dubbed the Convention the 'People's Reichstag',[130] and there was some truth in this jibe: prospective speakers had at the beginning of the proceedings to get their speeches approved by the Standing Orders Committee, while any interventions from the floor were dealt with in a peremptory fashion.[131] Despite claims to the contrary, the Convention was not intended as a 'People's Parliament'[132] but as a demonstration of popular unity behind a pre-arranged set of slogans.

As such, it undoubtedly impressed most of the delegates,[133] who seemed content to voice their enthusiastic approval while political differences went undisturbed. Especially warm welcomes were given to Dutt, to a Church of England vicar, to Krishna Menon and to two soldiers who, in defiance of army regulations, appeared in uniform.[134] 'The biggest applause of all', wrote a Mass-Observer, 'was received by Harry Pollitt simply on announcement of his name . . . more people were trying to *see* him than had been in the case of any other speaker'. Further comments by the same investigator throw an interesting light, not only on Pollitt's legendary oratory, but on the nature of the proceedings in the Royal Hotel: 'Several people after the meeting thought "Harry was marvellous", but on being questioned by Inv. could not remember anything he had said.'[135] Not surprisingly, the business of the Convention was carried out without a hitch and its existing programme was more or less automatically ratified: the original six points in more detailed versions than those quoted earlier, together with new commitments to colonial liberation and to the taking over of 'the banks, land, transport, armaments and other large industries in order to organise our economic life in the interests of the people'.[136] Likewise, the conference endorsed the Standing Orders Committee's twenty-six nominees – Communists or their very close allies – for the National Committee which henceforth would run the affairs of the movement.

Over the coming months the National Committee issued a good deal of literature elaborating the Convention's eight points and stating its attitude to current political developments. During its existence the Convention later claimed to have issued 632,000 pamphlets and 1,336,000 leaflets and manifestos.[138] Locally the work of the Convention was carried on by twelve regional and reportedly as many as 200 local committees.[139] In the summer it was announced that the Convention was to hold a still larger recall conference at the end of August, but this never took place. By the time August arrived, the 'character' of the war had been 'transformed' by the German invasion of the USSR, and much of the programme on which the Convention had campaigned had been discarded by the CP. Moreover, the impetus behind the movement was now being diverted into other channels, for the burgeoning movement of Anglo–Soviet committees offered the prospect of a unity far broader than had been achieved by the People's Convention on a political basis more in accord with the CP's new priorities. The convention languished for a few more months, issuing calls for unity behind the government and increased production which bore only a tenuous relation to its original programme until at last, at the beginning of 1942, it finally wound up its affairs.[140] So what, apart from the expulsion of a number of Socialists from the Labour Party, had it achieved, or at least set out to achieve, during its brief existence?

Obviously, one of its aims was to fill the vacuum left by the Labour leadership's perfidious alliance with the ruling class. 'Workers have said to me time and time again that our message is pulling together the Labour movement', wrote Harry Adams, the Convention's Chairman:

> Most important is the effect upon organised workers who have found that their normal avenues of activity . . . have been deliberately closed by the Labour leadership.
> The Convention pushed open the doors and, in place of despondency, confidence in their power to achieve unity and concessions from the ruling class even in war time is possessing growing numbers of workers.[141]

The aim of the movement was thus to give shape and expression, 'a common policy and leadership', to the fragmented and rudderless opposition to Labour's official policies.[142]

However, while it was constantly stressed that the Convention was intended in this way to reinvigorate the Labour movement, the process worked both ways. According to Adams, it was through its industrial base that the Convention stood the best chance of realising its political objectives:

> Especially do I appeal to shop stewards, trade union branch secretaries, delegates to trades councils – you who represent the real life-blood of the Labour movement. . . . You hold the key positions. You have the mass influence in the decisive places; you have the power to change things. Be proud of that power and proud to use it.[143]

The Convention thus challenged the right of Transport House to the leadership of the Labour movement and hinted that it aimed to use local Labour organisations to achieve its own political ends. One can well understand why

Transport House in its turn should accuse the Convention of deliberately disrupting the Labour movement with the intention of building up a new political party.[144]

The Convention's spokesmen repeatedly denied this charge, claiming that the Convention movement had 'developed from within the Labour Party' and drew most of its support from the Labour rank and file. The Labour Party could not be identified with the careerists who occupied its higher echelons; it drew its strength from the mass of selfless activists in the localities. It was not, said Pritt 'to much laughter and clapping', the first time that an army had proved better than its generals.[145] The Convention, it was claimed, not only embodied 'the spirit of those who founded our great Labour and Trade Union movement'[146] but stood by the principles laid down more recently by those who still led the Labour Party. Fourteen Berkshire Socialists protested against their expulsion from the Labour Party in a pamphlet demanding, not a break with outdated reformist policies, but 'a return to an independent policy based on Labour's Immediate Programme of 1937'. This programme, they felt, was 'nowhere contradicted by the eight points of the People's Convention'; and to prove this, they juxtaposed extracts from the two programmes and begged readers to note the similarity. They publicised the story of their expulsion, they said, 'because we wish to win back the right to belong to the movement which our fathers built and which we have gladly served' and thus ' "to keep alive the Labour organisation in our own areas . . . until full working class unity and activity can be achieved" '.[147]

Running parallel with this portrayal of the Convention as a movement of disenchanted Labour was a series of vigorous, if unconvincing, denials that it was a Communist front organisation, the 'Innocents' Club' derided by the National Council of Labour.[148] Dutt's papers reveal just how much the movement owed to his thinking – and how little to its 'non-Party' figureheads like Pritt and Adams – and how many of its most important statements were drafted by him,[149] although they also reveal, as we shall see, that the policies of Dutt and his Party were very much conditioned by the need to find common ground with the 'innocents'. In any case, the NCL's suspicions were not to be allayed, and it called on 'all members of our Movement to combat all Communist attempts to divide their ranks in this supreme moment in our history':

AS WORKERS: STRENGTHEN THE TRADE UNIONS!
AS CITIZENS: STRENGTHEN THE LABOUR PARTIES!
AS CONSUMERS: STRENGTHEN THE CO-OPERATIVE SOCIETIES![150]

But it was precisely because of its commitment to strengthen these organisations, and the NCL's alleged indifference to their fate, that the Convention claimed the allegiance of Labour activists. It did not 'seek to destroy existing organisations; usurp their authority; nor supersede useful machinery or negotiations' but rather to 'inspire new life and confidence into these movements'.[151] Its purpose was to challenge the existing leadership of the Labour movement, not to replace its basic organisations.

Thus the Convention never took on the normal functions of a political party. There was no membership as such and the Convention had no real organisation below the level of the local committees, and possibly very little even at this level: in the recollection of two Convention delegates interviewed, the movement 'only existed in terms of the national organisation' and 'there were no local branches'.[152] At a London conference, where it was again stressed that 'the Convention is *not* a new party, and does not cut across any of the existing parties', the main task laid down for supporters of the Convention was individual propaganda: 'each individual must keep the subject under discussion among his friends and in his organisation'.[153] Similarly, although the CP had previously put up 'independent' candidates in by-elections, no nominee of the People's Convention put its programme before the electorate; when Malcolm MacEwen did so in Dunbartonshire in February 1941 it was as the representative of the Communist Party.[154] In short, the Convention never projected itself as an alternative to the Labour movement. Its relationship to Labour was summed up by a resolution passed at a mass rally on Tyneside:

> The Convention movement is one of unity based on active, functioning trade union branch life, shop steward and workshop organisation and a vigorous local Labour Movement. . . . A People's Government can neither come to power nor function unless it is based upon and led by the Labour and trade union movement.[155]

But if a People's Government was unthinkable without the support of organised Labour, the People's Convention was nevertheless intended to represent far more than that section of the working class which opposed the government.

From time to time during the development of the Convention movement, Communist spokesmen explained why it was that the CP campaigned, not for 'the seizure of power . . . and the establishment of Socialism', nor even for a Labour government which would 'have the advantage of being a class Government, and opening the way for further developments', but for the apparently much vaguer aim of a People's Government. During the war, as before it, the Party's main objective was to resist the development of Fascism; and Fascism, it was argued, advanced the interests of only a tiny minority of the people. Everybody else could be mobilised against it provided they understood how Fascism manifested itself, what it stood for and how it achieved its aims. Thus it was that, just as during the 1930s, the idea of 'the People' was invoked with monotonous regularity in Communist propaganda: a People's War, a People's Peace; a People's Parliament, a People's Army; a People's this, a People's that. If anything, this incantation grew even more repetitive in the months leading up to the People's Convention, as the Communist press articulated the wartime grievances of the various components of this anti-Fascist majority. Despite their diversity, these groups were bound by their common interest in removing the Churchill Government, along with its policies of imperialist war and encroaching Fascism, and the specific demand for a 'People's Government' was held to express 'the wide character of the movement that will bring it into power and the wide support on which such a Government will rely'.[156]

Put in this context, the People's Convention appears very much as a reincarnation of the pre-war People's Front. It was an attempt to give a national, political dimension to the agitations to which Communists had long devoted so much energy, as well as to overcome the sclerosis of the Labour movement. Its manifesto was conceived as 'a call to all working men and women; Socialists, trade unionists and Co-operators; professional and intellectual workers; small shop-keepers, small business-men and farmers; democrats and anti-Fascists; in short, to all workers by hand and brain'. This distinction between 'the people' and the parasitic minority living off the people goes back at least to the days of the Chartists, who often counterposed the 'productive' and the 'unproductive' classes. That the Convention programme called to mind the Six Points of the People's Charter, and that the Convention was originally to have been held in Manchester, where the National Charter Association had been formed a century earlier, was no accident. As a Communist historian put it to readers of the *Daily Worker*, the Convention followed 'in the footsteps of the Chartists'.[157]

During the run-up to the Convention, the *Worker* printed statements of support for its programme from individuals of disparate views from all walks of life: engineers, railwaymen, academics, clergymen, pacifists, disenchanted supporters of the Conservative and Liberal Parties and, of course, Labour activists and Communists. The image presented was that of a broad movement of democratic challenge, and the Convention organised a variety of activities to give substance to this image. Thus, to give one example, were a series of Student Conventions held to bring home to students the wartime neglect of education.[158] Another of the movement's particular objectives was to arouse the women of Britain on the issues which concerned them most, and indeed the Convention was to be as successful in this field as any.

In the first part of 1941 it ran a sustained campaign on the food question and set up the London Women's Parliament, an initiative which survived the demise of the Convention itself and took root in other parts of the country.[159] The Convention was equally concerned to stand forth as a protest against the cultural debasement of capitalism. It formed a Committee of Arts and Entertainments Professions and enlisted a number of illustrious names in its support: the bandleaders, Lew Stone, Phil Cardew and Sidney Lipton; the composers, Alan Bush and Rutland Boughton; the sculptor, Henry Moore; the actors, Michael Redgrave and Beatrix Lehmann; and the writers, Patrick Hamilton, Rosamund Lehmann and Sylvia Townsend Warner, not forgetting 'L. Kellett, the well known wrestler' and Mick Mariano 'who can do anything with a piano accordion'.[160] Fundraising events included a variety show featuring the Saxes and Sevens, the Convention Swingsters and the People's Choir and a concert of orchestral works by Bach and Mozart.[161] The Convention portrayed itself as a genuine people's movement, representing the forces of progress and enlightenment in revolt against the political and cultural decay of capitalism. It was not meant to appear as just another scheme worked out in King Street.

The very heterogeneity of the support claimed by the Convention provoked widespread scepticism as to the nature of the common objectives which held it together. The consensus on the anti-Communist left was that the Convention's followers were, by and large, honest men and women who were unwittingly advancing the defeatist intentions of the disingenuous, conspiratorial Communists who controlled the movement.[162] This argument rested on the assumption that the CP was bent on a Leninist line of opposition to the war and that all its activities were directed towards precipitating a revolutionary crisis in Britain. However, when the *Daily Worker* – in effect the organ of the Convention as well as the CP – addressed these criticisms, it expressed no immediate interest in revolution:

> The Press has sneered at the extremely varied character of the Convention. How can soldiers agree with clergymen, constitutionalists with revolutionaries and co-operators with shopkeepers? How, indeed? Because they all speak for the people, because they are all determined to find a basis for agreement in face of the common danger . . .

But this was still rather nebulous. What basis of agreement could possibly unite such disparate interests? The *Daily Worker* gave its answer:

> The eight points adopted by the Convention are wise and solid. No pipe dreams of a new world, but a realistic programme for uniting all sections of the working people in the fight for the conditions of life and democratic rights of to-day and the

People's Government and People's Peace of to-morrow.[163]

This is all a bit mystifying. The CP was ostensibly the Party of revolution, taking its inspiration from pipe dreams of the new world of Socialism for which alone it existed. Moreover, the Party's leading theoretician had described the imperialist war as the death throes of capitalism, the harbinger of 'the greatest revolutionary crisis this world has ever known',[164] the opportunity for the workers to take power and turn their dreams into reality. With this revolutionary task before the Party, alliances with shopkeepers and constitutionalists could appear as irrelevant or worse:

> in time of war . . . all the pre-requisites for a Popular Front on the old model have disappeared. . . .
> For we are in the midst of an Imperialist war in which the forces which might have co-operated together in time of peace have been split asunder by the war and when the duty of Socialists is to utilise the crisis created by the war to bring about the overthrow of the capitalist system.[165]

Thus J. R. Campbell wrote in June 1940; and yet for the best part of the next year the 'main task' of the Communist Party was to attempt to rebuild a broad popular movement around a 'realistic' programme of immediate demands – very much a Popular Front on the old model.

The rationale for the CP's strategy was provided, as usual, by Dutt. In answering the detailed indictment of Communist policy in *The Betrayal of the Left* in April 1941, Dutt reaffirmed the CP's commitment to the revolutionary, Leninist analysis of imperialist war: of course the Communists had their 'ulterior aims'! However, he went on:

> the ultimate issues of the final struggle for power and the solution of the crisis let loose by imperialism and its war are not yet the immediate issues which confront the masses of the people for decision to-day or to-morrow. An enormous development of the political situation and mass awakening . . . will be necessary before such a stage is reached; and the fulfilment of such a development will leave few of the landmarks familiar in present controversy standing as they are at present. Hence the barren, abstract, metaphysical character of much of the present controversy on the left, which speculates on future hypotheses *as an excuse for opposing and sabotaging present elementary simple common tasks*.[166]

The gist of Dutt's argument would have been familiar to readers of the *Labour Monthly* before the war. The Communist Party was, by definition (and perhaps only by definition), the revolutionary party which would lead the people to Socialism. However, the necessary revolution was not yet the issue, and to speculate on this future event was therefore abstract and metaphysical. Far more important were the simple, common tasks with which the masses were currently concerned. And of course, these elementary tasks were all defensive – defence of democratic rights; defence of living standards; and, literally, defence from German bombs. As in the 1930s, there was no clear connection drawn between these immediate struggles and the final, necessarily offensive, innovative, creative revolutionary act. Instead, the revolutionary development of defensive mass struggles was more or less assumed. Dutt's 'Notes' frequently referred to the profound crisis of capitalism which had led to and was then deepened by an imperialist war which brought with it the promise of revolution. But that was in the long term. In the short term revolutionaries always seemed to have their backs to the wall:

> War is a forcing house of all development, sharpens all contradictions, telescopes the evolution of years into months and days, shatters old and decaying social and political systems, states and empires, and in this sense, by its destructive role . . . prepares the way for future revolutionary change. This is the long-range significance of imperialist war, which is the expression of the profound crisis of the dying capitalist system. But in its short-range effect imperialist war, because of its reactionary character, means an enormous strengthening of all reactionary forces.[167]

As before the war, the CP's primary objective was to mobilise resistance to Fascism, thereby preserving the liberties and developing the political consciousness and will to struggle necessary for the future advance to Socialism.

In this light, the People's Convention does not appear as the hub of a new Communist strategy for exploiting the possibilities of imperialist war. It seems rather to have been an attempt to give some cohesion to the diverse defensive struggles in which Communists had been engaged for many years and to rebuild the links between Communists and others on the left. Towards the end of 1941, Dutt argued in a letter to Pollitt that 'the Convention represented the first beginning . . . of a coming together of all types of people in a broad democratic movement for immediate democratic aims', in which Communists would play a guiding, but not a controlling, role. In practice however, as Dutt admitted, the Convention had operated as a 'small auxiliary organisation run by us, peopling its committees with our own members and close associates, instead of drawing in the new forces and giving them a free hand, with only political assistance from a few of our politically capable representatives'. Significantly, Dutt believed that the Convention was as capable of performing a positive role after June 1941 as before, an indication that he at least regarded it as more than just an anti-war 'front' organisation.[168]

So the People's Convention can be seen as an attempt by the Communist

Party to construct a non-sectarian front around the immediate needs of wide sections of the population. Into this picture the first six of the Convention's eight points fit neatly as the programmatic basis of an immediate defensive struggle in the interests of which more fundamental differences should be set aside. But the final and most contentious points of the Convention's programme – for a People's Government and a People's Peace – were, as the *Daily Worker* hinted, slightly different; these were the issues, not of today, but of tomorrow. The achievement of these aims would require something more than a common adherence to civilised values, and the enunciation of these demands would seem likely to bring up the political differences which Communists appeared anxious to avoid. Revolutionaries and constitutionalists could no doubt come to an agreement about the need for bombproof shelters, but on the question of a People's Government taking power in election-free Britain their differences were seemingly insuperable. Similarly, while clerics and soldiers (figuratively speaking) might very likely stand side by side in the defence of democratic rights, the question of a People's Peace was just as likely to keep them asunder.

These two points therefore require more detailed consideration. It is not enough to say that the CP opposed the war; it is crucial to establish the circumstances in which Communists envisaged the war being ended and the way in which their activities were designed to bring about those circumstances. During the 'phoney war', the CP's proposals amounted to little more than an endorsement of Hitler's peace offer. However, after the fall of France the CP issued no more calls on the people to 'stop the war' and no longer implored the British Government to sue for peace. Their proposals for the ending of the war were more comprehensive and at the same time more ambiguous.

7.8 People's Peace, People's War

We are not pacifists; we do not believe that there is nothing worse than war. There are some kinds of peace that are worse than war. What we want is a people's peace that will end the causes of war. We believe that only a people's government can achieve this kind of peace.

Many people say that this is all wishful thinking; that we imagine that the people of Germany would rise against Hitler as soon as we get a people's government here.

We do not know what the people of Germany will do. But we believe, as most people believe, that *until* Hitler is got rid of the war cannot stop. We believe that our task is to *help* the German people to do this.

(Ivor Montagu, speech, February 1941[169])

On 19 July 1940, Hitler, temporarily satiated, renewed his offer of a peace settlement with Britain. Undeterred by the disasters which had befallen it, the British Government pledged itself to fight on. The British Communist Party, shaken out of some of its illusions by the Blitzkrieg, echoed Churchill's rejection of Hitler's overtures, though with very different reasons:

> a People's Peace can never come from imperialism. It can only be won by the working people, taking the control of affairs into their own hands, in unity with the working people of all countries.[170]

This, more or less, was to be the CP's attitude until June 1941. When towards the end of 1940 the ILP contingent in the Commons put down a motion in favour of a negotiated peace settlement, the *Daily Worker* dismissed the suggestion as an 'entirely false issue' and derided the ILP's arguments as a 'pacifist bleat':

> Peace through an appeal to Hitler! The proposal is farcical. . . .
> The real issue . . . is action by the people themselves to end the war in their own way and over the heads of their Hitlers and Churchills.[171]

The CP's demand for a People's Peace was obviously something quite removed from the pacifist bleating which it had awkwardly combined with revolutionary growling during the early months of the war. The CP had apparently adopted a line on the war which accorded rather better with the internationalist and the anti-Fascist principles of Communism.

The main vehicle for the CP's campaign for a People's Peace was the People's Convention; and it was because it stood for this ill-defined objective that the Convention was particularly prone to allegations of defeatism. Time and time again the Convention's leaders refuted these persistent 'misrepresentations'[172] until at last, in the early part of 1941, they felt compelled to call upon Commander Edgar P. Young to clarify beyond doubt this most contentious point. Young's pamphlet began with a summary of the full Convention programme for the very good reason that the attainment of a People's Peace was held to be impossible without the prior implementation of its first seven points. The demand for a People's Peace had quite deliberately been left to the end of programme, and to take this last point out of sequence, to judge it in isolation, was ridiculous, fruitless and misleading. Young rejected 'futile half-measures or quack remedies', by which he specifically intended the suggestion of a compromise peace with Hitler:

> we very definitely do NOT want Hitler to win the war, and . . . would not negotiate peace *with anyone* on any terms which would permit the survival of the revolting systems represented by Hitler and Mussolini, *or by their admirers and imitators.*

But Young viewed with equal horror the prospect of victory for those who were fast introducing Fascism in Britain. He advocated instead an international struggle against Fascism in which Britons would play their full part:

> We want the British people to win, *in conjunction with the German and Italian peoples and with all other peoples,* by achieving a victory over Hitler, Mussolini and all those, here and throughout the world, who love Fascism or who are merely determined to maintain their own position of power and privilege (*which must lead, in the end, to Fascism*).

The scenario painted by Young was of a People's Government coming to power in Britain and offering a peace so attractive to the German people that they would be stimulated into overthrowing their oppressors.[173]

The main flaw in this argument is easily spotted. It is almost unbelievable that Palme Dutt, viewing the prospects for revolution in Europe at the beginning of 1941, could write that 'the danger . . . is that our movement may not develop rapidly enough for the pace of advance on the Continent, so that the Anglo–American millionaires can still dream of using the British people for the role of the gendarme of counter-revolution against the advance of the socialist revolution in Europe'.[174] More ludicrous still, the egregious Pritt apparently felt it 'almost certain' that the prospect of a 'People's Peace' would 'at once' release the German workers' pent-up hatred for the Nazi regime, so that the latter, 'even if not immediately succeeded by a German People's Government, [would] be compelled to accept . . . the terms of the peace proposed, or face immediate and widespread revolt'.[175]

Pritt's lack of political insight was admittedly unsurpassed, but this fantastic assessment of the supposedly precarious balance between Fascism and democracy on the continent – so precarious, indeed, that the formation of a democratic government in Britain would be enough to tilt the balance decisively in favour of the forces of democracy – was fundamental to the demand for a People's Peace. The CP did not feel able completely to drop its demand for peace, but neither would it contemplate a peace which would leave continental Fascism intact. It cut this Gordian knot by insisting on the vigour of the anti-Fascist movement in Europe, thereby implying that a democratic peace was a feasible objective. Thus, when the greetings of the 'real Germany' to the People's Convention reached London in March 1941, they were widely circulated by the Party to show that 'the workers in Germany are still fighting for solidarity between the workers of all lands'.[176] When it adopted a more principled, internationalist line on the war, the CP fell into the trap of vastly overestimating the capacities of the democratic opposition in Germany. Unable to claim that whether or not Germany won the war was immaterial to the British people, it produced worthless evidence to show that peace need not involve any German gains. Worthless, because by 1941 the 'real' Germany had been crushed by the other, very real Germany of barbaric reaction.

But if Communists clung to their hopes of a popular revolution in Germany, they were nevertheless prepared to admit that such a revolution would not inevitably follow the formation of a People's Government in Britain, even if it was very likely to. Possibly, even when offered the hand of friendship, the German people would fight on under Hitler. In that case, the argument ran, a People's Peace would be secured by a progressive war, as the formation of a People's Government would 'change the character of this war, while it continued'.[177] Moreover, Communists repeatedly insisted, 'for such a real defence a People's Government would be enormously more powerful than any previous imperialist Government conducting war for imperialist aims'.[178] The reasoning was by now familiar to readers of the Communist press. Under a popular government, the British people would fight with unequalled zeal in their own interests, unhampered by the forces of reaction, and would find willing allies in the peoples of Europe, of the Empire and of the USSR.[179]

The CP was, then, fairly clear as to the policies to be followed by a future People's Government. The prospect of such a government coming to power was nevertheless remote. The question remained of the Party's attitude to the imperialist war still in progress. Several of the Party's critics asked it to state in forthright terms whether or not they supported the existing war against the Axis powers, but no such statement was ever forthcoming.[180] Dutt justified this evasiveness, and the CP's failure to state explicitly the Leninist attitude to the war, by reference to the threat of retaliatory action by the authorities.[181] The implication that all that prevented Communists from expressing a Leninist line of opposition to the war was Defence Regulation 2D was nonsense. Whether out of genuine political convictions, a desire to build broad political alliances or just an astute assessment of the political situation, Communists were inhibited from expressing forthright opposition to the war because they could or would not countenance the idea of a Nazi victory.[182] Instead they criticised the policies by which the Churchill Government waged the war, very often adding that their own policies – the immediate demands of the People's Convention – would improve morale and strengthen the war effort.

Typical of the Party's ambiguous stance on the war was Malcolm MacEwen's Dunbartonshire by-election campaign on the programme of the People's Convention in February 1941. In his address, MacEwen described the war in traditional Leninist terms, as a resurgence of the longstanding conflict between the British and the German imperialists which had given rise to the First World War. But then he invoked a more recent tradition, stating that 'the Communists here, as elsewhere, fight for the defence of the people against fascism'. Matters were further complicated when he proceeded to accuse the British imperialists, who were struggling for world domination, of impeding the war effort:

> It is the Government which undermines 'morale' by the injustices for which it is responsible; which stands between the people and air raid precautions; which allows waste and inefficiency to sabotage industry . . . the way to improve 'morale' is not to suppress those who voice genuine grievances, but to remedy the grievances. But only a People's Government is prepared to take the necessary action against vested interests and profiteers, to organise industry efficiently, and to create a democratic People's Army . . .[183]

Clearly, MacEwen was not opposed to the war in the simple sense of wanting it stopped. According to the Home Intelligence report on the campaign, 'at no time did a Communist speaker state that he was "for peace" '.[184] 'As usual', commented a Mass-Observer at one big Communist meeting, 'Campbell explained that the Communist Party had no formula for an immediate peace'.[185] 'The Communist Party couldn't promise them peace to-morrow', said another Communist, 'but it could promise them an earlier peace than they would get under a Churchill Government, and in the meantime fair distribution of food and adequate ARP'.[186] And in the meantime, too, a People's Government would wage war more effectively than Churchill; thus, for example, MacEwen's call for a 'People's Army freed from the class barriers and distinctions which disfigure the armed forces to-day. These are the conditions of a successful defence of the people against fascism from abroad.'[187] MacEwen, in line with his Party, adopted an ambivalent attitude to the war in which the criminal struggle of British imperialism and the necessary struggle of the British people were intertwined. In the short term, this meant opposing the policies of the British imperialists as implemented by the Churchill Government, while advocating measures which would assist a democratic war effort. Thus can we explain the confusion within the Party's ranks as to its immediate attitude to the war. However, the Party was quite sure of the way to resolve this contradiction: a People's Government would repudiate the war aims of British imperialism, leaving only the legitimate struggle of the British people against Fascism. War might still be necessary for the survival of a People's Britain, but out of a People's War would come a People's Peace.

But how was one to obtain a People's Government?

7.9 A People's Government

> They're a bit impractical, as usual. A people's government must be made but they don't say how.
>
> (Streatham man's reaction to the CP leaflet *The People Must Act*, 1 July 1940[188])

If a People's Government was to be anything more than an ear-catching slogan, two crucial questions had to be answered: how was it to come to power and of whom would it consist? The first question was the more fundamental, if only because, if its accession to power involved protracted, violent conflict within Britain, then clearly the successful defence of the people from 'their enemies without' would be impossible while this went on. At some point in the projected campaign for a People's Government, either its supporters would have to make their contribution to a situation of such chaos as to make a mockery of the idea of resistance to Germany; or else the prospect of a People's Government would have to be abandoned until the threat of a Nazi invasion had receded.

To pose the alternatives in this way is to make the assumption that the CP was not banking its hopes on a peaceful transfer of power. Certainly, a recurrent criticism directed at left-wing champions of the 'People's War' was that they took for granted the readiness of Britain's rulers to accede to changes of a socialist character. The hopes of a 'revolution by consent' entertained by Labour theorists like Harold Laski were dismissed on the grounds that 'changes which would be of real value to the workers must be such as to meet with the sharpest and most violent resistance by the capitalists'.[189] From this one would infer that the call for a People's Government was a call for violent revolution and one would expect to find the CP preparing its supporters for this eventuality. To spread illusions to the contrary would be to follow in the steps of the renegade Laski. In practice, however, the CP was extremely vague as to the means by which a People's Government would come to power.

The prevalent confusion on this matter was personified by Pritt, the most prolific publicist for the People's Convention. When John Strachey, utilising his extensive knowledge of Marxist doctrine, warned that until the Convention pointed out the constitutional route to power it must be supposed to stand for revolution, Pritt's response was unexpectedly timorous. Not once, he protested, had he suggested that a People's Government should come to power 'by any but constitutional means'. Whether or not the ruling class was prepared to give up power 'without a fight', and Strachey thought not, was a 'big topic' which Pritt did not propose to discuss. But, he went on:

if it is suggested that it is wrong even to advocate a constitutional change of government because the ruling-class might resort to arms against us in the middle of the war rather than accept the change, I do not accept that double-distilled defeatism.[190]

While thus disavowing revolution, Pritt was in no way explicit as to how a constitutional change of government would be effected. This is hardly surprising for, as Pritt was the first to point out, constitutional means of change were systematically being denied the British people. And as to whether Britain's Fascist-inclined rulers were likely to relinquish power peacefully, Pritt himself had not long previously maintained that 'only political infants would be naive enough to suggest that the whole ruling class will give up without a struggle'.[191]

To say that Pritt was mixed up is a gross understatement. In a book published in 1941, he seemed at first to stand by the constitutional approach he had adopted in the controversy with Strachey:

> That the workers will have to take charge I have no doubt; but I believe it to be still possible for them to do so without revolution.

And yet two pages later he poured scorn on this very notion:

> It would be flying in the face of history to ask that the ruling class should recognise that its own continued existence involves a grave social evil, and should accordingly abdicate . . . it will defend its positions as stoutly as it can, regardless of the true interests of the community.[192]

All Communists were well aware that this stout rearguard action would involve the use of the armed forces and possibly collaboration with the Fascist enemy without; that the ruling class would not remain supine while its power was destroyed by constitutional methods, 'without revolution'. This, according to Pritt, was why it was discarding time-honoured constitutional procedures and turning to Fascism. But it is unfair to pick on Pritt. He differed from other Communists only in that he made a feeble attempt to anticipate the problems involved in the coming to power of a People's Government, thus revealing his thorough confusion. For the most part Communists were content to leave these problems until they had to face them.

Their reticence about the coming struggle for power was in part an indication that Communists did not regard a People's Government as an immediately attainable objective. The first task was to organise mass campaigns on immediate demands which would build up to a crescendo of anger against the government. Thus would the demand for a new government 'take on an irresistible character' leading to 'forms of political crisis' in which the masses would 'find the means' of securing their objective.[193] On more than one occasion, Dutt pointed out that 'the change from the Chamberlain to the Churchill Government took place, not by the arithmetic of the Parliamentary vote, which still registered a majority for Chamberlain, but in consequence of the rising feeling in the country', and cited the examples of the Hands Off Russia campaign, of Red Friday and the Invergordon Mutiny, and of the resistance to the new UAB regulations in 1935 as proof of the efficacy of mass struggle.[194] This was disingenuous, for Dutt knew very well that none of these agitations had touched upon the question of power. Mass discontent with Chamberlain had certainly played its part in his removal from office, but the decisive factor was the possibility of drawing from the existing Parliamentary representation an alternative government which could command a massive majority in the Commons. But Communists did not envisage a People's Government taking power merely through a reshuffling of the existing political élite; after all, Parliament was dominated by 'one totalitarian bloc' and a People's Government would therefore have to recruit the bulk of its personnel from outside Parliament, from the 'hundreds of signatories of the People's Convention' and not from the 'conventional Party leaders and Parliamentarians, who have completely exposed their bankruptcy'.[195]

A People's Government would require not the rearrangement of Parliament but its overthrow, and yet this conclusion was wilfully avoided by Dutt. Instead of a clear appraisal of the problem of political power, there was the customary glorification of militancy and a blurring of the distinction between this militancy and revolutionary politics such as had long characterised the politics of the Communist Party. Back in 1935, Dutt, extolling the mass resistance to the new unemployment scales, had written that 'never was there a clearer demonstration of the power of mass action to override all constitutional forms' and that 'the path of the workers' struggle to victory has already been shown'.[196] In the absence of any opportunity for revolutionary action, the CP had long distinguished itself from more insipid currents on the left by its commitment to militant class struggle on immediate issues. Theoretically, the Party never lost sight of the 'final solution'; struggles for partial demands were related to the final solution by the dubious assumption that an accumulation of militancy added up to a revolution. The revolutionary task of the Party was to set the ball rolling, to show the *'next step forward'*, to:

> organise the struggle of the working people on the basis of those mass issues which

can already win the support of the overwhelming majority against the big propertied interests . . . and thus to build up the class front of the workers, the broad front of all sections of the people, which can alone, by its advancing strength and mass activity, make real and practical the question of a change of government, and thus lead the way to the final solution of the present crisis in the interests of the people.[197]

The problem was that during this period Communists never managed to advance beyond the first stage of 'dogged defensive struggle'.[198] The transition to the fundamental struggle against capitalism itself never occurred. Between defensive militancy and the struggle for power there lay the obstacles of satisfaction with partial successes and demoralisation by defeats, to say nothing of the qualitative transformation required to turn the demand for greater justice within capitalism into the determination to do away with capitalism. In 1941 Communists were still on the first stretch of the path which the unemployed struggles of 1935 had mapped out. The more ambitious slogans which the Party imposed on this defensive militancy – whether for a People's Government or for a Soviet Britain – were so little related to current tasks as to be virtually meaningless.

The clouds of equivocation which obscured the route to a People's Government gave rise to a degree of scepticism as to the credibility of the Convention's political alternative. From his London factory, J. T. Murphy reported that the Convention movement began to disintegrate after the climax of the January conference because the road forward was so poorly marked:

> Maybe the suppression of the *Daily Worker* had something to do with this, for two things became apparent in the workshop. First, after the delegates to the Convention had given their reports, they did not know what to do next; they had no specific objective before them beyond that of popularising the eight points of their programme. Secondly, the Communists switched their energies into a campaign for the lifting of the ban on the *Daily Worker*. Within a month or so the Convention was almost forgotten.[199]

Murphy's view was endorsed by one of the Convention manifesto's signatories:

> It's always been a problem, I think, that you build a campaign up and you get a conference like that and that's like a crescendo. Now, unless you've got another objective that people can easily see to carry the momentum on, you tend to go right down. There probably wasn't a sufficiently realisable perspective of what the People's Convention itself could do.[200]

Even as they left the Royal Hotel on 12 January, some delegates were heard to express their dissatisfaction with the Convention's failure to point the way forward:

> People don't want to be told about [the] food shortage – we know that all right for ourselves. We want to be told what to do about it.
>
> I wish there'd been something definite – we could go back and do.[201]

If the imprecision with which the Convention's spokesmen defined its aims made it difficult to motivate its supporters to fight for these aims, so did it hamper its efforts to secure wider public support. Fighting the Dunbartonshire election on the Convention programme, Malcolm MacEwen obtained a creditable 15 per cent of the poll.[202] However, he might well have polled higher had the support generated by his stand on immediate issues been accompanied by the belief that he stood for a realistic alternative to the governing coalition:

> It would . . . appear that the Communists succeeded in mobilising more goodwill than was reflected in the actual vote. In election discussions people heard expressing sympathy for the point of view of the Communist candidate remained unconvinced that the Communists in any way represented an alternative Government. The vagueness of their general arguments was commented upon . . . .[203]

The ambiguity of the CP's attitude to the war, compounded as it was by its failure to clarify political issues in a way that might have alienated potential allies, meant that it failed to persuade any large number of people of the feasibility of its alternative of a People's Government.

It is worth taking up Murphy's point that the Convention movement was weakened by the diversion of its supporters' energies into the campaign against the ban on the *Daily Worker*, for it is clear that the ban prompted the CP to broaden still further the scope of the alliances it was prepared to make. The necessity for a new approach was spelt out in a document in which Dutt described the ban as 'the signal of a new political situation, which raises sharp new questions for the Party' and attempted to answer these questions.[204] The ban demonstrated more clearly than ever that British politics must move in one of two directions – 'either to full fascism, or through successful working class and democratic resistance to the alternative popular democratic programme of defence of the people's liberties and standards and the people's way out of the crisis'. Of course, there was nothing new in this. What was new was the immediate threat to the legal existence of the Communist Party; Dutt pointed out the 'halfway character of the present position. D. W. banned. General organisation and propaganda goes forward. This position must move one way or the other.' Thus both the general interests of British democracy and the particular interests of British Communism – and Dutt would not have separated the two – demanded as an *urgent* necessity that an *immediate* stand be taken against the present 'totalitarian drive'. However, the two most contentious demands of the People's Convention were certain to impede the building of the broad unity necessary if this stand were to be effective. Dutt therefore advised that a distinction be made between 'propaganda slogans' and 'organising slogans for immediate action'. A People's Government and a People's Peace were propaganda slogans; they should not be neglected, but 'the conditions are not yet present for carrying them out'. On the other hand, 'the essential organising slogans for action, which show what to do now, and thus build up and extend the movement, turn on daily issues and needs'. This distinction underlay the suggestions Dutt made as to the future development of the movement. The first of these was that the awkward 'propaganda slogans' be played down within the Convention movement, for Dutt specifically criticised the 'concentration on ultimate aims as if immediate solution of all problems, in such a way as to weaken attention to present tasks to develop broad People's Movement on daily needs. Hence speculations "how" etc.' The second was that Communists should move beyond the confines of the Convention and organise 'co-operation on special issues on a still wider front, with all sections opposed to the totalitarian drive, irrespective of outlook on other questions'. As so often, Dutt's recommendations were quickly put into practice.

To many who were generally unsympathetic to Communism, the suppression of the *Daily Worker* and the BBC's subsequent decision to banish prominent supporters of the People's Convention from the airwaves appeared as ominous, and yet needless, infringements of civil liberties. When the BBC's ban was retracted as a result of some popular and some very influential pressure,[205] the potential of alliances of all progressives, whether pro- or anti-war, was made clear. Under the impact of these events, the CP manifested a new willingness to offer its political embrace to those who supported the war. This was first indicated by its warm commendation of the fifteen MPs who voted against the suppression of the *Worker*, in some cases even while expressing their 'detestation' of its policy; this crack in the single totalitarian bloc was hailed as 'the beginning of a common front of opposition in Parliament . . . of the greatest significance for the growth of . . . a broad movement throughout the country'.[206] The following month, Dutt opened the pages of the *Labour Monthly* to prominent opponents of the ban who were nevertheless openly antagonistic to the CP; the 'Press Freedom in Wartime' symposium featured the likes of H.G. Wells, Sir Richard Acland and Lord Ponsonby, and Dutt later welcomed the formation of a Press Freedom Committee representing a comparably broad range of opinion. There clearly existed the potential for a movement to defend democratic rights far more extensive than that which would endorse the demand for a People's Government and a People's Peace. By April Dutt was therefore portraying the Convention not as itself the broad movement needed to check the totalitarian offensive, but as a 'first beginning', the foundation on which such a movement could be built. The main objective now was a 'united stand of supporters of democracy, irrespective of their opinions of the People's Convention and its programme'.[207]

At the same time it was stated more explicitly than ever before that the Convention itself was not a 'peace movement' and that progressive supporters of the war were welcome in its ranks. Already, the ambiguity of its programme had ensured that advocates of a British victory would be found among the Convention's backers. A prominent example was Michael Redgrave, whose endorsement of the Convention's programme earned him a brief spell of notoriety and a short-lived ban by the BBC. Alarmed by allegations that his reputation was being exploited by the Communists for defeatist purposes, Redgrave felt compelled to send a statement of his commitment to a British victory both to the press and to the Chairman of the Convention. The latter wrote back to assure Redgrave that the Convention was 'not a "stop the war" movement'. The eighth of the Convention's points merely expressed 'the aim of a just and democratic peace based on the freedom of all peoples' which was shared 'by millions of people, whatever their viewpoint on the origins of the war, the present conduct of the war, or the present policy of the government'. By its very nature the Convention necessarily allowed a 'considerable latitude of opinion even on very important matters'. It was indeed, Adams went on, sketching what was by now the official portrait of the Convention, a movement of those who realised that differences over the nature of the war and the means of attaining a People's Peace did not 'prevent collaboration on the common aims on which all can agree'.[208]

So by the spring of 1941 the aims of the People's Convention was, to quote another of Dutt's political reports, 'to mobilise the broadest front of the workers on elementary class issues irrespective of the attitude to the war'. Acknowledging the strength of pro-war sentiment among the population at large, Dutt argued that Communists 'must not run ahead, from the present stage of mass consciousness but must relate the practical tasks we set before ourselves clearly to what the workers are ready to respond to'; and this meant concentrating on 'the Fight for Democratic Rights' and an 'Economic Class Programme'.[209] Thus, for example, the Convention produced a mass of literature on the food question without ever relating it to the war in a way that might alienate potential supporters of its 'Economic Class Programme'.[210] The vision of a People's Government and a People's Peace, which had never been anything more than a vision in any case, receded further and further into the distant future as the CP endeavoured to build a democratic opposition out of the materials to hand. As Britain's military position deteriorated in the spring of 1941, the People's Convention came at last to rest its hopes on the formation of a patriotic opposition within Parliament:

> In this situation a great responsibility rests on all Members of Parliament. They have still time to act and speak for the people, it is still possible for men of goodwill in all parties to end the paralysing grip of coalition policies. . . .
> *The time has come to form an effective parliamentary opposition which will come out boldly in the interests of the people.* . . .
> There is a growing movement throughout the country which will respond to a bold and resolute stand.

At the close of the 'imperialist war' period, just as at the beginning, the CP invoked the name of that imperialist warmonger *par excellence*, Lloyd George, who had 'felt compelled to voice many of the demands which the People's Convention has been insisting on for months'. In this at least, the Party line had now turned a full circle; and with this appeal to all men of goodwill, 'regardless of their politics',[211] we can take our leave of the movement which has been described as the culmination of Leninist policy of revolutionary defeatism.

7.10 Communists and the war effort, 1940–41

> Mr. Henry Strauss (Norwich): Would the hon. Member tell the Committee whether the Communist party is now in favour of fighting this war?
> Mr. Gallacher: Again the intervention is quite irrelevant.
> (Exchange occurring during William Gallacher's speech on the government's budgetary proposals, 23 July 1940[212])

We noted earlier that during the 'phoney war' there existed a fairly rigid dividing line between the CP's policy of opposition to the war and its activities in industry.[213] However, once the Party had adopted a more credible line on the war, it became possible to attempt to break down this informal demarcation between the different elements of Communist politics. The Party's uneasy relationship with union bureaucrats and the limitations imposed by total war remained, but after June 1940 Communists had fewer inhibitions about expressing their Party's political views in an industrial context. Previously, the CP had declared its opposition to the war in blunt terms. The ambivalence of its position lay in its unwillingness to echo these statements in an industrial context; trade union struggles were justified on narrow, economic grounds. After June 1940 the Party developed a far more ambiguous political programme, but its very vagueness meant that it could be expounded more freely in industry. Industrial struggles were still justified on economic grounds, but they were also related to the conduct of the war and to the political demands associated with the People's Convention. The ambivalence of the Party's position now lay in the Party line itself; the CP's political pronouncements were so nebulous that they could be transmitted and interpreted in quite different ways. The Party's aims could now be articulated in the workshop without implying opposition to the war. It is with this relationship between Communist politics and the war effort that we are principally concerned here; for more detailed accounts of industrial struggles during this period, the reader must turn to other works, notably Croucher's *Engineers At War*.

The Party's industrial strategy remained that of defending the rights and standards of the working class by independent, militant trade unionism organised on as wide a basis as possible. When wage demands accumulated towards the end of 1940, the Communist press reverted to a campaign for all-round wage increases similar to that of a few months earlier. To secure these increases, Pollitt argued in a Party pamphlet, workers should 'press forward their demands under all circumstances'. No matter how beguiling the calls for national unity, they should remain mentally and organisationally prepared to strike whenever necessary, and necessity was to be judged not in terms of capitalist war production but of working-class self-interest.[214] Throughout this period, workers led by Communists struck, or 'went on holiday' in the current euphemism, though in much smaller numbers than a purely economic view of the situation would lead one to expect; and these strikes received full support from the *Daily Worker* and the *New Propellor*.

Industrial struggle was considered necessary by Communists not merely on economic grounds. At a time of strenuous efforts to enmesh the unions in the industrial apparatus of the state, an amenable, docile Labour movement would be powerless to resist these Fascist developments. An intransigent, class-conscious Labour movement, on the other hand, would form an irremovable obstruction on the British road to Fascism. Moreover, campaigns on immediate demands were held to constitute the first stage of the movement to end capitalism itself, and of all types of immediate struggle that in industry was considered of the greatest revolutionary potential. Pollitt especially had an almost mystical faith in the lasting effects of wage struggles. In December 1940 he described the 'fight for increased wages' as 'a vital part in the fight to end war, save the lives of the people and go forward to the full future realisation of Socialism', just as in June he had argued that the fight to defend working conditions would stimulate 'a re-awakening of political thought and class consciousness . . . a new purpose, interest, activity and aim'.[215] Somehow the fight of the workers to raise the price of labour transcended itself into a challenge to the continued rule of the bourgeoisie, but how this was to occur, and why it had not occurred before, was never clearly spelt out. In practice, how far did Communists try to imbue economic struggles with a revolutionary political consciousness? Into what political context, if any, did they fit industrial disputes? Above all, how were they related to the imperialist war?

For the most part, the CP justified its commitment to industrial struggles by reference to the domestic political situation and the hardships caused by the war. However, the Party's leaders were well aware that the 'attack on the workers' was not simply a continuation of the pre-war conflict over wages and conditions, but was motivated to a large extent by the desire of Britain's rulers to devote labour and resources to war production. Thus, for example, did William Rust greet the new year in 1941:

> as British capitalism swings over to armament production and yet more armaments, so will the production of goods required by the people be brought to a stop. . . . The iron ration will become a reality and the road cleared for the depression of wages.[216]

But if the iron ration was dictated by the needs of war production, then surely the fight against the iron ration and the depreciation of real wages was tantamount to the sabotage of war production? The CP's opponents never tired of pointing this out, and in unguarded moments leading Communists seemed to acknowledge the fact:

> If we could imagine the two sides to have equal industrial resources and one side devotes two-thirds of the available capital and labour to maintaining and extending its war machine and the other side devotes only half of its resources to this purpose, then other things being equal the first side will win the war.[217]

The preservation of living standards and established conditions of employment, quite apart from the withdrawal of labour that might be necessary to secure these, was apparently incompatible with the effective prosecution of the war. However, with the words 'other things being equal' Campbell left himself an escape clause, and his implicit admission of defeatism was qualified by Communists in three crucial ways.

The first has already been described. Briefly, it was argued that if the government deprived the working class of its rights and attacked its living standards, then it also undermined the popular will to resist the enemy. Shortly after writing the above, Campbell himself argued that there could be 'no greater mistake than to assume that Fascist methods make for efficiency in countries where the overwhelming majority of the people are free from the Fascist infection. The opposite is the case.'[218] For political reasons, measures of compulsion would prove counter-productive.

The second justification for the struggle of the workers in factories and pits was that capitalist control of industry was itself detrimental to the war effort. The capitalist's lust for profits led to inefficiency and corruption, while his class interests did not dispose him to resist to the full the Fascist enemy without. Thus in the summer of 1940 the CP formulated the demand for Workers' Control Committees in which the defence of working-class conditions and stiffening of resistance to Nazism were portrayed as complementary. These committees were to concern themselves not just with traditional trade union questions but 'with all questions hitherto regarded as the inviolable province of management, i.e., the organisation of the work, the character of the work undertaken, costing and finance, etc.' Management would have no representation on these committees; they would be elected by and accountable to the workers alone, 'closely linked up with the Trade Union organisation, but directly based on the factories'.[219] In the expression of this demand, the strength of the workers' commitment to their own defence was contrasted with the recidivism of their bosses, demonstrated now in Britain as earlier in France.[220] The message was that private enterprise, mismanagement and treachery went hand in hand. No such committees appear ever to have been formed, but this theme shaped the ideas of Communist industrial militants right up to June 1941 and beyond.

The shop stewards at the Napier's Aero works in London, where the CP was very strongly organised, took it up almost immediately, demanding workers' control and the nationalisation of the aircraft industry on the grounds that 'maximum production of the type of engine on which they were engaged was essential to the defence of the people and that they were determined that nothing should be allowed to stand in the way'.[221] London AEU stewards adopted the same defencist tone in condemning the Men of Munich:

> They impose 'sacrifices' on the working class, and while in pursuit of profit they disorganise production, leaving our boys without arms, without planes, and without defence.[222]

Some months later Fred Pateman reported that 'starting with their own firm a group of shop stewards have set themselves the herculean task of cleaning up the mismanagement, inefficiency and downright corruption in the aircraft industry'.[223] A particular source of bitterness towards the employers was the 'cost plus' system, which was taken to mean that profits were no longer tied to output and that employers therefore stood to gain by lengthening the amount of time spent on a given job.[224] At least one strike was threatened over the needless moving about of machinery in what was felt to be a deliberate attempt to slow down production.[225] Of course, enforced idleness had its effect not only on the war effort but also on piecework earnings. It is nevertheless significant that the stand against the employers' offensive was so frequently related to the grave damage this offensive was inflicting on the war effort. The case was brought together in an issue of the *Daily Worker* which, thanks to Herbert Morrison, never saw the light of day:

> War production is in a parlous condition, due to the reckless profiteering and incompetence of the ruling class.
> ... the workers have done their utmost to end the waste and inefficiency. Faced with the fact that in factory after factory thousands of labour hours are being lost every week due to the criminal neglect of the employers, the workers have made innumerable protests. ...
> The workers have made many sacrifices, the employers none ... the Government and the employing class stand convicted of having placed profit before the interests of the people ...

The *Worker* went on to put the 'disruptionist' activities of the Communists in their proper perspective with the claim that 'more working hours have been lost in certain factories as a result of mismanagement than in all the strikes of recent months'.[226] If Britain were defeated, the blame would not rest with strike-prone Bolshies.

The CP's resistance to the extension of working hours provides an interesting illustration of how it sought to identify the maintenance of working conditions with the needs of national defence. Everybody knows that in the summer of 1940 the people of Britain became possessed with the spirit of Dunkirk, meaning that they devoted every possible minute of their lives to keeping out the invader, whistling pluckily while they worked. As was to be expected, Britain's Communists denounced this intensification of the exploitation of labour. Less predictable, perhaps, was the extent to which these denunciations too were imbued with the Dunkirk spirit.

Communists took their cue from the eminent Communist scientist, J. B. S. Haldane. On 30 May, under the heading 'The Seven Day Week *Will Reduce Production*', Haldane argued in the *Daily Worker* that, through a mixture of 'Fifth Column work' and 'sheer blind hatred of the workers', Britain's rulers were 'sabotaging the war effort as surely as a trainer would sabotage a mile race if he told a runner to sprint the first hundred yards'. Drawing on the lessons of the First World War, he demonstrated that, if workers were forced to work flat out for any length of time, the certain result would be exhaustion, absenteeism and a slump in production. The defence of the workers' immediate interests and the defence of the nation therefore amounted to much the same thing, and those union leaders who abandoned the former thereby imperilled the latter. These arguments were soon taken up by Communists in industry, who demanded relief from the pressures of excessive overtime 'in the interests of efficiency and production'.[227] The way in which these Communists assumed an air of responsibility for the proper conduct of the war is brought out well by the following report compiled by the EATSSNC:

> Reports from many districts show that where Shop Stewards have taken up the inefficiency of excessive hours, and the adverse effect on production through excessive fatigue caused by the workers doing their best to get the maximum production, it has been possible to secure rest days. . . .
> In Glasgow, particularly, and also in other places, Shop Stewards, in accordance with a Government announcement, have been able to arrange in discussion with their managements for holidays to be taken on the staggered system . . . so that production is not interrupted or any shop closed down. Here again the results will be beneficial.[228]

To a far greater extent than before the industrial activities of British Communists were explicitly related to the prosecution of the war, but in a fashion that implied that war production was not an irrelevance, nor a murderous evil, but a vital necessity.

Haldane's contribution to this debate is a reminder that military and technical personnel were as deeply involved in the war effort as industrial workers, and shared many of their concerns. Despite his allegiance to the CP, Haldane was employed in highly sensitive areas by various departments of the forces, including 'the Air Ministry's top-secret Air Intelligence 4', and the *Daily Worker* was proud to advertise the fact.[229] Another Communist scientific worker, Hyman Levy, described his contribution to the war effort thus:

> I come down for two days breather every fortnight, but spend a good deal of that time working out details of anti-submarine and anti-aircraft devices. Most of my teaching time is spent in training young men for service in the technical war departments. I have all my spare time taken up with *free* consultations in connection with war problems.[230]

Levy, then, was neither a saboteur nor a defeatist: 'How could it be immaterial to a Jewish anti-nazi and anti-fascist if the Germans over-ran this country? I am not mad.' But for this very reason Levy had not the slightest confidence in Britain's rulers, as he explained in a series of revealing letters to Victor Gollancz.

Levy found the prosecution of the war on the scientific side terrifying. The dominant role played by big business meant that the profit motive and trade secrets played havoc with scientific and technical work, while the most vital matters were left to people 'who fundamentally have nothing against the nazis if they would only leave them alone in their position of social power'. Having tried to apply the CP's original 'war on two fronts' line, Levy felt it impracticable because he saw no evidence at all that the powers-that-be were:

i. able effectively to mobilise technicians and scientists to fight nazism.
ii. capable of being moved by politically conscious technicians and others to become effective on the basis of private enterprise.
iii. showing the slightest sign of an anti-nazi attitude developing into an anti-fascist attitude.

Indeed the opposite was happening. To the extent that British capitalism strengthened its war effort, it moved closer to Fascism; and the war could not be fought 'to the full extent of which Capitalism is capable without British and American Capitalism going completely fascist to the fullest extent'. The only acceptable alternative was a People's War:

> The crux of the matter lies here – that you either agree that a deepening of democracy is essential to fight a war on behalf of freedom or you hold that the best instrument for such a war is a population bound and gagged under a capitalist dictatorship. . . . If you hold that a deepening of democracy is essential then *the very first step* in the whole struggle is the fight against this growth of fascism at home. . . . That, as I see it, is broadly my case; it has nothing to do with Lenin's 'defeat of one's own imperialist government', where the circumstances were quite different.

The Napier's shop stewards would not have dissented from these views, for their political attitudes and the problems which they faced were much the same as Levy's. These letters express as well as anything the commitment of Communists to resist Fascism, within Britain and without, to the full, as well as their scepticism as to the capacity or inclination of Britain's rulers to organise an effective, democratic war effort against Nazi Germany.

Communists advanced a third argument to show that their economic demands were not incompatible with a successful war effort: that it was quite feasible for the rich to bear the brunt of the costs of the war, leaving working-class living standards relatively unimpaired. Tirelessly, the Communist press drew attention to rampant profiteering and the blatant inequality of sacrifice. Walter Holmes aptly described himself as 'a "layman" with a taste for reading, day by day, columns of company and financial reports and of tips to investors where to find the profits'[231] and his 'Workers' Notebook' in each edition of the *Daily Worker* was packed with his findings. A similar feature, 'The Money We Make For Others', was to be found in the *New Propellor*. The deduction made from these reports was that there was ample scope for shifting the burden of the war from the backs of the workers to those more able to bear it.[232] But if the attack on the rights and living standards of the people was not essential to the prosecution of the war, then neither was popular resistance to this attack equivalent to a struggle against the war. Implicitly or explicitly, the Communist Party now shared this assumption. In February 1941, for instance, Dutt advised that the Party's response to industrial conscription – 'the centre of the immediate issue' – should not be an 'abstract negative, which would be interpreted as indifference to war needs. The question turns on: for What and How?'[233] Dutt's advice was followed, not just with regard to industrial conscription but to all aspects of the war effort. Communists did not, for instance, contest whether or not the war needed to be financed at all. The question turned on: How?

In April 1941, Page Arnot stigmatised the 'Keynes Budget' as 'the first British Budget to be constructed on the principles of Nazi finance'. The Communist alternative to this budget was not, however, the ending of the war which gave rise to such innovations, but its own set of fiscal proposals by which the cost of the war would be 'put fairly and squarely on the rich through the only tax that really touches them – a tax on the wealth they have piled up from the labour of the workers'. Arnot entitled his *Labour Monthly* article on the budget 'Who Pays for the War?' and stuck meticulously to his brief. Like Gallacher in the Commons, he gave details of the potential revenue from a tax on property without ever considering the ends to which this money would be put.[234] Here it is interesting to note that a year or so earlier J. R. Campbell had dismissed such proposals as largely irrelevant. 'However the war is financed the consumption of the working class will be cut', he had written, and therefore *'the main danger to the workers lies in the logical development of the war economy itself'*. Working-class interests could not be defended properly 'within the framework of war economy' but only by 'bringing the Imperialist war to a close'.[235] Communists rarely said as much, and hardly at all by 1941. The question they raised, sometimes explicitly and between nearly every line they wrote on the subject, was: who should bear the cost of the war?[236]

From the foregoing it should be clear that, as from the summer of 1940, Communists did not counterpose industrial militancy with the successful prosecution of the war. This is well illustrated by the strike at British Auxiliaries in Glasgow in the autumn of 1940, of which we have a detailed account by Croucher.[237] The dispute was typical of the period in that the issue at stake was not wage rates but the dictatorial enforcement of managerial 'prerogatives', in this case the prerogative to sack three AEU convenors in four months. But the strike was untypical in that it lasted for several weeks. According to evidence cited by Croucher, it was actually CP policy to keep strikes short at this time,[238] and this is certainly borne out by the conduct of this dispute.

British Auxiliaries was not a large concern, but the strike against the victimisation of the third convenor, a Communist called Cunningham, became, according to Croucher, 'a *cause célèbre* amongst trade-unionists throughout Scotland'. That it became so was due in part to the circulation of strike leaflets by the Shop Stewards' Committee. What interests us here is the tone of aggrieved patriotism with which the stewards levelled their accusations at the management:

> It has been obvious for a considerable period that this management has, for trivial reasons, lost the essential harmony of the men and are, therefore, frustrating our war effort. The culmination of this mismanagement has now made itself manifest in the dismissal of our shop convener. . . .
>
> Because of the serious situation facing our country, the attitude of the management has been of great concern to the men for some time. The latest statement of the manager will bear out the need for this concern: '*It makes no difference how long the employees stay out, I am insured against loss, as my profits are guaranteed.*'
>
> The employees are very anxious to be back at work . . . so that their services in the country's dire need may be utilised.[239]

This is hardly the language of men determined to build up a mass movement to topple the government and end the war, *pace* Pollitt. Indeed, Cunningham himself advised a meeting of the strikers to return to work without him, but was shouted down. An interesting historical parallel suggested itself when the local CP invited David Kirkwood MP to intervene in the interests of a speedy settlement, for twenty-five years earlier 'Davie Kirkwood of Beardmore's' had himself combined the defence of the rights of engineers with expressions of solicitude about the supply of munitions to the front. Certainly, the Communists at British Auxiliaries stood more in the tradition of Davie Kirkwood than of John Maclean. Of course, one cannot generalise from this one case; but even if Communists were occasionally indifferent to the military consequences of industrial militancy,[240] whenever they did stop to consider the impact of industrial struggles on the war it was invariably to express concern at the loss of production or else to put these struggles in the context of the 'real defence' of the people. No doubt they read Pollitt's pamphlets, but they showed little urgency about progressing to his long-term objectives.

The new emphases and omissions in Communist politics now enabled Communists to rebuild industrially rooted alliances with an overtly political content. We saw earlier how Communists in the SWMF and the EATSSNC had tended to keep their distance from their Party's original anti-war policies and tried to maintain their influence by the strength of their commitment to free trade unionism and the material interests of the working class. As from June 1940, these Communists felt far more comfortable with the Party line. Arthur Horner, for example, gave his full public backing to the policies of the Communist Party. In doing so, he no more gave vent to anti-war feelings than he had before, but this course no longer required that he occupy himself wholly with trade union questions. Rather, Horner felt free to express his concern about Britain's security, as J. L. Hodson discovered in February 1941:

> I said: 'I think that Hitler has to be fought.' He interrupted: 'So do I.' . . . I tried to discover how far he is prepared to go in fighting Hitler. He seemed a little vague – whether deliberately it was hard to say. Finally, he said: 'I stop short at defence.' I said: 'But isn't our attack on Mussolini, for instance, defence?' He said he doubted the wisdom of our strategy in the Mediterranean, and went on: 'Of course we've got to protect our food routes.'[241]

Unknown to Hodson, Horner was already serving on the Invasion Trade Union Committee for South Wales, making preparations to 'fight against Nazi tanks with picks and shovels' should the Germans invade.[242]

Fully exploiting the flexibility offered by the new Party line, Horner re-entered the mainstream of Labour politics in South Wales, as a Communist as well as trade unionist. Horner gave vocal support to the People's Convention and had no compunctions about serving on its National Committee, for open advocacy of Communist policies no longer carried with it the risk of estrangement from majority opinion in the coalfield. Horner attended the Convention as one of four delegates sent by the SWMF EC, which regarded its decision to support the Convention as 'quite consistent' with the Federation's previous declaration of support for the war. True, a number of lodges protested at this decision and one lodge official demanded that Horner now make his choice between his union and his Party.[243] But Horner's loyalties no longer conflicted and it was not necessary that he make this choice, as it apparently had been a year earlier. At the subsequent SWMF conference the question of support for the People's Convention was left in abeyance, but at the same time Horner was returned unopposed as President, a striking display of confidence in his leadership.[244] The unity of the South Wales miners remained intact, and it was no longer necessary for

Horner and his comrades to avoid political questions to ensure this. But this was not, of course, unity against the war, and the SWMF's support for the People's Convention was, more or less, consistent with its earlier resolution of critical support for the war. The Party, not the Federation, had shifted its position. One piquant episode brings out the flavour of the period. In the midst of deciding on various measures of support for the People's Convention, the SWMF EC discussed 'the form of a contribution by the Federation to the war'. The outcome was a donation of £3,000 to finance the work of the Young Men's Christian Association among the troops. Horner, as President, attended the presentation ceremony. Quite possibly it was a fellow Communist who signed the cheque.[245]

A similar pattern of events occurred in the EATSSNC. When the campaign against the Men of Munich was launched, political questions were once again aired in the *New Propellor* and, moreover, explicitly related to the tasks of the shop stewards' movement. No doubt, as J. T. Murphy found in the London engineering shop where he worked,[246] many Communists still hesitated to address the subject of the war in their workplaces. However, the People's Convention, which was strongly supported by the EATSSNC and the *New Propellor* with the result that a very large proportion of its delegates came from the engineering industry, gave these Communists the opportunity to raise political as well as economic issues without in any way implying hostility to the war:

> The programme . . . was attractive to the workers. Naturally they wanted higher wages, better conditions, bomb-proof shelters, etc. Naturally they wanted friendship with the USSR, a Government less tarred by the brush of friendship for Nazi Germany, and a peace that would be a People's Peace. Hence, when this programme was advanced as the means for dealing with Hitlerism more effectively it 'caught on' with many workers.[247]

We reiterate, the politics of the Communist Party were now being expounded more freely in the workplace and related to industrial issues; but these were not, in any clear sense, the politics of opposition to the war.

To sum up, the CP advocated working-class militancy to combat the employers' offensive and the integration of the unions into the economic apparatus of the state. However, keenly aware of the political and military context of strikes, Communists took a fairly cautious approach to industrial activity, because of the pro-war sentiments of most workers; because of the friction with the trade union machines which was bound to arise from automatically unofficial disputes; and because, verbally at least, Communists had no desire to disrupt the war effort. Pollitt and Dutt attempted to fit this industrial activity into a revolutionary theoretical framework, describing it as the first stage in the mass awakening which would lead to a People's Government and thence to Socialism. The flaw was that the revolutionary transformation of the struggle for reforms and palliatives takes place only in very specific circumstances. Dutt, Pollitt and the Comintern, however, held that the character of a whole epoch was conducive to such a development and, moreover, that this epoch would not come to an end until this transformation *did* take place. The course of subsequent events, guided by the Communist Parties of Europe in ways unanticipated by Dutt in 1940, has decided this question. In any case, while this train of events remained in the future, revolutionary trade unionism differed from that of the reformists mainly in its firmer commitment to the immediate interests of the working class. Jack Owen, who had as much experience of industrial politics as any Communist, argued that Communists would avoid isolation and 'get the men moving' by 'asking for things that matter IN THE SHOP':

> There is no need to wear a red tie and shout slogans. Don't be worried by the thought that your Right Wing shop steward utters the same things. The difference is that you have a revolutionary outlook, you are bound to keep at it, whereas your 'pocket Bevins' usually shout their slogan and go to sleep again.[248]

The revolutionary might utter the same things as the reformist; but the revolutionary was prepared to fight for these things.

7.11 The Communist Party and the establishment

> The other day I had an argument with some prominent Communists about the People's Convention. I was opposing it. One of the objects of the Convention was the promotion and defence of democratic and trade union rights in Great Britain. I pointed out that there were no greater evidences of the vitality of democratic rights in this country than the publication of the 'Daily Worker' and the holding of the People's Convention. I cannot say that to-day.
> (Aneurin Bevan speaking in the Commons debate on the banning of the *Daily Worker*, 28 January 1941)

It is a most significant fact that the British Communist Party escaped suppression even during its period of opposition to the war, as indeed it has throughout its existence. The freedom to work openly to achieve its aims distinguished the CPGB from most other sections of the Comintern and perhaps helps to explain some of the British Party's most striking characteristics. The remarkable continuity of the Party's leadership owed much to its comparative security from arrest, clandestinity, exile and political murder. The fact that the Party's acknowledged leadership remained in London, remote from the decision-making centre of world Communism, helps to explain its responsiveness to local pressures and its adeptness at balancing these with Comintern directives. The legality of Communism in Britain enabled Communists to embed themselves in the left wing of British political culture, developing interests and contacts, positions of influence and political priorities, which made the concept of international Bolshevik discipline somewhat problematic.

Paradoxically, if the legality of British Communism engendered a fairly pragmatic political approach, this pragmatism was reinforced by the very precariousness of the Party's legal position during the early part of the war. Quite apart from the suppression of the *Daily Worker* and numerous instances of harassment and victimisation, Cabinet records reveal that a comprehensive ban on Communist publications, the internment of Party leaders and the proscription of the Party were all considered, and rejected on grounds of expediency rather than principle. And of course, the CP's whole conception of the development of Fascism in Britain ensured that, even without access to Cabinet records, it was acutely aware of the possibility of such actions being taken.

Although the government armed itself with extraordinary powers as early as August 1939, it was not until after the formation of the Churchill Government that rigorous action was taken against opponents of the war. Even then, with the Nazis sweeping across Western Europe and British Fascists interned in their hundreds, the CP was treated with relative leniency. The Home Secretary, Sir John Anderson, gave three reasons for this: that the Party generally refrained from direct anti-war propaganda, that it was free of any suspicion of 'Fifth Column' tendencies and that it was making no organised attempt to disrupt production. Anderson therefore advised against full use of the government's powers against the CP, but recommended that specific transgressions by Communists be dealt with firmly.[249] This is indeed what happened in the summer of 1940.

One of the more stringent actions taken by the government at this time was to prevent the distribution of the leaflet *The People Must Act* which presented the new, more compelling arguments advanced by the CP after the fall of France. At the same time Anderson put it to the War Cabinet that the *Daily Worker* too be suppressed, for its pages were filled with the very same arguments. At this juncture, however, ministers were unwilling to take such a step: one consequence of the proven bankruptcy of the French authorities was that 'public opinion was, at the moment, very sensitive to the issue of free speech' and Anderson had therefore to be content with sending the *Worker* a formal warning to modify its editorial stance.[250] With the lessons of France fresh in people's minds, the government judged it wiser to intimidate than to suppress the Communist press and the Party itself. Instances of such intimidation were rife.

The most scandalous of these was the internment of John Mason.[251] The apparently arbitrary selection of this individual, against whom no specific charges were brought, suggests that the government was concerned mainly to demonstrate to the CP its readiness to make full use of its powers if and when it felt it necessary. Although only a handful of Communists were interned, the summer of 1940 saw numerous minor acts of oppression. The police made frequent use of the criminal law to carry out basically political arrests, the usual charge being that of using 'insulting words':

> On these grounds a number of workers . . . have been sent to prison. Distributors of leaflets have been similarly treated. Home searchings are now resorted to for no ostensible reason and the police also make attempts to obtain the dismissal of factory workers who are suspected of holding militant views. Even school children have been questioned in order that the police may obtain information regarding the political views of their parents and relatives. Some 40 people have been arrested for carrying on the normal activity for working-class organisations.[252]

Even if, as was usually the case, no charges resulted from police raids, the police could still contact employers in the hope that they would dismiss Communist miscreants.[253] Indeed, as Croucher has shown,[254] many employers needed no such encouragement to victimise Communists, although it is not easy to separate overtly political from managerial motives in these situations. Moreover, especially when workers attributed victimisation to the latter, management ran the risk of provoking industrial unrest and so this weapon had to be used with discretion. An alternative tactic was to shift Communists to smaller establishments where they could do less damage,[255] and later on we shall witness the *reductio ad absurdum* of this method. All in all, then, the British authorities did enough to make their presence felt without taking really decisive action against the CP.

Before turning to the ban on the *Daily Worker* in January 1941, it is worth noting the CP's reaction to the threat to its main organ. Earlier it was noted that Dutt gave the risk of suppression as the reason for the *Worker*'s equivocation as to its attitude to the war.[256] In fact a letter from Dutt to Rust, the *Worker*'s editor, reveals that the Party's attitude to legality was more complex than was admitted in public:

> For explaining the line to the staff, we need . . . to warn not only against provocation, but also against a wrong approach to legality, that is as if the mere fact of the continued appearance of the paper, irrespective of contents, were itself victory (i.e., the conception of 'legality at any price' short of open pro-war

matter). It is obvious that under certain conditions this could be a victory for the other side, not for us.

Dutt then outlined the main issues to be dealt with in the paper: the independence of the Labour movement; democratic rights; economic and social demands; opposition to monopoly capitalism and profiteering; and the advocacy of Socialism, internationalism and support for the Soviet Union. Evidently, although Dutt was obviously aware of the danger of allowing the government to define the limits of Party propaganda, the failure to enunciate the Party's opposition to the war was not to be regarded as a 'victory for the other side'. Dutt also stated that, even if the *Worker* had to tread cautiously, 'at the same time we aim, by pamphlets and leaflets, to put a general political line before the movement'. However, prevarication about the war was not, as we have seen, a special prerogative of the *Daily Worker*. The fear of provoking retaliatory action by the authorities might have been one factor restricting the scope of the Party's anti-war propaganda, but it was one of many and not the most important of them.[257]

The main emphases of Party propaganda remained fairly constant during the latter months of 1940, and yet it was only in November that the question of drastic government action against the Party was raised anew. The reasons for this are not quite clear. The most likely is that the Cabinet was apprehensive lest the People's Convention gain widespread public support. However, the Home Office memorandum recommending the suppression of the *Daily Worker* stated that the paper's circulation was falling and that Communist propaganda was having an appreciable impact only in particular factories. The main risk in allowing this propaganda to continue, it went on, lay in the potential threat to morale 'if and when circumstances become more difficult'.[258] It is hard to understand why this consideration should have been more urgent at the end of 1940 than a few months earlier, when a German invasion seemed imminent. Perhaps it was felt that public opinion was less sensitive to the issue of press freedom than it had been just after the collapse of France. Another possible explanation for the Cabinet's belated decision to strike at the Party was the appointment of Herbert Morrison as Home Secretary in October 1940. Within the Labour movement Morrison had long been at loggerheads with the CP, and it is tempting to see his instigation of moves against the Party as an extension of his earlier campaigns to root out Communist influence in the Labour Party. Alternatively, it might have been felt that the measure was less likely to arouse opposition on the left when introduced by a Labour minister. Whatever the reasons, on 21 January 1941 the *Worker*, and with it *The Week*, were suppressed under the draconian Defence Regulation 2D.

At the same time, a Cabinet committee was set up to explore the possibilities of further action against the Party. For the most part it concerned itself with the alternative forms of propaganda with which the CP was very soon endeavouring to fill the gap left by the disappearance of the *Worker*.[259] Duff Cooper, the Minister of Information, recommended a comprehensive ban on Communist periodicals to silence the Party, while the committee as a whole formulated a detailed scheme to prevent the distribution of seditious leaflets, although for some reason these proposals were never put into effect.[260] However, the most interesting of the committee's deliberations were those relating to the possible suppression of the Party itself.

On this question ministers were divided. Morrison himself had informed the Cabinet that the ban on the *Worker* was not to be treated as 'the first step in a movement for the suppression of the Communist Party'.[261] A 'strong section' of the Home Defence (Security) Executive, on the other hand, advocated that the CP be made illegal and its leaders interned in which case, it was felt, many rank-and-file Communists would abandon the party.[262] One minister to endorse this proposal was Ernest Bevin, the Minister of Labour. Bevin felt it inadvisable to proceed against Communist militants in industry, where it was 'difficult to distinguish between subversive propaganda and genuine grievances', but nevertheless, and characteristically, favoured prompt action against the 'small number of intellectuals' who he believed to form the 'central pivot of Communist activity'. Morrison, who had little more affection for Bevin than for the Communists, argued precisely the opposite: further action against the Party must inevitably extend to Communists in industry, and this could well provoke industrial unrest on the sort of scale seen on Clydeside twenty-five years earlier.[263] The same point was put to the War Cabinet by Anderson: the workers were not likely to feel aggrieved at government action against the Party as such, but moves against Communists in industry would be construed as victimisation and 'would cause discontent among workers who are not themselves in sympathy with Communism'.[264] On this point there was seemingly a consensus; the question was whether it was possible to decapitate the CP while leaving its industrial membership unmolested. The government's restraint in dealing with the Party was due mainly, it would seem, to its trepidation lest decisive action provoke more industrial unrest than the allegedly subversive activities of the Communists were ever likely to.

The CP's leaders were no less aware than the Cabinet that Communists were less vulnerable as trade unionists than as members of the Party. During the campaign for the release of John Mason it was not mentioned that Mason was a Communist, nor was the specific threat to the Party invoked. His internment was depicted instead as an attack on basic trade union rights.[265]

It was partly for this reason that the Party instructed a number of its leading officials, such as its Industrial Organiser, Peter Kerrigan, to return to their trades as the best guarantee of habeas corpus. It was felt that this might deter the government from clamping down on the Party leadership, as the arrest of a factory worker could be represented as 'an attack upon trades unionism' and might be resisted as such.[266] The sagacity of this tactic, which was adopted even by so exalted a figure as Harry Pollitt,[267] is already evident from the Cabinet discussions described above.

That ministers were unwilling to risk a head-on collision with the trade union consciousness of the British proletariat did not at all mean that they were impotent to deal with the Communist presence in the factories. In February 1941 Anderson informed his indignant colleagues that Communists as prominent as Ben Francis, formerly the *Daily Worker*'s industrial correspondent, and Wal Hannington were having little trouble obtaining positions in concerns engaged in vital war production.[268] So shocking was this revelation that the wheels of British government were immediately set in motion. The sequel, as recorded by Hannington, is entertaining enough and evocative enough to merit quoting at length.

In January 1941 Hannington took up employment at an engineering works in Neasden. After only a few weeks, however, it became apparent that his presence there was unwelcome. Whether or not the authorities were putting pressure on the firm, Hannington was not in a position to know. He knew only that the management, having first of all tried to sack him only to back down at the threat of strike action, then decided to try 'another bright idea':

> The machine shop was a large single ground-floor structure with angled glass roofs for daylight. In the corner of this spacious area there was a small brick-built department. It had a glass roof and no side windows. Painted on the door were the words 'Strictly Private, Keep Out'. There were only half a dozen men in this department, engaged on some top level security work. So I was amazed when a few days after the attempt of the management to discharge me I was ordered to pack up my tools and move into it. When I entered I found that the group that worked there were hurriedly moving out and the heavy-gang were on the job of unbolting and lifting all the machines, except a centre-lathe and small tool-grinder and removing them. . . . I was put to work on the remaining lathe and next morning, when the removal of the other machines had been completed, the door was closed and I found myself completely isolated. Alone all day within those four plain walls, with no window to see what was going on outside, I felt like a prisoner again in a large prison cell.[269]

The whole affair is slightly ludicrous, but nevertheless instructive. A notorious Communist of twenty years' standing is engaged to produce vital equipment for fighter aircraft; the issue is raised in the War Cabinet and it is agreed that it is undesirable that revolutionaries should occupy such positions where they can exercise an 'unwholesome influence' on key sections of the workers; and yet the authorities are so apprehensive about provoking an adverse reaction that they do not dismiss, let alone intern, this Communist, but devise a quite ridiculous scheme to isolate him from his workmates. And Hannington, of course, was merely one of thousands of Communists employed in war work, many of whom were shop stewards or occupied official union posts.

The contrast with Germany, with Italy, with France could hardly be greater. One gets the impression that both the authorities and the Communist Party were persuaded of the wisdom of acting cautiously; the authorities, because they knew that the Communists were doing no grave damage to the war effort – this is stated several times in Cabinet records – and that intemperate measures against them would antagonise those who knew Communists primarily as dedicated trade unionists. The Communists, on the other hand, knew that if they overstepped certain limits the government would very likely make use of its emergency powers, as it had against Mason and one or two other Communists in cases which served mainly as a warning of possible things to come.[270] Moreover, to carry out blatant anti-war activities would be to alienate those workers on whose solidarity their security depended; the workers would not come out in support of someone victimised for some 'heroic gesture' which did not concern them, as Communists had known for years.[271] Pragmatic rather than doctrinaire, it seems almost as if the two sides had arrived at one of those 'typically British compromises'. And so, the threat of suppression remaining but not being put into effect, the situation remained until June 1941.

7.12 Postscript: towards 22 June 1941

In April 1941 we had a speaker from King Street to explain the Party line. It was a most curious sensation which I could never forget, because when he began to speak everybody began to look very puzzled and were scratching their heads, and every now and then they suddenly began to smile until almost everyone in the whole meeting was smiling. They realised that what in fact was happening was that he was expressing support for the war.
(Eric Scott, then Chairman of High Wycombe CP[272])

Every historian who makes use of oral sources is aware that the retrospective testimony of the makers of history does not consist simply of the recollection of historical facts and personal experiences but is also something of 'an imaginative reconstruction . . . built out of the relation of our attitude towards a whole active mass or organized past reactions or experience'.[273] Eric Scott's recollection of a Communist Party spokesman 'expressing support for the war' in April 1941 might appear to be just such a case of 'imaginative reconstruction' in the light of subsequent developments in Communist politics. However, this 'reconstruction' bears an important relation to historical reality for, by April 1941, if the CP did not actually express support for the war, neither did it express or even imply opposition to it. The thrust of its criticisms was against the government's *conduct* of the war and against its imperialist war *aims*. Typical was the Commons motion of no-confidence in the government proposed by Gallacher and Pritt in May 1941:

> by submitting to the dictates of vested interests it has hampered the democratic initiative of the people; by failing either to overcome the waste, corruption and inefficiency prevailing in many branches of industry, or to organise production and equitable distribution of food supplies, it has imposed heavy and unnecessary suffering on the people; by not adopting and proclaiming progressive peace aims it has stifled the forces of resistance to Hitler and Mussolini in Europe; and by refusing to follow a policy of friendship to the USSR it has increased our burdens and difficulties; and . . . has therefore forfeited the confidence of the country.[274]

Just as typical was Dutt's demand that 'the reactionary imperialist aims and oppression of other peoples, *which only serve to prolong the war*, be ended. . . . Only so can the appeal of the people reach out with an honest and trusted voice to the rising movement of the peoples in the other countries and win them as allies in the common cause.'[275] Implicit in these statements was a recognition of the necessity for the war itself; for what else was the 'common cause' if not the cause of democracy against the Axis powers? Already it was accepted, as it had not been a few months earlier, that 'attacked people, like the Yugoslav and Greek peoples, are waging a valiant and just war for liberation'.[276] As the war shifted eastwards and the latent Soviet–German antagonism grew sharper, the war was no longer characterised simply as an inter-imperialist struggle. The imperialist aims of the Anglo-American ruling classes coexisted with, and undermined, the legitimate struggle of the peoples – including the British people – against Fascist aggression. By the beginning of June the *Daily worker* was presented as the paper which would, if permitted, 'continue its fight for a People's Government, against Hitlerism, and for a People's Peace';[277] and the insertion of this specific reference to German Fascism summed up the current trend in Communist propaganda. When the Soviet–German antagonism broke out in open war in June, the CP need only have made relatively minor adjustments to its political line, had it decided that the new situation demanded a policy of critical support for the war; but in fact it went a good deal further than that.

To commemorate the twentieth anniversary of the *Labour Monthly* in July 1941, Dutt wrote a massive tome of 640 pages, *Crisis of the British People*, which used material from twenty years of Dutt's 'Notes of the Month' to trace the crisis of British imperialism back to the First World War and beyond and demonstrate that the only solution to this crisis lay in the victory of Socialism. It was no doubt, as the advance publicity claimed, a 'veritable handbook of Marxist–Leninism':

> That selections from writings spread over 20 years are valid when reprinted in 1941, makes CRISIS OF THE BRITISH PEOPLE a supreme vindication of Marxist method. That is but one of the really important purposes served by this remarkable work. A second is the comprehensive understanding it gives of the world as it is. A third is its conclusive demonstration of the one and only way forward out of capitalist anarchy into Socialist order.

But if these selections were supremely valid in April 1941, they were no longer valid by July. For a few months, advance subscribers were asked to remain patient as publication was held up by the need to incorporate 'additional material' and the 'increasing and well-known difficulties of the printing trade'. Then, at the beginning of 1942, it was announced that this 'encyclopaedic' work would no longer be appearing after all; and subscribers were asked to accept in its place a very different book, *Britain in the World Front*.[278]

This curious episode is of considerable symbolic value, for the consequences of the CP's decision to support the war in June 1941 were that it abandoned not only the particular slogans of the 'imperialist war' period but the 'understanding of the world as it is' which had underlain its activities since its formation; not two years, but twenty years of 'Notes of the Month'. In this sense, what occurred after June 1941 was far more than a 'change of line'; it was a change of world outlook symbolised by the dissolution of the Comintern, which will be considered very briefly in the conclusion to this book.

Notes

1 The title of an article by George Strauss, *Tribune*, 12.7.40.
2 M-O TC 25/8.
3 RPD K4, Dutt to W. Cowe, CPGB Scottish DC, 19.5.40.
4 'Notes', June 1941, 248–9.
5 *LN*, July 1940, 1,498–9; VG MSS.157/3/DOC/1, Strachey to I. Montagu, 22.7.40.
6 *Tribune*, 12.7.40; M-O TC 25/8, reactions to the CP leaflet *The People Must Act*, Romford

and Streatham, 1.7.40, 2.7.40, cited *Thesis*, 290–1.

7 CPGB PB, 'Political letter to the Communist Party membership', 15.7.40. It should be pointed out that many Communists felt at that time that the Party should have moved much further in the direction of 'national defencism' than it was yet to do. One such was Bert Ramelson (interview, Imperial War Museum). Another, who confided his feelings only to one or two very close associates in the London District leadership, was Phil Piratin (interview):

> I decided that I couldn't conceive of a situation where I as a young man, strong and healthy personally, would allow or expect, let alone welcome, a German invasion of Britain when, as I mentioned before, Lord Haw-Haw announces on the radio in that summer of 1940 sometime that among the people they are going to immediately destroy would be myself. I couldn't help thinking personally that no-one's going to destroy me until I can destroy some of them. My whole attitude was that there's something wrong in the [Party's] calculations. My ordinary human but politically motivated attitude leads me to the conclusion that we ought to now contend against these people as a Communist Party. Officially, now Churchill was in the saddle and made his speech about fighting on the beaches and quite frankly I welcomed that because it sounded very different from anything that Chamberlain had ever said.

8 See e.g. the 'Political letter' of 15.7.40 where it was stated that, although Britain was going through a 'serious political crisis', it was not yet 'deep or fundamental'. This conclusion, however at variance with some of the CP's more extravagant statements, was implicit in the Party's political practice throughout this period.
9 CPGB PB manifesto, *DW*, 22.6.40. The nine demands are given here as summarised *DW*, 28.6.40.
10 IBA statement, *DW*, 12.6.40; see also *DW*, 4.6.40.
11 *DW*, 14.6.40.
12 *DW*, 10.6.40, 11.6.40.
13 'Spectator', *DW*, 13.9.40.
14 *DW*, 19.7.40.
15 CPGB PB statement, *DW*, 15.6.40.
16 Gallacher, *WNV*, 3.8.40, 420.
17 *DW*, 12.6.40.
18 *DW*, 18.6.40.
19 Gallacher, *WNV*, 3.8.40, 421.
20 'Military correspondent', *DW*, 12.6.40.
21 *DW*, 19.8.40.
22 *DW*, 9.7.40.
23 Gallacher in the Commons, *DW*, 22.6.40; Ted Bramley, speech at London rally, *DW*, 25.6.40.
24 E. M. Winterton, 'Is this a war for democracy?', *LM*, July 1940, 485–94, where this question is discussed.
25 M. Johnstone in Attfield and Williams, *op. cit.*, 32–3.
26 Pritt, *DW*, 5.6.40; on this, see e.g. P. Sloan, 'The country of Socialism and the war', *LM*, July 1940, 392–8.
27 See e.g. Gallacher's speech to the Commons, 20.8.40; 364 *H.C. Deb.*, 1253.
28 First published in 1939, this compilation was reprinted as *Spokesmen for Liberty* in the first part of 1941.
29 Connolly, Bolingbroke and Wordsworth, quoted *DW*, 6.8.40, 26.8.40, 8.8.40.
30 In Gollancz (ed.), *The Betrayal of the Left*, 137.

31 See e.g. the *Daily Worker* editorial, 'Bring the guilty to account!', 18.6.40.
32 *New Statesman and Nation*, 14.12.40, 621.
33 Attfield and Williams, *op. cit.*, 33.
34 See pp. 70–3.
35 'Notes', Nov. 1940, 564–5.
36 RPD K4, draft political letter, 8.7.40.
37 'Notes', Nov. 1940, 563–72. Dutt took the same perspective in his pamphlet *We Fight For Life* (CPGB, 14.11.40), e.g. 7–11, 14–15.
38 I. Montagu, *The Traitor Class* (1940), 7, 30, 33, 72, 130–3.
39 'Imperialism and counter-revolution', *LM*, Nov. 1940, 606–7.
40 RPD K4, Dutt to Edmund Dell, 25.11.40.
41 RPD K4, 'Report of R. Palme Dutt to the special meeting of the Central Committee of the Communist Party during the week ending May 24, 1940', 25.5.40.
42 R. Goodman, *WNV*, 24.8.40, 453–4.
43 E.g. *DW*, 28.10.40.
44 Gallacher, *WNV*, 18.1.41, 39.
45 E.g. CPGB statement on the Hess mission, *WNV*, 24.5.41, 323–4.
46 'Notes', Jan. 1941, 11–12.
47 Published as a *LM* War Pamphlet in about June 1941. For a hostile examination of the CP's anti-Americanism, see 'Note III' and J. Strachey, 'The American question' in V. Gollancz (ed.), *The Betrayal of the Left*, 70–9, 83–106.
48 *The Empire and the War* (CPGB, 12.6.40), 10–12.
49 'Notes', May 1940, 267; Aug. 1940, 419; Dutt, *We Fight For Life*, 11.
50 C. Dutt, 'The colonial question and the war', *LM*, June 1940, 350.
51 Dutt, *India Today* (1940), 17, 476.
52 'Spectator', *DW*, 4.1.40.
53 *The Empire and the War*, 12.
54 M. Carritt, *India* (CPGB, 21.1.41), 6–7; Carritt, 'India before the storm', *LM*, May 1940, 295; Dutt, *India Today*, 480–1.
55 Ibid., 17, 481–4.
56 Ibid., 15.
57 Dutt, *DW*, 24.5.40.
58 CPGB Colonial Bureau, *PO*, Jan. 1940, 6–7.
59 *PO*, Jan. 1940, 6–7; Mar. 1940, 19–21; PRO INF 1/910, Roger Hollis to J. M. Ross, 8.2.41; *DW*, 4.12.40. See also *Thesis*, 318–19, for the limited circulation of Party pamphlets on colonial affairs. It should also be noted that the appearance of Dutt's massive tome on India in 1940 was coincidental: it had been in preparation since 1937.
60 M-O TC 25/8, e.g. report on People's Convention (Holborn Hall), 12.1.41; report of Convention meetings, Holborn Hall, 22.2.41; Royal Hotel, 16.3.41. See also PC *Organising Bulletin*, no. 1, 12.5.41, 3 (MML).
61 RPD K4, 'Suggestions of line of policy statement (introducing programme and policy resolution)', 1.1.41.
62 Dutt, *India Today*, 31–2, 529; R. P. Arnot, 'India To-day', *LM*, Sept. 1940, 495–8.
63 M. McInerney, *DW*, 10.1.41; Gallacher, *Ireland, Can it Remain Neutral?* (CPGB, 9.4.41), 16–20; M. Milotte, *Communism in Modern Ireland* (1984), 196–7. In this field, as in others, there was thus no return to the 'leftism' of the Third Period.
64 'Notes', Jan. 1940, 3.
65 'The Labour movement discusses the war', *LM*, Feb. 1940, 108.
66 For which see ch. 1 above.

67 A. Horner, 'The war on the home front', *LM*, Nov. 1939, 661–3.
68 See e.g. J. Johnson, *The Men Behind the War* (CPGB, 31.1.40).
69 M. Hudson, 'British monopoly capital and the war', *LM*, Apr. 1941, 182.
70 *WNV*, 22.2.41, 121.
71 See the articles by P. Field in *LM*, Feb.–Apr., 1941.
72 'Notes', Jan. 1941, 13; see also e.g. Campbell, 'The scaffolding of servitude', *LM*, July 1941, 321.
73 *Ibid.*, 326.
74 Campbell, 'Trade unions in the strait jacket of war', *LM*, Oct. 1940, 542.
75 *DW*, 16.8.40.
76 *WNV*, 4.1.41, 10; *DW*, 28.12.40.
77 E. Burns, *WNV*, 1.3.41, 140.
78 *Choose Your Future* (1941), 124.
79 'Notes', Oct. 1940, 517; May 1941, 200.
80 *DW*, 27.5.40.
81 361 *H. C. Deb.*, 151–7, 22.5.40.
82 See Gallacher's speech in opposition to the Bill, *ibid.*, 163–5.
83 *DW*, 24.5.40.
84 R. P. Arnot, 'The political black-out', *LM*, Dec. 1939, 738.
85 'Notes', Dec. 1939, 711.
86 Campbell, 'Trade unions in the strait jacket of war', 544–5. See *A Brief Outline of the Life of John Mason* (John Mason Defence Committee, 1940) and also Branson, *op. cit.*, 298–301, for this case and that of T. E. Nicholas, another Communist who was interned.
87 For the ban see pp. 239–40.
88 Dutt, *WNV*, 8.2.41, 81, 88; Rust, *WNV*, 15.2.41, 101–2.
89 'Notes', Mar. 1941.
90 'Before the Labour Party conference', *LM*, Apr. 1940, 230.
91 See ch. 2 above.
92 *DW*, 4.11.39.
93 See Dutt, 'Socialism versus National Socialism', *DW*, 17.5.40; Arnot, 'The fate of the Labour Party', *LM*, June 1940, 338–42; Rust, 'National Socialism: Labour Party brand', *LM*, Sept. 1940, 479–84.
94 See pp. 153–64.
95 Dutt, report to CPGB CC, *WNV*, 1.6.40, 312.
96 Aneurin Bevan, *Tribune*, 7.2.41; Garry Allighan, *New Statesman and Nation*, 1.2.41, 106.
97 See p. 75.
98 Of 25.5.40, i.e. for the current policy of the CP.
99 RPD K4, 'Revised draft memorandum on the Labour Party', 1.6.40.
100 See *Thesis,* 349, note 16.
101 See *Thesis,* 343.
102 See H. Pelling, *A Short History of the Labour Party* (1972 edn), 156.
103 H. Pelling, *A History of British Trade Unionism* (1976 edn), 215.
104 Pollitt, *WNV*, 22.2.41, 113–14.
105 P. Kerrigan, 'The trade unions: what now?', *LM*, Nov. 1940, 589. For a discussion of these problems from the contemporary Communist standpoint, see A. Hutt, *British Trade Unionism. An Outline History* (1941), ch. 10, entitled 'Trade unions – or Labour Front?'
106 Pollitt, *DW*, 7.10.40.
107 See e.g. Kerrigan, *op. cit.*, 593–4; W. Hannington, 'The AEU and the shop stewards'

movement', *LM*, Feb. 1941, 69.
108 *DW*, 20.12.40.
109 CPGB CC statement on 'The Communist Party and the Labour Party', *LM*, Dec. 1939, 760.
110 See *Thesis*, 246, n. 33.
111 E.g. Arnot, 'Before the Labour Party Conference', *LM*, Apr. 1940.
112 D. N. Pritt, 'Where are we now?', *LM*, June 1940, 335.
113 Pritt, 'The People's Convention', *LM*, Oct. 1940, 526–9.
114 Pritt, *Forward to a People's Government* (PC, 1940), 16.
115 See L. J. Macfarlane, *The British Communist Party. Its Origin and Development until 1929* (1966), 189–93, 210–20, 223–9; B. Pearce, 'The Communist Party and the Labour left, 1925–1929' in M. Woodhouse and B. Pearce, *Essays on the History of Communism in Britain* (1975), 179–83.
116 'Notes', Feb. 1937, 76. See also p. 35.
117 The CP's official position was that trade unionists should continue to pay the levy; CPGB CC statement on 'The Communist Party and the Labour Party', *LM*, Dec. 1939, 760.
118 RPD K4, 'Draft resolution on the Labour Party' and 'Memorandum on organisation', 10.2.40.
119 Here it should be borne in mind that, in London at least, where there was a sharp decline in Party membership, the CP decided to concentrate on factory rather than area organisation; see *Thesis*, 521.
120 RPD K4, 'Revised draft memorandum on the Labour Party', 1.6.40.
121 RPD K4, 'Development of the campaign for a People's Government (draft resolution)', 8.8.40.
122 The leading speakers at the conference, D. N. Pritt, Harry Adams and W. J. R. Squance would become the People's Convention's Treasurer, Chairman and Secretary respectively. None was formally a member of the Communist Party.
123 Manifesto reprinted *LM*, Nov. 1940, 601–6.
124 *The People Speak* (report of People's Convention, 12.1.41; PC, 1941), 3–4.
125 See e.g. R. Croucher, *Engineers at War* (1982), 113, 137; *Daily Herald*, 17.1.40. For repudiations of these allegations, see M-O TC 25/8, report of PC meeting, Holborn Hall, 2.2.41.
126 Murphy, *Victory Production!* (1941), 39–43.
127 The report is reproduced in Attfield and Williams, *op. cit.*, pp. 189–90; for further reasons for approaching it sceptically, see *Thesis*, 356–7.
128 M-O TC 25/8, 'General Report' on PC, 12.1.41; extracts from this can be found in A. Calder and D. Sheridan (eds), *Speak For Yourself. A Mass-Observation Anthology 1937–1949* (1985 edn) 198–202.
129 Harold Marsh, interview.
130 *Daily Herald*, 14.1.41.
131 M-O TC 25/8, reports on PC, Royal Hotel and Holborn Hall, 12.1.41.
132 The title of an article on the Convention by Pollitt, *LM*, Dec. 1940.
133 M-O TC 25/8, report on PC, 12.1.41, lunch-hour conversation.
134 *Ibid.*, reports on PC, 12.1.41. One of the soldiers, Ted Willis, was accordingly booted out of the army a few weeks later.
135 *Ibid.*, report on PC, Royal Hotel, 12.1.41.
136 *The People Speak*, 54–6.
137 For their names see *ibid.*, 62.
138 Printed statement by Squance embodying PC National Committee resolution, 3.1.42

(MML).
139 See e.g. *WNV*, 22.2.41, 122; *The People's Convention Bulletin* no. 4 (c. Feb. 1941) (MML); PC *Organising Bulletin* no. 4, 15.8.41 4 (MML).
140 See PC National Committee resolution, 3.1.42, in printed statement by Squance (MML).
141 *People's Convention Special* (c. Mar. 1941), 2 (DNP).
142 PC National Committee resolution, 1.12.40, in *The People's Convention Bulletin*, 8.12.40, 10. In this respect the Convention's contribution appears to have been inspirational rather than organisational.
143 *The People Speak*, 17–18.
144 *Report* of the 40th Annual Conference of the Labour Party (1941), 21.
145 *The People Speak*, Adams, 8–10; Pritt, 25; M-O TC 25/8, report on PC (Holborn Hall), 12.1.41.
146 Adams, *Why Britain Needs a People's Government* (PC, Dec. 1940), 5.
147 *Labour Party Members Expelled for Advocating Labour's Own Programme* (PC, 1941), 1, 3, 5–7.
148 E.g. *The People's Convention Reply to the National Council of Labour* (PC leaflet, Mar. 1941) (MML).
149 See *Thesis*, 382–3.
150 NCL statement on 'The People's Convention', *Report* of the 40th Annual Conference of the Labour Party (1941), 184–5.
151 Squance, *The People Speak*, 29.
152 Malcolm MacEwen and Harold Marsh, interviews.
153 M-O TC 25/8, report on PC meeting, Royal Hotel, 16.3.41.
154 According to MacEwen (interview), the CP's initial instinct was in fact to put up a Convention candidate. In effect, of course, given the lack of an effective Convention organisation at grassroots level, this would have been a Communist candidacy in all but name. It was the banning of the *Daily Worker* which led to the decision to put forward a declared Communist candidate, standing on a Convention platform but at the same time bringing to the fore the issue of the ban. MacEwen himself was on the staff of the *Worker*'s Scottish edition.
155 *DW*, 20.11.40.
156 Emile Burns, *DW*, 7.12.40; report of London and Home Counties PC conference, 16.3.41, *People's Convention Supplement* (c. Mar. 1941) (MML). For a discussion of some of the groups to which the Party tried to appeal, see *Thesis*, 367–74.
157 Dona Torr, *DW*, 25.11.40. One banner noted by a Mass-Observer in the Royal Hotel proclaimed:

CHARTIST MOVEMENT MANCHESTER JULY 20, 1840
to the
PEOPLE'S CONVENTION LONDON JANUARY 12, 1941
100 YEARS OF STRUGGLE

158 *DW*, 6.12.40.
159 For the CP's work amongst women at this time, see *Thesis*, 369–71.
160 *DW* e.g. 12.10.40, 22.10.40, 29.10.40, 13.11.40, 6.12.40, 23.12.40.
161 M-O TC 25/8, '3 big shows!' leaflet, c. Feb. 1941.
162 E.g. J. Strachey, 'The People's Convention' in V. Gollancz (ed.), *The Betrayal of the Left* (1941), 154–72.
163 *DW*, 14.1.41.
164 Dutt, *DW*, 5.8.40.

165 Campbell, 'Immediate programme or social-democratic utopia?, *LM*, June 1940, 361.
166 'Notes', Apr. 1941, 155, 162–4.
167 'Notes', Mar. 1941, 99.
168 RPD K4, Dutt to Pollitt, 13.11.41. This letter has been published with a commentary by James Hinton in the *Bulletin* of the Society for the Study of Labour History no. 39 (1979), 27–32.
169 M-O A TC 25/8, report of PC meeting, Holborn Hall, 2.2.41.
170 *DW*, 22.7.40.
171 *DW*, 7.12.40.
172 E.g. *Let Us Fight Now in Defence of the People* (PC, Feb. 1941).
173 Young, *A People's Peace* (PC, 1941), 3–6.
174 'Notes', Feb. 1941, 53.
175 Pritt, *Forward to a People's Government* (PC, 1940), 13.
176 Printed in Young, *op. cit.*, 15–16 and as a separate leaflet, *The Real Germany Speaks* by the CP. According to Borkenau, 'this was a swindle pure and simple, since not only were no such documents distributed in Germany, none ever appeared during that period in *Die Welt*'; *European Communism* (1953), 261–2.
177 Young, *op. cit.*, 7.
178 Dutt, *We Fight For Life* (CPGB, 14.11.40), 23; Burns, *DW* 14.11.40.
179 E.g. Young, *op. cit.*, 6–7.
180 See Sean O'Casey's wordy evasion of such a question put by George Strauss, *DW*, 3.10.40, 4.10.40.
181 'Notes', Apr. 1941, 162.
182 Dutt himself shared these inhibitions. The peroration to his speech to the People's Convention was originally to have ended with the rousing cry to 'End this criminal imperialist war!' but, on second thoughts, he changed this to the less controversial 'For a govt. of people's representatives'. The change was obviously prompted by Dutt's reluctance to alienate supporters of the Convention and had nothing to do with fear of government action; RPD K4, 12.1.41.
183 M-O A TC 46/10, MacEwen's Election Address.
184 PRO INF 1/292, no. 22, 5.3.41.
185 M-O A TC 46/10, 'Big Communist meeting at Alexandria', 16.2.41.
186 *Ibid.*, Cllr Hugh Macintyre speaking at Black Diamond Hall, Duntocher, 9.2.41.
187 MacEwen's Election Address. Interestingly, both MacEwen and J. R. Campbell, with whom he had long discussions on the matter, were of the opinion that the fundamental condition of success in this struggle was an Anglo–Soviet alliance. It was this which accounted for the surprising omission of any reference to the USSR in MacEwen's election address. 'The truth was', he explained, 'that as we could not say the one thing that would have made sense, that only through an alliance with the Soviet Union could Fascism be defeated, Johnnie thought it was better to say nothing than to repeat the Convention's vague formula about friendship with the Soviet Union' (interview).
188 M-O TC 25/8.
189 M. Heston, 'Following Ramsay MacDonald', *LM*, Dec. 1940, 656.
190 *LN*, Feb. 1941, 1,665–71.
191 'The People's Convention', *LM*, Oct. 1940, 526.
192 *Choose Your Future* (1941), 88, 90.
193 Pollitt, 'The People's Convention. What Next?', *LM*, Feb. 1941, 63. As Gollancz pointed out in *The Betrayal of the Left* (p. 51), the CP used such phrases as 'find a way' (or 'find the means') as a 'nauseating formula, which covers a loose and lazy refusal to think with

clearness and precision'.
194 *DW*, 29.6.40; *We Fight For Life* (CPGB, 14.11.40), 24–5.
195 S. Blackwell, *Birmingham Today. The Role and Record of Neville Chamberlain and others* (CPGB, Midlands DC, 1941), 45. See also the draft of Dutt's speech to the Convention, RPD K4.
196 'Notes', Mar. 1935, 139.
197 'Notes', May 1941, 201.
198 'Notes', June 1940, 33.
199 *Victory Production!* (1941), 43–4.
200 Eddie Frow, interview.
201 M-O TC 25/8, report on PC, 12.1.41. The investigator commented that 'there was definitely a certain amount of feeling that there had not been enough concrete decisions taken'.
202 3,862 votes, as against 21,900 for a Labour candidate.
203 PRO INF 1/292, no. 22, 5.3.41.
204 RPD K3, 'Outlines of political report', 14.2.41.
205 Honourable figures like E. M. Forster and Vaughan Williams withheld cooperation with the BBC in protest at the ban.
206 Dutt, *WNV*, 8.2.41, 82; *Let Us Fight Now in Defence of the People* (PC, Feb. 1941).
207 'Notes', Mar. 1941, 115–25; Apr. 1941, 151–2.
208 Text of letter from RPD K4, 14.3.41; published over the signature of Adams, *People's Convention Special* (c. Mar. 1941) (DNP). See also Redgrave's *In My Mind's Eye* (1984 edn), 162–72.
209 RPD K4, 'Draft outline of political report to enlarged meeting', 15.4.41.
210 E.g. *More Food and How to Get It* (PC, Apr. 1941) (DNP).
211 *Call to MPs from the People's Convention*, PC printed letter dated 2.5.41; *WNV*, 10.5.41, 295.
212 363 *H.C. Deb.*, 696.
213 See pp. 122–47.
214 Pollitt, *Wages – a Policy* (CPGB, 24.12.40), 17–21.
215 *Ibid.*, 23; *The War and the Labour Movement* (CPGB, 12.6.40), 8.
216 *DW*, 1.1.41.
217 Campbell, 'The workers in the total war economy', *LM*, July 1940, 386.
218 *DW*, 12.7.40.
219 RPD K4, draft of 'Political letter', 8.7.40. Interestingly, similar sets of proposals had been advanced by the Party as far back as 1922 and again in 1937; see Pollitt, *Serving My Time* (1941 edn), 162–3; *It Can Be Done* (CPGB, report of 14th Congress, 1937), 280.
220 *DW*, 27.6.40.
221 *DW*, 23.7.40.
222 EATSSNC circular, 16.7.40 (WCML).
223 *DW*, 2.11.40.
224 See G. Crane, *WNV*, 7.6.41, 357.
225 *DW*, 22.10.40.
226 *DW*, 21.1.41. That there was 'very little report of Communist activities adversely affecting production' was acknowledged privately by the government; PRO CAB. 98.18, 'View of Production Executive', 29.1.41.
227 Telegram from South Wales armaments workers to Bevin, *DW*, 8.8.40.
228 EATSSNC, 16.7.40.
229 *DW*, 28.5.40; see R. Clark, *J. B. S. The Life and Work of J. B. S. Haldane* (1968), ch. 7.

230 This and the next paragraph drawn from VG MSS.157/3/DOC/1, Levy to Gollancz, 14.1.41, 5.2.41, 7.2.41, 2.3.41, n.d. (c. Mar. 1941), 8.5.41.
231 *DW*, 23.7.40.
232 E.g. Pritt, *Choose Your Future*, 37; 'Notes', Mar. 1941, 99–100.
233 RPD K3, 'Outlines of political report', 14.2.41.
234 Arnot, 'Who pays for the war?', *LM*, May 1941; *The Keynes Budget* (CPGB, 25.4.41; includes Gallacher's Commons speech of 7.4.41).
235 Campbell, 'The workers in the total war economy', *LM*, July 1940, 389–91.
236 See for example how in its campaign on the food shortage in the first part of 1941 the Party took great pains to show that the war itself did not require that the people go hungry; *Thesis*, 420–1.
237 References to Croucher, *Engineers at War*, 100–4, unless otherwise stated.
238 *Ibid.*, 86.
239 British Auxiliaries Shop Stewards' Committee, 'Victimisation of shop steward' leaflet (WCML). Another leaflet, expressing similar attitudes, is cited by Croucher.
240 E.g. the Coventry shop steward quoted *DW*, 5.10.40.
241 Hodson, *Towards the Morning* (1941), 91.
242 Horner, *Incorrigible Rebel* (1960), 163.
243 SWMF EC minutes, 17.9.40, 15.10.40, 22.10.40, 5.11.40, 3.12.40, 10.12.40, 24.12.40, 21.12.40, 4.1.41, 7.1.41, 21.1.41; *Western Mail*, 1.2.41; Broomfield, 'South Wales during the Second World War', 588–94.
244 *Western Mail*.
245 SWMF EC minutes, 5.11.40; *Western Mail*, 27.12.40.
246 Murphy, *Victory Production!*, 25.
247 *Ibid.*, 40–1.
248 *DW*, 2.8.40.
249 PRO CAB 98.18, Home Office memorandum, 27.7.40.
250 PRO CAB 65 WG 193(40)2, 4.7.40; WG 194(40)10, 5.7.40; *DW*, 13.7.40.
251 See pp. 193–4.
252 CPGB PB statement, *DW*, 15.6.40. A number of such incidents were reported in the *Daily Worker*; see also R. Kidd, *British Liberty in Danger* (1940), 263–5, and, for personal accounts, D. Hyde, *I Believed* (1951), 85–8 and *Thesis*, 533.
253 Branson gives an example, *op. cit.*, 297.
254 *Engineers at War* (1982), 95 ff.
255 This was the experience of Eddie Frow, a CP steward in Manchester; interview. See also the report in *New Leader*, 25.1.41. However, this too could provoke unrest, as with the fortnight-long strike at De Havilland's in protest at the transference of stewards without consultation; *DW*, 9.8.40, 19.8.40.
256 See p. 216.
257 RPD K4, Dutt to Rust, 1.6.40.
258 PRO CAB 66 WP(40)482, Home Office memorandum on 'The "Daily Worker"', 23.12.40.
259 See *Thesis*, 536.
260 PRO CAB 98.18, 20.1.41, 28.1.41, memoranda from Home Secretary, 27.1.41, and Minister of Information, 3.2.41; CAB 66 WP(41)27, report on 'Communist activities' by Lord President of the Council, 10.2.41.
261 PRO CAB 66 WP(41)7, 11.1.41.
262 PRO CAB 98.18, memorandum by Chairman of Home Defence (Security) Executive, 16.1.41.

263 PRO CAB. 98.18, 20.1.41.
264 PRO CAB 66 WP(41)27, report by Lord President of the Council, 10.2.41.
265 See *A Brief Outline of the Life of John Mason* (John Mason Defence Committee, 1940).
266 PRO CAB 98.18, memorandum by Home Secretary. 17.1.41; Ted Bramley, interview. A second reason for some leading officials returning to their trades in reserved occupations was to exempt themselves from conscription and thus minimise the dispersal and dislocation of the Party leadership. According to Bramley this was an equally important motivation. Bramley himself worked in Park Royal for a time, later returning to full-time Party work. He had in any case by this time been given a low army medical rating as he had had tuberculosis. It should of course be pointed out that the Party's general policy was for all members in the appropriate age groups to respond to military call-up.
267 See J. Mahon, *Harry Pollitt* (1976), 267–8.
268 PRO CAB 66 WP(41)27, report by Lord President of the Council, 10.2.41.
269 Hannington, *Never On Our Knees* (1967), 336–7.
270 And for the authorities, perhaps, as a means of testing the depth of feeling aroused by such actions.
271 See pp. 50–1.
272 Attfield and Williams, *op. cit.*, 128.
273 Sir Frederick Bartlett cited by T. Harrisson, *Living Through the Blitz* (1978 edn), 321.
274 *WNV*, 10.5.41, 289–91.
275 'Notes', May 1941, 211 (my emphasis).
276 F. Ring, 273–6. See also CPGB CC, 'Political letter to the Communist Party membership', 19.5.41.
277 M-O TC 25/9, *Daily Worker* leaflet, 2.6.41.
278 No script of the book appears to exist, but a description and full list of contents are to be found in a publicity leaflet inside *LM*, Apr. 1941.

Chapter eight
Ruptures and continuities
two case studies, 1936–41

Throughout this book the aim has been to balance the broad generalisations which the historian of any organisation has necessarily to make with insights into the diverse pressures which shaped Communist politics in particular localities, particular industries and particular organisations. Only thus, indeed, are possible the sort of enlightening generalisations which encompass rather than obliterate the particular. It is with this in mind that this chapter explores in greater depth the issues faced by Communists moving in two very different spheres of activity: the highly-charged and articulate debates within the Left Book Club, and the common struggles for their immediate interests of ordinary people, especially ordinary women, in Birmingham.

In the case of Birmingham, we shall find, as previously when trying to understand the pressures faced by Communists in industry, that the Party's decision to oppose the war brought with it surprisingly few changes in the nature and direction of Communist activities. But if we look first at the Left Book Club, we shall observe a marvellously vigorous movement for unity sinking into insignificance as the granite realities of international politics on which it had so largely been constructed turned out to be as of quicksand. These two studies therefore provide an exceptionally stark picture of the ruptures and continuities in Communist politics. Possibly too stark, indeed, and too facile; for never let us forget that many of those Communists who remained so sensitive to the problems involved in mobilising people around their most immediate concerns were at the same time posting off intemperate letters of resignation from the Left Book Club.

8.1 The rise and fall of the Left Book Club

The aim of the Club is a simple one: it is to help in the terribly urgent struggle *for* World Peace & a better social & economic order & *against* Fascism . . .

(Left Book Club application form)

Life and politics are unfortunately not very simple things: and progressives are, as they always knew they would be if war came, in a desperate dilemma.

(Victor Gollancz, May 1940[1])

It is symptomatic of the climate of left-wing politics in the late 1930s that Victor Gollancz should have regarded his aim in setting up the Left Book Club (LBC) as a simple one. To many on the left, like the Communist, Ralph Fox, the successive international crises which threatened to engulf Europe in war presented themselves almost as straightforward moral issues:

> There are rare occasions in history . . . when the demands of life fully correspond with the dignity and intensity of man's desires. Such an occasion confronts us to-day when the conflict of classes throughout the world has 'created an object of love and of hatred – of apprehension and of wishes – adequate (if that be possible) to the utmost demands of the human spirit'.[2]

Above all, the principles of world peace and anti-Fascism were embodied in the heroic struggle of the Spanish people, sustained by the aid and the lives of the European left and by the Soviet Union. Fox himself demonstrated the force and sincerity of his words when he gave his life in the defence of Madrid. The barbaric support of international Fascism for Spanish reaction provided the other half of this Manichean picture of world politics, the object of apprehension and hatred; the rights and wrongs of the bombing of Guernica were not open to debate. It was the unspeakable brutality of their common adversaries which led to the blurring of differences on the left. There were, of course, dissenting voices asking uncomfortable questions about the Moscow show trials, the suppression of the POUM and indeed the whole conception of the Popular Front; but the most vigorous sections of the left were temporarily united on what appeared to be an uncomplicated set of issues. But then the events surrounding the outbreak of war revealed unexpected and unwelcome complexities which cut sharply at the slender ties binding the left together. One result was the disintegration of the Left Book Club, which had been not merely a forum of opinion but the nearest thing that Britain had to a People's Front movement on a national scale. A study of its break-up will reveal that the roots of the wartime divisions on the left were firmly embedded in the politics of the People's Front.

The Left Book Club was formed in the summer of 1936 as part of the publishing house of Victor Gollancz, already renowned as a brilliant innovator in the world of books. The basic idea was that Club members would receive each of the Club's monthly choices, and such of its supplementary selections as they desired, at a fraction of their normal price, as well as a free monthly copy of *Left Book News* (later *Left News*).[3] The books were all intended, in some way or other, to contribute to the 'terribly urgent struggle *for* World Peace & a better social & economic order & *against* Fascism'. The interest stimulated by these books was such that there arose a 'wholly spontaneous demand' for discussion groups in which to debate the issues raised by the selections.[4] Gollancz encouraged this growth by setting up an LBC Groups' Department headed by Dr John Lewis. By 1939, the Club had reached the peak of its influence. That April Gollancz reported a Club membership of about 57,000, many of whom were active in one of the twelve hundred or so LBC groups. Of the latter, at least thirty-nine had their own premises, while some published their own bulletins. More than two million books had by this time been distributed by the Club.[5] The Club had emerged as a real political force drawing its inspiration from the ideas associated with the Popular Front; so much so, in fact, that in 1939 the Labour Party not only instituted its own, rather dreary Labour Book Service, but also threatened to declare membership of the Club incompatible with membership of the Labour Party.[6]

But if the Left Book Club constituted a challenge to the authority of Transport House, it nevertheless disclaimed any intention of forming a political party in the normal sense of the word. Gollancz even denied that it was committed, as an organisation, to the building of a People's Front, though he admitted that 'the very existence of the Left Book Club tends towards a Popular Front'.[7] In retrospect, the Club seems to have fulfilled the sort of political functions in which the Labour Party has traditionally been deficient: disseminating literature, organising educational and cultural activities, public meetings and national rallies. Some local groups also took part in more overtly 'political' activities of the sort which Transport House felt were the exclusive concern of the Labour Party,[8] but the Club as a national organisation tended to keep its distance from such goings-on.[9] Early in 1937, John Lewis stressed that only groups which unanimously wished to do so should take part in agitational activities and recommended the Manchester group's declaration of purely educational intent as a guide to the Club's role.[10] Two years later, when a number of groups got involved in Cripps's National Petition campaign, Gollancz issued a circular asking them to desist, despite his personal sympathy with the campaign's objectives.[11] It may be that by this time Gollancz's main concern was to prevent the exacerbation of the Club's already poor relations with the Labour Party. Nevertheless, the Club was shaped very much by the belief that its success as a broad unifying force would be best secured if differences over political tactics were sorted out outside its organisation rather than within it.

The Club's value in unifying diverse tendencies on the left is undeniable. Most frequently the Club is associated with the political awakening and leftward drift of the liberal-minded middle classes, and with the penetration of progressive opinion into the more reactionary parts of England where the Labour Party had still to make an impact. While this is undoubtedly correct, it would be a mistake to ignore the social diversity of the Club's membership. In a by no means untypical issue of *Left News* we read of the formation of a Doctors' and Scientists' Group based in Birmingham; of the Poets' Group with its journal, *Poetry and the People*; of a new Engineers' Group based at the Irlam works at Cadishead, Manchester; of a Schoolgirls' Group in East London; and of a thirty-strong group of Aberdeen tramwaymen meeting monthly to discuss the Club choice.[12] A Communist shop steward in Manchester gave his assessment of the value of the Club:

> The Left Book Club books did have an impact. After the outbreak of war I went into the factory at ten o'clock to address the nightshift and as I walked up the aisle a man opened the door of one of these great big cupboards and showed me row after row of these books. They were reading them on nights, so they did have an influence. I knew personally quite a number of engineering workers, on the District Committee of the union and active shop stewards, who were members of the Left Book Club and did read the books, and used the arguments in them as well – particularly on the issues of Fascism and war.[13]

And according to its local organiser the Club was 'a real Popular Front – middle class, working class, white collar – a real Popular Front in Manchester.'[14] As an instrument of political enlightenment, the Left Book Club is unique in the history of the British left, and has often been cited as a factor contributing to the Labour landslide of 1945. And in the short term, of course, it was central to the broad campaigns against Fascism and war to which the Communist Party was so committed.

The question thus arises of the extent of Communist influence over the Club. A glance through the files of *Left News* reveals that this was considerable. The early issues of the paper included monthly contributions on 'the USSR Month by Month' by Ivor Montagu, while the journal's most substantial feature article was nearly always written by John Strachey expounding some or other aspect of Communist policy. Quite apart from these regular features, there were numerous occasional contributions by Communists, while Club selections were in many cases the work of writers in or close to the CP. Indeed, leading Party members, particularly Emile Burns, were privately very much involved in the Club's selection procedures and on one or two occasions, as we shall see, were able effectively to veto undesirable scripts.[15] In addition, Club members were offered every title published by the Communist publishing house, Lawrence and Wishart, at two-thirds of its normal price, and special subscription rates to Claud Cockburn's *The Week*.[16] Clearly, the Club did a great deal to make the views of Communists known to those who otherwise would have remained ignorant of them.

Communists also played a significant role in the discussion groups movement spawned by the Club. Although the political allegiances of the vast majority of group convenors cannot be ascertained, we have no reason to doubt Harry Pollitt's testimony that 'it was the work of the Communist Party which gave the Left Book Club its mass basis, and enabled it to carry through all its manifold activities'. Indeed, Pollitt, himself a notable participant in the Club's affairs, revealed that 'out of their experience in the Club, many splendid new members came into the Communist Party, the majority of whom today [1958] hold responsible positions in our Party'.[17] Furthermore, of the Club's paid organisers, at least four – Sheila Lynd, Jane Conway, Betty Reid and William Paul – were Communists, while the head of the Groups' Department, John Lewis, was very sympathetic to the Party although he did not become a member until after the outbreak of war.

However, this is not a simple question of 'Communist domination' but one of a convergence of views on the left at a time of deepening crisis. Thus, while it is certainly significant that one of the Club's three selectors, Strachey, was a Communist, it is equally significant that for three years he could cooperate fairly amicably with Gollancz and Harold Laski, a member of Labour's NEC. The very essence of the CP's strategy at this time was the building of a broad front embracing a wide range of opinion but united on the most pressing issues of the day. John Lewis recalled that those Party members 'who entered a group to flog the Party line, acted contrary to that line',[18] and this paradox gives a good idea of the value of the Club to the CP. Communist influence was felt, but it was felt as much in the publication of books by Acland and Attlee – indeed by virtually any anti-Fascist writer who steered clear of 'Trotskyite attacks on the Soviet Union'[19] – as in the dissemination of the views of Communist writers. At a time when Transport House was trying to drive the CP into political quarantine, it was enough for Pollitt and Strachey that they should appear on the same platform as clerics and trade union leaders, as Liberal and Labour MPs; they would have gained nothing by packing the platform with Party members.

The Party line, then, was not to 'take over' the Club but to ensure that it remained as inclusive an organisation as possible. When later the CP's influence over the Club began to disturb Gollancz, Sheila Lynd, who at Pollitt's request had given up all Party work to devote her energies to the Groups' Department, suggested to Gollancz that he 'go through all the folders at the office, which contain all the correspondence I have ever sent concerning the Club: you will not find one instance of my "using" the Club for the benefit of the Party, but many of my preventing foolish local groups from doing so . . .'[20] The restraining hand of the Groups' Department can perhaps be detected in the following story of a Club member in Leicester, whose development shows the sort of long-term advantages which might accrue to the CP if it refrained from overwhelming LBC groups and alienating the Club's non-Communist supporters:

> When I joined the Left Book Club, three years ago [1937], I was a member of the Labour Party (had been for 16 years). I was amazed to find the local Group in control of Communists and wrote you accordingly. . . . Came a change in the Group by which the active Communists gave place to an increasing moderate view represented by Labour and Liberal opinion, with a consequent steadying of the 'balance of opinion'. Throughout the whole period one has been actively engaged in the Group; leading discussions, fostering the cultural development of members, and generally taking a prominent part in the progress of the Group. . . . Thanks to these activities, and the study of Marxist writings, I have arrived today – a Communist![21]

This indicates as well as anything that the crucial importance of the Club for the CP lay in the fact that neither its active membership nor its propagandists were predominantly Communists. In addition to its intrinsic importance in the fight against reaction, the Club provided an essential breadth of contact for the Communists who played such an enthusiastic part in its activities.[22]

But if the Left Book Club seemed perfectly designed to carry out the CP's Popular Front strategy, it was nevertheless very much dependent on one individual, Gollancz, who was not a Communist. The Club remained an integral part of Gollancz's publishing house and it is therefore impossible to extricate the finances of the Club from those of the company itself. However, it is clear that the Club's manifold activities were heavily subsidised.[23] Moreover, according to Betty Reid who worked full-time for the Groups' Department in Henrietta Street, the Club was 'not only financially dependent but his was the motivating power'. While Laski and Strachey contributed little to the day-to-day running of the Club, Gollancz was constantly at work, devising scheme after scheme which 'kept the whole pot boiling'. On his appointment as Groups Organiser, Lewis assured Club members that 'Mr. Gollancz reads every letter that comes into the office, and discusses with me every day the activities of any group from which we have heard that morning', and apparently Gollancz maintained this level of interest throughout the massive expansion of the Club.[24] Gollancz was, in short, a dynamic personality in the right place, with the right resources at his disposal, at the right time. Without him and his publishing house, the Club in the form that it emerged would have been inconceivable.

However, there was also a less attractive side to Gollancz. The ardour with which he furthered the Club's activities was accompanied by a manifest desire to keep a tight personal grip on his progeny. Symptomatic of his rather proprietorial attitude towards the Club was his insistence that the only article in *Left News* expressing '*Club policy*' was the editorial which he himself wrote. 'Everything else', he insisted, 'must be taken as representing nothing but the views of the writer himself.'[25] That Gollancz felt he bore exclusive responsibility for the policy and image of the Club was borne out when well-advanced and well-publicised plans for a 32-page *Left News Weekly* were suddenly abandoned late in 1937, for reasons which Gollancz felt it necessary to disclose only a year later. Not only were the financial and technical difficulties insurmountable, he claimed, a bit too self-deprecatingly in view of his record in publishing, but 'it was felt that I personally had insufficient time to give to the supervision of a weekly, and that if it lacked this supervision it would not be an organic part of the Left Book Club'. Instead, Gollancz announced an arrangement with *Tribune* by which he would assume editorial responsibility for a small LBC section in that paper.[26] Finally, and significantly in view of later developments, Gollancz resisted pressure to put the groups movement on 'some democratically organised national basis . . . through which members can express themselves'. According to these proposals, which were put forward at a conference of group convenors in 1937, the groups would have been headed by an elected national council and guided by a written constitution.[27] Had the proposals been put into effect, and the Club transformed into an accountable organisation, its wartime history might have been very different. However, Gollancz had no need to bargain, knowing full well that the movement could not survive without his support; the malcontents could not afford to force the issue.

So while there can be no doubting Gollancz's sincerity and enthusiasm, the fact remains that he tended to see the Club very much as his private property. The success of the Club, however, depended neither on Gollancz alone nor simply on the members who kept the Club going in their different parts of Britain, but on the partnership between them. If ever there occurred a serious difference of opinion between the man who led and financed the Club and the Communists and near-Communists who constituted much of its active membership, the Club would inevitably face a severe crisis.

For the first year or two of the Club's existence there was little indication that this would ever happen. Gollancz later recalled that 'for about fifteen months I was as close to the communists as one hair to another',[28] the result being that his personal dominance within the Club did not conflict with the CP's short-term aims. Emile Burns, who worked closely with Gollancz on Club matters, subsequently conveyed to him his appreciation of the way in which he had originally led the Club:

> I thought you handled this work not merely well in a technical sense, but with a very sound political approach, one that really led numbers of people forward. I felt that you really understood what the Party was working for, and that even on questions of tactics there was no serious difference.[29]

The nature of this understanding is brought out well by the case of August Thalheimer's *Introduction to Dialectical Materialism*.

In March 1937 this volume was announced as an 'Additional' choice and warmly recommended as a lucid introduction to its subject by John Lewis. Two months later, however, the book was withdrawn before publication without a word of explanation and replaced by a philosophical textbook emanating from the Leningrad Institute of Philosophy. In the meantime Gollancz had been made aware that Thalheimer was *persona non grata* in the Communist movement, from which he had been expelled in 1928. Harry Pollitt himself implored Gollancz to suppress the book. Gollancz, of course, refused; so Pollitt repeated his request, whereupon Gollancz gave way, withdrew the book and concocted a 'cock and bull story' to explain his action to anybody interested enough to enquire.[30] But for Harold Laski threatening to resign from the Club, a similar fate would have befallen a volume of H. N. Brailsford's which concluded with unacceptable criticisms of the Soviet authorities; these no doubt constituted a 'Trotskyite attack on the Soviet Union'. In initially rejecting the book, Gollancz against stressed his personal responsibility in deciding what should and should not be offered LBC readers, although he was also careful to seek the opinion in the matter of the CP, in the shape of Burns.[31] At this time Gollancz was responsive enough to the views of the CP, and his personal preferences in these matters were close enough to those of the majority of the Club's members, that his ascendancy over the Club was not widely resented.[32]

That this symbiotic relationship might one day come to an end first became apparent at the time of Munich. The official position of the Communist Party was that the Munich war scare was manufactured by Chamberlain with the aim of perpetrating a betrayal of democracy and proclaiming it 'peace for our time'.[33] But, just as some Communists were swept away by the feeling that war was imminent, so too did Gollancz make it clear that he anticipated that Chamberlain would fight Hitler and, moreover, committed the Left Book Club to support of a war in which 'anti-fascist democrats would be fighting, and rightly fighting . . . in the same ranks as anti-democratic imperialists'.[34] And when Chamberlain returned from Munich with his worthless guarantee of peace, Gollancz's immediate reaction, like that of the *Daily Worker*'s leader writer, was one of relief:

That was a very human characteristic of his. He couldn't help feeling relief that the immediate danger of war had lifted, partly because he had a deep hatred of war and was in essence a pacifist. That was a strong influence which he submerged because he understood in his head that pacifism was not enough and that you had to stand up to Fascism, but it was really a rather difficult thing for him. I think Munich was tied up with this hatred of violence and hatred of war.[35]

Looking back at the Munich crisis, one detects for the first time the possibility of a rupture between Gollancz and the Communists if it came to a point where the issues of war and peace could no longer be side-stepped by references to collective security. In both his declaration of support for war and his subsequent relief that this support would not be required, Gollancz showed a readiness to fall in with the Chamberlain Government which was not shared by the Communist Party.

As well as momentarily exposing these potential political differences, the Munich crisis brought to a head Gollancz's misgivings about the role of the Communists in the Club. In his next *Left News* editorial Gollancz revealed that 'the events leading up to Munich, Munich itself, and most of all the situation in which we find ourselves as a result of Munich, have inevitably led to a searching re-examination of policies, values and ideas'.[36] Although the language in which Gollancz expressed the results of this heart-searching was diplomatic, if not cryptic, it was apparent that he had come suddenly to regret the influence which Communists wielded over the Club. Only a month earlier he had offered a spirited defence of the Club's willingness to publicise the views of Communists,[37] but in 'Thoughts After Munich' he struck a quite different note:

> I have allowed myself, I think . . . to become too much of a propagandist and too little of an educator . . . my eagerness to express certain ideas had . . . tended to overlay what I hope I have never forgotten: namely, that only by the *clash* of ideas does a mind become truly free . . . I think it right to add that in my view the publications of the Club have tended to concentrate to too great a degree (though by no means exclusively) on two or three points of view . . .[38]

Gollancz was careful to make no direct reference to the CP, and the possibility of open recrimination within the Club's ranks was avoided. Indeed, it is the opinion of Betty Reid – and she, of course, was a Communist in daily contact with Gollancz – that this was an ephemeral difference of opinion and that Gollanz remained in general agreement with the CP until the Nazi–Soviet Pact.[39] It is true that Gollancz's article did not presage an immediate schism. Strachey appears to have written to Gollancz to indicate his agreement with 'Thoughts After Munich',[40] while Dutt found 90 per cent of what Gollancz had written 'perfectly correct'.[41]

Despite such pleasantries, there are clear indications that the understanding between Gollancz and the CP had been seriously undermined by the Munich crisis. Emile Burns, for example, claimed that after Munich Gollancz appeared unwilling to see him and never consulted him on any political issue; previously they had been in regular contact and basic agreement over Club matters.[42] Another indication was Gollancz's disclosure in 1941 that his financial contributions to the *Daily Worker* had 'ceased, for reasons into which I will not enter, many months before the outbreak of war'.[43] One can hardly doubt that the unspoken explanation was Gollancz's disillusionment with Communism from about the time of Munich. It was precisely this disillusionment which led Gollancz, within weeks of Munich, to commission Leonard Woolf to write for the Club a defence of the values of freedom and tolerance whose suppression in the interests of Socialism he could no longer condone.[44]

Subsequently Gollancz was to regret having given Woolf *carte blanche* to write as he saw fit on such contentious matters,[45] but there is further, conclusive evidence that his desire to distance himself from the CP was no passing mood. This is a letter sent to Pollitt in January 1939 in which Gollancz addressed certain criticisms of his behaviour made by the Communist leader. The reproach which most galled Gollancz was that he had omitted to confer with the CP during the Munich crisis, and his response merits quoting at length:

> The very essence of the value of the Club to the socialist movement, and more specifically to the Popular Front movement, was precisely that it *honestly* wasn't an organ of the Communist Party; and it was also this fact which, in my view, has made it so valuable to the Communist Party . . . here was a body in radical agreement with the CP over a great part of the field, but at the same time *genuinely* (I specially underline the word genuinely) independent. I can't imagine anything of greater value to the Popular Front movement.
>
> But as time went on the situation began to change in a way that disturbed me considerably. Our growing contact, my joy in working with people of your type, and the force of your own personality, meant that gradually the independence was being lost. Almost insensibly the club *was* tending to become an organ of the Communist Party. . . . And this was having a really serious effect on the club as a broad educational instrument of the kind I had envisaged. Moreover, it was doing grave danger to its Popular Front work . . .

For these reasons, Gollancz went on, he had felt disinclined to consult the CP about the line the Club should take on the Munich crisis:

> It seemed to me absolutely vital that the club should recover, and recover as rapidly as possible, the character it was in danger of losing. . . . If, during all that

hectic time, there had been the same very close contact, it would have been impossible, in my view, for the club to have regained this character.

His *Left News* editorials, he said, laid down 'not the Party line, but what I felt to be the imperative function of the Left Book Club'. But this did not necessarily portend a split between the two organisations because they still shared broadly the same aims and, moreover, were still in 'really close and friendly touch with each other'.[46] For the best part of a year, it is true, the cracks in the People's Front were papered over by Left Book Club leaflets damning reaction in unexceptionable terms. But the differences were to re-emerge and cripple the Club in the period opened up by the Nazi–Soviet Pact. The new war crisis precipitated by the Pact raised the same political and organisational questions for the Club as had the Munich crisis. On this occasion, however, the crisis developed inexorably into war itself, opening up divisions within the Club over which there could be no compromise.

The dissensions within the Club arose in the first place from different interpretations of Soviet policy and conflicting attitudes towards the British Government. Gollancz was appalled by the signing of the Nazi–Soviet Pact, which he construed as a retreat into isolation on Russia's part. The CP, on the other hand, insisted that an Anglo–Soviet pact remained possible and urgently necessary, and in the week or so before war broke out devoted itself to a campaign around this demand.[47] Gollancz refused to allow the Left Book Club to be associated with this campaign. Instead, he issued a circular to group convenors insisting that the Club was not, as yet, to give any political lead on the issue. He was subsequently confirmed in this position by Laski threatening to resign from the Club if it issued statements on the Pact conflicting with those of the Labour Party.[48] Indeed, Laski was soon to press for a declaration unequivocally distancing the Club from Soviet foreign policy and aligning it instead with the Labour Party.[49] Gollancz resisted this pressure on the grounds that the Club could not survive as a broad forum of left-wing opinion if it committed itself on such contentious issues.[50] But it was precisely this reluctance to mobilise the Club on the issues of the day which so antagonised the Communists working for the Club, such as Betty Reid. In a letter to Gollancz, Reid went on to voice the suspicion that his prevarication was due, in part at least, to his unwillingness to offer any challenge to the Chamberlain Government:

> I may be wrong about your attitude, but from one or two things you said it seemed to me that you suggested it was impossible to continue the campaign against Chamberlain in the present circumstances. This seems to me an absolutely extraordinary attitude. I think the Club should have been mobilised on this very issue, because every member could agree about it. To say that it will weaken the

country or that we must have national unity in time of crisis is to fall headlong into the trap set for us by the Government.[51]

The political differences which had briefly surfaced at the time of Munich had now acquired a new and ominous significance. Long before the CP had stated its opposition to the war, indeed before the war had even been declared, the Left Book Club was already encumbered by fundamental disagreements: over the question of support for the Soviet Union and that of opposition to Chamberlain.[52] These political divisions coincided with organisational problems to bring to a head the question of who it was that controlled the Club.

As the war crisis deepened, Gollancz put into effect a pre-war plan to move himself and the bulk of his publishing concern to his country house at Brimpton, near Reading. As part of this arrangement he invited first Sheila Lynd and then Betty Reid to accompany him to assist in the running of the LBC groups. Both Lynd, who consulted Pollitt on the matter, and Reid refused, arguing that the Club could hardly be run effectively from a country house in Berkshire. Thwarted in this way, Gollancz sacked the entire staff of the Groups' Department. Only later did he relent to the extent of delegating Lewis and Reid to deal with the groups from London on a provisional basis. This they did until the summer of 1940.

This bare statement of events gives little idea of the bitterness which this issue aroused. To the Communists who worked for the Groups' Department, it seemed obvious that Gollancz's objective in dissolving the department was to prevent them from having any real say in the affairs of the movement which they had done so much to build up. The correspondence between Gollancz and Sheila Lynd was particularly envenomed, partly because Lynd was a 'very tough Party member' and partly because she had been working for Gollancz since well before the Club's formation and had 'come through into the Party with him, so to speak, and she felt he'd betrayed'.[53] This sense of betrayal clearly coloured her response to the proposed move to Brimpton:

> since the beginning of the Groups we have worked at building them, regarding it as our main Party work, using our position in the Party to win greater understanding of the importance of the Club. We understand the Groups and the way the Club must work as well as you, and have hitherto worked with you in everything the Club has done. We have been regarded as officers of the Club. But when the situation becomes critical, we find that we are not officers but office boys – and apparently office boys who are not to be entirely trusted in the building, just because they are Communist office boys.[54]

The implications of Gollancz's refusal to allow any dilution of his personal control over the Club could no longer be ignored, and the Communists in his employ were quick to reproach him for the inequity of the situation:

> I feel that you entirely equate yourself with the Club . . . here is an enormous organisation for which we have asked members to sacrifice their time and energy to build. Yet this vast organisation is entirely dependent on one man (leaving aside the Laski Strachey myth) who may at any moment decide that the whole thing has been wrong, that it should be shut down, that it is *necessary* to shut it down, that it should be swung behind the Government (this, of course, is just an example), and in fact that the whole organisation is dependent on your individual judgement.[55]

Feelings were running high, but the rebuke was nevertheless justified. Early in September Strachey offered to deal with the groups' correspondence in London to make up for Gollancz's removal to Brimpton. Gollancz declined the offer; in view of Strachey's political loyalties and his daily contact with Pollitt, 'nothing in the world could prevent the whole thing gradually taking on the King Street tinge'. In justifying this stance, Gollancz made no attempt to uphold the 'Laski Strachey myth'. On the contrary, he insisted, as he was often to do in the coming months,[56] that the Club was 'technically simply a publishing department of Victor Gollancz Limited' and that he could not, therefore, abdicate personal responsibility for its activities:

> I do feel that I must keep the day-by-day direction in my hands; and the day-by-day direction could not be in my hands, if you, up in London, were doing the Group correspondence.[57]

The CP would have to adjust to the revelation that the most conspicuous success of its Popular Front strategy was in reality nothing more than a department of a London publishing house; a publishing house, moreover, whose proprietor was beginning to exhibit an emphatic aversion to Communism.

For the time being, however, a compromise was worked out and John Lewis continued to attend to the groups assisted by Betty Reid. Gollancz's preference of Lewis to Sheila Lynd was not fortuitous, nor was it based purely on his personal feelings in the matter. As far as Gollancz was concerned, Lynd's consultation with Pollitt on the question of her moving to Brimpton demonstrated that her allegiance was primarily to the CP and only secondarily to the Left Book Club.[58] Lewis, on the other hand, was not yet a member of the Party, and Gollancz felt it safe to accord him a measure of responsibility 'on condition that the groups were run as *genuinely* "all-in" bodies'.[59] In coming to this decision, Gollancz was no doubt influenced by the rough draft of a possible statement on 'The Function of the Club in War' sent him by Lewis at the beginning of September. In this statement Lewis argued that the Club should steer clear of controversy over Communist policy and the Nazi–Soviet Pact and that it was not the business of the Club either to attack or defend the Chamberlain Government, nor should it formulate a war programme. In the interests of maintaining unity within the Club and averting Laski's threatened resignation, Lewis emphasised the importance of the Club's educational work and summarised his case in words which echoed the stated opinion of Gollancz himself:

> We do not stand for *one* point of view in carrying on such work. There must of necessity be great variety of opinions. *Our responsibility is to see that opinion, whatever it is, is well informed.* That is all.[60]

So Lewis remained at his post and his approach was officially adopted by the Club for the next few months. A variety of opinions were indeed expressed, and the columns of *Left News* reverberated to the sounds of political discord.

The first really jarring note was struck in the December issue, which featured lengthy and conflicting statements on the war, expressing their respective 'party lines', by Laski and Strachey. Not entirely fortuitously, this controversy coincided with the publication of two monthly choices representing different and now irreconcilable elements within the Club. The November choice was the defence of liberal values which Gollancz had commissioned after Munich, Leonard Woolf's *Barbarians at the Gate*. Within it was expressed, for the first time in a Club selection, a fundamental antipathy towards the Soviet Union, which elicited a tart response from Strachey in a hostile review for *Left News*. If Woolf's volume shocked Communist sensibilities, those of less Russophile members of the Club were no less perturbed by the December choice, Hewlett Johnson's offensively naive *The Socialist Sixth of the World*, published just as it seemed poised to become the Socialist Sixth and a Bit by invading Finland.

The exposure of differences of opinion over the Soviet Union, just as it was playing an apparently villainous role on the centre stage of world politics and just as the LBC was visibly at odds over the nature of the war, led to an outburst of recrimination in the pages of *Left News*. The letters printed were fairly evenly balanced between those supporting Laski and Woolf and those supporting Strachey and Johnson. Some of the contributions made serious attempts to address the issues, while others were merely abusive. The words of one writer indicate the obstacles in the way of a genuine dialogue within the Club:

> You will maintain . . . that the LBC is showing both sides of the question. Such an attitude is, in my opinion, not only out of date and fallacious, but positively dangerous . . . There can be no two sides to the question of Russia, just as there can be no two sides to the question of slavery or whether the earth is round.[61]

Given this sort of mentality – which was basically that of the CP expressed in a particularly sharp form – and the existence of real political differences, it was futile to attempt to reconcile the Club's warring factions. Nevertheless, Gollancz persevered with his efforts until May 1940.

For instance, although Lawrence and Wishart terminated its special arrangement with the Club at the end of 1939,[62] works by the likes of Hannington and Dutt continued to appear in Club bindings. Moreover, precisely because he identified the Club so closely with himself, Gollancz was notably circumspect about expressing his own view of Communist policy. His pamphlet *Where Are You Going?* was admittedly a strongly worded indictment of the CP, but its very outspokenness meant that Gollancz was unwilling to publish it through the Club in case it was interpreted as a statement of Club policy.[63] Likewise, when he sent Raymond Postgate of *Tribune* a denigratory article incorporating some of the themes of *Where Are You Going?*, he requested that it be published anonymously because, he said, 'my troubles are enough already'.[64]

It was the German advance into Western Europe at the beginning of May that finally persuaded Gollancz that the differences within the Club were insuperable. As late as its May issue, Gollancz was scrupulously even-handed in allocating space in *Left News* to the different tendencies within the Club, and even without it.[65] Even after the subjugation of Denmark and Norway, even after Strachey had broken with the CP leaving the selectors unanimous in their opposition to the Communists, even after *Where Are You Going?*, Gollancz endeavoured to maintain the precarious balance within the Club. But between the printing of this issue, on 7 May, and its distribution the Nazis turned their offensive westwards, thus posing a direct threat to British security. The phoney war was over, not only within Europe but within the Left Book Club. On 11 May Gollancz drafted an appeal to the patriotic and anti-Fascist instincts of Club members and had it distributed with that month's issue of *Left News*. While insisting on his willingness to publicise all viewpoints which did not endanger military security, Gollancz wrote that in the present life-and-death situation he could no longer remain silent as spokesman for the Club.[66] As far as Gollancz was concerned, there was no further possibility of a *modus vivendi*, and the same was true of those Communists who expressed their disgust with his leaflet by resigning from the Club.[67] Henceforth books by Communists could no longer be bought through the Club. Indictments of policy, usually by Strachey or Gollancz, began to appear in *Left News* with some frequency, and Gollancz was no longer unwilling to have them regarded as expressions of Club policy. By July, the Left Book Club was as firmly committed to a 'People's War' as it had earlier been to a People's Front.

About this time, too, Gollancz decided to wind up the Groups' Department, or what remained of it. As early as February he was unhappy with Lewis's management of the groups. He complained to Betty Reid that, although Lewis had begun the war with the honest intention of running the groups as 'all-in' bodies, he had since lost interest in maintaining the Club as a broad educational body. 'I believe a very simple thing has happened. Under the growing stress of events, Lewis, though not a member of the Communist Party, more and more not only takes the communist point of view, but adopts the whole communist idea of propaganda for that point of view.'[68] However, it seems again to have been the German assault on the West that finally convinced Gollancz that action was necessary. In May, Lewis and Reid were given their notice and Gollancz took personal responsibility for the running of the groups from Brimpton.[69]

The movement which had sprung up in an atmosphere of optimism and unity ended not only in failure but in acrimony. Gollancz's *Where Are You Going?* elicited a predictably vituperative response from Communists, who did not always draw the line between political criticisms and personal calumnies and on one occasion provoked Gollancz to the point of threatening to initiate libel proceedings.[70] It would be wrong to think that Gollancz's former colleagues were necessarily chastened by this experience. When he later suggested that the Club be renamed the 'League of Victory and Progress', Sheila Lynd retorted that he might just as well call it 'Strength Through Joy'.[71] Examples of this sort of language could easily be multiplied, to little purpose. The point is that the break in the Left Book Club could never be repaired, even when the CP reverted to support for the war; and that the CP was incapable of maintaining its contacts from the People's Front period in a situation where the issue of the war, with the related question of Soviet foreign policy, was paramount.

The Communist members of the Club appear to have reacted to this polarisation of attitudes in one of two ways. The first was to exercise a blatant control over LBC group activities in a way that defeated the Club's original purpose. It was this tendency to reduce the groups to what one convenor described as a 'sort of bastard CP local' that prompted Gollancz to do away with the Group Department. The same convenor went on to suggest that by behaving in this fashion the Communists were losing all the advantages which the Club had previously provided:

> I have done my best to prevent this happening. The treasurer and chairman, who were respectively Labour Party and Liberal, having gone, this has left me more or less fighting a lone battle.[72]

It would seem that the CP was holding onto the organisational forms, but losing the essence, of the People's Front. Gollancz was certainly of this opinion, claiming that 'certain powerful Left Book Club groups in which communists were in a majority actually refused to allow any expression whatever to the opposing point of view'.[73] At Welwyn Garden City, for example, where the local LBC group was very much involved in Communist-initiated campaigns, most of the committee at the group's AGM were not even receiving Club selections, while *bona fide* Club members were told nothing of the group's activities.[74] An astute assessment of the futility of these tactics was provided by a Club member in Sheffield:

> The branch of the LBC of which I am a member has become completely dominated by the local CP and on that account does not carry out the objects for which the club was founded nor appeal to the wide circles that it was the object of the club to reach.
>
> No-one would wish to deny to the individual members of the CP their exemplary devotion to their party, nor the self-sacrifice and tenacity with which they carry out the policy of the party as they understand it. Their devotion is however worse than useless. . . . It tends towards the narrowing of activity to the relatively tiny group of party members and is observed to leave untouched or even alienate the vast masses of middle and working class radicals who are thirsting for progressive leadership.[75]

This sectarian attitude brought advantages neither to the Club nor to the Party; for if the groups were little more than CP locals, they might as well have designated themselves as such and done away with the pretence of some sort of broader unity. Within the LBC, Communists seemed to find it impossible to maintain a non-sectarian style of politics around an unpopular, and therefore implicitly 'sectarian', political line. One can well understand why, in other environments where it was more feasible, Communists often chose to play down their opposition to the war.

The other tendency, apparently contradictory but in its effects very similar, was for Communists to abandon the Club altogether. Again, it is difficult to distinguish political defections from the general effects of wartime conditions, but the results, as described by Gollancz, were devastating:

> In the old days, the Communist members were the most active recruiters . . . because the very existence of an open forum for all progressive opinion tended to strengthen the Popular Front movement, in which communists passionately believed. But now the Popular Front movement is in abeyance; and while only a very small minority of communist members is actually resigning for 'political reasons' – the majority wish to be able to buy at the cheap price . . . such of 'their own' books as we are publishing and shall publish – they show little energy in recruiting new members, for they do not feel the old enthusiasm for an organisation which exists to give free expression to all Left opinion.[76]

A small illustration of the effect that the withdrawal of Communist goodwill could have is given by Eddie Frow, who had previously made the monthly trip to Collet's in Manchester to collect the latest Club selection for himself and five workmates. He left the Club in 1940 and presumably, if they still wanted the books, the other five had to go and fetch them themselves.[77] Indeed, according to its founder the Manchester group, at one time the largest in the country, ceased its activities shortly after the outbreak of war: 'the war killed it'.[78] From the middle of 1940 there was not even the incentive of cheap Communist books to stay in the Club. Gollancz was trying to rebuild the Club on a new basis and was no longer concerned about retaining the allegiance of Communists, nor were Communists anxious to give it. When Gollancz put forward the idea of a League of Victory and Progress, John Lewis announced that the time had come for 'a final secession from the Club of all those remaining members who understand what is meant by the struggle against Fascism'.[79] From this point on, it is impossible to speak of the Left Book Club as a political movement. Although it dragged out its existence until 1948, henceforth the Club was little more than a means of distributing cheap books.

This series of events raises a number of interesting points. It reveals, first of all, that the exhilarating movement for left-wing unity in the late 1930s had been built on too insubstantial a basis, had left too many questions unanswered, to be able to survive the upheaval of a war which destroyed so many illusions. The Left Book Club grew out of a feeling of boundless optimism, a conviction that if only the arguments of the left were heard then unity would be achieved; and that, given unity, then the left would emerge from the crisis triumphant. The birth of the Club coincided with, and shared the buoyancy of, the People's Front victories in France and Spain. But the French and Spanish People's Fronts were defeated, while that in Britain never got as far as the battlefield. Optimism gave way to a new, divisive reality: Chamberlain was not driven from office, war was not averted, and the Soviet Union reached its own agreement with Fascism. The questions that had been suppressed in the interests of unity now demanded an answer; and Britain's People's Front disintegrated without ever emerging from its chrysalis.

Secondly, these events demonstrated the vulnerability of political movements dependent on the wealth and influence of one or two individuals. In 1940, and with good reason, Lewis and Dutt reproved Gollancz for his exercising a 'one-man dictatorship' over the Club.[80] But as long as it had been convenient to them – as long as that one man 'thought in substantial harmony with the real trend of events' – Communists had been more than willing to take the political short cuts provided by the reputations and resources of individuals who remained accountable principally to themselves. Such alliances, like all those of the People's Front period, were justified by the imminence and the extremity of the threat to the British left, but they did not provide the basis of a durable movement for social change; certainly not one durable enough to withstand the shocks of the autumn of 1939.

Finally, the annulment of the political understandings realised through the Left Book Club shows how opposition to the war narrowed the CP's breadth of contact and compressed its sphere of influence. The Party was now faced with the task of filling the gap left by the Club. How could it make up for the loss of an agency for the distribution of books of a Communist persuasion and of a monthly journal publicising the views of the Communists and their closest allies in the context of a broad left-wing movement? More importantly, what could fill the place of the network of LBC groups which had enabled Communists to participate in, and often lead, discussions on the affairs of the day from a left-wing standpoint? The answer, and a rather unsatisfactory one it was, lay in the *Labour Monthly*.

The *Labour Monthly* was founded by Palme Dutt in 1921 and Dutt was to remain its editor until his death over half a century later. Not surprisingly, then, the journal faithfully followed the twists and turns of Communist policy and reflected the alternative narrowing and widening of the alliances which the Party sought to create. But, while there was never any doubt as to the political reliability of the *Labour Monthly*, there was sporadic debate within the CP as to its precise political function.

From the beginning the journal presented itself not as an organ of the Communist Party but as 'A Magazine of International Labour'. The distinction might appear academic given Dutt's impeccable orthodoxy, but it nevertheless defined the *Monthly*'s original objectives. For over a decade Dutt insisted that his journal was not to be regarded as 'the theoretical organ of the party' but as 'a general propaganda organ, based on an editorial Communist outlook, but addressing itself primarily to non-party workers'. Even in 1930, when the CP's relations with just about everybody else were at an all-time low, Dutt calculated that two-thirds of the journal's circulation went to 'non-party workers'. At that time, however, the CP's Political Bureau began to question the feasibility of continuing to support both the *Labour Monthly* and the Party's official theoretical organ, the *Communist Review*, and put it to Dutt either that the two journals be merged or that one of them cease publication. Dutt was adamant that this should not happen, interpreting the proposals as a 'relapse to a narrow isolation in our work' which would entail the inevitable abandonment of the *Monthly's* current function.[81] On this occasion his arguments won the day. The *Communist Review* remained the Party's theoretical organ while the *Labour Monthly* continued to reach out to the wider movement, providing a link between Communist and 'non-party worker' which became increasingly valuable as the CP came to espouse the politics of the united front. This link was strengthened by a series of broad conferences convened under the auspices of the *Labour Monthly*; between the end of 1931 and the end of 1935 a dozen of these were held. In the same period the *Monthly* also issued a series of pamphlets intended to take its most important articles to a wider readership, while Dutt showed an increasing willingness to open the journal's pages to the CP's new-found allies on the left.

However, by 1935, when the *Labour Monthly* and presumably the *Communist Review* were faced with crippling financial problems,[82] Dutt's stance had apparently altered and it was agreed that the functions of the two journals should be combined through the *Monthly*. The *Communist Review* ceased publication and henceforth Dutt endeavoured to maintain the *Monthly*'s general appeal while accepting that it bore new responsibilities as the theoretical mouthpiece of the Communist Party.[83] For a year or two a balance between the two objectives was maintained, but from about mid-1937 onwards the scope of the journal grew perceptibly narrower until by 1939 whole issues merely presented different aspects of the Party line.

At the same time Dutt abandoned the attempt to promote wider activities through the journal: the last pre-war *Labour Monthly* pamphlet was published in 1936, the last conference held in February 1937. The main speakers at this conference were Laski and Cole, two spokesmen for the Labour left who were closely associated with the Left Book Club; and it is this association which offers the most likely explanation for Dutt's restriction of the scope of the *Monthly*'s activities. Dutt's efforts to induce such figures to speak from the same platforms as Communists no longer seemed necessary, for the Left Book Club was far better equipped for this task. The organisation of discussion conferences in which different viewpoints on the left could be presented was no longer essential now that a permanent dialogue had opened up within the LBC. If serious writings by Communists were to reach a wide public, then the best thing was to send them along for a perusal by Gollancz. Moreover, given the wide circulation of *Left News*, the *Labour Monthly* had no longer to combine the functions of a 'general propaganda organ' with those of the 'theoretical organ of the party'. Dutt could afford to restrict the scope of the *Monthly*'s activities to the articulation and elaboration of the Party line, knowing that the building of left unity could safely be left to the Left Book Club. Safely, that is, until the outbreak of war.

The period in which Gollancz gradually extirpated all traces of Communist influence over the LBC was also one of a new lease of life for the *Labour Monthly*. In the space of fifteen months, its circulation trebled, despite the imposition of an export ban,[84] and this dramatic increase coincided with a diversification of the journal's activities. Early in 1941, for example, it resumed the publication of pamphlets embodying and extending material from its pages, while in February 1940 there took place in London the first *Labour Monthly* delegate conference for several years, shortly followed by a number of regional conferences.[85] Most importantly of all, there was the proliferation of *Labour Monthly* Readers' Discussion Groups.

The first of these groups, like those of the LBC, appear to have sprung up quite spontaneously around the end of 1939, but very quickly Dutt seized on and publicised the idea.[86] The response was slow at first, but by the end of 1940 about fifty groups were being circulated with a monthly syllabus to aid discussion. By June 1941 there were over two hundred groups, many of which had sent delegates to the first Discussion Groups' conference, addressed by Dutt that May.[87] Thereafter their numbers increased still further in line with the general expansion of Communist influence.

There can be little doubt that the purpose of this movement was to fill the vacuum left by the collapse of the Left Book Club. There was no organisational continuity at the top, and Betty Reid insisted that 'the discussion movement round the *Labour Monthly* postdated rather than precipitated the disintegration of the Left Book Club'.[88] Nevertheless, it is clear that a number of *Labour Monthly* groups were simply reconstituted LBC groups. Thus in the first 'Discussion Groups Bulletin', which appeared in May 1941, Dutt pointed out that many of the groups had been formed 'from the nucleus of defunct Left Book Club Groups, a point that might be borne in mind by others'.[89] In the same bulletin Dutt outlined the purpose of the groups in words which made it clear that their main characteristics were inherited from the Left Book Club:

> The group is a meeting place where every point of view is welcomed and is open to criticism and discussion. The group must not be tied to a political line or programme. It does not exist to pass resolutions or to send delegates to conferences. Its function is *educational*. The activity which necessarily follows from effective political discussion is a matter for each individual member, *working in whatever organisation he belongs to*.[90]

These words might well have been written by Gollancz himself; but there was a crucial difference between the *Labour Monthly* and the Left Book Club which throws into doubt the value of the new movement.

In theory the groups were to be non-partisan. Dutt claimed that they embraced 'almost every point of view' and urged that the 'tendency of some members to use the group purely as a medium for active political propaganda instead of as a broad forum for education and discussion' be restrained.[91] But these intentions were incompatible with the contents of the *Labour Monthly*, from which Dutt systematically excluded 'almost every point of view' except that of the Communists and their closest allies;[92] it was after all, as Dutt reminded one Communist in November 1940, 'the theoretical organ of the party'.[93] Such a publication was obviously ill suited to its new task of stimulating a broad discussion movement; and yet, if anything, its links with the CP were strengthened during this period. In April 1940, for example, Emile Burns called on CP District Education Departments to take the initiative in forming *Labour Monthly* groups as 'popular mass forms of organisation'.[94] And some months later Dutt suggested that Ivor Montagu be co-opted onto the *Monthly*'s Editorial Board 'as a direct liaison with the Propaganda Department' of the Party.[95] Moreover, the threefold increase in the *Monthly*'s circulation was due principally to a concerted effort by Party organisations to popularise the journal *within* Communist circles. The result of this initiative by the Political Bureau was that of the increased sales of around 7,000 during the first year of the war over 3,000 were distributed through the Party itself, while a comparable number were distributed through 'progressive bookshops', a fair proportion of which must have gone to Party members. So satisfying were these results that in December 1940 Party organisations were given further instructions to renew their efforts in this direction.[96] In terms of its contents and its readership, the *Labour Monthly* was more thoroughly an organ of the Communist Party than ever before.

From the foregoing it is clear that the *Labour Monthly* groups could never adequately replace the Left Book Club. Circumscribed as it was by the rigid orthodoxy of the Communist Party, Dutt's journal did not provide the material around which a genuine dialogue encompassing a range of political tendencies could be conducted. At one time it might perhaps have fulfilled such a function; so too might *Discussion*, a monthly magazine set up by the CP in 1936 to promote the exchange of views between Communists and 'honest opponents of our Party':

> It will not ram an 'official' point of view down its readers' throats, nor will it ticket and docket as an -ist' . . . any contributor who presumes to differ from the Communist Party or, within our Party, expresses a divergent viewpoint, honestly held.[97]

However, *Discussion* failed to attract much participation by non-Communists and early in 1938 it ceased to appear – perhaps another casualty of the Left Book Club's success. Whatever the reason for *Discussion*'s early demise, the fact remains that after the break-up of its pre-war alliances the CP paid the price for having neglected to maintain its own channels of broad propaganda and broad discussion and for having concentrated its efforts on the Left Book Club. The Left Book Club has been celebrated in numerous books and articles, while the *Labour Monthly* groups are all but forgotten. In this instance the verdict of history is just, for by 1940 the *Labour Monthly* did little more than ram an official point of view down its readers' throats and the discussion movement it spawned was as blatant and as ineffectual a front organisation as ever was set up by the CP.

The foregoing pages demonstrate once more that, during the period in which it opposed the war, the CP maintained and even strengthened its own organisation and means of propaganda, but that it was politically more isolated than it had been in years. Communists were still committed to the theory, the rhetoric and the organisational forms of the People's Front, but in reality they were no longer the moving force in a genuinely broad political movement. Not only had the war uncovered latent differences on the left, but the Communist Party proved incapable of engaging in meaningful dialogue about the actions and intentions of the world Communist movement and especially of the Soviet leadership. Instead it resorted to abuse: the Communist Party, wrote one Party intellectual, 'can leave Mr. Kingsley Martin, Mr. Strachey and Mr. Gollancz to their dungheaps'.[98] Not surprisingly, Messrs Martin, Strachey and Gollancz would never again show much enthusiasm for the embrace of the Communist Party; where the war intruded, the People's Front was dead, beyond resurrection, and the CP's intolerance drove the final nail in its coffin.

There was, however, another side to the picture, for in many areas Communists remained active, dedicated and effective in trade union and other mass struggles. The catch was that this was nearly always at the expense of ignoring the central political issue of the day – the war – and the attitude of Communists towards it. Nationally, the Party's most significant initiative during this period, the People's Convention, owed its limited success in winning broad support to its determined stance on immediate issues and its equivocation on the more basic, but more divisive issues, of war, peace and the means of political change. Within the Left Book Club such equivocation was impossible, and these events therefore provide an invaluable illustration of the sort of isolation which faced the Party when the question of imperialist war intruded too greatly in its day-to-day activities. To view the other side of the picture, let us examine instead the contribution of Communists to mass struggles in Birmingham before and during the first part of the war.

8.2 Mass struggles in Birmingham, 1939–41

The ability of a Labour movement to modify its environment instead of being destroyed by it will depend upon its steadily and resolutely prosecuting the struggle of the wage workers against the conditions of life imposed upon them by capitalism. If, instead, it attempts to stifle that struggle in the hope of accommodating itself to the existing ruling class, it will wither and die. This, and not loosely and emotionally formulated questions of 'evolution versus revolution', is the supreme issue before a Labour movement.

(John Strachey, 1938[99])

It is one of the recurrent themes of this study that the CP's politics differed from those of the Labour Party less in its conviction of the eventual necessity of revolutionary change than in its insistence that, to secure *any* beneficial change or indeed to maintain existing conditions, mass struggle was needed. The issue, as Strachey had described it, was between accommodation and struggle, and the problem with the 'reformism' of the Labour Party was that it had never reformed anything.[100] The Popular Front was thus conceived not essentially as an electoral manoeuvre but as a comprehensive political strategy, the first objective of which was that the great masses of the people should become active and organised in the furtherance of their immediate, sectional demands. The aim was not merely to obtain palliatives but to check the advance of reaction and set in motion popular struggles which, growing in vigour and cohesiveness and led by the class-conscious proletariat, would culminate in the conquest of power. The prognosis was a dubious one, but the selfless commitment of so many Communists to these struggles was perhaps the most laudable, and certainly the most consistent, facet of Communist politics during this period.

To illustrate this conception of the Popular Front, both before and after the outbreak of war, a study of left-wing politics in Birmingham is particularly appropriate. Writing in 'Birmingham's Labour Weekly' in 1939, Richard Crossman stressed the fact that support within the Labour Party for the People's Front and its current spokesman, Sir Stafford Cripps, came predominantly from those constituencies still to be won by Labour.[101] This fact was certainly significant, and was certainly true of Birmingham, a city which returned a straight dozen Tory MPs in 1935.[102] However, the assumption – made by Crossman as by many others – that the appeal of unity in places like Birmingham was to be explained by the attractiveness of electoral alliances where Labour had no immediate hope of dislodging the Tories unaided is only partly true. Indeed, in Birmingham, at least, such electoral calculations carried no force whatsoever, for the Liberal Party there was electorally moribund. It had no representation on the city council and had contested not one of the city's Parliamentary constituencies in 1935. The Unionists' cast-iron grip on local affairs could thus hardly be attributed to the disunity of their opponents. Two other explanations for the phenomenon noted by Crossman offer themselves. The first is that in many 'backward' areas, like Oxford, Communists wielded considerable influence within the Labour Party and had indeed very often played an appreciable part in establishing a Labour presence in those areas. The second is that it was in those areas where Labour exercised little influence over municipal and Parliamentary affairs that the broad mass struggles which underpinned the Communist conception of the Popular Front seemed most necessary. Such was the case in Birmingham, where the impulsion towards unity was not electoral arithmetic but dissatisfaction with Labour's passivity towards Conservatism nationally and solidarity in the struggle against Conservatism within Birmingham. Birmingham's Communists, of course, maintained this struggle after the outbreak of war; and their very consistency in this respect led to embittered exchanges with the local Labour Party. This is the development we shall be tracing in the pages that follow.

It was perhaps to be anticipated that a Borough Labour Party which had already thrown up mavericks like Mosley and Strachey would share the Communists' impatience with the Labour leadership in the late 1930s. Indeed, such was Birmingham Labour's readiness to flout Labour Party orthodoxy and Labour Party rules, especially when it came to united endeavours on behalf of Spain, that it twice came into direct conflict with Transport House.[103] The rationale for this upsurge of Popular Front activity was a conception of politics far removed from the Parliamentary preoccupations of Labour's national leadership:

> Debates in the House, however forcible and convincing, are inevitably doomed to mere futility when the division bell rings.
>
> *The real victories are to be won in the constituencies*, and it is here that the effective value of leadership is tested. *It is the rank and file who are the deciding factor in the situation*, and we have no hesitation in asserting that the vast majority of Labour supporters in the country are *bewildered, not to say disappointed*, by the attitude of compromise adopted by our leaders. . . .
>
> We do appeal to our elected leaders to take serious stock of the situation before all that is best and virile in our ranks is driven to associate with what we are pleased to call the disruptive organisations.[104]

Matters between the national and local Labour leadership came to a head in the spring of 1938 when the BLP's active involvement in a broadly-based Birmingham Council of Action, set up at the instigation of Victor Gollancz, led to its being threatened with disaffiliation from the Labour Party. Reluctantly, the BLP toed the official line on association with 'non-affiliated' organisations and by 1939 the heresies of the Birmingham left appeared to have been extirpated by the inquisitional bureaucrats of Transport House. But, if the prospect of a formal, city-wide People's Front had receded, the greatest demonstration of unity in Birmingham was still to come: the municipal rent strike of 1939.

For the blighted regions of the North of England, the major social problem of the 1930s was unemployment, the product of industrial decay. For a city like Birmingham, in contrast, the most important problem of the decade was to provide sufficient housing for the thousands of workers attracted by the magnet of industrial prosperity.[105] While the private-sector housing boom of the 1930s met some of this demand, the only real solution to the problem was a massive municipal housing programme. The fairly progressive traditions of the municipal Toryism which dominated Birmingham ensured that some effort at least was put into easing this situation; 30,000 council houses had been erected by 1930, and this figure increased by about 2,500 a year until the war.[106] This achievement was nonetheless inadequate and by 1938, 30,000 applicants for housing were registered with the council and the figure was increasing by 25 to 30 a day.[107]

Towards the end of that year, therefore, the council unveiled its ambitious 'five year plan' to build 5,000 homes annually, 4,000 of them for displaced slum dwellers and 1,000 for registered applicants. This figure of 25,000 was, however, '5,000 less than the very conservative estimate of the minimum actually required',[108] and so the 'five year plan' included a further provision which the council presented as a partial remedy for the projected shortfall. The council was to impose an increase in rents ranging from 1s to 2s 6d, but at the same time was to create a rent pool of £30,000 from which tenants unable to pay the increase could draw a rebate on satisfying a means test. The aim of this scheme was ostensibly to induce better-off tenants to move into unsubsidised accommodation in the private sector, thereby vacating houses for the genuinely needy. It was, said a council spokesman, 'the greatest socialistic proposal ever launched in the city of Birmingham'.[109] So persuasive was this Tory egalitarianism that five members of the Labour group on the council, including its leader A. E. Ager, defied the party whip and voted for the scheme.[110] By and large, however, Birmingham's Socialists were united in their opposition to these socialistic proposals. The differential rents scheme was the cause of the Birmingham rent strike; and in this strike it was Birmingham's Communists who played the leading role.

Britain's Communists were no less aware than Birmingham's Tories of the dimensions of the housing crisis and by 1939 had already established their credentials as campaigners for tenants' rights. The most celebrated battles had been fought in the East End of London but just as important was the Party's work in organising the deracinated occupants of the new council estates and jerry-built semis of the Midlands and Home Counties. Indeed, council estates, like the huge municipal settlement at Wythenshawe on the outskirts of Manchester, were regarded as especially 'fertile soil for the Communist Party':

> Into these solidly working-class districts are coming the best and most socially conscious type of workers – those who are prepared to make the sacrifice of higher fares and rents in order to get out of the slums, so that their children will grow up in healthier and happier surroundings.[111]

The new council estates also provided a host of issues on which to arouse these socially conscious self-improvers: community facilities, which were so often lacking, public transport, which was so often deficient and overpriced, and of course rents. In short, the proposed rent scheme in Birmingham provided Communists with the ideal opportunity to put into effect their strategy of mobilising workers on issues of immediate concern to them; and this they did with conspicuous success.

The first action of the Birmingham Communist Party was to set out its objections to the scheme in a penny pamphlet, *49,000 Tenants Say No!* Essentially, the pamphlet gave two reasons for opposing the scheme: that Birmingham's housing shortage required much more drastic action than that envisaged by the council; and that differential rents would pit worker against worker, while the speculators who were responsible for and benefited from the housing shortage carried on just as before.[112] It was this second objection which, albeit very often for different reasons, was most widely shared by the tenants. Although the long-term housing shortage provided the context of the dispute, it was the prospect of rent increases and the insult of a means test that aroused widespread indignation in the city. The CP's assertion that 49,000 tenants said no was, as always, extravagant; but enough tenants said no to mount a sustained campaign against the increases.

Beginning with a protest meeting in Northfield in mid-December, Communists and Labour Party members worked together amicably and efficiently to establish ward committees on every estate in the city.[113] Local Labour notables, including some of generally orthodox views like Councillor Walter Lewis, Vice-President of the Trades Council, played an active part in the movement and did their best to air the tenants' grievances on the city council. Nevertheless, it was an open secret that the moving force behind the campaign was not the Labour Party but 'another organisation which shall be nameless, but which is characteristic for its enthusiasm in adopting and fostering demonstrations of a spectacular and provocative nature'.[114] This was of course the Communist Party, which by taking this initiative had deftly broken through the *cordon sanitaire* imposed by Transport House. One local citizen carped at Labour's inconsistency in expelling Cripps and yet turning a blind eye to this 'Popular Front in action'. 'The conundrum seems to be: "When is a Popular Front not a Popular Front" ', he complained in an inadvertent tribute to the city's Communists, 'and the answer seems to be "When it operates in Birmingham" '.[115]

The first task for the leaders of the agitation was to develop an organisation capable of bringing it to a victorious conclusion. Following the suggestion of W. H. Milner, formerly a Labour councillor but now a Communist, representatives of forty local tenants' associations met in February to establish the Birmingham Municipal Tenants' Association (BMTA). The BMTA's leading spokesmen, Billy Milner and Jessie Eden, were both Communists, as were its other officials, although the willing involvement of Labour councillors was equally striking. Given Labour's derisory representation on the city council (22 councillors out of 136, and falling), the BMTA had no real alternative but to develop a campaign of mass resistance to the scheme. Initially, however, it took a rather cautious line. The Labour councillors Walter Lewis and Julius Silverman warned against the precipitate strike action advocated by Milner, and the BMTA decided merely to collect blank 'means test' forms to demonstrate the extent of discontent with the scheme. This tactic was largely ineffective, and over three-quarters of the forms were filled out and returned by the closing date for rebate applications. A change of tactics was needed, and the BMTA decided to seek a mandate for a rent strike.

On Saturday 1 April the BMTA organised a city-wide strike ballot of council tenants. The ballot, which was run on the lines of a municipal election, was in itself a considerable feat of organisation. Each household was encouraged to cast its vote in a secret ballot in one of 250 polling stations – houses, schools, even a marquee – dotted around the council estates. The result was a resounding 13,000 majority for strike action on a 34 per cent turnout.[116] To put this achievement in perspective it is worth noting that in the St Paul's ward municipal by-election held at the same time the Labour candidate was soundly thrashed on a turnout of less than 20 per cent, the reason given by the candidate's agent being the pathetic level of assistance he received. 'In striking contrast to this deplorable lack of interest and enthusiasm', commented the *Town Crier*'s 'Observer', 'the Rent Strike Ballot stands out a mile. . . . Whatever one may feel about the policy and methods of our Communist friends one has to hand it to them when it comes to matters of organisation.'[117] But predictably, the council was unmoved, and on 1 May the strike began.

The number of tenants who responded to the call for strike action cannot be established with certainty, for the public statements of both sides to the dispute were very much geared towards influencing the morale of the strikers one way or the other. Perhaps the most plausible estimate was that of Albert Bradbeer, leader of the Labour group on the city council, that in mid-June around ten thousand tenants were still on strike.[118] Certainly, there are a number of reasons to doubt the MacGregor-like utterances of T. B. Pritchett, the chairman of the City Estates Committee, the main one being that, unlike MacGregor, Pritchett eventually gave way.

By the seventh week of the strike, influential voices in Birmingham – Labour and Tory – were suggesting the lines of a settlement to the dispute. These proposals came more than halfway towards meeting the tenants' demands, and the BMTA responded to them with studied moderation. This did not, however, entail any relaxation of the strike effort, despite the attempted use of distraint by the Estates Committee. Although the bailiffs moved in, they did not succeed in entering the house of any striking tenants, and after this abortive attempt to force the issue Pritchett very reluctantly came to terms.

By the agreement eventually reached on 3 July the BMTA received official recognition and a firm guarantee that no rent increases would be imposed. However, in one essential respect the settlement reached was extremely vague. The BMTA's main concession was to agree to cooperate with the council in formulating a scheme whereby better-off tenants would have the opportunity 'of voluntarily contributing to the Rent Pool, purchasing their houses or finding alternative accommodation'. As the war clouds gathered it became apparent that this key issue in the dispute had still to be resolved, for there was no consensus as to what constituted a 'wealthy tenant', nor how such a tenant would be identified without a means test, nor what was meant by 'voluntary contributions'. However, when the war clouds finally burst the issue was shelved indefinitely. The tenants had, in effect, won a famous victory.

The most outstanding feature of the strike was the active involvement of thousands of women. One of the objects of the CP's Popular Front strategy was to awaken and organise the millions, including millions of women, untouched by the Labour movement; and in this respect the Birmingham rent strike was a resounding success. The one woman to be found among the strike leaders, Jessie Eden, was undoubtedly the most popular figure to come to prominence during the dispute, largely because she represented a rank and file consisting almost exclusively of women. It was, said the *Daily Worker*'s reporter, 'a woman's war'.[119] Indeed, towards the end of the strike it was felt necessary to approach the traditional institutions of the Labour movement – the Borough Labour Party and the Trades Council – because 'the men folk are considered the weaker sex in the strike' and it was hoped that these bodies might be able to rectify the situation.[120]

There are two possible reasons for the predominance of women in the strike. Reporting a demonstration of 4–5,000 tenants in Chamberlain Square, a local journalist commented that:

> There were not many men, but the women, as chancellors of the domestic exchequer, raised shrill and forceful voices as they chanted the refrain 'We Won't Pay!'

and it may be that women felt more directly affected than men by any inroads into their household budget.[121] More importantly, most of the strike activity took place on the estates during working hours and so the responsibility for sustaining the strike necessarily fell on the women who remained at home. During the first week of the strike it was reported that rent collectors were being escorted around the estates by bands of women and children equipped with trumpets, bells, rattles and other 'noise-raising instruments'. Demonstrations of this nature, which were by all accounts good-humoured, were essential to maintain the solidarity of the strikers. And as the weeks dragged on, and the Estates Department tried to break the strikers' morale and intimidate their leadership by the use of distraint, it was the women who had the job of keeping the bailiffs out. This they did by those threatened locking themselves in their homes while other women formed shifts of pickets which used ARP bells to signal the arrival of the bailiffs to the rest of the estate. 'I feel sorry for the unfortunate bailiff who succeeds in getting into a house', said one picket, 'because once in he will never get out. The women will come from all over the place.'[122] Although there were one or two attempts to involve the men more closely, by the formation of a 'Tenants' Defence Corps', for example,[123] and by the women holding factory gate meetings, the strike was essentially conducted and won by the womenfolk.

To maintain the enthusiasm of the strikers and attract the eye of the public, the BMTA promoted a number of those activities of 'a spectacular and provocative nature' which were by this time a hallmark of the CP's mass politics. Best known of these are the antics which brought the NUWM national attention in the months before the Birmingham rent strike: the unemployed men lying down in Oxford Circus and the Dorchester Hotel, or chaining themselves to railings outside labour exchanges or, most famously of all, shouldering their black coffin with its inscription *He did not get winter relief.*[124]

The same zest and imagination characterised the Birmingham rent strike. At indoor meetings, mock trials and executions of a dummy representing Major Pritchett were staged, while 'street performances of plays written and acted by rent strikers' were another prominent feature of the dispute. The most popular of these was 'How to get rid of the bailiff' which 'brings the whole audience into participation and ends with the bailiff being chased over the garden wall'. Striking tenants proclaimed their defiance by displaying in their windows not only incomplete rent books but irreverent posters:

> Situation vacant. Bailiff wanted. Congenial job for man with experience of Hitler's S.S. Guards. Must be strong in the arm and head. Has to deal with Tenants' Committee.[125]

The CP's exuberant style of politics is perhaps best illustrated by the *Birmingham Mail*'s account of a demonstration by 3,000 women tenants at the official opening of Birmingham's 50,000th council house in Yardley:

> Lines of constables blocked the street near the front of the house where the opening ceremony was to take place, but the women demonstrators were determined to get through, and get through they did, time and time again, with cries that must have almost deafened the city officials and others. In the end they had closed in on the house and were over-running the next garden. Policemen held hands until their arms no doubt felt like breaking, but they were helpless to stop the onward rushes of the screaming, laughing women. . . .
>
> At noon, the time fixed for the opening ceremony, more women came streaming down from the top of the hill, and these were headed by a drum, a mock clergyman and a home-made coffin containing an effigy of 'a wicked bailiff' who had been hanged amid great rejoicing on a nearby estate. 'Mourners', some of them dressed in deep black, made up the make-believe cortege and pretended to be overwhelmed with grief. . . .
>
> Down [a] side street the procession found an excellent spot for the 'internment'. It was a dug-out drain trench . . . presently, while amused workmen looked on from the nearby unfinished Council houses, a sonorous voice arose intoning a mock burial service.
>
> According to this graveside orator, the body was that of a bailiff who had been 'apprehended in the act of unlawfully entering the house of one of the wealthy tenants on the estate'.
>
> One or two wits clutched handfuls of soil and threw them into the grave on top of the coffin, and this was the signal for a large number of wreaths to be dropped in as well, or laid lovingly on the side of the grave. The funeral over . . . the women felt they could return to their locked, bailiff-proof homes – and to their husbands' dinners.[126]

No doubt the proceedings were enlivened by the parodies of popular hits invented by the strikers – *Doing the Bailiff's Walk*, for instance ('Living rent free is easy / Do as you damn well pleasy'), or *We'll Make a Bonfire of our Notices* or 'Council tenants, give them your answer do / Show the Council we won't pay a blooming sou' sung to the tune of *Daisy Daisy*.[127] So successful was this spectacle that the BMTA proposed a day out to Ullenhall to stage another trial of Major Pritchett. In the event 4,000 tenants did make the trip, though not to display their theatrical talents but to celebrate their justly deserved victory.

For the CP the significance of the tenants' movement, in Birmingham and elsewhere, was not limited to its ability to extort concessions over rents. According to the *Daily Worker*, activities of this nature provided a quicker and surer path to political change than the narrow electoralism of Transport House, or indeed of certain advocates of a People's Front:

> Leading [the tenants] are the women. Time and time again we are told that the women are not interested in politics. Here, on an issue that affects them closely, they are willing not merely to go to the polls but to march for miles demonstrating for their rights.
>
> This is . . . a sign that if only the Labour Movement will give an active lead on 'bread and butter' issues, the people will sweep all obstacles from their path. . . .
>
> The rent battles have a lesson for Labour. The thing that counts is not the name but the Movement. If Labour will give an active lead on the issues before the people, there will grow in the place of so-called apathy a movement for a happier Britain that can sweep Chamberlain into the limbo of the past and replace him by a Government for the future.[128]

However, the connection drawn here between bread and butter questions and the government of the future was far too facile and there is not much evidence to substantiate the *Worker*'s claim that 'the political implications of the strike are being brought to the fore'.[129] The strike certainly livened up the local Labour Party and aroused the political consciousness of some of the tenants and might have led to a revival of Labour's fortunes at the November municipal elections.[130] But the relationship between a rent strike and the struggle for a new government in Britain, let alone the struggle for Socialism, was problematic to say the least; and it was a problem that the CP never really addressed.

Nevertheless, by its leadership of the rent strike the Party had enormously strengthened its position in Birmingham. Many new Party members were recruited as a direct consequence of the agitation, while the CP's 'Crusade for the Defence of the People' in the first part of 1939 brought better results in Birmingham, in terms of audiences, collections, literature sales and recruits (162), than anywhere else. All in all, Eden estimated much later, the Party in Birmingham doubled in size in 1939, while it had effective control of the BMTA, now an officially recognised body claiming over 20,000 members.[131] Moreover, Birmingham's Communists had developed close working relations with many members of the Labour Party and had managed to coordinate their mass activities with the efforts of Labour representatives on the city council.

All seemed to augur well for the CP, but the prospect of further steady progress along these lines ended with the outbreak of war. Following the Party's subsequent political convulsions, Birmingham's Communists, using the BMTA as a basis, continued to try to promote the sort of activities they had led so ably in the 1930s. However, their efforts no longer met with the approval of the Borough Labour Party. The bifurcation of Birmingham's left wing arose from conflicting attitudes towards the war, but the two camps which formed cannot simply be described as 'pro-war' and 'anti-war'. There were some on the left who supported the war and yet continued to associate with the Communists, while the bluntest of the CP's critics, Jim Simmons, held pacifist beliefs which he expressed almost provocatively in the early months of the war.[132] The debate over the war was indeed less fierce than that over immediate working-class interests. In the war of words which accompanied the bloodier battles over the Channel one can discern two completely different conceptions of how best to secure reforms from the capitalist class. The local Labour Party came to uphold those dubious virtues of patience and deference to its leaders that it had rejected so shortly before. The Communist Party, on the other hand, continued to work very much within the framework set by the Popular Front.

The clearest demonstration of the continuities in Communist politics occurred at the beginning of 1940 when the BMTA, and principally Eden and Milner, took the lead in organising a rent strike on the council estates just over the border from Birmingham in Solihull. The tenants' main grievance was again the introduction of a differential rents scheme, and in virtually every other respect – the proportion of tenants withholding their rent, the active involvement of the local Labour Party and the willingness of Labour councillors to voice the tenants' case – the dispute was a miniature replica of that in Birmingham the previous year.[133] The only real dissimilarity was that, after remaining solid for three-and-a-half months, the strikers gave way to the threat of legal action with practically nothing to show for their efforts. This otherwise inconsequential episode is instructive precisely because it bore such a marked resemblance to the dispute in Birmingham. The BMTA's approach to issues of this nature had been affected not at all by the CP's decision to oppose the war, and there is no evidence of the tenants' grievances being exploited for anti-war purposes. If anything, as for example when Eden justified the strikes with the assertion that 'the noble aim for which they were fighting should have its origin on their own doorsteps',[134] the opposite would appear to have been the case. For Communists like Eden and Milner these campaigns had their own intrinsic importance and were not conceived primarily as part of a mass movement against the war.[135]

While the BMTA remained active on housing matters, it no longer restricted itself to the grievances of tenants as tenants. Henceforth the CP used this organisation to wage campaigns on a whole range of domestic issues raised by the war. In November 1939 the BMTA issued a comprehensive immediate programme which appeared to one observer to have been 'designed to embrace every grievance which the Labour Party has been fighting to remedy ever since the war started'.[136] On the basis of this manifesto a conference was arranged to launch a city-wide movement of thirty-four Vigilance Committees to defend working-class interests during the war.[137] These committees, which encouraged the participation of 'all organisations interested in social questions', were concerned especially to promote the interests of dependants of men in the forces, an indication of the BMTA's determination to maintain its contact with the women of Birmingham.[138] For the same reason, on International Women's Day 1940 the Association arranged no fewer than eleven meetings, as well as a demonstration in the Bull Ring with an all-woman platform.[139] Shortly afterwards the BMTA formally established an Old Age Pensioners' Association and a Soldiers', Sailors' and Airmen's Dependants' League.[140] The CP's aim remained that of setting up autonomous organisations designed to mobilise people around their most immediate concerns, especially those people whose interests were poorly served by the orthodox Labour movement. The sectarianism that was perhaps implicit in the Party's anti-war line was not allowed to interfere with these activities. On the contrary, the stress was wholly on domestic issues[141] and Communists encouraged the broadest possible participation, for instance by organising tea parties for those whose menfolk had been called up:

> Forty children and twenty mothers turned up. After tea had been served, a number of our members organised games, etc., for the children, whilst the mothers went into another room, where an informal talk was given by Jessie Eden. . . . The response of the women was splendid, all agreed to serve on a committee, two agreed to act as joint secretaries.
> They have now met as a committee and prepared a plan of campaign in their area which includes street meetings, petitions, letters to the Press, etc.[142]

Overtly political questions seem hardly to have been touched upon, at least until the formation of the Birmingham Women's Emergency Committee to campaign for a People's Government in July 1940.[143] The BMTA had broadened the scope of its activities, but the emphasis remained very much as before.

The Birmingham Labour Party, on the other hand, no longer viewed such goings-on sympathetically. At the start of the war it had, along with the Trades Council and the Co-operative Party, set up a Joint Emergency Committee (JEC) to secure the redress of the legitimate grievances of the working class by the fullest use of constitutional channels; and Labour spokesmen did not take kindly to the BMTA's challenge to its exclusive prerogative to deal with such matters. The *Town Crier*'s 'Observer', whom we have witnessed applauding the Communists' initiatives on behalf of the tenants, now admonished them for setting up vigilance committees in words uncannily reminiscent of the 'appeals to loyalty' which Birmingham Labour had scorned before the war. Members of the Labour Party, he said, had 'no need to go outside their own organisation' to agitate for food control and higher dependants' allowances, for 'such matters as these can be safely left in the capable hands of our Parliamentary representatives'. 'While we may not all agree with Labour's official war policy – or lack of it', he went on, 'it cannot be denied that it remains the only political force . . . to see to it that [the workers] get as square a deal as possible in wartime'.[144] The issue, clearly, was not so much the war itself as how best to mitigate its effects on the working class. From the very outbreak of war the Birmingham Labour Party seems to have moved closer to orthodox 'Labourism' with its emphasis on representation and constitutionalism. For the time being, however, the polemics were muted. It was only a year later, when the bombs started to fall on Birmingham, that the invective began in earnest. For the local Labour Party was made to realise that it had accepted responsibility for the well-being of Birmingham's citizens without the power to enforce measures it deemed necessary; and when it was castigated for its ineffectiveness by the Communist Party, it felt obliged to reply in kind.

Communists, in Birmingham as elsewhere, had developed an interest in air raid protection well before the war,[145] but during the summer of 1940 this concern became something of a mania. This might seem curious, given the Party's stated opposition to the war: nobody believes that you can stop it raining by putting up an umbrella. But for the CP, ARP was the perfect issue around which to build a mass movement of the discontented, taking control of their own affairs rather than trusting to their callous and incompetent rulers. All over the country Communist-organised demonstrations and deputations, and street meetings and ARP Committees, sounded the red alert. Communists were very often especially active in cities which had been blitzed. In Bristol, for example, the *Daily Worker* Defence League issued leaflets giving advice to those bombed out of their homes and referring them to the Party-run ARP Campaign Committee's offices for assistance.[146] Better known is the occupation of the tubes and the formation of shelter committees in London,[147] and it is worth noting the emphasis which Party literature addressed 'To Shelterers in the Tubes' put on the efficacy of independent mass activity:

> I remind myself: I won the use of the Tube by going along with many people and taking possession. We did it by ourselves. We didn't wait for anyone. We didn't agree with the Government instructions to keep out. We came, we saw, we conquered.
> THAT'S THE WAY I MUST WIN THE IMPROVEMENTS NEEDED. Unless I get together with other folk, I won't get them. I must talk it over with the others. We must stick together. We must help each other. We must elect delegates to speak for us to the authorities.[148]

In short, the threat of air attack and the inadequacy of the protection available to Britain's population was perhaps the dominant theme in Communist propaganda at this time; and where raids actually occurred Communists were eager to offer assistance and above all political leadership to the victims.

The Party's criticisms of the authorities' precautionary measures were as applicable to Birmingham as to any city. Until the very outbreak of war its parsimonious Tory council rejected essential safety measures on grounds of expense, and in July 1940 Willie Gallacher told his fellow MPs that 'the very worst part of the country as far as defence is concerned is Birmingham which is represented by a bunch of die-hard Tories who are not interested in the people'.[149] The result was that the raids on Birmingham – seventy-three of them between August 1940 and May 1941 – caused chaos. According to Tom Harrisson's authoritative work on the Blitz, Birmingham:

> was not only caught unawares that winter, the December raids disclosed 'grave deficiencies' in the local system. The authorities failed to help the victims of bombing promptly or adequately . . . there were 'disorderly scenes'. Rescue workers, overstrained, were 'going crackers'. Looting became serious.

The government report from which Harrisson drew this information concluded that, had further raids followed without respite, the city might have been reduced to a virtually uninhabitable state.[150]

The raids thus provided plenty of material with which to indict the authorities, and the CP accordingly drew attention to the lack of bomb-proof shelters, the failure of water supplies, the need for mobile canteens and, especially, the indifference of the authorities to the plight of the homeless.[151] The local Labour Party, as we shall see, accepted the force of these criticisms but staked its reputation on securing improvements by pressure within the council chambers. Not only was it to be largely frustrated in its efforts but it had also to bear its share of responsibility for the council's record, for Labour councillors had accepted places on council committees and by this time inter-party cooperation was 'complete'.[152] Their problems were not eased by the pronouncements of Councillor Norman Tiptaft, the idiosyncratic Tory chairman of the ARP Committee who was prone to denounce even the mildest criticisms of his record as 'Fifth Column Activity'.[153] The Labour Party found itself in the invidious position of accepting a degree of responsibility for the policies of such as Tiptaft with which it did not necessarily agree and over which it exercised little control. The CP, unencumbered by commitment to the war effort, fully exploited its discomfort, and the controversy which ensued throws much light on the differences between 'Labour' and 'Communist' politics.

The CP's reaction to the raids on Birmingham was to try to bring pressure to bear on the authorities by means of mass deputations and public meetings.[154] At the same time the Party mounted an energetic campaign for the provision of bomb-proof shelters; an exhibition on the merits of the Haldane shelter organised by the ARP Co-ordinating Committee was reportedly visited by 'thousands of people'.[155] The local Labour Party was predictably unimpressed, however, claiming that the solid achievement of a Labour Party with its feet on the ground was to be preferred to the hot air of Communist demagogy.[156] DEEDS NOT WORDS, boasted the publicity accompanying the JEC's first interim report:

LABOUR HELPS BOMBED AND HOMELESS

THE COMMUNIST-INSPIRED MASS MEETINGS, CONVENTIONS, CONFERENCES (Addressed by Experts?) ACHIEVE *NOTHING*!

LABOUR'S JOINT EMERGENCY COMMITTEE
DELIVERS THE GOODS

The claim was seemingly justified by the list of very creditable achievements which followed. These included the 'taking over of large houses and furnishing as hostels for temporary homeless', the 'provision of mobile canteen services for homeless people' and the 'recognition by ARP Committee of need for deep shelters where practical'.[157]

However, the real picture was not quite so rosy. The following week John

Baird, Labour's municipal candidate for Small Heath, described how, in a situation where delay might well have led to loss of life, it was the methods of the Communist Party and not those of the JEC which brought results:

> During the severe raids last August, when in most cases the sirens did not sound until long after the raids had started, Small Heath and Yardley were among the chief sufferers. I got in touch with the Secretary of the Emergency Committee and asked that something should be done about it, but was informed that the Committee would not meet for another nine days.
>
> The situation was very urgent, and some of us, including members of the Communist Party, by our constant agitation, managed to get an enquiry into the question, and from that day to this we have had ample warning.
>
> That was one instance when the Emergency Committee did not 'deliver the goods'.[158]

If the JEC's credibility was dented by Baird's riposte, it was devastated by the raids on Birmingham that same week.

The nights of 19–22 November were the worst of the Birmingham blitz, and the effectiveness of the city's air raid measures and the value of the JEC's achievements were put to a severe test. Both were found wanting. The proudest boast of the JEC had been that it had secured the commitment of Birmingham's propertied classes to the requisitioning of large homes as required. However, the authorities made no preparations to meet this commitment and when thousands of Brummies were rendered homeless by the raids they received from the council nothing more comforting than a recommendation to go and stay with their friends or neighbours.[159] Even the *Town Crier* admitted that the council's formal acceptance of such radical proposals was of next to no value in the absence of any endeavours to carry them out.[160] Likewise, despite the vaunted provision of a mobile canteen service, the *Daily Worker* reported that 'in Birmingham it is almost impossible to find a mobile canteen even in the most badly bombed areas'.[161] The inadequacy of this service, and the unlikelihood of securing sufficient improvements to it from the council, is surely demonstrated by the fact that the Labour Party set itself the task of raising £500 for a 'Birmingham Socialist ARP Canteen', and indeed achieved its aim in May 1941 – the month after Birmingham suffered its 'last really heavy raid'.[162] The JEC's other claims were similarly without much foundation. The Council's ARP Committee was not convinced of the need for deep shelters, whether practical or not; in January 1941 Tiptaft bluntly stated that 'big shelters were "death traps" and the policy of the committee was dispersal'.[163] Indeed, the JEC itself, by demanding of the council improvements it claimed already to have secured, seemed implicitly to admit that its achievement fell short of what was necessary.[164] It had promised grand deeds in words which grossly exaggerated its ability to perform them.

The CP seized on these shortcomings and attributed them to the Labour Party having thrown in its lot with the Tories. In December it issued an 'Open Letter to the Birmingham Labour Movement' which dwelt nostalgically on the good old days before the war when 'Communist and Labour men and women spoke and worked with each other, and roused a wide section of people in its action, for their own vital interests'. This *ad hoc* united front, it went on, had been disrupted by the machinations of Transport House and its paid officials,[165] the result being 'the stagnation and decay of the Labour Movement in Birmingham. . . . At a period of greatest trial for the workers of Birmingham, the Labour Party is derelict.' The letter concluded with an appeal to revive the spirit of 1939:

> Let us get together again and tackle with new energy and enthusiasm the tasks which face us in the terrible situation of to-day.[166]

The JEC retorted with a 'smashing rejoinder', defending the record of Labour councillors and berating the CP for its ineffectiveness and the ambiguity of its stance on the war.[167] But if Labour spokesmen insisted on the efficacy of constitutional action in their polemics with the Communists, they also reproached the local Tories in words which betrayed a much more sober estimation of the influence of the JEC.

Birmingham's Tories showed scant regard for the views of the Labour contingent on the council and, as we have seen, Tiptaft even implied that their grumblings were tantamount to Fifth Column activity. In the uproar which followed this remark, one can sense the seriousness with which the Labour Party took the threat from its left:

> Councillor Tiptaft . . . should know that the treatment meted out to the Labour Movement by his Party is helping the Communists.
>
> Labour seeks to effect change and improvement by constitutional methods; they are insulted and rebuffed by the Tories and the Communists immediately say to the sufferers, 'You have nothing to lose, why not join in a "mass movement of revolt", under Communist leadership, the Labour Party will never get you anything by constitutional methods.' Who, we ask, are the 'Fifth Columnists?' Labour who seeks to use constitutional methods, or the Tories, who by their attitude seek to discredit these methods.[168]

This was almost an unconscious endorsement of Communist methods. The writer, Jim Simmons, did not sanction 'unconstitutional' methods, but he did realise that the threat of mass opposition might be the one thing to prod Tory councillors into action. In rebutting the 'Fifth Column' slander, he employed exactly the arguments with which the Communists had replied to his own allegations; the real Fifth Columnists were 'not those who reveal evils', he protested, 'but those who condone their perpetuation'.[169] Labour's complacency had been shattered by the November blitz, and Simmons was now openly apprehensive lest the CP profit from its failures. He virtually pleaded with the Tories to make the democratic process work:

> If they mistake the moderation hitherto displayed by Labour as a sign of weakness they are very much mistaken; we feel just as keenly on these matters as the Communists, but our object has been to get things done by the responsible authorities rather than seek to make the matter a political issue. . . .
>
> The services secured as a result of the pressure of the Joint Emergency Committee would have been a boon to the bombed and the homeless IF THEY HAD BEEN EFFICIENTLY CARRIED OUT. The fact that they were not will be seized upon by the Communists . . .[170]

By January 1941 Simmons had adopted a more threatening posture:

> IT IS NOT TOO LATE YET TO DO THE RIGHT THING IN THE RIGHT SPIRIT, but the time is short, and to our Birmingham Bourbons we say 'You have been warned'.[171]

The problem was that the Versailles Bourbons had been dealt with by a fine example of the mass unconstitutional activity which Labour in Birmingham had so categorically repudiated. Constitutional methods of change had almost broken down; the council meeting which most nearly coincided with Simmons's ominous words had been declared inquorate, giving Simmons cause to comment rather plaintively that the JEC's desire was simply to be 'helpful' and 'constructive' but that 'councillors who know that they are immune from elections for an indefinite period have shown nothing but resentment'.[172] The Labour Party was in an impasse. Its predicament was such that it tried to jolt the council's Tory majority into action by raising the spectre of a mass movement of the afflicted led by Communists, and yet was unable to take the leadership of any such movement itself, having accepted responsibility for the decision-making procedures of the Tory-dominated Council House. The final, ironic twist to this story was provided in March 1941 when the leader of the Labour group on the council filled the front page of the *Town Crier* with a justification of a recent council rate increase. The article was headed *Why Our Rent Will Go Up*.[173]

So far this account has not dwelt on the differences between Labour and Communist policy on the war, for these were indeed raised far less frequently than questions of immediate political tactics. However, it was sometimes suggested that the conflicting approaches to these immediate political questions arose from more fundamental differences over the war. Sam Blackwell, the CP's Birmingham organiser, argued that Labour's incapacity to win improvements for the people resulted from its entanglement in the war effort:

> It is true that Labour leaders find themselves very busy. But they are not busy fighting for Socialism. The Supply Committees, Emergency Committees and the Ministry of Information keep them busy smoothing the way for Capitalism.[174]

Labour spokesmen, in turn, argued that the CP was concerned not to right wrongs but to foster and exploit discontent for revolutionary, anti-war purposes. 'Fully intent upon the policy of revolutionary defeatism', intoned the JEC's report for 1940–41, 'they have no time for those who wish genuinely to help the people in a practical way'.[175] In fact, a far more accurate assessment of the CP's priorities came from the sarcastic pen of Jim Simmons:

> The CP is out to WIN, not the revolution, but bomb-proof shelters, to them the acme of perfection is a supply of bomb-proof shelters, in fact bomb-proof shelters are their King Charles's Head.[176]

But the securing of such tangible benefits as bomb-proof shelters was also the preoccupation of the Labour Party, and its claim on the loyalties of Socialists rested on its ability to 'deliver the goods'. The confrontation in Birmingham was not between reform and revolution but between Labour's reformism, deferential towards the establishment and paternalistic towards the working class, and the militant reformism of a Communist Party which banked its hopes on stimulating mass political activity. The difference was, in the words of John Baird, a disaffected member of the Labour Party:

> a difference of principle between Labour Party representation to the authorities and Communist Party mass action.
>
> Is the best method of the workers achieving their object to go cap in hand to the powers that be and appeal for action, or should we not rather use our organisation to stir up the masses and encourage them to demand action?[177]

This is as cogent a summary of the issues at stake as one could hope to find.

That Baird should have sided with the CP in this matter suggests that the Labour Party's renunciation of 'normal' political activity had opened up a political space which Communists could hope to fill as long as they did not isolate themselves from potential allies by explicit opposition to the war. Far from being a 'crypto-Communist', Baird had during the early months of the war expressed harsh criticisms of the ' "Yes Men" Communists' who slavishly followed where Russia led them. It was the CP's 'policy of "Russia right or wrong" ', he wrote, that had 'forced those who, in the past were its friends . . . to part company with it'; and yet over the coming months, despite his reservations about CP policy and his continuing support for the war, he renewed his association with the Communists because of their activities on immediate issues. Like the CP, Baird felt that 'the workers have never gained a concession of any worth from the Capitalist class without first of all being involved in a long and hard struggle', and towards the end of 1940 he ratified his understanding with the Communists by signing the People's Convention manifesto.[178]

For active Socialists like Baird, the problem with the Labour Party's doctrinaire constitutionalism was that, at a time when the balance of political representation remained fixed for the duration, it left Labour Party members with no way of effecting political change; in fact, with nothing to do. Nationally, the individual membership of the Labour Party fell by half during this period, and Birmingham was not exempt from this trend. In Aston, for example, the Labour Party 'nearly collapsed', while in Deritend 'there was almost an entire lack of political activity' – Divisional Labour Party meetings were infrequent and poorly attended and ward meetings non-existent.[179] In 1939, three of Birmingham's twelve DLPs affiliated to the Labour Party on the minimum permitted membership of 240; in 1940 the figure was five, and the following year, eight.[180]

The war itself obviously created problems for any mass political organisation, but there were political reasons for Labour's decline too. In 1941 it was reported that in King's Norton 'members do not understand the meaning of the electoral truce, and the Labour Party's decision to keep it has driven out 400 members – some have gone over to the Communists'. Even after this exodus, the King's Norton party was reckless enough to issue a statement recommending abstention in a by-election in that constituency, and for this act of insubordination was suspended by Labour's NEC.[181] However, where a local Labour Party continued to espouse a 'Popular Front' style of politics a healthier state of affairs could occasionally be recorded. The Olton Labour Party, for example, knowingly admitted Communists into its ranks, played its full part in organising and sustaining the Solihull rent strike and waged a vigorous campaign on ARP, as a newcomer to the district in 1940 recalled:

> We'd been in the house two days and there was a knock on the door: 'We're canvassing for support for a petition for getting rid of these [Anderson] shelters because they're a danger to life.' That's how I think the Labour Party in this area got going. There was this big campaign and it brought in a lot of people.

It did bring in a lot of people, and that was its significance; the Olton Labour Party continued to publish its own paper, it held regular monthly meetings and, in defiance of national and local trends, its membership *increased* by half as much again in 1940.[182] There were those in the Labour Party who continued to believe, as the official spokesmen for Birmingham Labour no longer did, that the real victories were to be won in the constituencies; and from these elements the CP was able to make recruits and build alliances. For, whatever the vagaries of its political line, the Party's attitude to immediate struggles had altered hardly at all since the days of the Birmingham rent strike.

The main value of this study is as a corrective to portrayals of the Popular Front in basically Parliamentary terms and of the CP as an organisation preoccupied with questions of foreign policy. Running parallel with and deeper than the CP's vacillating attitude to international affairs was its commitment to a popular mobilisation against the many and various injustices of capitalism. These mass struggles, according to Party leaders, would provide the necessary substructure for an invincible movement against the continuation of capitalist rule. However, for the Communists who led them these struggles had their own justification quite independent of the CP's wider political aims and therefore only marginally affected by the Party's decision to oppose the war. The CP remained constant in its opposition to Britain's, and also Birmingham's, Tory leaders, and its mode of struggle against them remained just as constant. It was, rather, the Labour Party which, having challenged the Tories only half-heartedly before the war, abandoned all semblance of opposition once the war had begun. Thus was the 'political space', already opened up by Labour's single-minded Parliamentarianism, widened, especially in a city like Birmingham where Labour's capacity to effect constitutional change was negligible.

However, the concept of 'political space' is an inadequate one, for political spaces do not exist as vacuums waiting to be filled, but are forced open by the struggle between conflicting political tendencies, between different conceptions of what is politically possible and necessary. The Birmingham rent strike was not lurking in a political space waiting to happen, but arose from the initiative and creativity of Communists and other left-wingers impatient with the passivity of Transport House 'Labourism'. How successfully the CP continued to occupy this territory after the outbreak of war is difficult to ascertain, given the paucity of hard evidence and reliable Party membership figures.[183] However, the preoccupation of the Birmingham Labour Party with the threat from its left is a sure indication that the CP was hardly reduced to irrelevance; for, paradoxically, while the Party's opposition to the war constituted something of a political liability, its lack of commitment to the war effort gave it fresh opportunities in the realm of mass struggles. It was only when it came to support the war, and the Tories who remained in control of the war, that the CP felt compelled to relinquish its leadership of these struggles, and thus too of its only conception of a British road to Socialism.

Notes

1 'Where are you going?' in Gollancz (ed.), *The Betrayal of the Left*, 11.
2 Fox, *The Novel and the People* (1944 edn), 152. Fox was citing Wordsworth.
3 For detailed accounts of the Club before the war, see J. Lewis, *The Left Book Club. An Historical Record* (1970); R. Dudley Edwards, *Victor Gollancz: a Biography* (1987); B. Reid, 'The Left Book Club in the thirties' in J. Clark *et al.* (eds), *Culture and Crisis in Britain in the 30s* (1979); S. Samuels, 'The Left Book Club', *Journal of Contemporary History* no. 2 (1965).
4 Gollancz, *LBN*, June 1936.
5 Gollancz, *LN*, Apr. 1939, 1,218.
6 Labour NEC minutes, G. R. Shepherd to Borough, Divisional and Local Labour Parties on 'The Left Book Club', Mar. 1939.
7 *LN*, Jan. 1937, 195; see also the speech cited by Dudley Edwards, *op. cit.*, 241–2.
8 See e.g. *LBN*, Oct. 1936, 107–12; Labour NEC minutes, 'Memorandum concerning activities of the Left Book Club', 23.11.38.
9 Betty Reid, interview. See however p. 279 for one of Gollancz's initiatives.
10 *LN*, Jan. 1937, 219.
11 R. Eatwell, 'The Labour Party and the Popular Front movement in Britain in the 1930s', (Ph.D., Oxford, 1976), 343–5.
12 *LN*, Jan. 1939, 1,133–4.
13 Eddie Frow, interview. However, Lewis later calculated that 75% of the Club's membership were either black-coated workers or left-wing intellectuals, many of whom had no record of political activity; Samuels, *op. cit.*, 75.
14 Frank Allaun, interview.
15 See Dudley Edwards, *op. cit.*, 234–7, 250.
16 The deal with Lawrence and Wishart operated from 1.8.37; *LN*, July 1937, 420; for *The Week*, see *LN*, Apr. 1938, 754.
17 Pollitt, 'Memories of a Communist leader. The Left Book Club period', *World News*, 19.7.58, 462–3.
18 *Op. cit.* 108.
19 See Laski, *LN*, Aug. 1937, 456.
20 VG MSS.157/3/DOC/1, Sheila Lynd to Gollancz, 13.9.39. Unless otherwise stated, all subsequent references to the Gollancz papers are to this set of documents.
21 VG, F. C. Cracknell to Gollancz, 22.5.40.
22 Especially perhaps in 'backward' areas. In urban districts, as Betty Reid recalled was the case with the Holborn Party branch, Communists were given no particular encouragement to become involved in Club activities and indeed there were heated arguments as to whether such distractions were not an unaffordable luxury given the pressure of Party work; letter to author.
23 See S. Hodges, *Gollancz. The Story of a Publishing House 1928–1978* (1978) 135.
24 Betty Reid, interview; *LN*, Jan. 1937, 194.
25 *LN*, July 1937, 422.

26 *LN*, Feb. 1937, 217; Mar. 1937, 257; May 1937, 343; Sept. 1938, 952–4.
27 Samuels, *op. cit.*, 71–2.
28 Gollancz, *More For Timothy* (1953), 357.
29 VG, Burns to Gollancz, 8.9.38.
30 *LN*, Mar. 1937, 253, 257; May 1937, 342; VG, Gollancz to Pollitt, 16.1.39.
31 Hodges, *op. cit.*, 141–2; Dudley Edwards, *op. cit.*, 266–8. The book was *Why Capitalism Means War*.
32 Thus, according to Betty Reid in a letter to the author, 'there was very little support for the so-called "democratic" demands. This would have strait-jacketed groups and members, and was really a non-starter'. And of course, any such formal organisational structure would certainly have invited some form of retaliatory action by Transport House.
33 See pp. 70–3.
34 *LN*, Oct. 1938, p. 997 (written 22.9.38). See also Dudley Edwards, *op. cit.*, 280–3.
35 Betty Reid, interview. See also Gollancz, *More For Timothy*, 371.
36 *LN*, Nov. 1938, 1,032.
37 *LN*, Oct. 1938, 996.
38 *LN*, Nov. 1938, 1,033.
39 Interview.
40 VG, Gollancz to Pollitt, 16.1.39.
41 RPD K4, Dutt to Gollancz, 19.12.38.
42 VG, letter by Gollancz published in the *Daily Herald* and the *News Chronicle*, 30.1.41.
44 See Dudley Edwards, *op. cit.*, 283–8.
45 *Ibid.*, 296–9.
46 VG, Gollancz to Pollitt, 16.1.39.
47 See ch. 5 above.
48 VG, Laski to Gollancz, 31.8.39.
49 VG, Laski to Gollancz, 12.9.39.
50 VG, Gollancz to Laski, 15.9.39. Interestingly, in view of later developments, Gollancz did not regard the 'smashing' of 'Hitlerism' as a contentious issue; rather it was 'implicit in the *whole purpose* of the Club'. However, see note 52 below.
51 VG, Reid to Gollancz, n.d. but Aug. 1939.
52 The issue so far, then, had nothing to do with the CP's decision to oppose the war. Indeed, Gollancz was not at first a committed advocate of the smashing of Hitlerism. Lloyd George's speech in favour of a compromise peace at the beginning of October, which was welcomed by the CP, was described by Gollancz as possibly 'the one sane utterance in an insane world'; Gollancz to Lloyd George, 4.10.39, cited by P. Addison, 'Lloyd George and Compromise Peace in the Second World War' in A. J. P. Taylor (ed.), *Lloyd George: Twelve Essays* (1971), 369.
53 Betty Reid, interview.
54 VG, Lynd to Gollancz, 30.8.39.
55 VG, Reid to Gollancz, n.d. but Aug. 1939.
56 E.g. *LN*, Apr. 1940, 1,466.
57 VG, Gollancz to Strachey, 11.9.39.
58 VG, Gollancz to Lynd, 18.9.39.
59 VG, Gollancz to Reid, 19.2.40.
60 VG, Lewis to Gollancz, 2.9.39.
61 *LN*, Jan. 1940, 1,426.
62 *LN*, Dec. 1939, 1,414.
63 Gollancz, *LN*, May 1940, 1,485.

64 VG, Gollancz to Postgate, 16.4.40.
65 In this issue both the CP and the ILP were given a platform from which to explain their anti-war policies.
66 VG, insert to *LN* dated 11.5.40.
67 A selection of such letters are to be found in the Gollancz papers.
68 VG, Gollancz to Reid, 19.2.40.
69 VG, Gollancz–Lewis correspondence, May 1940.
70 VG, correspondence between Gollancz, Lewis and Reid, July–Aug. 1940.
71 *LN*, Nov. 1940, 1,544–8; *WNV*, 7.12.40, 695–6.
72 *LN*, Apr. 1940, 1,465.
73 *LN*, Nov. 1940, 1,544–5.
74 *WNV*, 11.11.39, 1,084–5; *LN*, Feb. 1941, 1,640–1.
75 Arnold Tustin of Sheffield, *LN*, Feb. 1941, 1,462.
76 *LN*, Apr. 1940, 1,469.
77 Interview.
78 Frank Allaun, interview; *LN*, Oct. 1936, 112.
79 *DW*, 3.12.40.
80 *Loc. cit.*; *New Statesman and Nation*, 14.12.40, 621.
81 RPD K4, Dutt to CPGB PB, 4.1.30, 9.8.30.
82 RPD K4, 'The financial position of the Labour Monthly for 1935'.
83 RPD K4, Dutt to Pollitt on 'LM and CR proposal', 13.2.35. CPGB PB resolution, Nov. 1939, cited in 'Memorandum on the Labour Monthly', Dec. 1940.
84 The *Monthly*'s print run increased in fits and starts from 7,000 in August 1939 to 20,000 in December 1940. The export ban, imposed in July 1940, led to the loss of about 1,500 monthly sales; *LM*, Jan. 1941, 2; RPD K4, 'Memorandum on the Labour Monthly'.
85 *LM*, Mar. 1940, 131–9; May 1940, 320.
86 *LM*, Dec. 1939, 720; Jan. 1940, 56.
87 *LM*, Jan. 1941, 4; June 1941, 258, 291.
88 Interview.
89 *LM*, May 1941, 243.
90 *Ibid.*, 241.
91 *Ibid.*, 241–4.
92 At least until the March 1941 issue, for which see p. 223.
93 RPD K4, Dutt to Edmund Dell, 25.11.40.
94 'Party training and mass political education', *PO*, Apr. 1940, 7–8.
95 RPD K4, 'Memorandum on the Labour Monthly'.
96 *Loc. cit.*
97 *Disc.*, Editorial Committee statement, Jan. 1936, 1–2.
98 E. M. Winterton, ' "Left" intellectuals and the war', *LM*, July 1940, 360.
99 J. Strachey, *What Are We To Do?* (1938), 378.
100 For a detailed discussion of these issues see pp. 46–9.
101 *TC*, 3.2.39.
102 It should however be noted that the Lichfield constituency, where Labour won a by-election in 1938, included over 30,000 Birmingham electors in Perry Barr.
103 This paragraph is based on *Thesis*, 436–9. See also P. D. Drake's very informative 'Labour and Spain: British Labour's response to the Spanish Civil War with particular reference to the Labour movement in Birmingham' (M. Litt., Birmingham, 1977).
104 *TC*, 1.1.37. The writer, Harold King, was neither a Communist nor a fellow traveller.
105 At least in the second half of the decade, when 17,000 more people settled in the city than

left it; A. Sutcliffe and R. Smith, *Birmingham 1939–1970* (1974), 9. For an excellent study of this question, see *When We Build Again* (Bournville Village Trust, 1941).
106 *Ibid.*, 32.
107 *Birmingham Post*, 8.12.38.
108 *When We Build Again*, 33.
109 *Evening Despatch*, 6.12.38, 7.12.38; *Birmingham Post*, 8.12.38; *TC*, 9.12.38; *Birmingham Gazette*, 13.5.39.
110 See the resolution deploring this action, Birmingham BLP minutes, 14.12.38.
111 'Building a Branch (1) Wythenshawe (Manchester)', *PO*, Apr. 1939, 8–11.
112 *49,000 Tenants Say No!* (CPGB, Birmingham, 1938). The CP apparently issued 10,000 copies of this pamphlet; *DW*, 4.3.39.
113 The account of the rent strike which follows is based largely on reports in the local press which can be found in the collection of cuttings 'Housing in Birmingham, 1938–43' held in Birmingham Reference Library. Detailed references can be found in *Thesis*, 472–3. Also very helpful were the conversations I had with Ted Smallbone, the BMTA's Secretary, and Jean Gale, daughter of Billy Milner, the BMTA's Chairman. An account of the strike with a rather different emphasis from my own will be found in S. Schifferes, 'Tenants' struggles in the 1930s' (MA, Warwick, 1975).
114 'Observer', *TC*, 27.1.39.
115 *Evening Despatch*, 28.1.39.
116 'I am in favour of a rent strike'   14,438
'I am against a rent strike'   1,093
Spoilt papers   169
One or two areas were left without polling stations, and not enough independent observers came forward to cover the whole city; for the ballot, see *Birmingham Mail*, 15.3.39, 3.4.39; *Birmingham Post*, 1.4.39; *DW*, 4.3.39; *TC*, 31.3.39, 7.4.39.
117 *TC*, 7.4.39.
118 *TC*, 16.6.39.
119 *DW*, 4.5.39.
120 *TC*, 16.6.39.
121 *Birmingham Mail*, 7.2.39.
122 *Birmingham Mail*, 1.6.39, 19.6.39; *Birmingham Post*, 17.6.39.
123 *DW*, 5.5.39.
124 See W. Hannington, *Black Coffins and the Unemployed* (1939).
125 *DW*, 19.6.39.
126 *Birmingham Mail*, 20.6.39.
127 For these songs, see *DW*, 2.5.39, 19.6.39; *TC*, 16.6.39.
128 *DW*, 22.6.39. Note the curious echo of Bernstein.
129 *DW*, 11.5.39.
130 None were held because of the war.
131 'Building a Branch (2) Kingstanding', *PO*, May 1939, 4–6; *PO*, June 1939, 16–18; Eden, cited Schifferes, *op. cit.*, 112; *Birmingham Post*, 17.7.39. The BMTA's dues were only a shilling a year.
132 See *Thesis*, 473 n. 80.
133 See *Thesis*, 452–3.
134 *Warwick County News*, 16.12.39.
135 As we have seen was the case with Arthur Horner, one reason for this might well have been that they felt no great enthusiasm for the Party's anti-war policy. Jean Gale recalled that, although her father, Billy Milner, remained loyal to the CP for some time, it was his

disillusionment with the Nazi–Soviet Pact that eventually led him to rejoin the Labour Party.
136 'Observer', *TC*, 24.11.39.
137 *DW*, 14.11.39; *Evening Despatch*, 16.12.39, and especially Milner's article, 'Why the tenants are on the warpath', *Evening Despatch*, 20.12.39.
138 Bert Williams, report to CPGB Midlands District Congress, *DW*, 29.1.40.
139 *DW*, 6.3.40.
140 *DW*, 16.3.40.
141 See e.g. Milner, *Evening Despatch*, 20.12.39.
142 *PO*, May 1940, 7.
143 *DW*, 6.7.40, 8.7.40.
144 *TC*, 1.12.39.
145 See e.g. *Air Raid Precautions. A Plan for Birmingham* (CPGB, Birmingham, Aug. 1938).
146 PRO INF 1/292, Home Intelligence report, 4.12.40–11.12.40.
147 See e.g. P. Piratin, *Our Flag Stays Red* (1948), 71–7; Branson, *op. cit.*, 302–6.
148 London People's Convention Committee leaflet (n.d.) (MML).
149 Cited in CP statement, *DW*, 23.11.40; Sutcliffe and Smith, *op. cit.*, 17–23.
150 T. Harrisson, *Living Through the Blitz* (1978 edn), 247–8.
151 *DW*, 29.11.40, 2.12.40, 5.12.40, 9.12.40.
152 Sutcliffe and Smith, *op. cit.*, 24–5.
153 *DW*, 9.12.40; *TC*, 11.1.41.
154 *DW*, 25.10.40, 5.12.40.
155 *DW*, 9.12.40.
156 See Jim Simmons, *TC*, 22.9.40, 11.1.41.
157 *TC*, 16.11.40.
158 *TC*, 23.11.40.
159 *DW*, 29.11.40; M-O, Town Report, Birmingham, G.H., 24.11.40.
160 *TC*, 30.11.40.
161 *DW*, 2.12.40.
162 *TC*, 3.5.41, 28.6.41; Sutcliffe and Smith, *op. cit.*, 29.
163 *TC*, 11.1.41.
164 'Deeds not words', *TC*, 16.11.40.
165 The BLP had no full-time officials in 1939, but early in 1940 Harry Wickham was appointed paid organiser in which position he took a staunchly anti-Communist stance.
166 *An Open Letter to the Birmingham Labour Movement* (CPGB Midlands District 1940).
167 *TC*, 28.12.40.
168 Simmons, *TC*, 11.1.41.
169 *TC*, 8.2.41.
170 *TC*, 30.11.40.
171 *TC*, 11.1.41.
172 *TC*, 18.1.41.
173 A. F. Bradbeer, *TC*, 15.3.41.
174 S. Blackwell, *Birmingham Today. The Role and Record of Neville Chamberlain and Others* (CPGB, Midlands District, 1941), 28.
175 Birmingham Trades Council and BLP *Annual Report and Year Book*, 1940–41, 59.
176 *TC*, 25.1.41.
177 TC, 14.12.41.
178 *TC*, 6.10.39, 10.11.39, 16.2.40, 14.12.40. Baird was shortly to be involved, as Secretary, in the Socialist Discussion Group, a ginger group in the Birmingham Labour Party which

produced a pamphlet called *A Policy for Victory through Socialism* and, together with *Tribune*, convened a conference to be addressed by Bevan; *Tribune*, 13.6.41; *TC*, 28.6.41.
179 D. Rolf, 'Birmingham Labour and the background to the 1945 election' in A. Wright and R. Shackleton (eds), *Worlds of Labour: Essays in Birmingham Labour History* (1938), 136–7.
180 Figures from the relevant Labour Party Annual Conference *Reports*.
181 M-O TC 46/10, reports on King's Norton by-election, 2.5.41, 3.5.41. The official figures record a fall in membership of 323 in the first year of the war.
182 From 62 to 98 members. See reports of AGM, *TC*, 18.1.41, *Warwick County News*, 18.1.41. The quotation and information on Olton Labour Party come from Len and Winifred Turner, interview, and also Harold Marsh, interview. It goes without saying that other factors like population dispersal contributed to the disparity in different Labour Parties' fortunes, but the trend is striking enough to be significant in this context.
183 Although interestingly James Hinton writes of nearby Coventry that 'it was the November (1940) blitz rather than Russian entry into the war . . . that seems to have been the turning point for the Coventry Communists' and provides evidence to substantiate this; 'Coventry Communism: a study in factory politics in the Second World War', *History Workshop* no. 10 (1980), 94–5.

Postscript and conclusion

An alliance with the Soviet Union meant a war to the death against Fascism. Yet when Churchill took over our policy and put it into operation, out came the critics with the amazing charge: 'The Communists have changed their policy again.' Well, well, there's no accounting for the twists and turns these fellows can make.

(William Gallacher, 1947[1])

For the last decade of its existence, the general line of Comintern policy seems to have been as much the product of Hitler's foreign policy as of Stalin's. It was Hitler's accession to power in 1933 that led, within a year or two, to the Comintern's adoption of the new Popular Front strategy. Then, in 1939, it was Hitler's readiness to come to terms with the Bolshevik menace that led the Comintern, in the opinion of its finest historian, to brandish once again the torch of world revolution, 'and in the direction, moreover, of just those capitalist states that were soon afterwards to become the Soviet Union's allies'.[2] Finally, it was Hitler's assault on the Soviet Union in June 1941 that led to the formal abandonment of the Communists' programme for world revolution and of the international organisation which had been established for the specific purpose of leading that revolution.

For a week or two, the British Party attempted to fit the fact of Hitler's final, suicidal act of aggression into its existing scheme of things, reiterating its objections to Anglo–American reaction and renewing its call for a People's Government which alone could achieve a 'People's Victory over Fascism and a People's Peace'.[3] Very quickly, however, it was realised that Hitler's 'dastardly' act had brought about 'an immediate change in the entire world situation' which demanded far more than mere tinkering with the Party line. It was Harry Pollitt, now reinstated as the Party's General Secretary, who was called upon to explain the nature of the new situation:

> There is only one issue in politics today: who is for or against Hitler? Who is for or against the creation of a national front to smash Hitler? Who is for or against the

creation of an international front between Britain, Russia and the United States to smash Hitler?[4]

The unwilling participation of the Soviet Union, and this alone, had transformed the imperialist war into a 'people's war' pure and simple,[5] and for the remainder of the war the CP demanded that everything 'be seen in its military context, everything subordinated to carrying through the successful struggle against Hitler'.[6] In practical terms, the CP's commitment to the 'national front' against Fascism entailed unwavering, though not uncritical, support for the Churchill Government, strict observance of the electoral truce and the unconditional subordination of the workers' sectional interests to the needs of war production. Henceforth Communists were the most impatient partisans of a total, offensive war against Germany, the most sterling of patriots and the most fervent and intolerant critics of those who had the temerity to disrupt 'national unity', whether by strikes, the contesting of by-elections or the dissemination of anti-government propaganda. So attractive was this policy, coinciding as it did with a popular mood of awestruck, grateful Russophilia, a pervasive discontent with Tory politics and a relaxation of the conditions of Party membership, that the CP almost trebled in size within a year of the attack on the Soviet Union.[7]

The CP's policies during the latter part of the war are often regarded as a return to, indeed the realisation of, the anti-Fascist conceptions of the People's Front period, symbolised by Pollitt's re-emergence as the Party's main figurehead. However, even the most cursory examination of this latter period, which is all that can be attempted here, reveals that the CP did not simply take up in June 1941 where it had left off in September 1939. Most crucially, the CP's preoccupation with the defeat of Hitler as the 'only issue' in politics, and its view that the only meaningful political alignment was that for or against Hitler, signified the complete abandonment of the Party's perception of the 'Fascisation' of Britain, and thus of its conception of Fascism as the universal product of capitalism in its final crisis. Instead, Fascism was depicted in abstract, moralistic terms, as the apotheosis of 'scientific barbarism', as the 'bestial monster' already familiar from official war propaganda. In their passionate moral indignation and their lack of dispassionate political analysis, Pollitt's writings exemplified this approach:

There was never such urgent need as now to grasp what Fascism means. . . .

What Fascism touches it blackens and besmirches, fouls and degrades. Where Fascism is, there is the blackness of night, the suppression of everything that the Labour Movement has ever fought to attain. The rule of the knout, the swing of the hangman's axe, the terror of the concentration camp. . . .[8]

Of course, Pollitt had been prone to adopt this tone even before the war, but then there had always been Dutt to locate this phenomenon in the context of the global crisis of moribund capitalism. But now, even when he attempted a more 'scientific', class-orientated analysis of Fascism, Dutt appeared to understand Fascism, as he had previously warned it should not be understood, as 'a general descriptive term for German and Italian imperialism' by which 'the "fight against Fascism" is presented as identical with the fight of Anglo–American imperialism against German–Italian–Japanese imperialism'.[9] For of course, the corollary to this identification of Fascism with 'Hitlerism', with the system by which Germans had 'ceased to be human' and 'degenerated into creatures lower even than the most brutish animals', was that all those who, whatever their politics, retained their allegiance to basic human values should unite to extirpate this demonic presence:

> How deadly the menace of Fascism is to all that is decent, humane, and cultured in the civilised world is shown in the way the various countries making up the United Nations have been brought together in a common alliance of Unity and friendship to withstand the common danger. Differences of social system and rivalries of different Imperialist nations have all been submerged to meet a common menace.[10]

Fascism, then, was an issue which transcended the particular faults of particular imperialist powers, and their bloody rivalries, and transcended the issue of capitalism versus Socialism; no longer was it regarded as a logical and foreseeable stage in the development of imperialism faced with the rising challenge of the social system of the future.

The Communist perception of Fascism within Britain was now confined exclusively to those it suspected of sympathy with the external foe: the potential Quislings, the Mosleyites and other negligible Fascist sects. But from Britain's rulers the CP positively demanded, in the interests of defeating Hitler, the sort of measures it had previously identified with Fascism, as the highest form of capitalist organisation for war. Thus, for example, during the uproar following Mosley's release from internment in 1943, D. N. Pritt, erstwhile critic of untrammelled executive powers, recommended that the government incarcerate those whose 'political views make them a danger to the State' as unhesitatingly as it would a homicidal lunatic.[11] Just as novel was William Rust's insistence that to explain 'the decisions of the Government to the people' was 'an obligation that the Press must accept in the period of national unity'.[12] The provisions of the Essential Works Order, once seen as the 'scaffolding of servitude', were another obligation willingly accepted by Communists.[13] Indeed, the CP now wholeheartedly accepted the methods of the 'Labour Front' in order to increase production. Communists deplored the 'rigid line of division between the management and the workers in industry' and campaigned vigorously for the formation of Joint Production Committees and the extension of 'State Control and unification' (a 'really impartial State control', whatever that meant) to 'override all sectional interests'.[14] And for all those who resisted such measures, for all those who encouraged a 'defeatist mentality' or tolerated 'practices or vested interests that prevent the full mobilisation of our country', Pollitt had an authentically 'Fascist' solution: they 'should be shot out of hand'.[15]

Of course, the extremity of Pollitt's language was intended to convey the gravity and the immediacy of the danger facing Britain, and the measures advocated by the Communist Party were originally conceived as temporary devices, involving temporary sacrifices, to ensure the victory over Nazism without which no advance to Socialism would be possible. Indeed, such was the Party's preoccupation with the necessary military victory that until about 1943 it discouraged all speculation as to the choices which would face the British people after the war as a diversion from more pressing tasks.[16] However, in the last part of the war, with the nemesis of Nazism visibly approaching, the CP had inevitably to address itself to the problems of the post-war world; and, as it did so, it became apparent that, having abandoned the view that capitalism was everywhere driven by its mounting crises towards Fascism, the CP was now ready to admit of the possibility and desirability of democratic progress and social reform within the framework of a stabilised capitalist economy. The catchword of the hour, popularised by Soviet and, to a lesser extent, British successes in the war, was *planning*; and during the last year or two of the war the CP issued pamphlet after pamphlet advocating the planned utilisation of Britain's resources to achieve full employment, the avoidance of slumps and increased wages and profits all round. 'How can they [the British people] make sure of jobs, homes, security and a rising standard of living for all?' asked Emile Burns. *'Certainly not by leaving everything to chance'*, he went on, and it was this sentiment, along with the unquestioned assumption that 'in the period after the war, capitalism will still be capitalism', that placed the CP firmly in the mainstream of Britain's emerging social-democratic consensus.[17]

The CP's illusions as to the prospects for international peace and fellowship after the war constituted an even more startling departure from traditional Communist doctrine as to the nature of imperialism. Just as Fascism had come to be identified exclusively with the Axis powers, so too had the forces within imperialism making for war. The Communist solution to that thorny problem of imperialist war was thus a simple one, if not a Communist one: Germany should be incapacitated by a 'peace' settlement far harsher than Versailles, involving its military occupation, the 'pastoralisation' of its economy and forced labour from its workers by way of 'reparation'.[18] With the German menace to world security thus eradicated, the victorious imperialist powers would be free to develop new forms of collective security and international economic cooperation and thus secure a 'peace which will last for generations'. Imperialist rivalries and imperialist wars would simply be unnecessary, for there had been 'too great a tendency to quarrel over the division of the post-war world market, as if it was bound to be a static, or even a shrinking quantity' when, in fact, the enlightened development of 'backward' countries could provide markets expanding steadily enough to satisfy both Britain and the United States.[19] So much for stale Leninist dogma! The CP had, in fact, more or less completely abandoned the conception of the general crisis of capitalism – expressed in mounting class struggles, sharpening imperialist rivalries, Fascism, recurrent war and, finally, revolution – which had called the Party into being back in 1920.

Internationally, the new direction in Communist politics was most dramatically indicated by the dissolution of the Comintern in May–June 1943. Despite Dutt's assurance that this decision was not such as to require 'prolonged internal discussion',[20] this admission that the Comintern had outlived its purpose, without ever having achieved that purpose, raised questions of profound importance for the British Party. The most fundamental of these, already raised by some opponents of the Party, was: what was now the purpose of maintaining a separate Communist organisation in Britain? The establishment of the Communist International, with its distinctive revolutionary programme and distinctive organisational forms appropriate to that programme, had been based on the conviction that the reformist, nationalist parties of Social Democracy were inadequate to the needs of the new era of wars and revolutions. And yet by the end of the Second World War the British CP had more or less abandoned 'Bolshevik' forms of organisation and discarded the theoretical assumptions that had underlain the break with Social Democracy, while the Comintern itself had passed into history. What, then, was the purpose of the Communist Party, and why should it not have followed the Comintern's example and liquidated itself?

For other European Communist Parties, the problem was not nearly so acute. The PCI and the PCF, for example, after emerging from the war with extensive bases of popular support, managed to take on the functions of mass reformist parties of the working class, somewhat on the pattern of classical Social Democracy. But in Britain there was no room for another mass reformist party, and yet the Communist Party henceforth offered little but a reformist strategy, in all but name, to be carried out by a Labour government. Its role in British politics was thus unclear; certainly, if the Party had not already existed in 1945, nobody would have troubled to invent it. For decades now, the CP, squeezed out by the Labour Party on one side and those parties and sects which adhere to traditional communist values on the other, has been a declining force on the left of British politics. In terms of its size, its activities, its electoral performance and the distribution of its literature and of its daily newspaper, the post-war period has witnessed the gradual decay of Communist politics in Britain. Perhaps most importantly, it has never since been able to attract new adherents of the ability and commitment that made it, within its limits, such an effective force on the left during the period covered by this book.

The material presented in the preceding pages, meagre though it is, allows us to conclude with a somewhat teleological view of the years between 1935 and 1941 as a period of transition for the Communist Party. Some writers have argued, quite plausibly, that the logical sequel to the Comintern's adoption of the Popular Front strategy in 1935 was the liquidation of the revolutionary International.[21] The fact remains, however, that the Comintern was not yet dissolved, either organisationally or, more importantly, ideologically. The period which followed was thus a contradictory one in which Communist Parties acknowledged that the overthrow of capitalism was not yet the issue and adopted policies accordingly, and yet remained committed to the world-view that the doomed capitalist system was passing through its final crisis.

This tension between traditional Communist ideological constructions and organisational forms and the implications of the new Popular Front strategy was arguably the most significant feature of Communist politics in Britain during this period. There was, for instance, the tension between the maintenance of a rigidly centralised, monolithic Party organisation and the dispersal of Party members into diverse fields of political activity in which they inevitably developed diverse interests and priorities: the tension between the centripetal pull of Party organisation and the centrifugal pull of the Popular Front, exemplified by Arthur Horner's ambivalent position as a leader of the South Wales miners and also of the Communist Party during the early part of the war. There was the tension between the adoption of a strategy which required a flexible and sensitive response to British political conditions and the continued acceptance of disconcertingly unpredictable Comintern directives based on the transient interests of Soviet diplomacy; the tension expressed in the Party's manifestly unrealistic pronouncements during the early part of the war and in the failure of many Party members to take these pronouncements too literally. There was the tension between the Party's cultivation of patriotic sentiments and its unshakeable belief that loyalty to the interests of the Soviet Union, as defined by the Soviet leadership, remained the first duty of the class-conscious worker. There was the tension between the traditional doctrines of Communism and the Party's attempt to reclaim the heritage, and the language, of Labour and democratic struggles in Britain.

And there was, of course, the tension between revolutionary theory and 'reformist' practice. The Party adopted immediate policies which presupposed the continued existence of capitalism but, because of its views as to the nature of moribund capitalism, it made little attempt to develop a coherent, constructive 'reformist' strategy. Communist thinking was based on the idea of crisis, of universal, unremitting crisis, of Fascism, wars and revolutions; the idea of a placid, gradual advance to the new social order was thus ruled out. The Party proposed immediate reforms, and adopted temporary expedients, but simply as a way of meeting the crisis and building up the forces which would bring it to a revolutionary conclusion. Communists campaigned for 'peace' but they would not, before 1941, have succumbed to utopian hopes of a 'peace which will last for generations'. They campaigned for social reforms and democratic rights within capitalism but they did not, as during the latter part of the war, issue detailed proposals for the long-term amelioration of capitalism. The Party adopted an immediate strategy, but not a reformist strategy; and it believed that by this immediate strategy the masses of the people would be brought into the struggle to end capitalism itself. This belief rested on the assumption, central to Communist politics, that capitalism had entered its final crisis, that in the not-so-very-long term it was incapable of stabilising itself, of absorbing reforms. This belief was, of course, if not unfounded, then premature. There is not much in Henry Pelling's history of the Party with which this writer agrees, but he undoubtedly identifies the fundamental tension in Communist politics when he writes that 'all the absurdities of the history of the party spring from this one fact, that it has been a revolutionary party in a non-revolutionary situation'.[22]

But if the Party's follies and absurdities stemmed from this one fact, so too did its vigour and effectiveness in the 1930s. Consider the hunger marches, the growth of the shop stewards' movement, the untiring campaigns against appeasement and on behalf of Spain, consider the Birmingham rent strike, consider even the People's Convention; and then consider the record of Britain's non-revolutionary parties and politicians, particularly those of the left, during this period of non-revolutionary crisis, and the balance will be found rather in the CP's favour than against it.

Notes

1. W. Gallacher, *The Rolling of the Thunder* (1947), 216.
2. F. Claudin, *The Communist Movement: from Comintern to Cominform* (1975 edn), 23.
3. See e.g. CPGB statement, 22.6.41 in *WNV*, 28.6.41, 401–2.
4. Pollitt on behalf of CPGB Secretariat, political letter to CP membership, 8.7.41, reproduced in V. Gollancz, *Russia and Ourselves* (1941), 118–26. There is no satisfactory account of Communist politics during the latter part of the war. However, accounts of the Party's response to the attack on the USSR can be found in Gollancz, *op. cit.*, 91 ff. and Branson, *op. cit.*, ch. 24. For a useful local study, see J. Hinton, 'Coventry Communism: a study of factory politics in the Second World War' in *History Workshop* no. 10 (1980).
5. See 'Notes', Aug. 1941, 349.
6. Pollitt, *WNV*, 1.8.42, 321–2.
7. Figures in Pelling, *op. cit.*, 120–1.
8. Pollitt, *Workers of Britain, Unite!* (CPGB, Apr. 1943), 5–6.
9. 'Notes', Mar. 1941, 102–3. This, for example, is the approach taken by Dutt in his *Britain in the World Front* (1942), ch. 3.
10. W. Wainwright, *Why You Should Be A Communist* (CPGB, 1.1.42), 23; Pollitt in *Unity and Victory* (CPGB, report of 16th Congress, 1943), 7–8.
11. Pritt, *The Mosley Case* (*LM* pamphlet, c.1943), 12.
12. Rust, *Lift the Ban on the Daily Worker* (*DW* League, 1942), 2.
13. J. R. Scott, 'Production Problems Today', *LM*, July 1943.
14. *An Urgent Memorandum on Production* (CPGB, Mar. 1942), 15–17; *Trade Union Policy in the War against Fascism* (CPGB, Dec. 1942; J. R. Campbell, 'Labour's crisis and opportunity', *LM*, May 1942, 141.
15. *The World in Arms!* (CPGB, 1941 or 1942), 3.
16. E.g. Pollitt in *The Communist Party on the Way to Win* (CPGB, report of National Conference, May 1942), 38.
17. Burns, *Jobs, Homes and Security* (CPGB, 1944), 3, 7–8.
18. E.g. Pollitt in *Victory, Peace and Security* (CPGB, report of 17th Congress, 1944), 12–17; M. Dobb, 'Reparations', *LM*, Mar. 1945, 78–82; P. Field, 'Germany', *LM*, Jan. 1945, 349–52.
19. Campbell, 'Anglo–American economic conflict', *LM*, Feb. 1945, 48–9.
20. RPD K3, message from CPGB Secretariat on 'The Communist Party and the Comintern', 26.5.43.
21. E. H. Carr, *The Twilight of Comintern, 1930–1935* (1982), 427.
22. *Op. cit.*, 182.

Appendix
Communist Party membership, 1939–41

The effects of the Nazi–Soviet Pact and the CP's decision to oppose the war on the Party's membership figures have been difficult to assess. No detailed figures were released by the CP between the summer of 1939, when membership stood at 17,756, and the beginning of 1942, when the corresponding figure was 22,738.[1] However, by the latter date the CP was beginning to benefit from the popularity of the Anglo–Soviet alliance and the attractiveness of the Party's commitment to the successful prosecution of the war. These figures throw no light on the period of the Nazi–Soviet Pact.

The Party's failure to produce detailed figures for this period might seem to indicate that its previously steady growth had been arrested, or even reversed. Certainly, to have acknowledged a slump in its membership figures would have invited unwelcome questions about the more extravagant claims in the Party's propaganda. For this reason it might seem reasonable to accept Henry Pelling's estimate that the Party's numbers may have fallen even below the 10,000 mark, that is to below the figure for 1936.[2]

However, the recent discovery of a memorandum issued by Herbert Morrison as Home Secretary in January 1941 has led some writers to suggest that Party membership held up better than Pelling had suspected. Morrison revealed that the CP had issued 20,000 membership cards for 1941. 'It is reasonable to assume that at least 5,000 of these cards will be kept in reserve for new members won during the year', he wrote; but on taking into account Communists in the forces who 'would not hold cards' he concluded that there had been 'little change since the outbreak of war'.[3] This statement has been taken as gospel by the CP's official historian.[4] Another Communist, Andrew Rothstein, has gone much further than this, citing contemporary Communist sources to show that during this period 'thousands voted with their feet – *into* the Communist Party'.[5] Hampered by the paucity and incompatibility of the available evidence, one must therefore assess as best one can three quite different assessments of the Party's position: that its members left *en masse*; that its membership remained fairly constant; and that it was inundated with new recruits.

One can begin, like Rothstein, by presenting a sample of the sort of claims made by the Party at the time. In every case the implication is that the decision to oppose the war had inaugurated a period of burgeoning growth for the Party:

> 'nearly every branch of the Party in this district [the West Riding] can report that new members have been recruited since the Central Committee issued its last statement on the war'.
>
> (*Daily Worker*, 31 October 1939)

> 82 recruits in the North Midlands and between 20 and 30 in South East Lancashire announced.
>
> (*Daily Worker*, 6 November 1939)

> 30 new members in Swindon announced.
>
> (*Daily Worker*, 10 November 1939)

> 500 YCL recruits in London alone since the start of the war.
>
> (*Daily Worker*, 22 November 1939)

> Two Glasgow meetings to celebrate anniversary of Russian Revolution attract 3,400 people, 33 of whom join CP with 'other applications arriving with every post'.
>
> (*Party Organiser*, December 1939)

> Pollitt speaks at the Memorial Hall, London, and 20 people join the Party 'there and then'.
>
> (*Daily Worker*, 16 December 1939)

> Sam Blackwell reports a Bristol membership of 320 representing 'a steady growth of the Party since the war, offset by conscription. Very few people have been lost through disagreement with our political line.'...
>
> (*Party Organiser*, May 1940)

A comprehensive summary of this sort of information appeared in the pamphlet *The Communist Party in War Time*, which claimed a membership of 20,000 in March 1940, 'practically all Districts being able to report considerable growth'.[6]

Partial confirmation of this picture comes from a series of reports compiled by the MOI's Regional Information Officers early in 1940. From the North Midlands, from Manchester and from South Wales came reports of 'many people joining [the] party at meetings', of 'increased financial support for the Communists' and of 'more Communist literature in the factories'. Under the stimulus of an influx of aircraft workers, Communist activity in the South West was likewise flourishing, even to the point of a tenfold increase in *Daily Worker* sales in Hereford. From Leeds, where there was particular concern over Communist activities at Montague Burton's, came reports of a Party meeting at the Town Hall in March 1940 attracting a 'wholeheartedly Communistic' audience of a thousand – mostly young men – who demonstrated 'great enthusiasm for the triumph of Stalinism . . . there being a general assent to everything said'.[7] In short, we have a fair amount of evidence from both Communist and governmental sources which would seem to suggest at the very least that this period saw no diminution of Communist strength. However, closer scrutiny of this evidence will reveal a rather different picture.

To put our figures from Communist sources in perspective we need only consider the admissions made by Party spokesmen retrospectively. In 1942, for example, one Communist described the 'crisis' faced by the Party in London at the beginning of the war:

> Our membership was very much reduced by the call-up, evacuation and general dispersal. We were down to 3,000 members. Activity in the streets and localities, which had been mounting higher and higher before the war, was largely destroyed by the new conditions – transference to industry, black-out, 'blitz', and a variety of restrictions. Our weakness in factory organisation was strikingly revealed.

The crisis was such that the CP virtually abandoned area organisation in London except for those who could not be organised at the workplace. Whereas previously the 'main proportion' of London Communists had been organised for 'general local activity in the Borough', they were now instructed to join factory groups. Significantly, the District Congress at which this decision was announced gave a London Party membership figure of 7,000. By March 1940, 8,000 members were claimed; and yet Ted Bramley later disclosed that the London membership had fallen to 3,500, or half the pre-war figure, by January 1941.[8] This discrepancy is of enormous significance, for the London District of the Party was far and away the largest, comprising 40 per cent of the national membership prior to the war. True, the Party in London was no doubt disproportionately affected by wartime dislocation, but this sort of discrepancy was not peculiar to London. For example, the boast that the CP had recruited 30 new members in Swindon in the first month or two of the war carries less conviction when we discover that as late as January 1942 the Party had only 60 members in that town, of whom 'only some 20 were working in an organised way'.[9] Even before June 1941, Dutt had described frankly, albeit behind closed doors, the CP's 'organisational difficulties' – 'new problems and adaptation to the transference of members and the difficulties of the call-up; practical difficulties in the organising of meetings; slowness of recruiting at a time when there is the most widely expressed discontent with the official Labour leadership and the greatest interest in all our literature'.[10] But this was not the sort of information to find its way into *The Communist Party in War Time*.

If the CP's claims have to be handled with discretion, so too do the reports of the Regional Information Officers. These reports are to be found in a file labelled 'Pacifist, Communist and Fascist Propaganda' and their allegations that in some towns these very different anti-war movements were 'strong and to some extent united' suggest that the RIOs did not always take much trouble to distinguish between them.[11] The RIOs were trained to become 'impartial recording and assessing machines free from political or other bias', [12] but such reports indicate that this was not always possible. Perhaps the fault lay less with the RIOs than with the contacts on whom they relied: the police, for example:

> A Party member was in the army, in intelligence, and they seconded him into the CID and so he nicked my file out of the CID files and brought it for me to have a look at. It was an illuminating experience because it consisted almost entirely of inventions: meetings that I was alleged to have gone to and journeys that I was alleged to have made which I'd never made. Somebody had sat there at the CID and in order to justify his salary had invented all these things.[13]

It therefore seems inadvisable to place too much credence on those RIO reports which are not substantiated by other sources. The case that the CP consolidated its earlier advances after September 1939 rests on some rather flimsy evidence.

The thought that Party officials in London and elsewhere were simply lying about the Party's position will come readily to many minds, but there is a more convincing explanation for the contradictory figures cited. The discrepancy between the registered and dues-paying membership of any political party had always been an especially marked feature of the Communist Party, mainly because so many recruits to the Party never became integrated into its activities. In 1938, for example, a London Communist complained that 'many recruits never become Party members. Either they disappear from our midst or become that queer anomaly "a non-paying member" '.[14] That the inclusion of these queer anomalies could make a considerable difference to Party membership figures is shown by the figures we have for the West Midlands for 1945: 2,882 members, of whom only 1,771 (65 per cent) were dues-paying members.[15] This crucial distinction between a card-carrying Communist and a paid-up Communist will enable us to make better sense of our figures for the earlier part of the war.

When Ted Bramley admitted retrospectively that Party membership in London stood at 3,500 in January 1941 he was recording the dues-paying membership for that month. The 7–8,000 members claimed in 1940, on the other hand, no doubt constituted the total membership of the Party in London. As such, the figures may well have included those Communists who had moved out of London and were simultaneously swelling the Party's ranks in the West Country. Similarly, it is unlikely that all those individuals who were so carried away by Pollitt's oratory at the Memorial Hall that they joined the CP 'there and then' subsequently settled down to the life of an active, paid-up Communist. However, their impulsive filling-out of Party application forms no doubt added their number, as also similar cases elsewhere, to Party membership figures.

Most importantly, it seems likely that the majority of those Communists who were disenchanted by the events of the autumn of 1939 did not proceed to bare their stricken consciences to the readers of the *New Statesman*, but merely let their membership of the Party fall into abeyance. One would imagine that these were not, by and large, particularly committed Communists who had played their full part in Party activities, but rather conditional adherents to Communism who had joined the CP on the strength of its opposition, and that of the Soviet Union, to international Fascism; and then drifted out when this stance was compromised by the events of late 1939. This conjecture is quite compatible with the statement of a leading Manchester Communist that he could not recall a single defection from the Party because of its decision to oppose the war.[16] This was not so much a period of impassioned letters of resignation from active Communists as one in which a substantial number of Communists who were less committed to the Party, or less amenable to its discipline, dropped out so quietly that they cannot be distinguished from the evacuated, the conscripted and the dead.[17] According to Gabriel Carritt, few even of those who were unhappy with the 'new line' left the Party:

> Most of them were silent, like Pollitt; kept their peace. Very few left. Far more left over Hungary. Far more.[18]

Peter Kerrigan, too, recalled that there occurred 'nothing like what happened when the Hungarian events took place',[19] and Ralph Simons drew the same comparison:

> Well, I can't recall people leaving the Communist Party. For me to say none did, of course, would be crazy; but I can't recall any sort of exodus. For example, during the period of Hungary in 1956, when the Communist Party in Britain supported the Soviet intervention, large numbers left the Communist Party and I saw it for myself. But certainly there was nothing like that in 1939.[20]

The comparison is surely an apt one; for when one considers the brouhaha which occurred in 1956, and tots up the number of prominent Communists who broke with the CP at that time, one appreciates how little vocal dissent from the Party line took place during the 'imperialist war'.

The matter is further complicated by the protracted exodus of Communists and near-Communists from the Labour Party which began in July 1939. In *The Communist Party in War Time* these were treated as new recruits, who presumably bolstered the Party's membership figures.[21] However, some at least of these Communists had held both CP and Labour Party cards, and their leaving the latter would have had no impact on CP membership figures.[22] Although this merely adds to our difficulties in assessing these figures, the most conspicuous example of the abandonment of the official Labour movement for Communism does bear out our earlier conjectures as to the trajectory of Party membership. In July 1939, Ted Willis, Chairman of the Labour League of Youth, went over to the YCL, taking a good proportion of the LLY's membership with him. In London, for example, a number of Leagues of Youth defected *en masse* and by August 1939 it was claimed that 95 per cent of the East London LLY had entered the YCL.[23] Thus was the *Daily Worker* able to boast of 500 YCL recruits in London in the first couple of months of the war. However, as we have argued was the case with many CP members, and as Ted Willis later recalled, many of these new adherents were Communists only on paper:

> It was really very funny because it was like the seven lean cows swallowing the seven fat cows and it made no difference. I issued this big appeal that everybody should leave the League of Youth and follow me into the Young Communist League. We made strenuous efforts about it, and it appeared to me that they did. Frank Chapple and all of the people I knew and hundreds up and down the country left and joined the Young Communist League. Whether it was the imminence of the war which dispersed it all, or what it was, I don't know; but two years later the Young Communist League was smaller than it had been. It obviously had an immediate effect on the Young Communist League, but not long lasting. They drifted away or went into the army.[24]

Willis was Secretary of the London District Council of the YCL in 1940. His testimony is a further warning to approach the more extravagant of the CP's claims with caution.

Another complication concerns the question of Party members in the forces. The Home Office, we observed, assumed that these Communists would cease to hold Party cards, and in some cases this assumption appears to have been correct. Joe O'Reilly, for example, recalled that his Party membership lapsed after his call-up,[25] while Bert Ramelson received no Party cards and paid no dues while in the army abroad. Interestingly, though, Ramelson kept hold of his 1939 Party card and when he was demobilised he found that he was accredited with continuous Party membership through the war years.[26] If this was common, it would obviously help to account for the discrepancy between dues-paying and registered membership figures. For understandable reasons, Party officials would have been keen to include conscripted Communists in their public estimates of the Party's strength. The lesson, once again, is that our conclusions must be tentative.

Nevertheless, on the basis of the evidence presented here and elsewhere in this book, some suggestions can now be offered as to the trend in Party membership. It would seem that during the first year of war a combination of wartime dislocation and political disillusionment led to an appreciable fall in the paid-up membership of the Party. Nevertheless, the bulk of the CP's active membership stood by their Party and very few leading members dropped out. For this reason the CP was able to continue to play a significant role in trade union and other mass struggles. And of course, as the Party threw itself into these struggles, and as it adopted a more plausible line on the war in the summer of 1940, its membership began to recover well before June 1941, as figures from London and Coventry show.[27]

These conclusions are very much in accord with the political interpretations offered here. As our study of the Left Book Club showed, the anti-Fascist movement of the late 1930s was united on the insecure basis of a number of potential contradictions which was shattered by the impact of war. Thus did Britain's incipient People's Front fall to pieces and, to the extent that these contradictions reached into the Communist Party itself, thus too did the CP suffer a loss of members.[28] But for most of its active membership the Party's approach to day-to-day struggles and the wider issues of politics remained valid. The fabric of the Party remained intact, if frayed at the edges. The CP emerged from this difficult period robust enough to take full advantage of the Soviet Union's entry into the war and the new political situation this created.[29]

Notes

1 CPGB CC *Report* to 16th Congress (1939; not held), 13; *WNV*, 18.4.42, 206.
2 Pelling, *op. cit.*, 113–18.
3 PRO CAB 98.18, memorandum by Home Secretary, 17.1.41.
4 Branson, *op. cit.*, 315, 327.
5 *Bulletin* of the Society for the Study of Labour History no. 34 (1977), 19–20.
6 *The Communist Party in War Time* (CPGB, 1940), 19–21. A notable exception to the reported trend was South Wales, where the rate of growth had not 'kept up to expectations'. The figure of 20,000 appears to have been the official one throughout 1940; see e.g. Dutt, *DW*, 5.8.40.

7 Reports in PRO INF 1/319.
8 D. Grandjean, *Ward Groups – the Way Forward* (CPGB, London DC, n.d., 1942?), 3; 'Draft discussion statement' for CPGB London District congress, 26.1.40–28.1.40, 6, 13–14 (WCML); *The Communist Party in War Time*, 21; Bramley, *WNV*, 28.11.41, 743–4.
9 *WNV*, 7.3.42, 155.
10 RPD K4, 'Draft outline of political report to enlarged meeting', 15.4.41.
11 PRO INF 1/319, minutes of conference of RIOs, 6.1.40; reports on 'Anti-war movements', n.d. (1940).
12 PRO INF 1/292, 'How the weekly report is made', 6.4.42.
13 George Matthews, interview.
14 A. Fleming, *DW*, 29.6.38.
15 Etheridge papers, Modern Records Centre, MSS.202/CP339, 'Report of membership position', 1945–46. The appropriate figures for the Midlands District in 1943 and 1944 were 65% and 78% respectively; see *ibid.*, 'Agenda and resolutions submitted to congress by the District Party Committee', 24.2.45–25.2.45.
16 Edmund Frow, interview.
17 In this context it is worth noting that in London, where there was such a startling fall in membership, there was a disproportionate number of recent recruits. Of the CP's 1,758 new recruits in the six months to April 1939, about a thousand were from London; see *DW*, 13.1.39, W.R., 'Some organisational problems', *PO*, Apr. 1939, 1.
18 Interview.
19 Interview, Imperial War Museum.
20 Interview. For the events of 1956, see Pelling, *op. cit.*, 169–81; N. Wood, *Communism and the British Intellectuals* (1959), 182–213; and various articles in *The Socialist Register 1976*.
21 Pp. 19–20.
22 E.g. Norman Brown, Arthur Exell, interviews.
23 J. Ferris, 'The Labour Party League of Youth, 1924–1940' (MA, Warwick, 1977), 129–31; F. Chapple, *Sparks Fly! A Trade Union Life* (1985 edn), 28.
24 Interview.
25 Interview. He did however hold discussions with other Communists while on service and maintain contact with the Party when on leave.
26 Interview, Imperial War Museum. Some Communists, on the other hand, continued to pay their dues while on service abroad; see Etheridge papers MSS.202/CP/89, Trooper R. A. Bird to Etheridge, 29.12.45.
27 The dues-paying membership in London rose from 3,500 to 4,500 (by 28.5%) in the first six months of 1941; Bramley, *WNV*, 28.11.41, 743–4. In Coventry there were, in November 1940, only 70 members organised in one branch, and 'factory groups hardly existed in any real form'. By the following June there were 150 members and ten factory groups; Jack Cohen, *WNV*, 7.3.42, 155.
28 Especially, perhaps, in a town like Oxford where the CP had more or less submerged itself in a local People's Front based on the Labour Party.
29 A further point needs to be added in parenthesis. If, like Henry Pelling, one takes the Communist Party in isolation then the slump in its membership figures might suggest that the Party faced a fundamental political crisis. But if one turns to Pelling's *Short History of the Labour Party* one discovers that the individual membership of the Labour Party virtually halved during this same period. As an essentially electoral organisation the Labour Party was admittedly more vulnerable than the CP to the stultifying effects of the electoral truce, but this information nevertheless gives an indication of the problems faced by any political party operating in conditions of total war.

Select bibliography

The following note merely points out the main primary sources for this study and offers a few suggestions for further reading. Interested readers should consult A. J. Mackenzie's painstakingly-compiled 'Communism in Britain: a bibliography', in the *Bulletin* of the Society for the Study of Labour History no. 44 (1982). A full listing of sources consulted for the present study will of course be found appended to my original thesis of the same title (Ph.D., Manchester, 1987).

Unpublished primary sources

Government records held in the Public Record Office
CAB 65/66   War Cabinet minutes and memoranda
CAB 98.18   War Cabinet Committee on Communist Activities
INF 1/292   Ministry of Information Home Intelligence reports
INF 1/319   Reports by MOI Regional Information Officers
               on 'Pacifist, Communist and Fascist Propaganda'
INF 1/909–11   Relating to export of Communist and Fascist publications

Personal collections
R. Palme Dutt (British Library)
Victor Gollancz (Modern Records Centre, University of Warwick)
D. N. Pritt (British Library of Political and Economic Science)

Labour movement records
Birmingham Borough Labour Party and Birmingham Trades Council minutes (Birmingham Reference Library)
Oxford City Labour Party and Oxford Trades and Labour Council minutes (Abe Lazarus Memorial Library, Ruskin College)
South Wales Miners' Federation Executive Council and annual and special conference minutes (South Wales Coalfield Archive, University College of Swansea)

Mass-Observation Archive, University of Sussex
The most useful sources in this archive were the File Reports and the following Topic Collections:

TC 25 Political Attitudes and Behaviour 1938–56
TC 46 By-elections 1937–47

Oral interviews

One or more interviews with the following Communists and ex-Communists were recorded and transcribed:

Frank Allaun; Norman Brown; Ted Bramley; Dave Campbell; Gabriel Carritt; Winifred Doherty (née Low); Arthur Exell; Alec Ferguson; James Friell; Edmund Frow; Margot Kettle (née Gale); Malcolm MacEwen; Harold Marsh; George Matthews; Bill Moore; Joe O'Reilly; Phil Piratin; Betty Reid; Benny Rothman; Ralph Simons; Ted Smallbone; Lord Ted Willis.

Interviews with the following non-Communists were also recorded in connection with this research:

Bob Edwards; Jean Ferguson; Alec Murie; Len and Winifred Turner.

A number of those interviewed also answered particular queries by post, as did Bernard MacKenna, while Mrs Jean Gale recalled to me at length her memories of her father, W. H. Milner. Other interviews cited in this book will be found in the Imperial War Museum, Department of Sound Records, and among the *Television History Workshop* transcriptions held in Oxford Central Library.

Contemporary printed sources

The most useful contemporary newspapers and periodicals will already be evident from the footnotes. For contemporary books, pamphlets and ephemera I relied mainly on the Marx Memorial Library (where can be found files on the People's Convention and the London First of May Committee) and above all on the Working Class Movement Library, now in Salford.

Books, articles and theses

All books published in London unless otherwise stated.

M. Adereth, *The French Communist Party: a Critical History (1920–1984) from Comintern to 'the Colours of France'* (Manchester University Press, 1984).
P. Anderson, 'Communist Party History' in R. Samuel (ed.), *People's History and Socialist Theory* (Routledge and Kegan Paul, 1981).
J. Attfield and S. Williams (eds), *1939. The Communist Party and the War* (Lawrence and Wishart, 1984).
D. Beetham, *Marxists in Face of Fascism* (Manchester University Press, 1983).
E. Benson, *To Struggle is to Live: a Working Class Autobiography. Volume Two: Starve or Rebel* (People's Publications, Newcastle, 1980).
F. Borkenau, *European Communism* (Faber, 1953).

S. Bornstein and A. Richardson, *Two Steps Back: Communists and the Wider Labour Movement 1935–1945* (Socialist Platform, Ilford, n.d.).
N. Branson, *History of the Communist Party of Great Britain 1927–1941* (Lawrence and Wishart, 1985).
N. Branson and M. Heinemann, *Britain in the Nineteen Thirties* (Panther, 1973 edn).
S. Broomfield, 'South Wales during the Second World War: the coal industry and its community' (Ph.D., Wales, 1979).
S. Bruley, 'Socialism and feminism in the Communist Party of Great Britain, 1920–1939' (Ph.D., London, 1979).
A. Calder, *The People's War* (Panther, 1971 edn).
D. Childs, 'The British Communist Party and the war, 1939–41: old slogans revived' in *Journal of Contemporary History* vol. 12 (1977).
F. Claudin, *The Communist Movement: from Comintern to Cominform* (Penguin, Harmondsworth, 1975).
C. Cockburn, *Crossing the Line* (MacGibbon and Kee, 1958).
R. Croucher, *Engineers at War* (Merlin, 1982).
H. Dewar, *Communist Politics in Britain: the CPGB from its Origins to the Second World War* (Pluto, 1976).
P. D. Drake, 'Labour and Spain: British Labour's response to the Spanish Civil War with particular reference to the Labour movement in Birmingham' (M. Litt., Birmingham, 1977).
R. Dudley Edwards, *Victor Gollancz: a Biography* (Gollancz, 1987).
A. Exell, *The Politics of the Production Line: Autobiography of an Oxford Car Worker* (History Workshop, Oxford, 1981).
H. Francis, *Miners Against Fascism: Wales and the Spanish Civil War* (Lawrence and Wishart, 1984).
H. Francis and D. Smith, *The Fed. A History of the South Wales Miners in the Twentieth Century* (Lawrence and Wishart, 1980).
E. and R. Frow, *Engineering Struggles. Episodes in the Story of the Shop Stewards' Movement* (Working Class Movement Library, Manchester, 1982).
J. Fyrth (ed.), *Britain, Fascism and the Popular Front* (Lawrence and Wishart, 1985).
W. Gallacher, *Revolt on the Clyde* (Lawrence and Wishart, 1941 edn).
T. Harrisson, *Living Through the Blitz* (Penguin, Harmondsworth, 1981 edn).
J. Hinton, 'Coventry Communism: a study of factory politics in the Second World War' in *History Workshop* no. 10 (1980).
J. Hinton, *The First Shop Stewards' Movement* (Allen and Unwin, 1973).
J. Hinton, 'Killing the People's Convention: a letter from Palme Dutt to Harry Pollitt' in the *Bulletin* of the Society for the Study of Labour History no. 39 (1979).
A. Horner, *Incorrigible Rebel* (MacGibbon and Kee, 1960).
D. Hyde, *I Believed* (Heinemann, 1951).
M. Johnstone and A. Rothstein, controversy in the *Bulletin* of the Society for the Study of Labour History nos 33–7 (1976–8).
J. Jupp, *The Radical Left in Britain, 1931–1941* (Cass, 1982).
M. Isserman, *Which Side Were You on? The American Communist Party During the Second World War* (Wesleyan University Press, Connecticut, 1982).

J. Jacobs, *Out of the Ghetto* (Janet Simons, 1978).
J. Lewis, *The Left Book Club: an Historical Record* (Gollancz, 1970).
L. J. Macfarlane, *The British Communist Party: its Origin and Development until 1929* (MacGibbon and Kee, 1966).
S. Macintyre, *Little Moscows. Communism and Working-Class Militancy in Inter-War Britain* (Croom Helm, 1980).
S. Macintyre, *A Proletarian Science. Marxism in Britain, 1917–1933* (Cambridge University Press, 1980).
A. J. Mackenzie, 'British Marxists and the Empire: anti-imperialist theory and practice, 1920–1945' (Ph.D., London, 1978).
H. McShane (with J. Smith), *No Mean Fighter* (Pluto, 1978).
J. Mahon, *Harry Pollitt: a Biography* (Lawrence and Wishart, 1976).
R. Martin, *Communism and the British Trade Unions, 1924–1933. A Study of the National Minority Movement* (Clarendon Press, Oxford, 1969).
A. Merson, *Communist Resistance in Nazi Germany* (Lawrence and Wishart, 1985).
M. Milotte, *Communism in Modern Ireland: the Pursuit of the Workers' Republic since 1916* (Gill and Macmillan, Dublin, 1984).
K. Morgan, 'Eddie Frow: engineering struggles' in the North West Labour History Group *Journal* no. 13 (1988).
E. Mortimer, *The Rise of the French Communist Party 1920–1947* (Faber, 1984).
H. Pelling, *The British Communist Party. A Historical Profile* (Black, 1975 edn).
B. Pimlott, *Labour and the Left in the 1930s* (Cambridge University Press, 1977).
P. Piratin, *Our Flag Stays Red* (Thames Publications, 1948).
R. Samuel, 'The lost world of British Communism' in *New Left Review* nos 154, 156 (1985–6).
S. Samuels, 'The Left Book Club' in *Journal of Contemporary History* vol. 1 (1965).
J. Saville, 'May Day 1937' in A. Briggs and J. Saville (eds), *Essays in Labour History, 1918–1939* (Croom Helm, 1977).
J. Stevenson and C. Cook, *The Slump. Society and Politics During the Depression* (Quartet, 1979 edn).
H. Thomas, *John Strachey* (Eyre Methuen, 1973).
E. Trory, *Between the Wars. Recollections of a Communist Organiser* (Crabtree Press, Brighton, 1974).
E. Trory, *Imperialist War. Further Recollections of a Communist Organiser* (Crabtree Press, Brighton, 1977).
R. Whiting, *The View from Cowley. The Impact of Industrialisation upon Oxford, 1918–1939* (Clarendon Press, Oxford, 1983).
N. Wood, *Communism and the British Intellectuals* (Gollancz, 1959)
M. Woodhouse and B. Pearce, *Essays on the History of Communism in Britain* (New Park, 1975).
P. Zinkin, *A Man to be Watched Carefully* (People's Publications, Newcastle, 1985).

Index

Acland, Sir Richard, 54 n. 62, 84 n. 54, 223, 258
Adams, Harry, 206, 207, 224, 248 n. 122
Ager, A. E., 229
Aid Spain movement, *see* Spain, solidarity with republic
Aircraft Shop Stewards' National Council, *see* Engineering and Allied Trades Shop Stewards' National Council
Altmark incident, 118, 160
Amalgamated Engineering Union, 37, 101, 130–2, 200, 228, 233
Anderson, Sir John, 237, 240, 241
Anglo–Soviet committees, 206
Anglo–Soviet pact, CP campaigns for, 85–6, 264
Arnot, R. Page, 56, 111, 232
ARP, 175, 197, 204, 288–9
Artists International Association, 39, 145–6
Attlee, Clement, 193, 258; *see also* Labour Party

Baird, John, 290–1, 294–5
BBC, 194, 223–4
Bevan, Aneurin, 57, 148, 236, 301 n. 178
Bevin, Ernest, 37, 191, 197, 240
Birmingham, 40, 254, 257, 277–97; air raids on, 289–93; CP, 280–96 *passim*; housing question, 279–80; Labour Party, 228–9, 280–1, 283, 289–96 *passim*, weakness in, 277–8, 281; rent strike, 280–5; Trades Council, 101, 283, 288
Birmingham Labour Joint Emergency Committee, 288, 290–3
Birmingham Municipal Tenants' Association, 281–8

Black, Misha, 145–6
Blackwell, Sam, 294, 312
Boughton, Rutland, 210
Bradbeer, Albert, 282
Brailsford, H. N., 261
Bramley, Ted, 36, 94–5, 160, 253 n. 266, 313, 314
Branson, Clive, 148
Bristol, 150, 289, 312
Britain, as 'aggressor' power, 90–1, 117–19, 121–2, 147; appeasement of Fascism, 60–4, 70–4, 80–1, 87, 112, 175–6; and Germany, 60–4, 70–4, 85, 184, 186; and Italy, 62; role in world politics, 56–7, 60–4, 69, 73–4, 183–7; and Spain, 63, 175–6; and USSR, 61–2, 74, 91, 112–13, 128, 147, 186
Britain Without Capitalists, 49
British Socialist Party, 111
British Union of Fascists, *see* Mosley, Sir Oswald
British Youth Peace Assembly, 39
Brown, Isabel, 162–4
Brown, Norman, 50, 97, 133
Burns, Emile, 65, 190, 257, 261, 263, 275, 306
Bush Alan, 210
by-elections, Battersea North (1940), 161–2; Bow and Bromley (1940), 162–4; Bridgwater (1938), 54 n. 67; Dunbartonshire (1941), 208, 216–17, 222; Kettering (1940), 169 n. 178; King's Norton (1941), 295; Mid-Bucks (1938), 54 n. 68; Oxford (1938), 54 n. 67; Perth (1938), 54 n. 69; Southwark Central (1940), 155–8; Stretford (1939), 153–5; West Ham, Silvertown (1940), 158–61; Westminster Abbey (1939), 54 n. 67, 79

Campbell, J. R., 65, 81, 84 n. 58, 89, 90, 110, 151, 189, 211, 217, 227–8, 232, 250 n. 187
Cardew, Phil, 210
Carritt, Gabriel, 79, 98, 315
Chamberlain, Neville, *see* 'Men of Munich'; National Government
Chapple, Frank, 316
China, 182
Churchill, Sir Winston, 76, 81, 84 n. 54, 245 n. 7; *see also* Conservative dissidents
Churchill Government, 172, 179–80, 185, 217, 220, 304; considers action against CP, 236–42; 'Fascist' tendencies, 189–96 *passim*
'Class Against Class', 19–20, 34, 39, 134, 196–7
Clyde Workers' Committee, 111–12
Cockburn, Claud, 94, 98, 257
Cole, G. D. H., 273
collective security, 59, 65
colonies, colonial question, 57, 81, 174, 176, 177, 180–2, 185–8; *see also* imperialism, India
Communist International, 1, 3–4, 6, 14, 15, 20, 149, 303; adopts Popular Front, 20, 33–4; and British CP, 13, 14; congresses, (2nd) 3, (7th) 20–1, 25–7, 28, 33–4, 41; disbanded, 4, 303, 307; loyalty to, 95, 98
Communist Party of Great Britain, historical treatment of, 5–10, 15; membership, 20, 311–17; threatened suppression, 236–42
Communist Review, 272–3
conscription, campaign against (1939), 77–9
Conservative dissidents, 45, 75–6, 79, 81, 84 n. 54, 98
Conway, Jane, 258
Cooper, Duff, 240
Coventry, 301 n. 178, 317
Cox, Idris, 141–2
Crane, George, 167 n. 94
Cripps, Sir Stafford, 32 n. 48, 178, 256, 277
Crossman, Richard, 277
Curry, Patrick, 99
Czechoslovakia, 73; *see also* Munich crisis

Daily Herald, 205
Daily Worker, 10, 43–4, 72, 96, 127, 130, 162, 168 n. 151, 232, 243, 263; banned, 129–30, 194, 197, 221–3, 236, 237–40, 249 n. 154
Denmark and Norway, invaded, 118–19, 161
Dimitrov, Georgi, 98, 114, 174, 197; Seventh World Congress report, 20, 25–6, 28, 33, 41
'direct action', 146–8
Discussion, 275–6
Dutt, Clemens, 162
Dutt, R. Palme, 8, 47, 85, 96, 98, 110, 156, 198, 205, 207, 216, 232, 243, 262, 271, 307, 313; anti-war line expounded by, 105–6, 113–14, 120–2, 125, 171, 172, 184, 215; on appeasement, 56–64 *passim*; biographical details, 10–12; and change of line on war, 89–91; on conscription, 78–9; on *Daily Worker*, 10, 238–9; on Fascism, 22–8, 74–5, 91, 191–6, 305; on imperialism, 186–7; and 'invasion scare', 180–1; and *Labour Monthly*, 272–5; on Munich, 70–4; pacifism and economism criticised by, 115, 125–6; and People's Convention, 212, 222–4, 250 n. 182; revolutionary perspectives, 34, 49, 108, 211–12, 220–1, 235–6; Socialist Labour Alliance, 202–3; on Tory dissidents, 76
Dutt, Salme, 71

Eden, Jessie, 281, 282, 286–7
Edwards, Bob, 38, 153–5
Edwards, Jack, 94
elections, CP policy on, 35, 45, 116, 153, 163–4; *see also* by-elections; General Election
Elliott, Lon, 99
Elliott, Sydney, 45
emergency powers, 87, 193–4, 216, 237–42
Engineering and Allied Trades Shop Stewards' National Council, 37, 128–32, 230, 235–6
Exell, Arthur, 40, 51, 96–7

Fascism, Communist perception of, 4,

21–30, 54 n. 79, 182–3, 185, 189–96, 208–9, 231, 304–5; as organisation for war, 28–9, 61, 190–2
Fife, 44, 52 n. 7
Fife Miners' Union, 147
Finland, 28; *see also* Soviet–Finnish war
First World War, influence on Communists, 93, 94–5, 98, 124; Lenin and, 106–8; opposition to, 110–12
forces, Communists in, 100, 311, 316–17
Forster, E. M., 251 n. 205
Fox, Ralph, 41, 255
France, 62; capitulation (1940), 170–1, 174–8, 182–4, 237–8; CP, 15, 34, 41, 90, 99, 102 n. 30, 307; Popular Front, 20, 34
Francis, Ben, 241
Frow, Edmund, 101, 131–3, 148, 162 n. 94

Gale, Margot, 145
Gallacher, William, 52 n. 7, 70, 71, 85, 86, 103 n. 32, 110–11, 123–4, 142–3, 151, 225, 232, 243, 289, 303
General Election (1935), 35
Germany, CP, 20, 121; extends war, 118–19, 171, 303; hopes of revolution in, 215–16; peace offer (1939), 113, (1940), 214; punitive peace settlement called for, 307; Social Democracy, 1–2; *see also* Britain; Fascism; Munich crisis; Nazi–Soviet Pact
Glasgow 230, 232–3, 312; Trades Council, 151, 202
Gollan, John, 79
Gollancz, Victor, 230, 279; on CP's 'revolutionary defeatism', 13, 105, 119, 123, 173, 179; and Left Book Club, 255–72 *passim*; relations with CP, 261–9 *passim*
Gower, Eric, 153–5
Gramsci, Antonio, 3, 144
Greece, 243

Haldane, Charlotte, 93, 100–1
Haldane, J. B. S., 229–30
Hamilton, Patrick, 210
Hammersmith Labour Party and Trades Council, 204
Hannington, Wal, 29–30, 110, 241–2
Hereford, 313

Hess mission, 184
Hollins, J. H., 159
Holmes, Walter, 231
Horner, Arthur, 19, 134–42 *passim*, 144, 169 n. 170, 234–5, 308
'Hornerism', 134–5
Hungary, Soviet invasion of, 315–16
Hutt, G. Allen, 33, 196
Hyde, Douglas, 105

imperialism, Communist analysis of, 3–4, 22, 48–9, 57–8, 114, 183–9, 306–7; *see also* colonies
Independent Labour Party, 11, 35, 38, 116, 153–5, 165 n. 33, 214
India, 81, 175, 182, 186–8; *see also* colonies, imperialism
industrial conscription, 77, 191, 197, 232
industry, Communist activities in, 50–1, 122–52 *passim*, 225–36 *passim*, 240–1
Inside the Empire, 187–8
International Brigade, *see* Spain, solidarity with republic
'invasion scare' (1940), 180–1
Ipswich, 96
Ireland, 175, 188
Italy, 30 n. 16, 62, 176, 184; CP, 307

Japan, 176, 184
Johnson, Hewlett, 267
Jolly George, 159–60
Jones, Bill, 37–8
Joyce, Eric, 161–2

Kerrigan, Peter, 98, 123, 191, 199, 241, 315
Kirkwood, David, 233
Klugmann, James, 41

Labour Book Service, 256
Labour League of Youth, 39, 156, 316
Labour Monthly, 11, 96, 127–8, 223, 272–6; discussion groups, 274–6
Labour Party, attitude to CP, 35–6, 45–6, 207–8; by-election contests, 153–64 *passim*; Communists active inside, 36, 75, 198–9, 316; CP's attitude to, 19–20, 35, 43, 45–7, 64, 75–6, 89, 195–203 *passim*, 206–8; Immediate Programme (1937), 47,

207; political levy, 202–3; relations with CP in Birmingham, 277–97 *passim*, in Oxford, 96–7, in the Rhondda, 143; wartime inactivity, 198–9, 295

Labour Research Department, 11
Lanarkshire Miners' Union, 151
Lansbury, George, 162
Lansbury, Violet, 162
Laski, Harold, 218, 258, 259, 261, 264, 266, 267, 273
Lawrence and Wishart, 257, 268
League of Nations Union youth groups, 39, 79
Leeds, 150, 313
Left Book Club, 39, 254–72 *passim*; Communist influence within, 257–9, 262–4, 265, 269–71; differences over war, 267–8; Gollancz's influence over, 259–61, 264–6, 271–2; Groups' Department, 256, 258, 259, 260, 265, 269; and Labour Party, 256; and Munich crisis, 261–4; and Nazi–Soviet Pact, 264; wartime reorganisation, 265–7; *see also* individual authors
Lehmann, Beatrix, 210
Lehmann, Rosamund, 210
Lenin, 2–4, 22, 105–10
Levy, Hyman, 97–8, 230–1
Lewis, John, 256, 258, 266–7, 269, 271
Lewis, Walter, 280, 281
Lindsay, Jack, 41–2, 178
Lipton, Sidney, 210
Lloyd George, David, 116, 225, 298 n. 52
London, aircraft workers' strike (1939), 129; anti-Fascist struggles, 27; Busmen's Rank and File Movement, 37; CP, 34, 120, 126–7, 149, 248 n. 119, 313–15, 317; First of May Committee, 148–51; Labour League of Youth, 316; 'March of English History', 42, 44; tenants' movement, 40; tubes occupied, 289; Women's Parliament, 208; YCL, 312–16
Lowe, Winifred, 100
Luxemburg, Rosa, 2
Lynd, Sheila, 258, 265, 266, 269

MacEwen, Malcolm, 208, 216–17, 222
McGree, Leo, 94

MacKenna, Bernard, 95–6
McShane, Harry, 94–5
Mahon, John, 36, 44, 150, 169 n. 161
Manchester, 27, 39, 131–3, 153, 280; CP, 132–3; Left Book Club, 256, 257, 271
Mann, Tom, 159
Martin, J. H., 155–8
Martin, Kingsley, 276
Mason, John, 193–4, 238, 240
Matthews, George, 99
May Day, 148–52
'Men of Munich', campaign against (1940), 173, 174–5, 181, 228
Menon, Krishna, 205
Mills, Pat, 151
Milner, W. H., 281, 286–7, 300 n. 135
Miners' Federation of Great Britain, 138, 146
Minority Movement, 9–10, 19
Montagu, Ivor, 180, 181–3, 185, 213, 257, 275
Moore, Bill, 93
Moore, Henry, 210
Morrison, Herbert, 129–30, 197, 239–40, 311
Moscow show trials, 17 n. 54, 255
Mosley, Sir Oswald, 278, 305; Mosleyism and BUF, 22, 24, 26–8, 158–9, 192–3, 237
Munich crisis, 69, 70–3, 180, 261–2
Murphy, J. T., 144, 204, 221, 235

National Council for Civil Liberties, 39
National Council of Labour, 207
National Government, and 'encroaching Fascism', 23, 30, 41, 74–6, 77, 80; foreign policy, 56–62 *passim*, 70–4, 81, 87; war preparations, 29–30, 63–5, 74–5, 77–9
National Guilds League, 11
National Left-Wing Movement, 19, 201
National Unemployed Workers' Movement, 20, 31 n. 42, 39, 88, 283
National Union of Students, 39, 145–6
Nazi–Soviet Pact, 14, 86, 100
New Propellor, 128–32 *passim*, 226, 232

Olton Labour Party, 295–6
O'Reilly, Joe, 316
Owen, Jack, 200, 236

Oxford, 36, 40, 50, 96–7, 133, 151–2, 278

pacifists, CP and, 116, 143, 162
Papworth, Bert, 37–8
Pateman, Fred, 228
patriotism, CP's brand of, 40–3, 178–9, 182–5
Paul, William, 258
Paynter, Will, 134, 135
Peace Councils, 39, 93
The People Must Act, 171, 174–5, 180, 218, 237
People's Convention, 101, 131, 188, 201–13, 221, 234–5, 236, 239, 276, 295; conference (January 1941), 204–5; disbanded, 206; not a 'peace movement', 223–5; organisation, 205, 208; origins, 202–4; programme, 188, 204–5, 209, 210–11, 213, 214, 222–3, 235, see also People's Government, People's Peace; propaganda, 205, 208
People's Government, CP's campaign for (1940), 172, 174–80 *passim*, 204, 208–9, 213, 216, 218–25
'People's Peace', 204, 213–17, 223, 224, 303
Piratin, Phil, 104 n. 76, 245 n. 7
Poland, 86, 96, 112–13
Pollitt, Harry, 24, 35, 38, 66, 71, 110, 142, 151, 169 n. 170, 199, 205, 212, 226–7, 241, 303; anti-Fascism of, 59, 80–2, 87–8, 93, 160, 303–6; and change of line on war, 90, 93, 98; conscription pamphlet, 77; *Defence of the People*, 80–1; and Left Book Club, 258, 261, 263, 265, 266; Silvertown election campaign, 158–61
Ponsonby, Lord Arthur, 223
Popular Front strategy, 7, 12–13, 20–1, 25, 33–52 *passim*, 196, 210–13, 277, 296–7, 308–9
Portsmouth, 95
Postgate, Raymond, 268
Press Freedom Committee, 223
Priestley, J. B., 128
Priscott, Dave, 95
Pritchett, T. B., 282, 285
Pritt, D. N., 192, 201, 205, 207, 215, 218–19, 243, 248 n. 122, 305
production, CP's attitudes to, 141, 175–6, 225–35 *passim*, 306

profiteering, 89, 176–7, 231–2

Ramelson, Bert, 265 n. 7, 316–17
rearmament, 29, 62–3, 65, 93, 166 n. 84
'Red Clydeside', 110–11
Redgrave, Michael, 210, 224
Reid, Betty, 98, 258, 259, 262, 264–6, 269, 274
Renton, Don, 88–9
'revolutionary defeatism', 13, 105–8, 231
Rhondda, 52 n. 7, 134, 141; All-In Movement, 142–3
Rickword, Edgell, 178
Robson, R. W., 50
Ross, William, 169 n. 178
Rothman, Bernard, 94
Rust, William, 71, 92, 135, 147, 154, 180, 181–3, 194, 227, 238, 305

Saklatvala, Shapurji, 161
Scott, Eric, 242
Scott, Joe, 37, 131, 167 n. 94
Scottish Peace Council, 116
Searson, Charles, 155–8, 161
Sheffield, 93, 270
shop stewards, 193–4, 200, 228–30, 233, 236; see also Engineering and Allied Trades Shop Stewards' National Council
Silverman, Julius, 281
Simmons, Jim, 286, 292–4
Simons, Ralph, 315
Smith, Fred, 130
Social Democracy, 1–2, 23, 24, 27, 106–7, 149, 191–2, 194–7; see also Labour Party
'Socialist Labour Alliance', 200–1
Socialist League, 35
Solihull rent strike, 286–7
South Wales, 27, 150–1; CP in, 134–45 *passim*, 317 n. 6
South Wales Miners' Federation, 134–45 *passim*, 150–1, 202; debate on war (1940), 139–41; and People's Convention, 234–5
Southampton, 150
Soviet–Finnish war, 113, 115, 118, 124, 146–7, 154–5, 158, 267
Spain, 34, 160, 255; British policy towards, 63, 175–6; example of 'people's war', 177, 182; solidarity

with republic, 17 n. 54, 39, 40, 57, 59, 64–5, 93–4, 96, 129, 135, 160, 175, 278
Springhall, David, 90, 125, 160
Squance, W. J. R., 248 n. 122
Stone, Lew, 210
Strachey, John, 114, 173, 218, 277, 278; breaks with CP, 114, 119, 276; on 'British Socialism', 46–8; on Fascism, 28, 31 n. 47; and Left Book Club, 257, 259, 262, 266, 267, 268; and Nazi–Soviet Pact, 100; on 'new model party', 12
Strauss, George, 35, 148, 173
strikes, 7, 37, 40, 129, 137, 146, 149–52, 226, 229, 232–3
Student Christian Movement, 39
Swindon, 312, 313

tenants' movements, 40, 280–7
Thalheimer, August, 261
Thomas, George, 142–3
Tillett, Ben, 159
Tiptaft, Norman, 290–2
Townsend Warner, Sylvia, 210
Toynbee, Philip, 100
trade unions, Communists and, 36–8, 50–1, 130–45 *passim*, 149, 191–2, 198–200, 203, 205
Trades Union Congress, 199; 'Black Circular', 37
Transport and General Workers' Union, 37
Tribune, 260, 268, 301 n. 178
Trory, Ernie, 92
Trotsky, Leon, 4–5
Trotskyist approach to CP history, 5–7

United Peace Alliance, 45
Unity Campaign, 35, 201
University Labour Federation, 35, 99
USA, 23, 28, 73, 184–5, 307
USSR, Britain and, 61–2, 74, 85, 186; British Communists and, 9, 58, 60, 65–6, 82, 89–90, 99–100, 101, 109, 118–19, 121, 204–5; Germany and, 85–6, 112–13, 119, 243; possible assistance from, 172, 176, 177–8, 243, 250 n. 187; *see also* Nazi–Soviet Pact, Soviet–Finnish war

Van der Elst, Violet, 155, 157
victimisation, 50, 238, 241–2
Villiamuir, Jock, 151

war, CP policy on, ambiguities of anti-war line 1940–41, 180–5, 243; calls for armistice 1939–40, 112–16; line modified June 1940, 171–80; opposes 'imperialist war', 105–6, 108–10; pre-war attitudes, 56–67, 70–3, 81–2, 87; supports war 1941–45, 303–6; switch to opposition 1939, 82 n. 9, 84 n. 58, 89, 101; veers towards pro-Nazism 1939–40, 117–22; 'war on two fronts' September 1939, 87–9
The Week, 194, 239, 257
Wellard, Charlie, 167 n. 94
Wells, H. G., 223
Welwyn Garden City, 270
West, Alick, 92
Wild, Sam, 177
Wilkinson, Ellen, 197
Williams, Ralph Vaughan, 251 n. 205
Willis, Ted, 100, 248 n. 134, 316
Winterton, E. M., 153
Wintringham, Tom, 17 n. 55, 128
women, CP and, 209–10, 282–5, 287–8
Women's Committee Against War and Fascism, 39
Women's Co-operative Guilds, 39
Woolf, Leonard, 263, 267
Workers' Control Committees, 175, 228
Workers' Weekly, 11
World News and Views, 187

Young, Edgar P., 214–15
Young Communist League, 39–40, 79, 99, 156, 312, 316
Young Methodists, 39
Yugoslavia, 28, 243

Zinkin, Peter, 128